PLEADING THE BLOOD

STUDIES IN THE CINEMA OF THE BLACK DIASPORA
Michael T. Martin and David C. Wall, *editors*

PLEADING THE BLOOD

Bill Gunn's Ganja & Hess

Christopher Sieving

INDIANA UNIVERSITY PRESS

This book is a publication of

Indiana University Press
Office of Scholarly Publishing
Herman B Wells Library 350
1320 East 10th Street
Bloomington, Indiana 47405 USA
iupress.org

© 2022 by Christopher Sieving

All rights reserved

No part of this book may be reproduced or utilized in any form or by any means, electronic or mechanical, including photocopying and recording, or by any information storage and retrieval system, without permission in writing from the publisher. The paper used in this publication meets the minimum requirements of the American National Standard for Information Sciences—Permanence of Paper for Printed Library Materials, ANSI Z39.48-1992.

Manufactured in the United States of America

First printing 2022

Cataloging information is available from the Library of Congress.
ISBN 978-0-253-05921-5 (hdbk.)
ISBN 978-0-253-05920-8 (pbk.)
ISBN 978-0-253-05918-5 (web PDF)

CONTENTS

Acknowledgments vii

Ganja & Hess: *Credits* ix

Introduction 1

1 Awakening: Kelly-Jordan Enterprises and the Black Movie Boom 8

2 Vision: Bill Gunn and the Black Man Apart 32

3 Creation: The Making of *Ganja & Hess* 65

4 Judgment: The Reception and Revival of *Ganja & Hess* 145

5 Resurrection: *Ganja & Hess*'s Life after Death 190

Conclusion: *Ganja & Hess* after Gunn, Gunn after *Ganja & Hess* 225

Notes 239

Bibliography 263

Index 281

ACKNOWLEDGMENTS

THIS BOOK WOULD NOT EXIST WITHOUT THE SELFLESS assistance and infinite patience of dozens of individuals and institutions. Everything of value in *Pleading the Blood: Bill Gunn's Ganja & Hess* is attributable to their influence. All of its flaws are my own.

Much love to my immediate family: Christine Becker, Robert Sieving, Joy Beaulieu Young, my beloved aunt Judy Beaulieu (1944–2020), and my faithful friend Gus (2003–2020).

Thank you to my amazing colleagues at the University of Georgia: Nicholas Allen, Dave Marr, Winnie Smith and Lloyd Winstead at the Willson Center for Humanities and Arts, Antje Ascheid, Marla Carlson (and Tony and Eli Dardis), Clay Chastain, Kate Fortmueller, Freda Scott Giles and the Institute for African American Studies, Angela Hall, Catherine Jones, Rielle Navitski, Richard Neupert, the Office of Research, Ed Pavlić, David Z. Saltz and the Department of Theatre and Film Studies, and Irene Xia.

Thank you to my support system at Indiana University Press: Jennifer Crane (at Amnet), Gary Dunham, Janice Frisch, Michael T. Martin, David Miller, Peggy Solic, David C. Wall, Stephen Williams, and the incredibly encouraging anonymous readers of my manuscript drafts.

Thank you to the many wonderful friends and acquaintances I've made on this decade-long journey: Stig Björkman, Pearl Bowser, Gerald R. Butters Jr., Liz Coffey (and Jeremy Rossen and Amy Sloper) at the Harvard Film Archive, Allyson Nadia Field, Nicholas Forster, Steven Fullwood and the Schomburg Center for Research in Black Culture, Mobina Hashmi, Jonathan Hertzberg, Donna Lightfoot-Cooper at the Nyack Public Library, Paula J. Massood, Rebecca Petersen May and the Special Collections and Archives at ZSR Library at Wake Forest University, Beth Moran, Caryn Murphy, Sarah Neilson, Hayley O'Malley, Jacob Perlin, Chris Poggiali, Rebecca Prime, Alessandra Raengo, Steve Ryfle, Ronda L. Sewald and the Black Film Center/Archive at Indiana University, Jacqueline Najuma Stewart, Sandra Waters, Kate White, and Morgan Woolsey. Also, thank you to the baristas at Hendershot's and Jittery Joe's in Athens, Georgia, and the servers at the BFI Bar and Kitchen at BFI Southbank, London, England.

Finally, I want to extend my deepest gratitude to those who contributed so much to *Ganja & Hess* and who so graciously offered me their time and wisdom, some four decades later: Marlene Clark, Victor Kanefsky, Quentin Kelly, Samuel D. Pollard, Chiz Schultz, and Samuel Waymon.

This book is dedicated to Sam Waymon and to the memory of Bill Gunn.

GANJA & HESS: CREDITS

Directed and Written by Bill Gunn
Producer: Chiz Schultz
Music Composed and Performed by Sam Waymon
Director of Photography: James E. Hinton
Production Designer: Tom John
Film Editor: Victor Kanefsky
Executive Producers: Quentin Kelly and Jack Jordan
Associate Producer: Joan Shigekawa
Production Supervisor: Ed Dessisso
Production Manager: Lou Pastore
Assistant Director: Anthony Major
Script Supervisor: Renoir Darrett
Musical Director: Ed Bland
African Instruments Played by Nadi Qamar
"March Blues" Sung by Mabel King
Special Audio Effects by Mike Lobel
Costumes Designed by Scott Barrie
Sound: Ron Love
Second Cameraman: Charles Blackwell
Lighting Director: Bill Lister
Assistant Cameraman: Thurman Faulk
Camera Assistant: James Walker
Assistant Editors: Cynthia Castleman and Samuel Pollard
Sound Editors: Al Nahmias and Vincent Stenerson
Properties Master: James Walker
Key Grip: Rex North
Best Boy: Dennis Murphy
Rerecording: Emil Neroda, The Sound Shop Inc.
Assistant Sound: Bill Meredith
Makeup: Scott Cunningham
Hairstylist: Annie DeMille
Wardrobe: Celia Bryant

Titles Designed by J. Sands
Production Secretary: Janus Klein
Assistant to the Producer: Janus Adams
Assistant to the Director: Roger Wall
Production Assistants: Scotti Lyew, Alan Skog, and Lincoln Pasteur
Still Photographer: Charles Stewart
Stuntmen: Tony King, Tommy Lane, and Malcolm Drummond
"Bungeli Work Song" used by permission of Folkways Records Inc., recorded by Musee L'Homme
Released by Kelly-Jordan Enterprises Inc.
Restored by the Museum of Modern Art, with support from The Film Foundation
113 minutes

Cast

Duane Jones (Dr. Hess Green)
Marlene Clark (Ganja Meda)
Bill Gunn (George Meda)
Sam Waymon (Rev. Luther Williams)
Leonard Jackson (Archie)
Candece Tarpley (Girl in Bar [Rose])
Richard Harrow [Harris] (Dinner Guest [Richard])
John Hoffmeister (Jack Sargent)
Betty Barney (Singer in Church)
Mabel King (Helgda, Queen of Myrthia)
Betsy Thurman (Poetess [Mrs. Tyson])
Enrico Fales (Rico, Dr. Green's Son)
Tommy Lane (Pimp)
Tara Fields (Woman with Baby)
The Congregation of Evangel Revivaltime Church

PLEADING THE BLOOD

INTRODUCTION

> Jimmie Baldwin once said something to me—he might not remember this—but it was very important. . . . I said, "what is this . . . this whole thing?" because I was going crazy. He then says to me, "If you look at this as a conspiracy, you will understand it. You will understand everything. But if you see it as an accident, you will go nuts. But if you see it, then you can begin to break down the conspiracy."[1]
> —Bill Gunn, as quoted in C. Taylor, "Bill Gunn," 105

LIKE THE VAMPIRE FIGURE WHOSE LEGEND IT POETICALLY engages, *Ganja & Hess* has faced mortality again and again over the course of its existence; yet its heart has never been staked.

Bill Gunn's film premiered at a lone Manhattan theater in April 1973 and suffered an almost immediate ignoble demise (see fig. I.1). Dismissed or ignored by mainstream critics and seemingly unable to compete in a market saturated with movies directed at African American filmgoers, *Ganja & Hess* was pulled after just two weeks by its distributor, Kelly-Jordan Enterprises. Kelly-Jordan then sold it to Heritage Enterprises. The film doctors at Heritage promptly recut (and, in the process, destroyed) the picture's original negative and reworked Gunn's vision into a supposedly more formulaic exploitation property that was exhibited under the titles *Blood Couple* and *Double Possession*.

In the days before the institutionalization of archival preservation, the immediate removal of a motion picture from distribution in its initial run, coupled with the obliteration of its negative, ordinarily would have consigned it to cinematic oblivion. *Ganja & Hess* escaped that fortune because of the tireless efforts of its champions. Its first revival happened almost simultaneously to its initial withdrawal, when it was screened to great acclaim at the Cannes Film Festival. In late 1973, buoyed by the audience reception at a Museum of Modern Art (MoMA) program of selected Cannes titles,

Figure I.1 The original *Ganja & Hess* poster, a copy initially owned (and signed) by cinematographer James Hinton. Courtesy Black Film Center/Archive, Indiana University, Bloomington, Indiana; and Chiz Schultz.

Gunn bequeathed a 35 mm copy of his original edit to the museum. From its first MoMA showing, *Ganja & Hess* slowly built a cult following among devotees of African American cinema, art house aficionados, and horror fanatics. Critical reappraisals began trickling forth, as well, as signaled by the movie's twenty-first-place finish in *Take One*'s 1978 survey of the best American motion pictures of the preceding decade.[2]

One of the most requested films in MoMA's collection, *Ganja & Hess* was screened frequently until it was yanked from circulation in 1980 due to print damage. This setback was overcome through the perseverance of film historian (and festival organizer, archivist, and collector) Pearl Bowser, who raised funds for and supervised a 16 mm restoration for distribution outside the museum. *Ganja & Hess*'s public profile remained relatively low, however, for most of the eighties and nineties, because it was not issued on home video, and those film buffs aware of the unexpurgated version's reputation had to settle for the bastardized version that was obtainable on VHS under various outré titles. The uncut original's standing among cinephiles and connoisseurs of Black movies soared upon its DVD release by David Kalat's All Day Entertainment label in 1998. *Ganja & Hess*'s current status as one of the most highly esteemed works of independent African American cinema is confirmed by its recent restorations, its continued success at museum, university, and repertory screenings, and its official remake, Spike Lee's *Da Sweet Blood of Jesus* (2014). *Pleading the Blood: Bill Gunn's* Ganja & Hess, the first book-length study of this landmark picture, is a continuation of this ongoing rediscovery and heightened appreciation.

Its eminence notwithstanding, *Ganja & Hess* has attracted scant academic attention in recent years, with two major exceptions: Marlo D. David's provocative reading of the erotic dimensions of Gunn's films, including his only other completed feature, *Stop* (1970); and Harrison M. J. Sherrod's analysis of *Ganja & Hess*'s "viral pathogens and uncanny ontologies." Published three decades ago were perhaps the two most comprehensive analyses: Manthia Diawara and Phyllis Klotman's "*Ganja and Hess*: Vampires, Sex, and Addictions" and Tim Lucas and David Walker's "The Savaging and Salvaging of an American Classic."[3] This relative neglect by academics is attributable, perhaps, to the peculiar circumstances of the movie's original release and to its longtime inaccessibility. Fortunately, not only is Gunn's final cut of *Ganja & Hess* now widely available: so, too, are hundreds of archival materials willed by his estate. Many of Gunn's personal papers and manuscripts, including a wealth of finished screenplays and teleplays, reside among the New York Shakespeare Festival (NYSF) records at the Performing Arts Library at Lincoln Center and at the Schomburg Center for Research in Black Culture in Harlem. The Schomburg holds many documents pertaining to *Ganja & Hess* in particular: script drafts, artist's statements, promotional materials, and even rudimentary storyboards and a shooting schedule. This book draws heavily on these resources in addition to interviews conducted with *Ganja & Hess*'s living major creative participants, each of whom has generously shared valuable insights into the film's conception, production, and achievement.

The time is right for a thorough reevaluation of *Ganja & Hess* as the product of multiple intertwined contexts: this is my book's fundamental objective. Structurally, however, these contexts are separated out to varying degrees. The opening chapter mainly explores *Ganja & Hess* as the product of unique industrial conditions, situating it in relation to the early seventies boom in Black-themed filmmaking. Chapter 3 highlights Gunn's aesthetic accomplishment via a close narrative and stylistic analysis supplemented with observations about the film's story development, production history, and extratextual influences; readers who are primarily interested in a "viewer's guide" to the movie will likely find this chapter most useful. In contrast, film scholars might be especially attracted to chapter 4, which details the evolution of *Ganja & Hess*'s critical reception within academic as well as journalistic discourses.

Pleading the Blood also represents the most exhaustive inquiry yet attempted into the cinema of Bill Gunn, whose endeavors in the movie industry were consistently devalued and thwarted by studios, producers, and critics.[4] Chapter 2 traces the arc of Gunn's pre–*Ganja & Hess* artistic career up to his directorial debut *Stop*, a film commissioned by Warner Bros. albeit never released. Following the debacle of *Ganja & Hess*'s dissemination, as detailed in chapter 5, Gunn was persona non grata in Hollywood. After Columbia fired him from *The Greatest* (1977), Gunn never again worked for a major studio. Nor did he have much luck convincing independent producers to finance his projects. Though Gunn did complete two episodes of a made-for-television serial, *Personal Problems* (1980–1981), distributors evinced little interest in handling a lo-fi, Black-cast soap opera, and it vanished after a handful of showings and airings. Gunn's final attempt at making a movie for theatrical release, to be titled *Territory*, fell apart with the death of its intended lead actor. When Gunn himself died two years later, the most perceptive tributes came from those who appreciated what his example *should* have meant for African American cinema. Most eloquently, Greg Tate asked his *Village Voice* readers to "imagine a world where Miles Davis was disallowed from recording after *Kind of Blue* or where Toni Morrison was only known as the author of *The Bluest Eye*. I don't think, *I know*, that if Gunn had been making a film a year after *Ganja and Hess* our cinema would have been transformed as Miles and Morrison have transformed our music and literature."[5]

Tate's eulogy powerfully articulates the need for a more sensitive assessment of the creative work of the hundreds of Black filmmakers who were denied the opportunity to initiate or complete projects and whose resulting minimal productivity has been used to excuse scholarly neglect. In partly centering my study of *Ganja & Hess* through the frame of Bill Gunn's intentions and experiences, as most scholars have and do, I admittedly run the risk of obscuring the institutional priorities, artistic traditions, and colleagues' contributions that undeniably shaped the film. I should, therefore, clarify that I do not consider "authorship" to be the sole or even the most rewarding framework for understanding *Ganja & Hess*. Regardless, both academic film studies and popular film criticism continue to be oriented around the appraisal of directors. For authorship to become a more productive methodology, with renewed relevance to complement our current historical moment of reckoning, I maintain that we must enlarge the canon of "worthy" film artists and auteurs to include those whose careers were truncated, impeded, or sabotaged by structural forces outside their control. It is especially important that historians apply this perspective to the study of Black filmmakers, who often have been prevented from exercising their full potential due to a host of factors, from economic to cultural to ideological.

Lacking such a critical reorientation, we might be tempted to label Gunn as a filmmaker of limited historical significance and, therefore, an unlikely candidate for reclamation, given the severely abridged nature of his cinematic contributions: two completed features, both suppressed by their studios, and two additional credited screenplays. Indeed, it would seem counterintuitive to elevate a director whose entire cinematic corpus fits under the rubric of what James Kendrick has labeled "phantom" films: "those films that have been lost [or aborted], destroyed, or exist only in fragments."[6] Using Kendrick's designations, *Stop* would likely qualify as a *ghost* film, a film "known to exist in a complete or nearly complete state, but for various reasons, usually political or legal in nature, [is] being withheld" from release.[7] For years *Ganja & Hess* was a *shadow* film, an alternate yet rarely seen version of a picture widely accessible on home video as *Blood Couple*. (Today their positions are reversed; *Ganja & Hess* can easily be purchased or streamed, whereas *Blood Couple* is difficult to find.) And *Territory* is just one of many *aborted* film projects Gunn scripted for which "little or no footage was ever shot."[8]

Pleading the Blood contributes, in part, to the burgeoning scholarship on Black American cinema that applies speculative methodologies to "phantom" subjects. A good deal of reconstructive work has already been done regarding the nonextant films of the earliest "race movie" pioneers. To cite examples that span our current century, Pearl Bowser and Louise Spence's groundbreaking volume on the pioneering, independent black filmmaker Oscar Micheaux, Christina Petersen's survey of the output of the New York–based Reol Productions, and Allyson Nadia Field's examination of the "uplift cinema" of the nineteen-teens are excellent models of research and argument for scholars of Black film history to adopt, partly because they encourage scholars to, as Field phrases it, "look for the presence in the absence."[9] These authors hypothesize the possible forms assumed by the mostly lost works of early African American cinema, and they accomplish this by both skillfully plumbing contemporaneous sources for historical context and closely scrutinizing surviving preproduction, production, and/or promotional materials. This monograph builds on the achievements of Bowser, Spence, Petersen, and Field (among others) by asserting that informed speculation about disappeared, altered, or unrealized movies can serve to remind us, as Kendrick notes, that "accessibility is a complex process of economics, politics, and legal wrangling, not to mention the general social privileging of the mainstream and the familiar."[10] In determining the motives behind the regrettable dearth of Black-authored texts throughout much of film history, we can better influence contemporary understanding of the Hollywood cinema's long crusade to frustrate challenges to its dominance and of that crusade's substantial basis in white supremacy. With regard to my subject, this approach enables us to comprehend the variety of ways in which Gunn's creativity was compromised and negated by the racist and heteronormative imperatives that underlie the American culture industry.

As a quick review of recent catalogs will confirm, book-length exegeses of historically and culturally significant movies now number in the hundreds, of which *Pleading the Blood* is merely the latest. Several university presses claim their own signature monograph series. Yet, despite the continuing interest in African American cinema among media scholars and the increase in the number of college classes dedicated to the subject, no university imprint hosted a monograph series on Black films until the inauguration of Indiana University Press's Studies in the Cinema of the Black Diaspora, which published anthologies on *Nothing but a Man* (1964) in 2015, *The Spook Who Sat by the Door* (1973) in 2018, and *Killer of Sheep* (1978) in 2020.[11] What is more, as of 2021, no major college press has ever issued a book-length, single-authored study of an independent African American–directed motion picture. There have been no scholarly volumes devoted solely to any of Oscar Micheaux's movies, to Spencer Williams's *The Blood of Jesus* (1941), Edward Bland's *The Cry of Jazz* (1959), William Greaves's *Symbiopsychotaxiplasm: Take One* (1968), Melvin Van Peebles's *Sweet Sweetback's Baadasssss Song* (1971), Kathleen Collins's *Losing Ground* (1982), Spike Lee's *She's Gotta Have It* (1986), Wendell B. Harris Jr.'s *Chameleon Street* (1989), Cheryl Dunye's *The Watermelon Woman* (1996), Barry Jenkins's *Medicine for Melancholy* (2008), nor to Haile Gerima's *Bush Mama* (1979), Julie Dash's *Daughters of the Dust* (1991), or any other works by the directors associated with the Los Angeles rebellion.

In view of this void, it is the author's hope that this publication will not simply increase general awareness of an extraordinary yet still underappreciated film (and filmmaker); it will also encourage the cinema studies discipline to engage in more meticulously detailed analysis of and research into the rich tradition of Black independent film, just as previous monographs have done for key works from the classical Hollywood cinema, the international art cinema, and various national movements and genres. Though many excellent anthology chapters and article-length explications have been written on almost all of the Black-helmed pictures listed above, the monograph format allows for the most thorough and extensive exploration of the multiple contexts and intertexts that produce films deserving of a spot among the ranks of Black motion picture classics. *Ganja & Hess*, I contend, fully merits inclusion in that vibrant, diverse, and expanding canon. The proof lies in the remainder of this book.

1

AWAKENING

Kelly-Jordan Enterprises and the Black Movie Boom

> Larry met Pete near the middle of the long single line and as they stood, he tried to recall the first movie he had ever seen. He had been six-years-old [*sic*] when he saw *Shaft* [1971] with his family. Somehow, he could remember the experience but he just couldn't recall what the film was all about.[1]
>
> —J. Murray, "Futuristic Fable," 43.

THE WINTER 1973 EDITION OF THE SHORT-LIVED BLACK arts journal, *Black Creation*, was a theme issue on what this book refers to as the Black movie boom:[2] a cycle of low-cost films whose recent and unexpected profitability awakened the major Hollywood studios, along with the owners of the many failing movie houses in America's biggest metropolises, to the existence of a sizable African American audience. The issue features several essays penned in response to this explosion in the production and exhibition of Black-themed films, especially the urban-set crime- and revenge-centered pictures that brought out viewers in droves, most notably *Cotton Comes to Harlem* (1970), *Sweet Sweetback's Baadasssss Song*, *Shaft*, and *Super Fly* (1972). These films and their many copycats were pejoratively categorized as "blaxploitation" by critics following the lead of activist Junius Griffin, quoted in *Variety* in August 1972.[3] *Variety* indiscriminately applied the term to almost all Black-oriented movies for years thereafter.[4]

Several of the *Black Creation* essays document the efforts of African Americans working within the system to ensure fairer representation, both in front of and behind the camera. The issue concludes, however, with a short work of speculative fiction, written by James Murray, first-string reviewer for the *New York Amsterdam News* and the first African American member of the New York Film Critics Circle. Murray's piece, "A Futuristic Fable," tells the story of Larry, a twelve-year-old Harlem resident in the year 1978, and his love for the movies: "the movies," in Larry's world, meaning Black movies, which were now ubiquitous.

Whereas the real-world Harlem resident of 1972 typically had to go down to Times Square to see even a blockbuster Black film like *Super Fly*, in the Harlem of 1978, Larry merely had to walk out his front door, for across the street from his housing project sat the two-hundred-seat Micheaux Theater, one component of a twenty-two-building arts complex covering six city blocks. Moreover, the films that played the Micheaux were the products of a separate, vertically integrated American film industry, releasing hundreds of films each year and controlled at every level by Black people. Larry was kept apprised of developments within this rapidly expanding business by his cousin Frank, who worked for one of eight New York–based Black-owned production companies partnering with a Black-run distribution company headed by documentarian William Greaves. Also releasing independent productions through Greaves were Sidney Poitier and Melvin Van Peebles, who operated out of London and Paris, respectively. (A few other notable African American directors, including St. Clair Bourne and Gordon Parks Jr., had expatriated to Nigeria, the site of a new $12 million studio space commissioned by Ossie Davis.) The new films produced by Greaves's eight associates, 208 in 1977 alone, circulated throughout a network of 213 theaters, all located in Black communities and every one of them Black owned.

"A Futuristic Fable" succinctly captures the boundless optimism that pervaded the discourse on African American cinema at the height of the Black movie boom. In light of the sky-high profit margins for pictures like *Super Fly* (Parks Jr.) and *Sweetback*, each costing around $500,000 and grossing close to $15 million, and the widespread belief that Blacks comprised a disproportionately large percentage (perhaps even a majority) of the American moviegoing public, observers confidently predicted the onset and exponential growth of a parallel film industry independent of white influence. In Murray's alternate universe, the Hollywood majors, corroded by institutional racism and chastened by "a successful six-month boycott organized by Jesse Jackson and a group of prominent Blacks in Hollywood," simply ceased production of Black-themed commercial movies and ceded the market to their competition.[5]

Murray's vision recalls other kinds of utopian predictions that proliferated during the sixties and early seventies, predictions of the dominant cinema's gradual eclipse by other kinds of film practice appropriate for the "new" audience. There was, however, something of a precedent for what Murray forecast: the "race movie" business that catered to Black-only movie theaters from the midteens to the forties throughout the South and in major Northern cities. Yet, the situation depicted in "A Futuristic Fable" deviated significantly from the system that nurtured the pioneer independent filmmaker Oscar Micheaux and his peers, in that Murray envisioned all levels of this modern business to be controlled *completely* by African American artists and entrepreneurs. Black authority over this projected media empire is the vital component in his hypothetical scenario. To this end, Murray's prognostication downplays the issue of African American involvement in *production*, which for decades had been the major concern of civil rights organizations in Hollywood, in favor of a focus on *distribution*, the branch of the film business where true power most clearly resides.

Across the seventies, countless Black independent filmmakers learned hard lessons about the importance of distribution. The trials that afflicted K-Calb Productions provided an early cautionary tale. Most of the footage for K-Calb's first project, *The Bus Is Coming* (1971), was filmed by an integrated union crew in South Central Los Angeles with $30,000 personally raised by producer Horace Jackson. After funds were exhausted with only 75 percent of the footage shot, Jackson's efforts to solicit completion money from local banks and entrepreneurs quickly hit a wall. "I've been to every bank in town," Jackson inveighed, "and you know what they say? 'Why don't you see Sammy Davis Jr. or Sidney Poitier?'"[6] *The Bus Is Coming* was finished courtesy of a completion bond provided by a white-owned distribution company, and it enjoyed a moderately successful release in several major cities. Unfortunately, the distributor withheld owed receipts from K-Calb until Jackson and director Wendell Franklin threatened litigation.[7] Decades later, Franklin reflected on "the learning experience" of getting *The Bus Is Coming* into theaters: "Every one of the black-financed and produced films made money, millions of dollars. Yet there was one crucial area we did not know anything about—distribution—and we were beat at the bank by distributors. Financial reports in *Variety* and *The Hollywood Reporter* stated that *The Bus is Coming* made almost thirteen million dollars on 150-dollar investments. . . . The first check I got was for one thousand four hundred dollars. The distributors were running two or three sets of books on us, telling us we hadn't cleared a profit."[8]

The shift in emphasis displayed in "A Futuristic Fable," away from filmmaking and toward distribution, reflects a growing awareness of the need for Black control over their own images, a need that went far beyond the token employment of an African American screenwriter or director. The reality of the situation at the time of Murray's writing, however, was quite different from the utopian ideal he foresaw, particularly within the realms of distribution and exhibition. Certainly, the Black movie boom was a boon for the decaying picture palaces in America's most populous downtowns. The stunning performance of Black-centered films in Manhattan's Times Square and Chicago's Loop rescued (at least temporarily) numerous theaters from financial failure.[9] Yet, as Murray reminds readers in his 1973 book *To Find an Image*, only fifteen of the more than fourteen thousand movie houses in the United States operating in 1972 were Black owned. Furthermore, only two Black-owned firms had even attempted to distribute films.[10] Production was the single area where cause for optimism was justified: in 1973 alone, Black performers starred in forty-five movies, twenty-one of which were handled by major distribution companies.[11]

Especially striking about the slate of Black-themed commercial releases in 1973, the year of *Ganja & Hess*'s unveiling, is the diverse range of subjects and approaches these films embraced. Contrary to conventional wisdom, not all or even a majority of boom-era movies were violent action pictures about outlaws and cops warring in the inner city. In fact, as Eric Pierson has shown, "the first series of films to cater to African American audiences" post-*Sweetback* and -*Shaft* was a minicycle of Westerns, with Poitier's *Buck and the Preacher* (1972) leading the charge. "Urban dramas" only dominated during the latter half of 1972, just as mainstream news sources like *Newsweek* were publicizing Black cinema as a lucrative production trend.[12]

Perhaps because the Black action picture seemed to reach a saturation point in a very short time, in 1972, critics spoke of the boom as a fleeting phenomenon, or "a stage through which the Black film movement must pass" so that "many new vistas will be opened" thereafter.[13] As if in confirmation, the highest grossing Black movies (aside from *Super Fly*), in late 1972 and 1973, were the G-rated, period-set family drama *Sounder* (1972) and the musical biopic *Lady Sings the Blues* (1972), both of which outgrossed many studio event pictures. Nineteen seventy-three saw the release of not just urban crime dramas like *Cleopatra Jones* and *The Mack* but also family comedies (*Five on the Black Hand Side*), concert documentaries (*Wattstax*), romantic dramas (*A Warm December*), and horror films (*Scream Blacula Scream*). The profits generated by these varied subgenres were often modest. Still, given that the industry at large was in the throes of a recession, the predictability of steady returns made Black-themed film production an attractive option at all levels of investment. The production mode established by the major studios was soon replicated by independents, which began to specialize in the creation and distribution of Black-cast, low-budget genre pictures, and the fruits of their labors flooded the market circa 1973. Most successful among the second-tier studios, American International Pictures financed a series of medium-sized hits built around violent action and the appeal of rising stars Jim Brown (*Slaughter*, 1972), Fred Williamson (*Black Caesar*, 1973), and Pam Grier (*Coffy*, 1973).

The apparently insatiable demand for Black cinema also led to a dramatic surge in the number of genuine independents that were partly owned by African Americans or that specifically targeted a Black viewership. Whereas only fifteen such production companies were active in 1970, twice that number had pictures in the works as of September 1972, although roughly half of these never got past the proposal stage.[14] A cursory examination of the many projects announced during the peak months of the Black movie boom, however, indicates that most independents intended to quickly capitalize on the blaxploitation craze before it petered out, by imitating (on even tighter budgets) the relatively undemanding formulas then being refined by the majors and minimajors. A few of these projects, including *Super Fly* (Sig Shore Productions), *Cool Breeze* and *Hit Man* (both of Penelope Productions Inc., 1972), and *Trick Baby* (Cinema Entertainment, 1972), fit the studio "Black movie" prototype so snugly that they were picked up for distribution by majors: Warner Bros., MGM, and Universal, respectively.

Whereas some independents served essentially as subsidiaries of the big Hollywood studios during the boom, a select few were formed expressly for the purpose of financing and producing a different kind of Black movie, one that eschewed the blaxploitation conventions the studios were rapidly exhausting yet retained enough entertainment value to attract a relatively broad audience. Among these were the vanity shingles formed by a handful of African American entertainers, the most successful of whom were able to release their independent prestige productions through established distributors. Poitier, still a major box office draw following his late sixties pinnacle, enlisted Columbia to handle his films for E&R Productions: *Brother John* (1971) and *Buck and the Preacher*, the latter a coproduction with costar Harry Belafonte's BEI. Bill Cosby, a newcomer to feature moviemaking, contracted with the independent Levitt-Pickman to distribute *Man and Boy* (1971), the maiden effort from his company Jemmin Inc.

Several less impressively capitalized firms sprouted across the boom years as well, and their ability to start and complete a film sometimes depended on their luck in securing the assistance of wealthy African American businessmen, a group notoriously reluctant to get involved in an enterprise as volatile as filmmaking. Like Jackson and Franklin before him, Raymond St. Jacques, who became a bankable movie actor with *Cotton Comes to Harlem*, had to rely on the largesse of a white-run corporation, Fabergé, and its film division Brut Productions, to finance his directing debut, *Book of Numbers* (1973). This concession came only after St. Jacques appealed to "every black millionaire in America" and was turned down by all of them.[15]

Third World Cinema Corporation, the most publicized of the early seventies Black independent film enterprises, epitomizes the motivations and disappointments of those producers who sought an audience interested in Black movies that were not just *different* from but *superior* to the usual action-oriented fare. Conceived as a corrective to the racist images propagated by mainstream American film, Third World Cinema was founded in 1970 by a group of distinguished actors, artists, and authors, most of whom were people of color. Initially functioning as a grant-based training program for minority actors and technicians, Third World Cinema announced plans in April 1972 to produce narrative features. First on the docket was an adaptation of John O. Killens's novel about Black soldiers in World War II, *And Then We Heard the Thunder*, to be followed by a picture scripted by Piri Thomas, possibly based on his acclaimed memoir *Down These Mean Streets*, and then a Billie Holiday biopic starring Diana Sands.[16] None of these ventures came to fruition. Yet, they speak to a desire to make movies that engaged seriously with Black (and Latinx) history and subjects. Each constituted an implicit rejection of the blaxploitation model and an acknowledgment of the controversy that the trend's stereotypes had engendered within the African American artistic community.

Its lofty ambitions notwithstanding, Third World Cinema arguably ended up serving the main propagators of those stereotypes. The only completed projects to bear the Third World imprint were *Claudine* (1974) and *Greased Lightning* (1977), a pair of well-made yet comparatively conventional, star-driven melodramas handled by Twentieth Century-Fox and Warner Bros., respectively. As the case of Third World Cinema suggests, as long as Black-themed films were *distributed* by white-owned concerns and conglomerates, the possibility of a sustainable, "true" African American cinema rising from the ashes of the Black movie boom was remote, at best.

Accordingly, in a reflection of the optimistic projections of the growth potential of the Black moviegoing audience—and of Hollywood's ongoing neglect of "authentic" Black subject matter—a small group of independents emerged to purportedly serve the cerebral needs of that demographic. The most ambitious of these pioneers was Kelly-Jordan Enterprises, distributor of *Ganja & Hess*. As originally conceived, Kelly-Jordan represented a determined and even commendable attempt to meld progressive aesthetic objectives with capitalist business practices via the forging of a Black art cinema. Its failure to accomplish this goal is, therefore, instructive for what it reveals about the limitations imposed on African American filmmakers, even in the midst of seemingly limitless opportunity.

Kelly-Jordan and the Quest for an African American Art Cinema

Kelly-Jordan Enterprises was founded in 1971 by Quentin Kelly, an Irish American former supervisor at Westinghouse Electric, and Jack Jordan, an African American impresario based in Europe. Kelly, who as a young man worked briefly as a publicist for MGM, was by the late sixties employed by Westinghouse's radio and television division; there, he worked on Merv Griffin's and Mike Douglas's syndicated talk shows. Intrigued by the movie business, Kelly sought approval from Westinghouse's production subsidiary, Group W, to make a documentary about Oakland's Roller Derby. His proposal was rejected, but Kelly covertly began developing the project in violation of his contract. When *Derby* (1970) was distributed through Cinerama Releasing Corporation, Kelly was credited as "L. S. Fields," a pseudonym crafted from one of his daughter's initials and another's middle name. *Derby* was successful enough to attract the attention of *Variety*, which exposed "Fields's" true identity in its July 28, 1971, issue, and Kelly was forced to resign his position at Westinghouse Broadcasting. Now free to devote his full attention to filmmaking, Kelly was further empowered by a five-picture deal he had recently negotiated with Cinerama president, Joseph Sugar.[17]

Whereas Kelly's contract with Cinerama was vital to the company's financial launch, Jordan's connections secured the creative personnel to make its films. Jordan's background is difficult to ascertain, but he appears to have been a man of tremendous nerve and dubious ethics. After a stint as "a black marketer in Germany after the war," Jordan moved, in 1957, from his native New York to Sweden and became a performer's manager and booking agent.[18] During his years overseas, Jordan established contacts with several eminent African American expatriates, including Josephine Baker, Ada "Bricktop" Smith, and James Baldwin. Charming and persuasive, Jordan was able to entice Baker, who had been unofficially blacklisted in the United States due to her antiracist activism, to speak at the March on Washington in 1963; a decade later, he would sponsor her final American tour.[19] Jordan also nearly convinced a wary Baldwin to set up a production company to transfer his play *Blues for Mister Charlie* to the screen, but, ultimately, the entrepreneur could not deliver the promised funding.[20]

By the late sixties, Jordan acquired some production knowledge by overseeing television specials and documentaries on Black-related subjects, first for Swedish television and then for Group W. At Group W, he made Kelly's acquaintance, and the two men decided to go into business together.[21] Kelly-Jordan Enterprises was incorporated as a publicly owned entity in 1971, its base of operations a suite on the sixteenth floor of a Madison Avenue office building. Initially, Kelly-Jordan operated as a production company releasing films through Cinerama, and Kelly assumed the responsibility of raising money and securing Sugar's approval for the firm's inaugural project, *Georgia, Georgia* (1972).

Jordan's access to talent may have been the primary catalyst for Kelly-Jordan's founding, but it was just one of a variety of factors stoking Kelly's ambition to break into Black-themed commercial film production. Kelly had long noted the absence of opportunity for African Americans in the film industry and the paucity of movies specifically tailored to Black sensibilities. Convinced that the studios were neglecting a significant portion of the overall theatrical audience, he studied the domestic market and determined that Black viewers made up 25 percent of that audience.[22] This number was unrealistically high, probably, yet Kelly's estimate was fairly conservative compared to many of the figures circulating in the late sixties and early seventies, alleging to accurately represent the ratio of Black filmgoers to American filmgoers in general.[23]

Kelly and Jordan counted on the existence of an ample niche segment within this totality, one that yearned for higher-quality pictures to patronize. They were not alone in holding this assumption. Several of the early think pieces on the Black movie boom similarly advocated a view of the African American audience as large and heterogeneous enough to support not just action/crime flicks but also films with more evolved "plot and character development."[24] This message was the gist of an *Advertising Age* report, by ad agency executive Ted Angelus, on the opportunities created by the boom. Though he recognized that the bulk of revenue generated by box office titans *Sweetback* and *Shaft* was contributed by "blue collar" patrons, Angelus was (like Kelly) more intrigued by the "intellectual" class of Black filmgoer that had yet to be reached. "To classify all blacks in one broad grouping" is folly, he cautioned eager producers and distributors. "If you try to appeal to all blacks, you made the boat but you're heading in the wrong direction. If you understand the varied and interesting segments of the black population, it will be a rough voyage, but you'll make it."[25]

If Kelly-Jordan were to "make it," its success would be achieved thanks to the abilities of Black creative personnel. After *Georgia, Georgia*, which was helmed by Swedish native Stig Björkman, Kelly insisted on hiring African American directors and screenwriters for the company's projects. This was a policy that had been generally observed by Hollywood at the outset of the blaxploitation cycle, as well, owing to the recent fortunes of Ossie Davis (*Cotton Comes to Harlem*), Melvin Van Peebles (*Sweetback*), and Gordon Parks Sr. (*Shaft*). Many of the Black-cast commercial films of 1972 were (ostensibly) creatively controlled by African Americans, most of them occupying their credited positions for the first time, including directors Parks Jr., Poitier, Oscar Williams (*The Final Comedown*), Christopher St. John (*Top of the Heap*), Mark Warren (*Come Back Charleston Blue*), William Crain (*Blacula*), Ivan Dixon (*Trouble Man*), Yaphet Kotto (*The Limit*), and Hugh A. Robertson (*Melinda*), and screenwriters Lonne Elder III (*Melinda, Sounder*), Phillip Fenty (*Super Fly*), J. E. Franklin (*Black Girl*), Drake Walker (*Buck and the Preacher*), and Suzanne De Passe (*Lady Sings the Blues*). The number of first-time Black directors plummeted the following year, however, as the majors scaled back their slates of low-budget, low-return genre pictures. In 1973, producers were more likely to assign those projects to unproven young white filmmakers like Larry Cohen (*Black Caesar*) and Michael Campus (*The Mack*) or to seasoned veterans like Jack Hill (*Coffy*) and John Guillerman (*Shaft in Africa*). Founded at the start of this reversal of procedure, Kelly-Jordan flouted the budding presumption that African American writers and directors were not really necessary to make profitable "Black movies," given that the elements of the blaxploitation formula had already become so conventionalized.

In fact, Kelly-Jordan's commitment to Black directors inadvertently caused its sudden transformation from production company to full-fledged producer-distributor. By the terms of the deal struck with Cinerama, Kelly-Jordan's designated directors had to be approved by Joe Sugar. This stipulation led to friction when Kelly insisted that Maya Angelou and Bill Gunn direct their own screenplays. Both *Caged Bird*, an adaptation of Angelou's best-selling autobiography, *I Know Why the Caged Bird Sings*, and Gunn's *Night In . . . Night Out (Story of an Obsession)* had been green-lighted by Cinerama in early 1972, but Sugar tried to talk Kelly into recruiting more experienced (white) filmmakers to take the reins on both productions. Sugar proposed hiring British director Terence Fisher, who had overseen many of Hammer Films' Gothic horror movies, to direct *Night In* (eventually retitled *Ganja & Hess*), but Kelly would not move off his position.[26] Consequently, the agreement with Cinerama was scrapped, and Kelly-Jordan assumed responsibility for distributing its own pictures.

Fortunately, Kelly was successful in petitioning outside investors to bankroll his partnership's expansion, drawing on the resources of, as characterized in *Variety*, "an odd potpourri of corporate bigwigs, black-operated brokerage houses, Arab oil money and a group of small businessmen in Rhode Island."[27] The latter connection proved especially lucrative. At dinner parties arranged with the assistance of stockbroker William Goode, Kelly and Jordan pitched their business plan to a host of Providence-area bigwigs. By the middle of 1972, several credit union officers, banking regulators, and members of the Rhode Island General Assembly owned Kelly-Jordan stock.[28] Even as cautious a businessman as Bill Cosby tried to buy into Kelly-Jordan Enterprises, telling Kelly that the two of them "could take over Columbia Pictures" if they tried. It was a period, the producer later recalled, that was "fraught with possibilities."[29]

As the poster child for "respectable" African American cinema and "the darling of Wall St. types and venture capitalists interested in aiding 'minority' enterprise," Kelly-Jordan attracted a great deal of press attention in the latter half of 1972.[30] This attention was expertly cultivated by Jordan, who served the firm as both production chief and public face. Jordan promoted the operation as the only Black-oriented film company not solely motivated by commercial aspirations. "We're not interested in producing a colored Doris Day movie," he told the *New York Times*, referencing the ubiquity of "Black" versions of mainstream Hollywood genres. "We're only interested in quality films."[31] Rather than condescend to popular tastes, Kelly-Jordan would challenge Black (and white) viewers with artistic films that demanded reflection and interpretation. This was the type of viewer further solicited by Jordan's public advocacy for a three-day festival specifically for Black movies, culminating in an hour-long awards show broadcast from Lincoln Center. Though Jordan swore that he did not regard the "Black Oscars" as a means of promoting his own films, it is worth noting that his proposal was reported the week before the theatrical premiere of *Ganja & Hess*, the work of a filmmaker who Jordan had already pronounced as "the black Stanley Kubrick."[32]

Time would reveal Kelly-Jordan's plans to be rather outsize, as only three of its projects were completed before the firm folded around 1975. Nevertheless, the promise signified by Kelly-Jordan, feted for a time as the industry's sole independent Black-owned producer-distributor, generated considerable enthusiasm among those who believed the confident projections about the "maturation" of the Black film audience, who believed that "An EAGER New Audience," as trumpeted in Kelly-Jordan's promotional brochure, "Wants EXCITING New Movies."[33]

The complex reasons underlying this enthusiasm are highlighted by the two Kelly-Jordan projects with the most impressive pedigrees, Angelou and Björkman's *Georgia, Georgia* and Baldwin's *The Inheritance*. These two ventures illuminate the business plan executed by the founders: to distinguish their films in the marketplace by (1) capitalizing on the talents of Black artists and intellectuals with distinguished reputations in other media and, (2) whenever possible, filming overseas. Shooting outside the United States provided a means of trimming expenses, but the practice also enabled Kelly-Jordan to take advantage of a foreign country's exoticism and cultural cachet, to build camaraderie among casts and crews, and to provide a potentially safer work space for the Black personnel laboring on these films.[34] *Georgia, Georgia*'s critical and commercial success momentarily validated Kelly-Jordan's artistic and internationalist pretensions. Conversely, the failure of *The Inheritance* to reach even the preproduction stage highlighted the drawbacks inherent in these practices and, in hindsight, foretold the demise of the company that staked its claim on the strategy.

Another Country: Not-So-Innocents Abroad in *Georgia, Georgia* and *The Inheritance*

Released in March 1972, *Georgia, Georgia* arguably lived up to its marketing tagline as "the most unusual film of the year."[35] Certainly, the film broke new ground for female representation in Black commercial cinema.[36] Not only was *Georgia, Georgia*'s original screenplay supposedly the first ever attributed to a Black woman (Angelou); its lead character (Georgia Martin, played by Diana Sands) was supposedly the first African American female movie protagonist of the seventies. *Georgia, Georgia*'s narrative was assembled from ideas generated by several parties: Angelou, of course, but also Björkman, Jordan and Kelly, and editorial consultant Hugh Robertson. Despite the occasional awkwardness resulting from this synthesis of conflicting agendas, *Georgia, Georgia* met the essential criteria mandated by its producers in fairly ingenious ways.

Unsurprisingly, considering his longtime Stockholm residency and his experience managing entertainers, the preliminary idea appears to have originated with Jordan. The expat producer envisioned a movie about a beloved but volatile African American singer, modeled on Jordan's onetime client, Eartha Kitt, touring Europe.[37] To help him develop this premise, Jordan approached Björkman, whose first feature had impressed Jordan when he saw it at Cannes. After eavesdropping on a coffeehouse conversation between a Vietnam War deserter and his mother, Björkman wrote a ten-page plot outline, titled "Georgia on My Mind," that Jordan promptly purchased.[38]

"Georgia on My Mind" begins with separate plotlines tracking the lives of two disaffected Americans in Stockholm. Bob Rojack is a shell-shocked twenty-year-old white combat veteran who has been living in Sweden for eight months; Georgia Martin is an internationally famous recording artist on tour. The story paths converge when Bob wanders into a club where Georgia is rehearsing with her band and is moved to send her a bouquet of roses. Following that evening's performance, Georgia asks her admirer to accompany her to a party and then a taping at a television studio. In the station's news library, the couple watch documentary footage of an Atlanta race riot, which moves Georgia to comment that she "wants to be . . . where the fight is held" and that it is not enough to merely sing about social change. That night Bob confides in his newfound companion, confessing to his platoon's rape and murder of a captured Vietnamese girl. Following Georgia's second show, the couple make love for the first and probably the last time, for she must leave Stockholm in the morning. As they part, Bob considers returning to America, realizing that he "feels isolated and alienated" in his adopted homeland, where the sole outlet for his community of exiles is to "organize themselves in different political groups." In the end, he wonders, "what can they do in Sweden?"[39]

Björkman was hired as director on *Georgia, Georgia*, but writing duties were turned over to Angelou. Jordan contacted the writer after reading the text of a speech she had presented at Yale, in which she argued that the "true character of the Black woman remains undescribed on the American stage or screen."[40] Given an opportunity to remedy this lack, Angelou expanded Björkman's synopsis into a feature-length screenplay. Much of Björkman's story was retained, especially its exploration of interracial romance. This aspect was of such importance to Angelou that she refused to change the race of Georgia's love interest (whom Angelou renamed Michael) to Black, as Sugar requested.[41]

Angelou did, however, significantly alter the balance in the attention given to the two leads. Georgia is unquestionably at the center of the finished film and the focus of attention from all of the secondary characters: most notably, Alberta, a personal assistant whom Georgia keeps around in order to "remind me of what I escaped." Angelou's Georgia betrays little concern for the greater African American community.[42] She craves adulation from fans and lovers, and she regards her Blackness as a straitjacket that binds and constrains her. Georgia involves herself romantically with white men despite Alberta's admonitions, dismissing the older woman's aphorisms about the racial obligations of Black women as so much "handkerchief-head jazz." The war of wills between Georgia and Alberta erupts into full-scale tragedy in *Georgia, Georgia*'s final scene. Alberta's unadulterated hatred of whites, which stems from her late husband's castration by a lynch mob, drives her to a psychological breakdown that is triggered by Georgia literally sleeping with the enemy. In the shocking finale, Alberta beckons Georgia to sit and have her hair brushed while the older woman warbles "This Little Light of Mine," an ordinarily calming ritual that Georgia had submitted to earlier in the film. Without warning, Alberta attacks and strangles her employer to death; maniacally, she continues to sing and brush the dead woman's hair as the closing credits roll.

Whereas the haunted white GI was the protagonist of Björkman's synopsis, Angelou's draft reduces his significance and downplays his motivations.

In the final script, the male lead is a photographer assigned to document Georgia's Stockholm tour stop. Michael did a tour of duty in Vietnam, but the reasons for his expatriation are unclear. Angelou instead comments on the fate of American war deserters and resisters in Sweden through the invention of a Black defector character, Bobo, who hounds Georgia throughout her Stockholm stay, futilely demanding that she call a press conference and pressure the government to grant political asylum to military deserters. The figure of Bobo introduces a fascinating and extratextual dimension to *Georgia, Georgia*, as the part is not only based on but played by Terry Whitmore, who earned international notoriety in the winter of 1968 when he and several other American servicemen defected with the aid of a Japanese antiwar organization.

Encouraged by Jordan and Kelly, Angelou traveled to Stockholm and immersed herself in the culture of the deserter-resister community, though she talked mainly to its Black representatives. (About a dozen of the roughly one hundred African American soldiers in the country resided in Stockholm; the majority lived to the south in Malmö.)[43] The information gleaned from them surely influenced Angelou's decision to redirect the political critique in Björkman's original outline toward the specific experiences of Black Americans serving in Vietnam. Angelou's integration of authentic details from the African American deserter community in Stockholm, such as cultural and political isolation and limited employment opportunities, endowed her *Georgia, Georgia* script with a potent subtext, one that satisfied Kelly-Jordan's directive for a more serious and sophisticated treatment of Black issues (albeit couched within the narrative framework of the interracial romance). Björkman's envisaged censure of American imperialism had been expressed primarily through the figure of the tormented white Vietnam veteran, with the matter of Georgia's social consciousness relegated to the background. In transferring the military refugee's condition from one of white exile (Michael) to Black exile (Bobo), Angelou creates a counterpoint against which Georgia's own identity as a conflicted Black subject is defined and scrutinized, as a woman who has so internalized the racism directed at her that she becomes both its victim and its vessel.

Perhaps inevitably, the foregrounding of the Black deserters' drama in *Georgia, Georgia* resulted in an ideological rift among the creative principals, which, in turn, reinforced the necessity for Black directors to call the shots on future Kelly-Jordan projects. Björkman was forbidden from deviating from the final draft screenplay, an edict more or less enforced by Angelou, who was present for the entire Stockholm shoot.[44] Kelly and Jordan then rejected Björkman's cut and brought in Robertson, the first African American Oscar nominee for editing (*Midnight Cowboy*, 1969). Robertson cut down the scenes involving Michael, disrupting the expository balance between the romantic leads, and privileged the material featuring Bobo and the Black defectors. Björkman had felt that *Georgia, Georgia* worked best as a story about two emotionally distant people who find love despite the workings of prejudice and intolerance. The "political" plotline was not necessary, in Björkman's view; regardless, it was imposed at the behest of Angelou and Sands, presumably with the producers' backing.[45] According to the logic of Kelly-Jordan's business model, political controversy was a salable element, one that could serve to repel accusations of vulgar sensationalism.

More precisely, Kelly-Jordan's favored method for building a distinctive brand amid the Black movie boom was to court *respectability* rather than controversy. Named by *Essence* as "the most controversial film in the Black community since" *Sweetback*, *Georgia, Georgia* was passionately debated within African American critical circles, particularly with regard to what Angelou was saying about the taboo of interracial sexual relations and the concomitant "threat" posed by autonomous, liberated Black women.[46] Yet, much of the advertising material for the picture downplays this contentious discourse in favor of flattering portraits of Sands, who was regularly mentioned in marketing and newspaper profiles as a breakout talent—even though she had been appearing in movies since the fifties—poised for year-end award recognition. In contrast to Cinerama's blurb in the April 5 *Variety*, which groups *Georgia, Georgia* with exploitation items like the horror import *Tales from the Crypt* (1972) and the transgender-themed *I Want What I Want* (1972) and publicizes all three solely in terms of first-week grosses, Kelly-Jordan's full-page ad in the same issue touts Sands's excellent reviews and prematurely congratulates the actor on her "projected" Oscar-winning performance.[47] Kelly-Jordan's promotion of Sands as a great actor and highlighting of her star turn as award-worthy possibly contributed to *Georgia, Georgia*'s crossover appeal. The film's resonance with a white mostly female audience was attested to by Cinerama's general sales manager, who observed that white viewers comprised 20 percent of its clientele at Manhattan's Forum Theatre.[48]

The degree to which Kelly-Jordan's production policies were determined by the lofty celebrity and literary caliber of Jordan's friends is further verified by its ambitious production schedule for 1972. Following the rollout of

Figure 1.1 A brochure highlighting Kelly-Jordan Enterprises' projected production schedule for 1973, anchored by the soon-to-be-released (and -renamed) *Blood (Is the Truth of the Thing)*. Manuscripts, Archives and Rare Books Division, Schomburg Center for Research in Black Culture, The New York Public Library.

Georgia, Georgia, having cemented its reputation as an industry standard-bearer for quality Black movies, Kelly-Jordan commissioned five additional films, including *Ganja & Hess*, *The Inheritance*, *Caged Bird*, *Honeybaby, Honeybaby*, and *Patrice*, a biography of Congolese independence leader Patrice Lumumba, written by his onetime aide Thomas Kanza. Each was to be provided a $350,000 budget ($50,000 above *Georgia, Georgia*'s price tag) in anticipation of a 1973 premiere. Kelly-Jordan further guaranteed another sixteen "quality black-oriented motion pictures" over the ensuing four years, including a Bessie Smith biopic intended as a vehicle for singer Roberta Flack.[49]

The Smith project was planned as Bill Gunn's follow-up to *Ganja & Hess*, referred to as *Blood (Is the Truth of the Thing)* and billed as a "suspenseful love story of the ultimate in compulsions" in the company's year-end promotional brochure (see fig. 1.1).[50] Subsequent to *Ganja & Hess*'s disastrous release, after Kelly-Jordan abruptly terminated the film's theatrical run and sold it to an exploitation distributor, Gunn claimed to Maurice Peterson of *Essence* that he had been initially approached and invited by the firm to polish an existing property: "I was given a script called 'The Vampires of Harlem,' which was essentially just exploitive. But had I not begun with that premise, I wouldn't have been able to make a film at all."[51] Gunn later provided more specifics about his hiring in an interview with the Black arts journal *Impressions*, in which he repeated his claim that Kelly-Jordan owned a screenplay, "by a very good filmmaker and writer," that needed work. The production partners made Gunn an offer to earn a credit on the "first" Black horror movie, promising him "it's going to be dynamic; it's going to be fabulous and I'm embarrashed [sic] to [offer] it to you." Fighting the urge to reply, "you should be," the recruit instead put his head down and cranked out a rewrite.[52] After showing Kelly a print of *Stop*, Gunn was asked to direct as well.[53] Shooting commenced in New York's Westchester County in July 1972. (An exhaustive production history can be found in chap. 3.)

This early enthusiasm for Gunn's ability notwithstanding, Baldwin's *The Inheritance* was the most prestigious and the highest priority among Kelly-Jordan's five projected releases for 1973. According to his biographer, Baldwin had been moved to again join up with Jordan after witnessing *Georgia, Georgia*'s modest success: "If Jordan could do it for Maya, why not for him?"[54] The deal subsequently consummated for *The Inheritance* was the author's best opportunity yet to realize his long-standing dream of making a movie. In the sixties, Baldwin had written several screenplays, including versions of *Blues for Mister Charlie* and his novels *Giovanni's Room* and *Another Country*, and he was famously engaged for much of 1968 and 1969 working on an adaptation of *The Autobiography of Malcolm X* for Columbia, only to depart the project over the studio's persistent interference.[55] The *Malcolm X* ordeal forever soured Baldwin on working within the Hollywood system, a position he maintained even when the studios began massproducing Black-themed pictures in the early seventies. Baldwin dismissed this industrial shift as "a desperate effort to fit black faces into the national fantasy, and that won't work. . . . How can you fit black faces into fantasies largely based on their exclusion?"[56]

In the spring of 1972, Baldwin came to terms with Kelly-Jordan; he would receive $25,000 for the screenplay, which he himself would direct, with production in Germany scheduled for that autumn.[57] Once again, Sands would portray an African American performer abroad: Brigid, who travels to Berlin to confront her birth father. The father, Wilfred, is a sixty-year-old German who had journeyed to America in the early thirties, romanced and impregnated a Black Birmingham teenager, then returned home and thrived as an industrialist because of his membership in the Nazi Party. Simone Signoret, Baldwin's neighbor in Saint-Paul-de-Vence, France, was to play Harriet, the industrialist's sister, and Lucien Happersberger, Sands's ex-husband and the business intermediary between Jordan and Baldwin, would serve as assistant director.[58]

Whether Baldwin possessed the cinematographic acuity to translate this fiction to film will, regrettably, forever remain an open question, because preproduction on *The Inheritance* was aborted not long after its initial announcement. Kelly claims that the script Baldwin ostensibly mailed to New York never reached him and a promised second copy never materialized.[59] David Leeming attributes Baldwin's desertion to the fact that Jordan, once again, failed to come through with the necessary financing. Enraged, Baldwin canceled the agreement first by phone and then in public, reportedly driving Jordan from a Saint-Paul-de-Vence restaurant with a torrent of "verbal abuse."[60] The author's mistrust of his presumed benefactor would prove to be well founded. Not long after Jordan's botching of the company's potentially biggest coup, Kelly discovered that his partner had embezzled nearly half of the money allocated for the production budget for *Honeybaby, Honeybaby*.[61]

The possibility also exists that Baldwin simply sensed a basic incompatibility between his own prose aesthetic and Kelly and Jordan's conception of "quality," which, in turn, portended a repeat of earlier traumatic experiences with producers and studios. Though it does not pare down exposition and psychological motivation to the degree that *Ganja & Hess* does, Baldwin's *Inheritance* script does feature a highly fragmented temporality, freely moving back and forth across nearly a half dozen separate time periods, usually without cuing the implied reader/viewer. Having recently endured Columbia's constant second-guessing (if not first-guessing) of his *Malcolm X* screenplay, which used a similarly disjointed time scheme, Baldwin conceivably harbored reservations about his new employers' capacity, no matter their assurances of creative freedom, to accept a style of narration that challenged the primacy of the social realist storytelling template that liberal film critics and producers endorsed as most appropriate for movies about "race issues." Baldwin's mode of storytelling, particularly in his late career, would have placed significant demands on even those viewers who fancy themselves as connoisseurs of "quality" cinema, making it eminently possible that Kelly would intervene during the postproduction stage, as he did on *Georgia, Georgia*. Despite his geographic distance from Kelly-Jordan's

Manhattan headquarters, Baldwin surely understood that Kelly, not Jordan, made the final executive decisions. And, while Quentin Kelly was no typical studio executive, he saw himself as chiefly accountable to stockholders, not to Baldwin and not to an "authentic" Black cinema.

The Black Movie Bust and the End of Kelly-Jordan

The sudden termination of *The Inheritance* was a bad omen for Kelly-Jordan, which struggled to follow through on its announced production schedule. Nothing ever became of *Patrice*, the Lumumba project hyped in promotional materials throughout 1972. The company did devote considerable effort to initiating a Bessie Smith biopic, in the wake of Motown's smashing success with its own film portrait of a legendary Black female vocalist, *Lady Sings the Blues*. Filming on *Bessie* was scheduled to begin in mid-1973, with Porter Bibb producing and Gunn directing his own script based on Chris Albertson's biography. The estimated budget, however, was nearly five times the usual expenditure for a Kelly-Jordan picture. An attempt to strike a coproduction deal with a Hollywood major was stymied by a dispute over ownership of the rights to Smith's life narrative, and, eventually, Kelly-Jordan abandoned its stake.[62] The aspiration to tell the story of the "Empress of the Blues" would not be fulfilled during the Black movie boom, although some of the era's top creative personalities tried their best; after Gunn dropped out, Bibb enlisted Lonne Elder III to rewrite the *Bessie* script and Gordon Parks Sr. and Melvin Van Peebles, in succession, to direct.[63] Gunn was approached again in 1987 about directing an adaptation of Albertson's book, this time adapted by his friend Ishmael Reed, with Aretha Franklin in the lead role.[64]

No Kelly-Jordan project was nurtured for so long without going into production than the proposed screen version of *I Know Why the Caged Bird Sings*. Angelou's desire to direct it was the result of frustration over Björkman's supposed inability to understand the nuances of her *Georgia, Georgia* screenplay.[65] Determined to have final say over her filmic creations, the writer took an intensive two-month course in cinematography in preparation for directing *Caged Bird*. Angelou optimistically set a production start date of the spring of 1972 and hoped to cast Abbey Lincoln and Robert Hooks as the parents of the child protagonist. The shoot was initially intended for Stockholm, but Angelou sold the producers on Stockton, California, as a more credible stand-in for her hometown of Stamps, Arkansas, despite the subsequent inflation in production cost.[66] The state of the script, however, was of more pressing concern for Jordan, who pushed Angelou to further develop her characters and to make the narrative more "cinematic." He implored Angelou to seek out feedback from one of the many "old and experienced" screenwriters "laying around Hollywood." *Caged Bird* was "far too important to take ro [*sic*] risk any chances on," Jordan reminded her, "despite your anxiety to get on with casting and final stages of preproduction." Furthermore, he cautioned, this time they should not assume that someone like Hugh Robertson "could come in and 'fix' what should be very clear and in the can in the first place."[67]

The ill-timed financial failure of *Ganja & Hess* in the spring of 1973, elucidated in chapter 4, pushed Kelly-Jordan's stock price per share to $7.25, down $11 from its August 1972 peak. By July, that figure plummeted to $2.50 per share, "half its initial offering price."[68] The downward spiral of its stock value crippled Kelly-Jordan's ability to begin production on *Caged Bird*, its lone presold property and the company's last chance at a hit. Although Kelly raised $750,000 at the eleventh hour from various Wall Street firms, a theater chain, and his Rhode Island network of speculators, he could not convince CBS, a potential new collaborator, to accept Angelou as director.[69] Reverting to its original title, *I Know Why the Caged Bird Sings* was eventually produced as a TV movie and telecast in April 1979. Angelou, who had been forced to surrender her goal of directing in order for the picture to be made at all, also suffered the indignity of seeing her final script draft rejected in favor of a rewrite by Leonora Thuna.

Compounding the losses incurred on *Ganja & Hess* and the delays in realizing *Caged Bird*, the chaos surrounding Kelly-Jordan's final released picture, *Honeybaby, Honeybaby* (1974), further hastened the firm's demise. Announced in early 1972, *Honeybaby, Honeybaby* was conceived as a romantic/comedic spy thriller and as another showcase for Diana Sands, this time paired with blaxploitation star Calvin Lockhart.

Shot in Beirut with the cooperation of the Lebanese government, *Honeybaby, Honeybaby* was marred by tension and animosity on the set. At one point, Sands, apparently suffering the onset of the as-yet-undiagnosed leiomyosarcoma that would take her life one year later, simply vanished; she later called Kelly from a fur shop in Paris, refusing to return until the company agreed to reimburse her for an expensive coat.[70] Her restlessness might also be attributed to her loathing of Lockhart, who reportedly felt similarly about his costar. To make matters worse, as director Michael Schultz later recalled, the native Lebanese crew was fractured along class lines between Arabs and their French-educated supervisors. All were united, however, in their contempt for Jordan, who rarely paid them.[71] Eventually, Jordan brought to the set a large briefcase filled with American dollars, from which he dispensed the crew's wages. Kelly struck deals for a soundtrack album and other cross-merchandising plans, but, without completion money, *Honeybaby, Honeybaby* languished in postproduction for two years.[72] Finally finished in late 1974, the movie died quickly from poor word of mouth and uniformly bad reviews; *Variety* excoriated the picture's numerous technical deficiencies, from its "washed out" color to its "chaotic" editing.[73] *Honeybaby, Honeybaby*'s plot, about a vacationing UN interpreter who gets ensnared in political intrigue involving a handsome soldier of fortune and the corpse of a deposed African leader, turned out so incoherently that new footage of a secondary character, the protagonist's sixteen-year-old cousin, addressing the viewer directly to clarify the confusing premise, was filmed and clumsily spliced into the final cut.

Honeybaby, Honeybaby was in release when Jordan's resignation was officially revealed in a November 1974 announcement made by Kelly, who attributed their split to "fundamental professional disagreements." (In fact, their legal association had by then been severed for a year.) The newly rechristened Quentin Kelly Enterprises would continue to, according to *Variety*, "provide opportunities for blacks in both the business and artistic ends and on all levels of responsibility."[74] But, in the absence of an active production slate, Kelly was reduced to acquiring cheap Japanese imports for distribution in specialized markets. In a deal brokered by Saladin Nader, a Lebanese-born actor mainly known today as the alternate (and obliviously fortunate) target of the Manson family on the night of the LaBianca murders, Kelly bought the American rights to *Admiral Yamamoto* (1968) and *Goyokin* (retitled *The Steel Edge of Revenge*, 1969), and the profits from their redubbed and reedited versions temporarily kept the firm afloat.[75] Kelly also purchased the theatrical rights to the closed-circuit television footage of the Muhammad Ali–George Foreman world heavyweight championship bout, the so-called "Rumble in the Jungle," in Kinshasa, Zaire, on October 29, 1974. The resulting featurette was booked in several Washington, DC, theaters and marketed to working-class African Americans who could not afford the $20 cost of the live broadcast. Unfortunately, by that point the fight had already run on ABC's *Wide World of Sports*. The featurette attracted minimal attention, and Quentin Kelly Enterprises soon folded up shop.[76]

Following his departure from the movie business, Jordan resumed his position as Josephine Baker's sponsor and spent the latter half of 1973 whisking the sixty-seven-year-old icon across the country for what turned out to be her farewell American performances. According to Baker's son Jean-Claude, Jordan disappeared during the tour's San Francisco run with "the last five thousand dollars in the box office."[77] Soon thereafter, an irate mobster visited Kelly's office, demanding to see Jordan about a $5,000 loan he had taken out for the Baker tour. Kelly reached his ex-partner by phone and advised him to flee the country immediately.[78] Josephine Baker ran into Jordan by chance in Stockholm in 1974, at the very club where Sands's performance for *Georgia, Georgia* was filmed. "I had to leave America because I lost everything," he lamented. "I came to Stockholm to start again."[79] Kelly and Jordan crossed paths, albeit circuitously, one final time at the end of the decade, when the former was contacted by mutual friend Ancky Revson, ex-wife of the founder of Revlon. By phone, Revson told Kelly that Jordan had "found" some original Rembrandts in a basement in Brussels and was offering them to her for $100,000. Kelly counseled her that the paintings were almost certainly fakes. He forgot about the call until several months later, when he saw Revson on *60 Minutes*, recounting the tale of how she had been swindled by an art forger.[80]

Due to the middling returns on *Honeybaby, Honeybaby*, his dubbed Japanese imports, and his Ali-Foreman featurette, Kelly exited the entertainment trade for good in 1975. After years spent gaining experience in the specialized water system industry, he founded WorldWater Inc., innovators and developers of solar-powered water pumping technology; he continues to serve as chairman and CEO of WorldWater and Solar Technologies Inc., headquartered in New Jersey.[81] His time as a would-be movie mogul now a footnote in a storied business career, Kelly looks back on *Ganja & Hess* with a measure of detachment. He claims no credit for the film's modern-day reputation. Yet, he is sensitive to the fact that he is painted as the villain in most accounts of its legend and that Gunn contributed significantly to this impression by maligning Kelly in public, both explicitly and indirectly, as illustrated by the caricature of a slimy movie producer in Gunn's play *Black Picture Show* (1975).[82] Without Kelly's initial support, of course, *Ganja & Hess* might never have existed, and his defense of Gunn's right to direct his own script over the objections of his corporate backers was undeniably courageous. Regardless, Kelly's domain was the world of commerce and the concrete, whereas Gunn's was the world of art and abstraction. And, though the immediate result of *Ganja & Hess*'s completion was financial calamity, the long-term effect has been the vindication of the artist's vision over the investors' bottom line.

His shadier attributes aside, Jordan's exit was, symbolically, the final blow to the company's viability. From its inception, Kelly-Jordan Enterprises had been publicized in trades and dailies as the best hope for a "legitimate" African American cinema largely on the basis of its partial ownership by a Black producer. During the press junket for *Georgia, Georgia*, Sands singled out Jordan for praise: "It took a Black producer to say, 'This is authentic; this is new and inventive; this is a good property to invest in.'"[83] She expressed confidence that Kelly-Jordan's future films would be equally honest given that "one-half of the partnership is black."[84] Jordan himself asserted that only a Black producer could be trusted "to go out and fight" for Black artists, adding that "Diana loves Mr. Kelly and she loves me—but she and I know where we came from."[85]

Without the participation of African American creative personnel, investors, theater owners, and distributors, Black commercial cinema could not have hoped to attain the self-sufficiency imagined by James Murray. As both optimists and cynics recognized, only Black people could guide a Black film industry to maturity: an industry capable of appreciating the broad diversity of its audience's interests, attitudes, and preferences and, therefore, capable of mobilizing a spectrum of appeals to satisfy as many viewers as possible. The loss of the Black "half" of the nation's only integrated independent film outfit heralded a premature end to this long-cherished dream, a fate that had already been foreseen by a small group of dissenters at the very peak of the Black movie boom. Initially, most pundits confidently predicted that Black-themed film production, distribution, and exhibition would remain constant from that point on. Doubt began to creep in, however, for a few perceptive observers near the end of 1972, when the market became saturated with Black-oriented pictures. "The [recent] flood of Black movies has been so swift and erosive that it seems the whole movement may soon be washed away," fretted *Essence* film critic Maurice Peterson. "For although there may have been enough resources in the Black community to make hits of *Sweetback* and *Shaft* when they were rare and novel, is it possible for the Black market to support five or ten films running concurrently?"[86]

As it turned out, the seventies African American audience may not have been large enough to warrant a substantial diversification of subject matter. Kelly-Jordan's demise is attributable not only to mismanagement but to unrealistic expectations about the size of the Black movie audience and that audience's ability to support a broad range of genres and production modes. The consequences of this misestimation came to pass in 1973, when several Black-cast films, which did not fit established commercial formulas yet were just as inexpensive as *Sweetback* or *Super Fly*, failed even to make back production costs, including *Ganja & Hess*. Thus, by 1978—the very moment of Murray's prophesied renaissance—Black films, in general, almost completely disappeared from the American marketplace. The expurgation of Black creative talent from the film industry was devastating, both for underused Black artists and for the quality of the American commercial cinema in general. Nevertheless, several of the actors, directors, and writers who vanished from the screen at decade's end left behind a record of considerable accomplishment amid so much discouraged potential. The following chapter, accordingly, probes the creative career of the artist who perhaps best exemplifies Black cinema's enduring promise, both actualized and deferred.

2

VISION

Bill Gunn and the Black Man Apart

> The black artist, thank God, does not find himself struggling in the clutches of Sigmund Freud, as does his white counterpart. His creativity still *struggles* to survive the *struggle*. And then to *prevail*. (Tell story of producer who wants to retire in south of France. Therefore he thought the fastest way would be to produce a black movie. This is presented to me, and the only way I could survive was to write it for him.) This sort of thing has got to stop. The results of these pathetic unions have sent many a white man to the south of France and many a *black* man to Hell.[1]
>
> —Bill Gunn, in Gunn, "I Deal Only in Abstractions."

BILL GUNN BEGAN MARKETING HIS TALENTS IN HOLLYWOOD in the late sixties, a time of maximum insecurity for the industry on multiple fronts, race relations among them. Gunn was then regarded as a perpetual up-and-comer, an actor and writer with a proven record of ability, making him, thus, a suitable token candidate for industry promotion at the "appropriate" time. That time seemingly arrived in 1968–1969, in the midst of renewed pressure exerted by the federal government on the major studios and Hollywood's creative and technical guilds to become more fully integrated.

In the two decades following World War II, many of the Hollywood films that featured Black protagonists or privileged Black-centered subject matter, from *Pinky* (1949) to *The Defiant Ones* (1958) to *To Kill a Mockingbird* (1962), adopted a "problem picture" framework, with racial prejudice being the (usually surmountable) "problem." In such movies, the beleaguered Black heroes must measure themselves against the attitudes and values of a white majority that may or may not allow them to assimilate. Whereas any white lead in a classical Hollywood film may possess a multiplicity of traits and a relatively complex inner life, a Black character is Black to the exclusion of everything else: a racialized subject, whose essence precedes their existence. For a movie to even acknowledge the fact of Black "private life," as James Baldwin acidly remarks in *The Devil Finds Work*, "is to violate white privacy." The situation in which Bette Davis or Joan Crawford finds herself "must always transcend the inexorability of the social setting, so that her innocence may be preserved," whereas "the situation of the black heroine, to say nothing of that of the black hero, must always be left at society's mercy."² For Baldwin, as Ed Pavlić suggests, Hollywood movies promote "the delusion that experience could be *only* personal," except where Black people were concerned: in which case, it could be "*only* social."³

This formulation did not change even when the violent Black separatist became a semiregular presence in American film, in racial problem pictures such as *Uptight* (1968), *The Lost Man* (1969), and *The Liberation of L. B. Jones* (1970). Yet, even though this figure superficially represented a departure from previous practices, under which African American characters were either powerless neurotic foils for white supremacists or pragmatic assimilationists, the Black militant of late sixties Hollywood cinema still primarily defined himself as a social being, always in opposition to the white oppressor.

Gunn's public statement about such movies—"The only two black men the white filmmakers can deal with are the Uncle Tom character and the militant. They can't understand the black man *in between*"—captures only part of his larger objectives as a filmmaker.⁴ Although his observation seems to suggest that he wanted Hollywood to do more to recognize the politically moderate African American, Gunn's artistic practice reveals a keen interest in the person who exists *apart* from or outside of simplistic ideological dichotomies: an autonomous human being molded by (and acutely conscious of) socially constructed identities like race, class, gender, and sexual orientation but not defined by them. His works are populated by outsiders, often artists, estranged from society and family, who are both tested by unceasing indignities and torturous negotiations of identity and, occasionally, pushed to the brink of suicide. At times, their failures are attributable to a broad societal conspiracy; often they self-sabotage. Either way, to paraphrase the narrator of Gunn's 1964 novel *All the Rest Have Died* when speaking of his father, it would be a mistake to disparage their "not being able to swim" lest we "miss the beauty of [their] ability to survive."⁵

By many accounts, Gunn was himself an outsider, battered by "rage and self-loathing," or, at least, he cultivated that impression.[6] Ishmael Reed remembered him as essentially "remote" and "alone" and noted the significance of the way in which Gunn's favorite promotional photograph shows him looking "like a German baron in a medieval castle" (see fig. 2.1).[7] Even with those closest to him, Gunn could be purposely enigmatic. Chiz Schultz, who knew Gunn for close to thirty-five years, never knew his friend's actual age; he long assumed himself to be Gunn's senior by a few years.[8] In fact, Gunn had shaved five years off his "official" age back when he was a young aspiring actor, and he kept up this deception for decades. Late in life, Gunn acknowledged the ruse to Clyde Taylor, admitting that his extremely youthful appearance allowed him to pass at age nineteen for a fourteen-year-old kid.[9] Nevertheless, the inaccurate birth year of 1934 continues to be listed in many articles on Gunn, even those circulated online by the New York Public Library system, which houses Gunn's personal papers.[10]

Despite the buffers he placed between his associates and the "real" Bill Gunn, Gunn generously revealed himself to the public through his art. His formal and thematic preoccupations reflected the liminality that he himself embodied.[11] The phrase "black man in between" is both an apt and an ironic metaphor as applied to Gunn, who, for his many critics and detractors, was never quite "Black" enough due to his middle-class upbringing and something less than a "man" due to his queer identity. In nearly every aspect of his existence, Gunn breached borders and upset hierarchies. He displayed considerable intellectual precocity at a young age yet became a high school dropout. He made a decent living in the fifties acting on stage and in television but abandoned it to take up writing full time. Refusing to be pigeonholed as a "race writer," Gunn's fiction is frequently set in both white and Black milieus, in a reflection of the circles in which he himself moved. Much of his oeuvre addresses the mutability of race and class, and this narrative concern is complemented by a juxtaposition of markedly disparate styles and tones.

This chapter endeavors to verify the details of and correct misperceptions about Gunn's body of work up to *Ganja & Hess*. In my analysis, I hope to reconcile two of Gunn's singular strengths: the creative repurposing of material from his own life in his art *and* his facility for imagining and inhabiting characters—women, the elderly, heterosexual couples, and whites and other ethnicities—with supposedly little relevance to his personal identity or experience. Representative of that latter aesthetic tendency,

Figure 2.1 "Like a German baron in a medieval castle": Bill Gunn's favorite publicity photo, taken by Charles Stewart in 1970. Courtesy Black Film Center/Archive, Indiana University, Bloomington, Indiana; and Chiz Schultz.

Stop, Gunn's debut as a film director, serves as the chapter's concluding case study. Although *Stop*'s sexual frankness is usually blamed for its shelving by Warner Bros., a close examination of the surviving edit and of Gunn's various script drafts suggests that the author's general refusal to respect the narrative, thematic, and formal constraints imposed on African American artists was, in all likelihood, the element that rendered his movie unassimilable within the commercial movie marketplace.

The Young Gunn: From West Philly to the East Village

The circumstances of his childhood and adolescence confirm that Gunn was indeed, as he himself appreciated at the time, a bit of a prodigy. One might justifiably draw a comparison to another child prodigy who eventually excelled in many artistic fields before becoming primarily identified with cinema, Orson Welles. The analogy is especially beguiling when one recalls that both men ultimately experienced an irreparable rift with the Hollywood studios and, therefore, completed far fewer films than they wanted to. Yet, despite the parallels in their career trajectories, formal eclecticism, and commitment to artistic independence, the comparison breaks down along the color line. Whereas Welles's creative inclinations were indulged practically from infancy, Gunn's moody introversion was diagnosed by authorities not as the manifestation of a rich interior life but as borderline mental disability.

Skin color was certainly the primary motivation for this distinction, and Gunn's upbringing needs to be understood in that context. A member of the remarkable generation of African American writers, musicians, actors, dancers, comics, and visual artists born between the early twenties and the midthirties, whose formative years coincided with the deepest valleys of the Great Depression, Gunn navigated past innumerable structural barriers to achievement. Such obstacles conspired to impede the accomplishments of even the Black middle class in which Gunn was raised, as was the case also for Maya Angelou, Chuck Berry, Miles Davis, Lorraine Hansberry, Adrienne Kennedy, and Melvin Van Peebles, let alone the poor and working-class populations that nurtured Alvin Ailey, James Baldwin, James Brown, Ray Charles, Dick Gregory, Toni Morrison, and Nina Simone.

Later modifications to the contrary, William Harrison Gunn Jr. was born on July 15, 1929, six months to the day after the birth of Martin Luther King Jr. Like the civil rights leader, Gunn was perhaps destined to follow in his parents' footsteps, but their path led to the stage rather than the pulpit. The narrator's description of his parents' background in each of Gunn's novels, *All the Rest Have Died* and *Rhinestone Sharecropping* (1981), seems generally faithful to the Gunn family record. Bill Sr. (1889–1987), like Sam Dodd's father in *Rhinestone Sharecropping*, was "a quick, intelligent, . . . humorous, attractive, blunt, worldly country man from Winston-Salem."[12] A touring musician and actor during the twenties, Bill Sr. married Louise Alexander (1900–1995), a showgirl and beauty pageant winner. Louise was an accomplished performer in her own right, who danced at the Cotton Club and appeared with Bessie Smith at Harlem's Lafayette Theatre.[13]

Thanks to a stable job as a delivery truck supervisor for a major Philadelphia newspaper, the elder Gunn was eventually able to provide for his family amid a comfortably middle-class environment.[14] Louise gave birth to Bill Jr. in Cincinnati, but, shortly thereafter, the Gunns left the grind of the road and settled in West Philadelphia, where they lived in a row house at 636 North Fifty-Sixth Street until Bill Sr.'s death nearly six decades later. Though the neighborhood boasted a comparatively high concentration of Black professionals, post office workers and Pullman porters among them, the Gunns were one of the few Black families there to own their residence, no small feat in a city in which eight of nine African Americans in 1939 were tenants rather than homeowners.[15] They were thus spared the horrors of the city's notoriously substandard housing and the interracial conflagrations that resulted when Black citizens, one hundred forty thousand of whom relocated to Philadelphia during the Great Migration, moved to traditionally Irish American and Italian American enclaves.[16]

The Gunns remained involved in the arts after coming to Philadelphia: Bill Sr. was a prolific poet and songwriter, and Louise started her own theater company. These and similar interests were passed down to their son, who displayed uncommon aptitude at a very young age. The Gunn collection at the Schomburg Center contains numerous drawings, sketches, and watercolors, the earliest of which was executed by the artist at age twelve. Another piece, an elegant self-portrait probably painted in the midforties, depicts an appropriately pensive Gunn on the cusp of adulthood (see fig. 2.2). As a child, Gunn was especially enthralled by the cinema, possibly in response to meeting actor Fredi Washington at age six and then seeing her films.[17] In short order, Gunn began organizing his weekend free time around the local movie house schedule: "On Saturdays, I would be gone to the cinema by 10 a.m. and my father would come look for me at 7 p.m."[18] He

Figure 2.2 Untitled self-portrait of the artist as an adolescent prodigy. Manuscripts, Archives and Rare Books Division, Schomburg Center for Research in Black Culture, The New York Public Library.

reveled in the overheated passions of Laurence Olivier and Vivien Leigh's historical romances and the South Seas epics of Dorothy Lamour and Jon Hall; their heightened artificiality appealed to his own self-described "sense of beauty."[19]

Gunn's childhood love of the movies perhaps compensated for his social awkwardness among his peers. Acutely aware that he "didn't fit in with everything as I was supposed to," Gunn spent more time with his parents and their friends than with his own age group.[20] His adolescent hypersensitivity to the outside world was crippling though not debilitating, if the experience of *All the Rest Have Died*'s narrator can be considered an accurate approximation of the author's youth. "I was not a strong child," Barney Gifford recalls near the book's opening: "I was, as I've been told many times, oversensitive, tearful, anemic and impressionable." Yet, he also resists the temptation to romanticize that period, realizing that "it could not have been a very hard road to travel."[21]

Johnnas (1966) presents an alternate version of Gunn's childhood in which the boy does not survive the journey. The one-act play's backstory involving the courtship of the protagonist's parents is transcribed nearly word for word from *All the Rest Have Died*.[22] Once the central character is born, however, play and novel sharply deviate over his fate. Barney Gifford goes on to live Bill Gunn's life, in essence: reaching adulthood in Philadelphia, moving to New York City, becoming a successful actor, and so on. Johnnas's future is, in the play's heartbreaking climax, violently arrested before it has a chance to unfold. Though he generally avoids interacting with other children, preferring instead the solitude of the bedroom where he composes poems and stories, Johnnas arranges a date between Hank, a neighborhood bully, and Loretta, whom Johnnas secretly loves. Afterward, Hank beats Johnnas for purportedly lying to him about Loretta's appearance; although Hank himself is dark skinned, he berates Johnnas for setting him up with "a black nappy-haired bitch like that Loretta. You told me she was beautiful, with pretty hair."[23] Crushed, Johnnas takes a trolley car to the city center and is next seen on the ledge of an office building, twenty stories off the ground. A crowd gathers, mocking him and encouraging him to jump, and he does. "Why?" his dazed father wonders in the final scene: "[A]ll that writing things down all the time, livin' in the movies, sittin' around . . . if we had talked . . . if I had told him that I've never liked it here either."[24]

Johnnas is perhaps Gunn's most deeply personal work, for it provided him with a vehicle to creatively interrogate the factors that, under marginally different circumstances, might have led the author himself to the ultimate act of negation. Several of the known details of Gunn's childhood match those of his fictional stand-in. A seemingly unbridgeable chasm separates the gifted child from his traditional-minded parents, neither of whom can really understand him despite their mutual love. Like his protagonist, Gunn was bullied and called "toasty" by the other Black kids at his integrated school.²⁵ Johnnas also gives voice to the adolescent Gunn's troubling estrangement from the world, a world from which the boy persistently fantasizes about escaping. Reading books, particularly boys' adventure stories from the late nineteenth century like Edward Stratemeyer's *The Last Cruise of the Spitfire* and the novels of Horatio Alger, provides Johnnas with an effective means of transport out of his dismal reality.²⁶ But *writing*, as the boy tells his teacher, signifies "the closest I can get to it without actually being there." Only through solitary acts of creation can Johnnas travel to "where I belong," a place filled with "colors and things of all kinds of shapes and they have no names and I'm one of them, and we're underwater, and the sun is everywhere."²⁷

These particulars of social ostracism and intense interiority are suggestive of what cultural theorist Kathryn Bond Stockton classifies as a quintessentially "queer" childhood: "queer" signifying not just "attract[ion] to same-sex peers" but being or feeling "different, odd, out-of-sync."²⁸ Gunn's recollections of his early years, whether recounted in interviews or reworked in fiction, further correspond to Michael Moon's conception of "modern" queer childhood. Such a childhood is characterized by processes "of uncanny perception and imitation, of initiation and self-initiation, of the gradual recognition of one's desires and the production and transmission of images and narratives of these desires."²⁹ The term "queer" is never mentioned in *Johnnas*, but the similarly coded designation "sissy" is. Specifically, it is Loretta, the object of Johnnas's unrequited love, who speaks the word in reference to her admirer's effeminate style of dancing. If the author's later remembrance of his childhood—"I went to bed with a little girl, that was wrong. So I went to bed with a little boy, and that was wrong"—is indeed accurate, Gunn may have intended the "sissy" reference in *Johnnas*, as well as the allusion to Alger and that author's "particular brand of male homoerotic domestic romance," as encrypted references to bisexual experimentation in his youth and the concomitant fear and/or shame of its exposure.³⁰

What seem to have been particularly damaging to the young Gunn's sense of self-worth are the conflicting implications behind that shaming. *Johnnas* dramatizes the effects of American society's disavowal of Black adolescent sexuality, a disavowal that Black adolescents themselves are obliged to police. In supposed defiance of their own "queering" by the mainstream on the basis of skin color, Johnnas's African American peers, even Loretta, who mocks Johnnas for dancing "like an ofay," equate whiteness with effeminacy and sissified behavior.[31] This same peer group nevertheless enforces the ideology of light skin as the only acceptable standard of beauty and heterosexual desirability, and any deviation from that cultural norm is punished with brutal violence. Such mixed messages about racial and sexual hierarchies could hardly fail to adversely affect a confused, discomfited child fumbling his way through a contradictory and haphazardly enforced socialization process.

Johnnas's most psychologically bruising clashes, however, are not with his peers but with teachers, and it is in this realm where the overlap with the author's own life is perhaps most salient. Though he was an avid reader and writer on his own time, Gunn showed no interest in structured lessons and spent most class periods staring out a window.[32] One of his instructors, frustrated by the boy's persistent indifference, reportedly told Gunn that "'natural laziness' was a racial heritage he must fight against."[33] The remark made a lasting impression. Gunn would eventually place this patronizing sentiment in the mouth of Johnnas's teacher, who warns his precocious pupil of his predisposition "to be lazy and happy-go-lucky." This laziness, he cautions, "is a trait that Negroes are born with and adds to their charm, but in a writer it is death."[34] This is the point at which Johnnas, like his creator two decades prior, becomes hyperaware of being *raced*, of being categorized, and by the very person who simultaneously compliments the boy for being "gifted" and "special."

Gunn suffered one final indignity at the hands of the Philadelphia public school system: expulsion. Though he later assumed a philosophical attitude about his dropout status, remarking in 1973 that "now I have less to unlearn," Gunn was humiliated over being thrown out of high school.[35] He plumbed the depths of this trauma in an unpublished reflection from 1979. In this blistering essay, Gunn foregrounds the contributions made by the city's schools to the unending cycle of grinding poverty ensnaring the local African American population. Black Philadelphians, Gunn claims, have long been exceptional, "different from any black people I have ever seen on the face of the earth. From these streets and houses of West Philly, South Philly, North Philly have come some of the most brilliant black men and women" on the planet. Yet, due to structural policies of segregation and neglect, many of West Philadelphia High's most intelligent and talented Black teens were, like Gunn, corralled into "special learning" classes and ignored. "It was quite obvious to everyone in the class except the teachers that at least a third of those black students were at the genious [sic] level," Gunn laments. "The really complicated interesting black students always found their way into the hard to teach category."[36]

Once Gunn left Philadelphia, he never lived there again, but his progress out of the city was fitful. Facing a future of limited employment opportunities in his hometown, Gunn enlisted in the Navy (as his father had during World War II) and served for eighteen months. Though Gunn never finished high school, his painting talent earned him a fine arts scholarship at the University of Pennsylvania. He worked as an orderly in the anatomy room at Penn's School of Medicine, and then as an aide in the library at the Wharton School, where he covertly sat in on business classes. Later, while working as a scenery painter at the Neighborhood Playhouse, Gunn was asked to play a small role in a production of *Street Scene*, Elmer Rice's play about the tenants of a New York City brownstone. Soon, thereafter, Gunn moved to Manhattan with $35 in his pocket plus four $25 war bonds, which got him through the week.[37]

Gunn arrived in New York at an inopportune time for Black dramatic actors. In the fifties and early sixties, on- and off-Broadway featured roles for African Americans were generally restricted to social problem plays about racial conflict. The African American actor was expected to, in Gunn's phrasing, "represent a race, not a character."[38] Typically, such plays were staged in ways that maximized visual contrast, and casting directors were thus reluctant to hire a Black actor with a light complexion or, in Gunn's case, "red nappy hair." Nevertheless, Gunn soon found his forte playing "a pleasant college type."[39] From the summer of 1952, which he spent touring luxury hotels in the Catskill Mountains, performing the lead role in an all-Black production of *Golden Boy*, Gunn did not lack for work for several years.[40]

Near the end of his stage career, Gunn wrote *All the Rest Have Died*, a fictionalized look back at his formative decade in Manhattan as experienced through the eyes of Barney, an erudite young Philadelphia transplant trying to make a living as an actor in New York. One of the more striking aspects of this highly contemplative chronicle is Gunn's disinterest in analyzing the craft or dishing on the theatrical scene. "If anyone were to ask why I wanted to go to New York, or how I became an actor in the first place," the narrator confesses early on, "I'm afraid I couldn't remember any spectacular reason or inspirational experience that made me decide on the actor's life."[41] The peak moments of Barney's theatrical career—an offer of a lead role on Broadway, the rehearsals, the premiere, the fawning reviews, the demands of publicity, his promotion to star billing, and his eventual exasperation with fame—are handled in fewer than three pages.[42] The far more significant markers of Barney's growth are the relationships he develops with three intimates: Taylor, a first cousin who precedes Barney in making the move to Manhattan, where he dies in a freak accident; Maggie, a blonde model who becomes Barney's fiancée; and Bernard, a troubled poet and writer of short stories. Dozens of pages are devoted to exquisitely detailed conversations between Barney and these confidants.

The cohort that Gunn himself joined in New York would eventually achieve near-legendary status, thanks to the mythology that developed around its most famous member, James Dean. Dean and Gunn met in 1954 when they read at the same audition for the original Broadway production of *The Immoralist*, based on André Gide's novel about a repressed gay scholar on his honeymoon who is seduced by an Algerian houseboy. Dean was cast as the houseboy, while Gunn played a secondary Arabic role and served as Dean's understudy. The two men bonded immediately, though they were not costars for very long: Dean departed for Hollywood soon after the show opened.[43] But Gunn remained part of the future icon's core group of East Coast pals, along with actors Robert Heller and Martin Landau. Gunn posed with a saxophone for Dean's most celebrated painting, allegedly the last he completed before his fatal car crash in September 1955. In a final favor to his friend (and rumored lover), Gunn, along with Heller and some others, broke into Dean's West Sixty-Eighth Street apartment the morning after his death and removed "pictures they thought might be embarrassing to Jimmy's memory."[44]

Dean's influence on *All the Rest Have Died* is concealed but palpable. Like Dean, Taylor and Bernard also die from injuries sustained from ejection from a moving vehicle: a cab and a sailboat, respectively. As Taylor lies on his hospital deathbed, he describes to Barney a recent bad dream in which he is confronted by a deceased friend: the friend tries to speak to Taylor, but no sound comes forth from his mouth, only an unceasing gush of blood.[45] Taylor's nightmare slightly revises a dream Gunn himself experienced on a winter's night soon after Dean's death. Penniless and bedridden with a fever, Gunn decided to commit suicide by opening his windows and "lay[ing] down to die." As he slept, he dreamed he was in Dean's apartment. He walked toward his friend, who "suddenly turned around and said, 'Beware of Death. He has sharp teeth,' and all this blood poured out of his mouth."[46]

All the Rest Have Died culminates in a moody rumination, narrated by Barney as he reminisces over those who have moved on from his social circle, whether due to death, marriage, or the lure of Hollywood: "The process of growing up had begun to take place with the falling away of old friends. In the long swim to the shore some never made the other side, but were swept out to sea and out of sight. There is the code of self-survival dealing with not looking back; once past and over the dangerous ground on which friends have fallen it is surely death to linger or to reminisce. Or to look forward to those who have sped ahead to success. I must not at any time feel left behind."[47] Yet, as signaled by the novel's elegiac title (borrowed from Emily Dickinson's poem "My Wars Are Laid Away in Books"), Barney *does* spend a good deal of time mourning those losses. In the final scene, he returns to Philadelphia, ostensibly to tell his parents of his engagement but mainly to visit Taylor's grave for what he tells himself will be the last time. This final revisitation of traumatic experience illustrates the tragic dimension of the intimacy that otherwise nourishes the main character. The paradox of our need for other people, whom we know we will someday lose forever, is one that Gunn would return to throughout his artistic life.

An Actor's Work, a Writer's Life

The biggest triumph of Gunn's stage career came in 1956, when he headlined the New Theatre Company's revival of Louis Peterson's social problem play *Take a Giant Step*. As Spencer Scott, a Black teenager attending a white New England high school, Gunn's sensitive performance earned him plaudits from *Times* critic Brooks Atkinson, who proclaimed Gunn "a likeable young actor with an easy grace, a ready smile and extraordinary awareness."[48] The off-Broadway revival of *Take a Giant Step* amassed three times as many performances as its original run, and Gunn was suddenly poised for theatrical stardom, albeit of the limited kind reserved for African American actors in the fifties.

Movie stardom, on the contrary, was closed off to Gunn almost immediately. Eager to play Scott in the 1959 screen adaptation of Peterson's drama, he was rejected by the independent production company Hecht Hill Lancaster in favor of pop singer Johnny Nash. Later, Gunn bitterly recalled being told by Hecht Hill Lancaster's casting director that he looked too old for the part of the eighteen-year-old lead, even though, as he claimed, "I was 21 at the time."[49] He was actually in his late twenties (and passing as five years younger), but the youthful appearance that enabled Gunn to play teenaged roles onstage was not sufficient for circumnavigating Hollywood's age discrimination, at least with regard to featured roles. He did, nonetheless, in 1959, play a fifteen-year-old in Twentieth Century-Fox's adaptation of William Faulkner's *The Sound and the Fury*.

Though Gunn did not sustain the leading man status he temporarily earned with *Take a Giant Step*, he managed to carve out an impressive niche as a character actor and (very) occasional lead on both stage and screen. Along with such luminaries as Ethel Waters and Lillian Gish, Gunn appeared in one of seven one-act plays presented at the International Building Exhibition of 1957 in West Berlin.[50] Off Broadway, he played a student in Ettole Rella's *Sign of Winter* and acted in a revival of Errol John's *Moon on a Rainbow Shawl*, amid a stellar ensemble including Cicely Tyson, Vinnette Carroll, and Robert and James Earl Jones. Gunn also performed as part of Joseph Papp's NYSF across three seasons at Central Park's Delacorte Theatre, in racially integrated productions of *Antony and Cleopatra*, *Winter's Tale*, and *Troilus and Cressida*.

Fortuitously, Gunn's decade-plus as a New York–based performer coincided with television's first "golden age." Being one of the city's relatively few Black stage actors of prominence, Gunn found steady employment within the nascent medium. His earliest TV work (ca. 1954) was undertaken for Black-oriented productions for WOR-TV, notably two programs from African American writer William Attaway: *Harlem Detective*, starring William Marshall; and the *Spotlight* episode "Carmen in Harlem," a Black-cast modernization of Bizet's opera, costarring Billie Allen.[51] Around 1957, Gunn began to appear frequently on the networks, in shows dedicated to race relations issues. After making a strong impression as a Black college student turned away by a white church congregation in CBS's public affairs program *Look Up and Live*, Gunn guested on the anthology dramas *Studio One*, *Danger*, *Kraft Television Theatre*, *The Kaiser Aluminum Hour*, *The Outer Limits*, the Canadian Broadcasting Corporation's *Perspective*, and standalone specials like CBS's *Americans: A Portrait in Verses*.[52] When the anthology series began to die out in the early sixties as more television producers shifted to programming filmed in Los Angeles, Gunn played similar roles on episodes of *Route 66*, *Naked City*, *The Defenders*, *Stoney Burke*, *The Man from U. N. C. L. E.*, *Dr. Kildare*, *The Fugitive*, and *Tarzan*. Both the late-fifties anthology series, with its rotating story topics, and the social problem–oriented "special episode" format of sixties serials permitted the networks to continue the movie industry's long-standing structure of discriminatory casting. Producers benefited from the talents of actors of color in one-off parts, in teleplays that condemned overt forms of racial segregation, while effectively shutting out those actors from recurring series work. Gunn almost subverted the standard pattern, however. By his account, Gunn was offered his own television series in the early sixties but turned it down, though he was "very tempted," because he would have had to move to Hollywood and sign a seven-year contract.[53]

Gunn's close relationship with James Dean during his years in Manhattan leads one to speculate on the extent to which Gunn, like his famous friend, was a student of the Method, the naturalistic, supposedly more authentic acting style popularized in the fifties by pop culture idols Marlon Brando and Montgomery Clift and taught by Lee Strasberg at the Actors Studio. Dennis Hopper later recalled that Gunn and Dean took acting courses with Strasberg and that the two friends would "meet under the gingko tree on the side of the 42nd Street Library . . . to do sense memories."[54] Gunn also became a confidant of Clift himself, one of the studio's most famous alumni. The men shared a teacher, Mira Rostova, but Clift functioned as Gunn's unofficial acting coach, teaching him how to analyze teleplays and dispensing advice to his protégé in the wings during stage performances.[55] These details lend credence to Ishmael Reed's identification of Gunn as "one of the first black actors to experiment with The Method," though this assertion undersells the not-insignificant number of African Americans who received Actors Studio training in this era, including Billie Allen, Roscoe Lee Browne, Rupert Crosse, Al Freeman Jr., Ellen Holly, William Marshall, Sidney Poitier, Raymond St. Jacques, and Frank Silvera.[56]

Despite his acquaintance with Method techniques, the earliest surviving records of Gunn's performance style, his television appearances, do not suggest a strict adherence to Stanislavskian principles (as modified by Strasberg). Contemporary historians characterize fifties-style Method acting as a system of techniques grounded in "a conception of the psyche in which the individual's inner drives are at war with the socially acceptable forms of human expression" and enacted through "painful struggle."[57] In contrast, Gunn's portrayal of men in psychological anguish, such as Roy, a Black Torontonian threatened by the potential breakup of his engagement to a white woman in "Crossroads" (*Perspective*), or Hank Plummer, a musician embittered by his father's abandonment and facing the impending death of his mother surrogate in "Goodnight Sweet Blues" (*Route 66*), are marked by subtlety and restraint. Even as those characters lash out, Gunn's vocal inflection and physical mannerisms barely waver. Granted, the more intimate nature of television acting encourages self-discipline. Yet, the reviews of Gunn's stage work confirm that his theatrical performance was likewise distinguished, as Atkinson verifies, by "reticence" and a disinterest in histrionics and overt "pathos."[58]

Gunn ceased acting altogether in the midsixties; aside from appearing in his own projects, he did not perform again in theater, television, or movies until the early eighties. His seeming disenchantment with acting, and with theatrical performance in particular, possibly owes something to the ubiquity of the Method, the predictability of its mechanics, and its implicit insistence on the experiential as the only legitimate wellspring for creativity. In other words, the budding playwright may have sensed a widening chasm between the text as written and the increasingly solipsistic and inarticulate acting styles promoted by the Actors Studio. Virginia Wright Wexman and Shonni Enelow have explored the ramifications of Strasberg's rewiring of Stanislavski's teachings to encourage actors to, as Wexman notes, "*substitute* their own feelings for those of the characters they played rather than to merge the two together."[59] As Gunn began to regard himself as a writer first and foremost, he likely objected to the notion that the actor's interiority and affective memories should supersede those of the written characters rather than simply shape them. Furthermore, as his art arguably became more race conscious in the later sixties, Gunn perhaps shared the disillusionment of James Baldwin, who wrote and directed *Blues for Mister Charlie* for the Actors Studio in 1964, with the essentialist underpinnings of the Method. Although the Method's emphasis on "the individual consciousness" initially appealed to him, Baldwin eventually came to realize that its "model of identification and the universalism that went along with it led to an erasure of difference and of history that produced the same effect as the political imposition of a unified American identity: the invisibility of marginalized people and the silencing of dissent."[60]

Indeed, despite hopes that the dissemination of this new realist style would lead to more "authentic" and complex roles and increased opportunities for African Americans, the advent of the Method did little to diversify the American theater. In the 1961–1962 season, Black actors portrayed only 173 parts both on and off Broadway, out of 2,400 roles total, and many of those roles were relegated to plays that followed the familiar social problem prototype.[61] In 1963, Gunn publicly decried this state of affairs. That summer, in a *Herald Tribune* feature on the effects of racial bias in the entertainment business, he issued a blunt demand to be "hired as an actor who is a Negro" rather "than as a Negro actor."[62]

Gunn incurred Hollywood's wrath the following year via a highly provocative interview in *Variety*. Though the profile was filed ostensibly to promote Gunn's just-published debut novel, the writer took the opportunity to air his grievances regarding the film industry's discriminatory casting practices. "When a good part for a Negro actor does come along, they always offer it to Sidney Poitier," Gunn fumed. "If he turns it down, they rewrite it for a white actor."[63] Gunn's accusation showed remarkable staying power within industry discourse. A year later, the *Pittsburgh Courier* reported that the "if we can't get Poitier" quotation was then "making the rounds" in Hollywood, to Poitier's irritation, and, as late as 1972, *Variety* cited Gunn's complaint as a widely accepted industry truism.[64] Given that Gunn rarely acted in films and television after the midsixties, it stands to reason that he was the victim of an unspoken blacklist: a possibility later broached by Reed, who cited Gunn's "reputation for being difficult" as the main reason for his dwindling opportunities as a performer.[65]

Perhaps Gunn felt sufficiently emboldened by his writing achievements to let his acting career drop. *All the Rest Have Died* was published in October 1964 and nominated as one of the seven finalists for a $10,000 Dell Book Award.[66] Gunn did not complete a follow-up novel for nearly two decades, but he wrote short fiction throughout the sixties. One of his stories, "The Bedlamite," was published in 1967 in the men's "lifestyle" magazine *Swank*.[67] "The Bedlamite" is narrated by Alexander Cruze, an eighty-five-year-old man passing his final days in a New England rest home. Alexander suffers from a selective memory lapse: he not only recalls nothing from the previous day; he cannot remember anything that happened to him after age thirty-five. The narrator is visited daily by a longtime friend, Hyacinth, whom he jilted fifty years earlier. Everyone else in his life is a complete stranger to him, though he feels oddly comfortable around a young man from the institution's library. As the reader learns by the end of the story, the librarian is in fact Alexander's own son. When Alexander's wife passed away ten years prior, the old man dealt with his grief by abandoning his remaining family and erasing from memory every detail of his life from the moment he met her in an effort to avoid the pain of losing her. After years of searching, the son found Alexander at the nursing home and took a job there to be close to the father who, of course, has no clue as to his real identity. Despite its circumscribed format, "The Bedlamite" is a quintessential Gunn text. Its haunting meditation on mortality and loss is expanded on in many of Gunn's fictional endeavors, including the similarly Gothic *Ganja & Hess*.

Gunn's preoccupation with painful memory and ambiguous paternity dates back to his first major work as a writer, *Marcus in the High Grass* (1958). A comedic drama about a young man obsessed with his long-dead mother and unaware that his drunken uncle is his true father, *Marcus in the High Grass* was staged by the Theatre Guild, a society devoted to the discovery and nurturing of young playwrights. Following a late summer tryout in 1959, *Marcus in the High Grass* premiered off-Broadway in 1960 with David Wayne and Elizabeth Ashley in the starring roles.[68] Because the actors in the play were white, several of its reviewers were unaware that its author was not. Their reference point thus became Tennessee Williams rather than, say, Baldwin, who had recently provoked the critical establishment with his incisive study of white Parisians and American expatriates in the novel *Giovanni's Room*.[69] Presumably stimulated by this initial effort at exploring the psychology of non-Black characters, Gunn further delved into Anglo-American milieus in the unpublished play *The Owllight*, completed around 1961. Set in a "large Greek Revival house" on the coast of Maine in 1899, *The Owllight* concerns a brooding poet who falls in love with the woman he believes to have broken up his parents' marriage, which led to his father's suicide. At play's end, the poet uses his father's razor to take his own life.[70]

In the midsixties, Gunn hit his stride as a playwright. *Johnnas* was first staged in 1966 at the Chelsea Theater Center, with Roscoe Lee Browne and Colleen Dewhurst in the roles of the parents.[71] Following its publication in *Drama Review*, *Johnnas* was frequently performed in repertory, and its script was adapted for television in an Emmy-winning production for an NBC affiliate in Washington, DC. The full-length drama *The Celebration* earned Gunn a "Most Promising Playwright" prize upon its 1965 premiere in Los Angeles.[72] Elia Kazan optioned the play to be produced at Lincoln Center in Manhattan but, ultimately, passed, denying Gunn a shot at far greater exposure.[73]

The Celebration was nevertheless responsible, in part, for changing the course of Gunn's life. After seeing the production at the Mark Taper Forum in Los Angeles, Hal Ashby hired Gunn to replace Erich Segal as screenwriter on Ashby's directorial debut, *The Landlord* (1970), adapted from a novel by Gunn's West Philadelphia contemporary, Kristin Hunter.[74] Gunn's

Landlord screenplay transformed Hunter's satirical exploration of race relations into a deeper, more serious (albeit absurdist) character study of a dim-witted WASP who, defying his conservative parents' low expectations for him, buys a Brooklyn tenement and becomes entangled in the lives of his Black tenants. Gunn seems to have enjoyed a cordial working relationship with Ashby, and he occasionally stopped by the set to observe the shoot and chat with Diana Sands, who played a featured role.[75] Yet these outings also reinforced Gunn's awareness of the screenwriter's fundamental anonymity in studio filmmaking practice. On one such call, Gunn expressed his reservations to a visiting reporter. Cinema, Gunn observed, is a "medium for the eye, not the ear. So the most important thing is what the eye sees.... It's very difficult for a writer's ego to make that transition.... All the beautiful description is in the script, and no one sees that."[76]

Despite these misgivings, Gunn quickly became one of the most in-demand scribes in Hollywood and one of very few Black freelance writers in an industry castigated by the Equal Employment Opportunity Commission for its chronic underemployment of African American talent. Soon after joining the *Landlord* project, Gunn was signed by Universal to develop *Friends*, an original story by and for novice filmmaker David Zeitlin.[77] Gunn exited the project early, however, due to Zeitlin's failure to flesh out the personal history of the Black protagonist, specifically his experiences with the inner city's "rotton [sic] school system." Without these added dimensions, Gunn stressed, the character would likely be understood as just "another super Negro on his way to white aceptance [sic]," thus excusing white viewers from thinking too deeply about institutional racism.[78] Though his departure from the project foreshadowed his later disputes with producers, Gunn accepted similar assignments during this period. Among the unproduced properties he worked on were *Moon*, an adaptation of Don Asher's novel *Don't the Moon Look Lonesome*, and *The Fame Game*, based on a Rona Jaffe potboiler about a girl group built up and torn down by the tawdry machinations of the music business.[79]

In the late sixties, Gunn forged a relationship with Harry Belafonte's production company, Belafonte Enterprises Inc. (BEI), through his acquaintance with Chiz Schultz. Schultz worked extensively in television in the fifties and early sixties as a production assistant; he was then enticed by Belafonte to leave Hollywood and head up BEI's motion picture division. Schultz's first BEI film credit was for a property that Belafonte optioned for his return to movie acting after a decade's absence. *The Angel Levine* (1970) was based on a Bernard Malamud short story about a Black angel on probation who must convince a Jewish tailor of his divine provenance or face excommunication from heaven. As BEI began the search for a screenwriter, Schultz recalled meeting Gunn years before, when he struck up a conversation with the actor at Downey's, a popular Manhattan hangout for show business workers.[80] Gunn was recruited to inflate Malamud's twelve-page story to feature length, which necessitated inventing new characters and developing the secondary character of the tailor's dying wife.[81] David Picker, president of United Artists, *The Angel Levine*'s distributor, pronounced Gunn's first draft to be the best he had ever read. But the film's director, Ján Kadár, felt that Gunn "didn't know how Jews talked," so Schultz had the script rewritten by Ronald Ribman. Though both writers felt they were deserving of sole screenplay credit, they were awarded joint attribution on the finished picture. Fittingly, given the film's pessimism about Black-white collaboration, both men were furious with this outcome and neither spoke to Schultz for over a year after *The Angel Levine*'s release.[82]

As Gunn worked on *The Angel Levine* throughout 1968, his name became attached to several of BEI's many movie projects, including proposed versions of his own plays.[83] Gunn was slated to write the book for a musical version of Ray Bradbury's play *The Wonderful Ice Cream Suit*, a longtime passion project for Belafonte. The writer's top priority, however, following *The Angel Levine* was to author the script for *House of Flowers*, adapted from Truman Capote and Harold Arlen's ill-fated Broadway musical set in a Haitian bordello.[84] *House of Flowers* offered Belafonte the opportunity to revisit the West Indies roots that propelled him to singing stardom in the fifties. Unfortunately, the property proved to be a poor fit for Gunn's sensibility, and his first draft inspired little enthusiasm from either United Artists or Belafonte, who stewed over the "total loss" of Gunn's $25,000 fee.[85]

Of the ten or so movie projects Gunn labored over in the late sixties, only *The Landlord* and *The Angel Levine* were completed and distributed. Nevertheless, the pay he collected from these jobs, combined with the income from his television appearances, provided the once penniless high school dropout with unprecedented financial security. In 1969, Gunn purchased a twenty-three-room mansion on the Hudson River in Upper Nyack, thirty miles north of Manhattan. Constructed in 1730 and formerly owned by writer Ben Hecht, the exquisitely furnished, mahogany-frame dwelling sat on an expansive estate complete with swimming pool, tennis court, stone tower, and private beach, and the interiors were copiously decorated with candles, flowers, antiques, and framed photographs and artworks. Schultz, who Gunn persuaded to move to the nearby artist's colony Sneden's Landing, recalled that his friend's bathroom was so large that parties were held in it.[86] Interviews with Gunn conducted at the time of *Ganja & Hess*'s release invariably comment on the house and its opulence; Maurice Peterson in *Essence*, one of many to posit a link between Hess Green's estate and Gunn's palatial abode, speculated on the latter's role in nurturing its owner's creativity.[87] *Essence* returned to Upper Nyack five years later to photograph Gunn next to his bed for an essay on the "sleeping rooms" of notable Black male artists. The velvet-trimmed walls of Gunn's room instilled, the correspondent reported, "an atmosphere of quiet contemplation and serenity," while his overstuffed bookshelves contributed to a sense of "sleeping in a gentlemen's study."[88]

Gunn's life was further transformed at the end of the sixties when he met Samuel Waymon. Waymon, in his midtwenties and already an accomplished musician, managed and served as organist in the band backing his older sister, the renowned vocalist Nina Simone. At the time of their initial meeting, Gunn was in preproduction on *Stop* and Waymon was living above the garage at his sister's house in Mount Vernon.[89] Waymon became Gunn's partner and housemate, and he further enlarged the latter's impressive social circle of accomplished artists. In their years in Upper Nyack, the two men hosted parties, readings, and receptions attended by the likes of Muhammad Ali, James Baldwin, Amiri Baraka, Ossie Davis, Ruby Dee, Helen Hayes, Toni Morrison, Simone, and the president of Nigeria.[90] Waymon became Gunn's closest artistic collaborator as well, making invaluable contributions as composer and musical performer to *Ganja & Hess*, *Black Picture Show*, and the stage musical version of *Rhinestone* (1982), as well as actor in *Ganja & Hess* and *Personal Problems*. He also served as Gunn's typist, editor, and sounding board, making it all the more impossible to isolate his influence on, or minimize his importance to, Gunn's seventies and eighties output.

In many ways 1969 was the most momentous year of Gunn's personal and professional life. Years of gainful employment had granted him the opportunity to acquire his dream house. He met the man who would become his lifetime companion and collaborator, and he was about to embark on his film directing debut. Yet, even in his annus mirabilis Gunn remained absolutely clear-eyed about his position within the American culture industry and society in general. A near-calamity from that year reaffirmed his cynicism. Gunn was walking along Central Park South wearing an expensive leather coat that he bought with some of his *Angel Levine* earnings. Suddenly, he was thrown up against a car by police officers, who demanded he tell them "where's the money." One of the cops bellowed that a woman down the street had just been robbed, and Gunn, evidently the most viable suspect in proximity, had been fingered as the thief. As he later related to Schultz, Gunn viewed the encounter as the essence of being Black in America, distilled. In an echo of his painful recognition decades earlier in high school, he was starkly reminded that "no matter how high up you are, you're still a nigger."[91]

Ready, Set, *Stop*: Gunn's Transition to Film Directing

At the end of 1969, both *The Landlord* and *The Angel Levine* were in postproduction and generating ample publicity and high expectations. Correspondingly, Gunn's reputation in Hollywood was strong enough to elicit an offer from Warner Bros.-Seven Arts to make his own movie, *Stop*, despite having no directing experience aside from theater workshops.[92] With the studio's announcement of its deal with Gunn and producer Paul Heller, Gunn became only the fourth African American to helm a Hollywood studio picture, following Gordon Parks Sr., whose Warner Bros.–backed adaptation of his novel *The Learning Tree* (1969) had debuted in June, and Ossie Davis and Melvin Van Peebles, who were then finalizing *Cotton Comes to Harlem* for United Artists and *Watermelon Man* (1970) for Columbia, respectively.

Gunn's ascension to the role of film director represented the culmination of an artistic ambition dating back to his early boyhood, when he arranged objects on a miniature model stage and surveyed his homemade mise-en-scène through the lens of a Brownie box camera. That the cinematic medium appeared to offer superior world-building opportunities was swiftly grasped by the child Gunn, who at the age of seven was already cognizant of the filmmaker's powers: "If a couple was walking down the street in a movie and there was a building behind them or a traffic jam or whatever, it was he that created that. He made me see what he wanted me to see."[93] Gunn's promotion by Warner Bros.-Seven Arts also provided him the means to best protect his scriptwriting efforts from inept directors and boorish producers. Although wary of the compromise and "dependen[ce] on so many people" that distinguish filmmaking from the comparatively private art of literature, Gunn nonetheless appreciated the film director's prerogative to "put the focus where you want it to be."[94] And, while being a scenarist for hire padded Gunn's finances, it also potentially condemned him to a professional existence of, in the words of *Rhinestone Sharecropping*'s screenwriter hero, "shoveling shit against the tide." Without gaining more control over his scripts, Gunn ran the risk of finding himself trapped within the cycle of "writing Race for money" and unable to refuse the next assignment "because the whole thing might come to a halt anytime."[95]

A studio movie such as *Stop* could perhaps only have been made in the late sixties. The picture's engagement with frankly "adult" themes, including polyamory and bisexuality, was enabled by the studios' abandonment of the Motion Picture Production Code in 1968 and their simultaneous implementation of a content-based ratings system, which allowed for greater leeway in representations of sexuality. Economically, *Stop*'s production was made possible by a crippling industry recession brought about by the desertion of older filmgoers. As a result, the venerable Hollywood majors increasingly entrusted filmmaking duties to unproven counterculture-identified directors and production companies such as Francis Ford Coppola's American Zoetrope. Warner Bros.' association with filmmakers like Coppola reflected policies initiated by its young production chief Kenneth Hyman, who succeeded Jack L. Warner when Seven Arts Productions bought out the studio founder's controlling interest in 1967. Hyman was acclaimed by *Variety* in early 1969 for demonstrating that a "carefully-selected production program can succeed sans bestselling properties or star-filled 'packages.'"[96] Hyman's willingness to back innovative low-cost projects bolstered Warner Bros.' reputation as a haven for film artists. And, although ownership of the studio changed hands once again in late 1969, this time to the multiconglomerate Kinney National Company, the new bosses promised to preserve these low-cost policies and eschew blockbusters.[97]

Against this optimistic backdrop, Gunn was given a budget of less than $1 million and a two-month shooting schedule in San Juan, Puerto Rico, at a magnificently restored nineteenth-century house, starting in late December.[98] Two white actors were cast in the lead roles of Michael and Lee Berger: Edward Bell, a former drama professor, and Linda Marsh, a rising star whom Kazan had directed in *America, America* (1963). Rounding out Gunn's cast were two newcomers: Richard Dow, a Hispanic actor with few film credits before or after *Stop*, and Marlene Clark, an African American model-turned-thespian. Gunn captured, by his own reckoning, "fantastic" raw footage for *Stop* despite working with a relatively unproven crew, including first-time director of photography Owen Roizman and a team of Puerto Ricans who did not speak English, alongside the obligatory white technicians mandated by the Hollywood craft guilds.[99]

Years later, Gunn described *Stop* as

> the story of an American writer and his wife, both white, who went to Puerto Rico. Two years [earlier], the writer's brother had committed suicide there, after having murdered his wife without apparent reason. The writer had inherited his house but had never gone there. With his marriage taking a turn for the worse, his wife and he decided to spend some time there together. What caused the murder and the suicide for his brother happens again. The only thing that can stop another murder and another suicide would be that the husband pulls himself together. But he is incapable of that.[100]

Reduced to its basic components, *Stop* could have developed into a recognizable genre picture, perhaps an erotic thriller. This is, in fact, how Heller framed the project for the *New York Times*, as "a study in the Hitchcockian sense."[101] Yet, the studio cut of the film, currently the only version available to view, contains little in the way of Hitchcockian elements. Nor is it a thriller in the conventional sense, despite the plot intrigue established by the backstory. *Stop*'s true antecedents are more literary and theatrical than cinematic, in the traditions of the absurdist, existentialist fiction of Albert Camus and the harrowing, finely observed character studies of Harold Pinter and Edward Albee. Yet, *Stop* also owes a narrative debt to the heavily psychological art cinema of celebrated European auteurs such as Ingmar Bergman, Federico Fellini, and Alain Resnais. Additionally, its concluding sequences gesture toward the equally ambiguous but more commercial "trip film," the short-lived, late sixties movie cycle exemplified by Roger Corman's *The Trip* (1967), in which a character explores her inner consciousness through the aid of hallucinogenic drugs, the net effect of which is less emancipatory than incapacitating.

The studio edit of *Stop* is half the length of the three-hour director's cut that Gunn delivered to Warner Bros. in early 1970.[102] Gunn's *Stop* possibly no longer exists, but one can get a sense of what his expanded cut might have incorporated based on a comparison of the extant semiofficial version with Gunn's final two screenplay drafts: one dated November 10, 1969, and bearing the title *Mandala*, and one dated December 6, which apparently served as the shooting script. Like many a Gunn protagonist, Michael is an aesthete of worldly sophistication and a writer of some ambition. Yet, he struggles mightily to complete a commission: an English translation of the writings of Camus. Michael regards the move to San Juan as an opportunity to clear his mind and focus his efforts. Almost immediately, however, he finds himself unable to work. He sleeps into the afternoon and spends his waking hours on the living room sofa, drinking, listening to classical music, and ignoring Lee, the implication being that he is lapsing into the behaviors of his brother John (played by Gunn's friend John Hoffmeister) in advance of the latter's mental break. Michael claims to have never been close to John, but their metaphoric kinship is suggested by several shared interests, including French literature. Fluency in French is an attribute shared by many of Gunn's characters, but, in *Stop*, this detail acquires an especially decadent resonance due to the Bergers' racial and social privilege and to the story's "underdeveloped" setting.

His physical attraction to his wife increasingly dissipated, Michael brings home a prostitute for sex while Lee is out for an afternoon. As he climaxes and falls, exhausted, to the side of the bed, the prostitute notices Lee watching silently from the doorway, having just returned. The woman nonchalantly dresses and demands payment from Lee, who numbly hands her a wad of bills. After an awkward attempt at reviving her unresponsive husband's ardor, Lee flees the house. Michael catches up with her on a secluded street and steers her toward a patio restaurant. Once seated, Michael stuns his wife with a stream-of-consciousness tirade, calculated "with the idea of hurting way deep, yet explaining himself."[103] His deeply personal and vicious attack, which fills nearly three pages in Gunn's screenplay but is slightly abridged on film, subtly exposes the protagonist's hypocrisy and that hypocrisy's foundation in the prison of compulsory heterosexual masculinity:

> I masturbate in the shower at least four times a week because the effort it takes to drag my exhaustion into that bedroom and assure you of my deep respect . . . my admiration . . . my passion . . . my humility . . . that there is a difference between a whore and a wife in the sack. . . . and that difference is my husbandly benediction of your sacred parts . . . I can't make that with every screw. There are times when I want you to be a whore for me. In the shower I think of whores and pick ups. I never think of you! . . . I'm leaving you. I am leaving you because you exhaust me. I'm leaving you because I don't know who I am. I'm leaving you because I no longer know the difference between love and duty. I'm leaving you . . . I'm leaving you.[104]

Edward Bell's understated rendition of this scalding broadside speaks volumes about how Gunn directs his actors: specifically, how he gives his actors space to interpret their roles based on their convictions about those characters in *individual* scenes rather than holding them to a consistency of motive and attitude for the duration of the narrative. Gunn's characters often act differently from one scene to the next, in ways that seem to contradict their deeply held beliefs about the world. This endows Gunn's characters with a complexity that arguably reflects how real people actually behave, even when those characters inhabit a fantastical story world (as they do in *Ganja & Hess*). The license that Gunn extends to his actors thus complements the freedom he allows himself as a writer to develop interesting and unpredictable narratives, rather than familiar, predigested experiences.

No sooner does Michael finish his monologue than the story's other principals arrive on the scene: Richard and Marlene Mathiesen, a glamorous and exotic young couple, who will serve for the Bergers as, in Gunn's description, "the people that wander into our lives, into our cafes, into our rooms. The people we hope can transfuse us with a new excitement."[105] Michael, recognizing Richard from an encounter at a Manhattan party, reintroduces himself and joins their table. Lee shortly follows and shocks her husband by openly flirting with the new acquaintance. The flirtation between Lee and Richard, and then between Michael and Marlene, continues into the afternoon, which the couples spend sunbathing on Richard's yacht, and, eventually, the evening, when the Bergers host a dinner for their new friends.

The dinner sequence mainly consists of aimless chatter, first in pairs (Michael/Richard, then Lee/Richard) and then among the entire group at the table. Their conversation strikes the ear as superficial and pretentious and thus reflective of the characters' labored efforts to convey an aura of worldly sophistication and, consequently, enhance their desirability as sexual partners. This unspoken desperation is the crucial subtext, and, because of its importance to his conception of the characters, Gunn rehearsed the scene repeatedly with his actors, all of whom except Marsh had very limited movie experience.[106] Perhaps inevitably, the committing of this particular sequence to film prompted one of the rare occasions when the director intervened with his actors on set; at one point, Gunn was even obliged to take Bell aside and explain to him that "there are scenes where we improvise and there are scenes where we do not. This is one of the scenes where we do not."[107] Through such tactics, Gunn elicited performances in *Stop* that give the impression of spontaneity even when his actors stick closely to the lines in the script.

The air of extemporization intensifies in *Stop*'s final half hour, during which the characters further shed their inhibitions under the influence of psychoactive and psychedelic drugs. After a meal supplemented with champagne and cannabis, the couples go out to a nightclub and take in a flamenco act. Halfway through the show, Richard excuses himself and, with Marlene's blessing, leaves with another woman. Marlene goes home with Michael and Lee, initiating an underlit, soft-focus sequence of sexual couplings. As noted in Gunn's revised screenplay, there follows a "series of almost subliminal shots of the three of them getting together" in various combinations: Michael and Lee, Michael and Marlene, Lee and Marlene.[108] The breaking down of repressions continues past the break of dawn, when Richard arrives and prepares a pitcher of orange juice mixed with mescaline. He presents, "in an almost Communion Ceremony fashion," each of the just-awakened Bergers with a tall glass of the spiked liquid.[109]

The hallucinogenic effect of the mescaline motivates the apparently subjective style and fragmented narration of *Stop*'s climax. After his hosts drink the concoction, Richard seduces them in succession. In the study, a prone and disoriented Michael "allows himself to be possessed by Richard." Afterward, in the bedroom, Lee tells Richard that she would rather see Michael dead than let him abandon her, and she asks, "If I make love to you will you kill him?"[110] In a surrealistic montage, Michael is then transported to a forest of gnarled trees, where he is pursued by Richard, who stalks him with a Luger in hand. Gunn's script, which possibly reflects his final edit prior to Warner Bros.' intervention, intercuts flashback images of the previous evening's merriments with shots of Michael's brother murdering his wife. Richard fires at Michael three times, but the latter escapes to a beach, where he encounters a group of indigenous children who "shoot" him with toy guns. After a long stretch of wandering, Michael finds his way home and takes a seat opposite his wife at their kitchen table; as the camera tracks in on Lee, she looks directly into the lens and shields her eyes with her palm, and the frame freezes in irresolution.

Perhaps in anticipation of filmgoers' inability to process this twisted story line, Heller attempted to clear up its ambiguities in the project's early stages of publicity, in which he helpfully observed that the three couples—Michael and Lee, Richard and Marlene, John and Ellen—are "all the same," metaphorically speaking, and that Lee's final gesture is "a reassurance to the audience that what had happened before would *not* happen again."[111] Yet, as evidenced by his movie's bewildering juxtapositions of objective and subjective realities, especially in its final third, Gunn certainly did not care about whether *Stop* provided "reassurance" to the audience, ideologically or narratively. His close adherence to his final draft script, even for scenes that seem to cry out for more spontaneous invention, indicates his commitment to ambiguity by design.

Although the deal for *Stop* predated Kinney's acquisition of its new motion picture division, the picture's tiny budget fit the cost-cutting policies implemented by incoming president Ted Ashley. According to Gunn, Warner Bros. executives were thrilled with the rough cut he assembled, and they subsequently offered him a three-picture contract.[112] Yet, within days, the studio took the film away from Gunn and commenced its own edit, rearranging the plot order and reconvening the actors for additional dubbing.[113] With only the Warner Bros. cut of *Stop* currently accessible, it is impossible to know precisely how far Warner Bros.' editors deviated from Gunn's rough cut. It seems probable, as Lawrence Cohn has speculated, that the studio added some voice-over dialogue, possibly lifted from the shooting script, to the film's ending in a largely futile attempt to clarify the final story events.[114] Bell, who assisted Gunn during postproduction, upon seeing the Warner Bros. version in 2010, insisted that *Stop* was reedited in order to make Linda Marsh's character the true focus of the story.[115] Unsatisfactory as the recut may have turned out, as of late 1970, Warner Bros. was still committed to releasing it. Official publicity stills were distributed, and, in November, the studio took out a four-page spread in *Variety* promoting its upcoming releases that included *Stop*, which was billed as an "ice-cold, white-hot probe of modern marriage and sex."[116]

From today's vantage point it might seem surprising, considering Gunn's reputation as a "serious" artist, that the most notable instances of advance promotion for *Stop* appeared in magazines marketed to devotees of the so-called "sexploitation" cinema. Warner Bros. publicists evidently regarded this largely male, largely heterosexual fan base as the only viewing public that *Stop* might potentially reach. Indeed, during this "highly mediated and increasingly permissive period of change," as David Church characterizes it, "the emergence of sexploitation fan magazines sold at newsstands and adult bookstores" played a vital role in ensuring the profitability of not only softcore pornographic features such as *I, a Woman* (1965) and *The Stewardesses* (1969) but sexually candid art films like Bergman's

The Virgin Spring (1960).¹¹⁷ Adult film aficionados and consumers of sexploitation media seemed most likely to seek out *Stop*'s unique mélange of difficult style and narrative and erotic frankness, and Warner Bros. hyped it accordingly.

The most substantial media bids to publicize *Stop*'s purportedly imminent release appeared in two softcore periodicals from Knight Publishing Corporation, *Adam Film World* and *Knight*, in October 1970.¹¹⁸ The former title publicized *Stop* in a ten-page spread that closely adhered to the sexploitation cinema fan magazine's tried-and-true format, which Church defines as "a brief plot synopsis . . . plus several fleeting critical comments," all of which are "far outweighed by lurid production stills."¹¹⁹ Unsurprisingly, given the vagueness of *Stop*'s plot, both profiles foreground the ambiguity and "mysticism" of the narrative. "A man has a passion for his wife Ellen, but he shoots her dead. Why?" asks the *Adam Film World* correspondent. "Richard and Michael get a passion for each other. Then Richard holds a pistol to Michael's head. Why?"¹²⁰ As the *Knight* reviewer astutely opines, any attempt to resolve these enigmas is beside the point because the director's true interest lies in exploring "Kafkaesque truths and [applying a] Pinteresque mystery approach to the sex-love-hate-cruelty dynamics of human behavior."¹²¹ The accompanying stills provide clues as to what Warner Bros. eliminated from Gunn's three-hour cut. Many of them capture the actors in various stages of undress, implying that the studio-employed editors were, paradoxically, instructed to trim the very elements that the studio would later exploit in *Stop*'s promotion. Judging from these images, shots of Marsh with her breasts exposed and of Marsh, Bell, and Clark asleep in the same bed were among those left on the cutting room floor.

Why, given its initial plan to sell *Stop* on the basis of its sexual content, did Warner Bros. then attempt to make the film *less* sexually explicit? Certainly, Warner Bros. hoped to avoid an X rating, which had become increasingly stigmatized as a marker of "dirty" movies in the two years since the creation of the age-based ratings system enforced by the studio-backed Classification and Ratings Administration (CARA). As Jon Lewis has shown, by late 1970, the major producer-distributors (including Warner Bros., of course) avoided the X classification at all costs, having been persuaded by Motion Picture Association of America president Jack Valenti "to resist the short-term profits earned by films that might eventually be labelled legally as obscene in favour of the long-term positive public relations exemplified in the studios' apparent restraint and social responsibility."¹²²

Despite its studio's preventive measures, however, *Stop* received an X rating from CARA, and this portended an uphill battle to attract positive critical attention. Warner Bros. could have scarcely been encouraged by the fact that many of 1970's studio-backed X-rated releases (including *Performance*, *Myra Breckinridge*, and *Beyond the Valley of the Dolls*) had been savaged by American reviewers, several of whom branded these pictures, in the description of *New York* critic John Simon, "indescribably sleazy, self-indulgent, and meretricious" and brimming with "mindless intellectual pretension and pathologically reveled-in gratuitous nastiness."[123] As Harry Benshoff has perceptively observed, such critical opprobrium, supposedly leveled in defense of standards of "aesthetic taste," was almost solely reserved for films that foregrounded "generic hybridity, stylistic experimentation, and queer content."[124] As an especially bold example of all three of those properties in combination, *Stop* stood little chance of getting a fair hearing from the mainstream critical establishment.

Of the elements isolated by Benshoff, "queer content" was probably the most unassimilable within this cultural context. Consider, for the sake of comparison, the critical acclaim and financial remuneration reaped by the roughly contemporary *Bob and Carol and Ted and Alice* (1969), which shares *Stop*'s spouse-swapping premise. Because it limits its sexual permutations to the heterosexual realm (and plays them out for comic effect), *Bob and Carol and Ted and Alice* was rewarded handsomely for its transgressing of social taboos. *Stop*'s depiction of same-sex coupling, in contrast, was likely the deciding factor in CARA's final judgment and thus in the project's disappearance. Whereas both Gunn's screenplay and the Warner Bros. cut are fairly circumspect about sexual activity between Lee and Marlene, alluding to such potentialities only in an abbreviated montage, the morning-after "possession" of Michael by Richard is played out face-to-face and instigated by a long open-mouthed kiss. Though filmed using low-key lighting and edited in a somewhat elliptical manner, Michael is obviously sodomized. This literal and metaphorical penetration lies at the heart of Marlo David's 2011 analysis of *Stop*. For David, the exposure of "Michael's queer desire ... forces him to experience vulnerability, fear, and confusion," in turn giving the lie to his privileged status.[125] This "symbolic displacement of the [white] patriarch" constitutes one of the most radical consequences of Gunn's appropriation of the tools of mainstream filmmaking, for it redirects the ongoing scrutiny of Black sexual and familial dysfunction onto its rarely investigated white counterpart.[126]

The racial dimensions of *Stop*'s critique of patriarchy probably had less influence on CARA's imposition of an X rating than the film's queer representations, but that might be because Warner Bros. had submerged the story's racial politics during the postproduction stage. *Stop* was filmed during a particularly volatile period of Puerto Rican history, one marked by acts of revolutionary violence by underground liberation movements opposed to the commonwealth government. Gunn later recalled being forced to work out of an apartment in Old San Juan because the hotels farther inland were "explod[ing] like matchboxes" due to terrorist bombings. For security's sake, due to the production's visibility as an emissary of American capitalism, Gunn employed around twenty crew members who were actual fighters within the *independista* movement.[127]

Surviving scripts indicate that Gunn did on some level conceive of *Stop* in terms of a neocolonialist critique and that he planned to incorporate indigenous elements to serve as an ironic counterpoint to the self-absorption and detachment from their environment displayed by the American leads. This strategy reveals itself in an early draft, when Michael's mescaline trip is interrupted by a group of "black natives" who encircle the white man and stare silently and "stone-faced" as he tries to reclaim his bearings.[128] Gunn's revised screenplay also features a remarkable scene in which Michael is introduced to a young freedom fighter brought to the house by the Bergers' maid. The American tourist betrays his disingenuousness with a series of condescending inquiries about what it "means" to be Puerto Rican and a revolutionary, yet his questions are nonetheless met with direct and thoughtful responses: "To be a revolutionary here in Puerto Rico, is having the courage to stand up in a country who denies itself. [It's] being aware of the unfairness, injustice, oppressive feeling of not [being] free in your own country."[129] Grasping for a common bond, Michael asks his houseguest whether he has read Camus. When the visitor continues his impassioned analysis of Puerto Rico's conversion into "an american [*sic*] industrial outpost," a bored Michael brings their discussion to a close by handing him a check; he then returns to reclining on his couch.[130] According to Gunn, the role of the revolutionary was played by a man who could not show his face on-screen because he was "the head of 'independista' in Puerto Rico" and, thus, wanted by the government.[131] The neophyte actor need not have worried; his character was dropped entirely from the studio's final edit.

Stop became the first of several Bill Gunn movie projects from which the writer-director's own contribution was effaced. The film has never received a proper theatrical or home video release, and most of the few people to have watched it have only seen a degraded VHS copy of the Warner Bros. version. For nearly three years after *Stop*'s completion the studio maintained the illusion of an eventual national release, and there is a remote possibility that the picture was shown in isolated test screenings in Texas.[132] In late 1971, Warner Bros. announced its fall of 1972 release schedule in the industry trades, and *Stop* was on it.[133] Yet, although the studio reassured Gunn that it was "only waiting for the right moment to send it into the theaters," Warner Bros. gave up on *Stop* the following spring, when the Ashley regime decided to sell several unreleased movies dating from the pre-Kinney era directly to television.[134] *Stop*'s sexually risqué subject matter mitigated against its network airing, and so it was shelved permanently.

Stop was screened publicly for the first time as part of the Whitney Museum's New American Film and Video series in the summer of 1990, a year after Gunn's death. Since then, rumors of both its pending reemergence and its total loss have circulated every few years. The Whitney retrospective reportedly screened a 35 mm print that had been found in the Warner Bros. archive in 1986, but that print then promptly vanished.[135] More recent museum screenings have used Sam Waymon's personal videocassette copy. The possibility of *Stop*'s restoration and circulation grew increasingly remote until it was announced in 2014 that Warner Home Video had remastered the film and would be releasing it through its DVD-on-demand subsidiary Warner Archive, once it had cleared up certain issues regarding rights and clearances.[136] As of 2021, however, these problems have not been resolved, and *Stop* has yet to appear via any video or streaming format in any of its various iterations.

"I think they make a lot of films with no intention of releasing them," Gunn mordantly replied in 1982 when asked why Warner Bros. never released *Stop*. "They take the film and get very excited about it and then they re-cut it and they don't like the cut so they shelve it. It's not even politics, just knee-jerk reaction to stupidities for no reason whatsoever."[137] He could have added that Warner Bros.' production philosophy of maintaining tight cost controls over movies helmed by "unproven" filmmakers—and African American directors in this era were always "unproven"—afforded the studio the luxury to cancel even completed pictures with minimal fiscal consequence. It is not surprising, then, that so many Black directors numbered among the era's industry casualties. Their talents remained "unproven" because they were, to begin with, never entrusted with projects that might have resulted in unqualified financial success.

The disappearance of *Stop* also implies second thoughts about inviting into the industry a Black filmmaker who refused to confine himself to "Black" issues. Gunn's instincts ran counter to the studios' impulse toward segmentation and categorization as a means of maximizing revenue, an impulse enforced during the concurrent blaxploitation cycle. *Stop* consequently became one of the more notable casualties of the constantly mutating production and distribution policies of the supposedly liberalized and supposedly meritocratic "New Hollywood."

3

CREATION

The Making of Ganja & Hess

> Bill and I used to laugh about how Black history would be even further distorted for decades to come. Suppressing the truth is a means of controlling people, controlling their history: a people's conception of themselves could be based on lies. Bill and I wanted to tell the truth about our belief system. *Ganja & Hess* was an original script based on the truth of our reality; everything in it came from reality.
>
> —Sam Waymon, interview with the author.

> The studios have absolutely no interest whatsoever in depicting Black culture or Black life.... So to be a serious filmmaker, you have to almost "steal" a movie.[1]
>
> —Bill Gunn, quoted in Peterson, "Interview with Bill Gunn," 27.

GANJA & HESS WAS BILL GUNN'S FURTHEST ADVANCE into the realm of genre fiction and the fantastic. What motivated this notoriously inner-directed aesthete's detour into such territory? The most obvious explanation stems from the fact that Gunn was at loose ends in the early seventies, his once-surging career having stalled after the shelving of his directorial debut. Burned by his initial association with a major, Gunn sought opportunities outside the studio system. While Warner Bros. deliberated *Stop*'s fate in late 1970, Gunn joined forces with Now Productions Cinema, founded by retired basketball star Don Barksdale, auto dealer Robert Bell, and Bell's brother (and *Stop* lead) Edward. Now Productions' maiden undertaking was to be *The Partisan*, which Gunn would write and direct with Edward Bell in the leading role.[2] In October, *Variety* optimistically predicted that

The Partisan would soon be filming on location "in Harlem, San Francisco and North Africa," but no screenplay was ever completed.³

The only other property to which Gunn's name was publicly attached in the years between *Stop* and *Ganja & Hess* was an original screenplay by Kathleen Collins. An early 1973 issue of *Chamba Notes* stated that Gunn was "tentatively scheduled to direct" *Women, Sisters and Friends*, with production scheduled to take place in the Bahamas, and, later that year, *Essence* reported that filming had actually wrapped.⁴ In fact, it never began. Collins herself had always planned to direct the script, and the project went unrealized precisely because she found no one willing to "give any money to a black woman to direct a film."⁵

The cancellation of both *The Partisan* and *Women, Sisters and Friends*, combined with the studios' disinterest in working with the independent-minded filmmaker, threatened to ground Gunn's directing career before it had a chance to take flight. Then, around the time of *Georgia, Georgia*'s premiere, Gunn met Quentin Kelly. A deal was struck between the two men by the end of March 1972, when Kelly-Jordan took out an ad in *Variety* plugging its upcoming pictures, including Gunn's *Night In . . . Night Out (Story of an Obsession)*.⁶ Three months later, *Night In* was reported by both *Jet* and the *New York Times*, which described it only as "a drama about vampirism," to be nearing production.⁷ By most estimates, the budget for what would eventually be known as *Ganja & Hess* was set at a measly $350,000.⁸

Little is known about *Ganja & Hess*'s preproduction and production histories other than those factors that influenced the (ill-advised) decisions about its release. This chapter thus aims to provide a relatively complete account of the film's conception, preparation, and execution. It attempts to settle the long-standing dispute over the project's origins and to clear up enduring misperceptions surrounding both Kelly-Jordan's rationale for commissioning *Ganja & Hess* and Gunn's rationale for accepting the commission. It further illuminates Gunn's creative process by dissecting the modifications undergone during the project's development and identifying those elements that contribute to its formal audacity and rich allegory. Those who have written about *Ganja & Hess* usually comment on the differences between the final cut and the shooting script, the latter of which has been available to scholars since its 1991 publication in Phyllis Klotman's anthology *Screenplays of the African American Experience* and which served as the basis for Spike Lee's remake. This chapter's analysis expands on this comparison while also incorporating observations on the screenplay's earliest surviving draft, from when the property was known by the title *Blood*.

Chapter 3 proceeds like a viewer's guide to *Ganja & Hess*'s complicated narrative, moving through it chronologically and pausing intermittently to clarify (or speculate on) plot information. Because previous efforts to interpret the film's meanings typically proceed from a contemplation of its story and characters, this chapter is additionally devoted to gauging the significance of visual and sonic style—editing patterns, framing and composition, performance methods, and overlapping and contrapuntal sound—with an emphasis on unexpected and occasionally uncanny stylistic juxtapositions and on how those dissonances harmonize with the director's thematic intentions. This focus leads to considerations of the essential contributions made by Gunn's creative associates. In their recent special issue of *Black Camera*, coeditors Nicholas Forster and Michele Prettyman make a compelling case for the "New York Scene" of independent Black filmmaking that nurtured Gunn (and Collins) as one based, despite the strong individualist streaks of its representative auteurs, in collaboration and "the intimacy of relationships."[9] In highlighting the invaluable influence of cinematographer James E. Hinton, film editor Victor Kanefsky, composer/sound designer/actor Sam Waymon, and lead actors Duane Jones and Marlene Clark to *Ganja & Hess*'s aesthetic achievement, the sections below should likewise serve as useful reminders that even the so-called director's cinema is a fundamentally collective endeavor.

Vampires of Westchester: *Ganja & Hess*'s Origin Stories

The question of who actually initiated contact between Gunn and Kelly-Jordan has long been a point of contention in the discourse on *Ganja & Hess*. Those with a stake in branding the producers as greedy barbarians have understandably taken the director's side of the story, as outlined in chapter 1. The claim that Gunn was contracted to make a film from a racially insensitive script that merely regurgitated *Dracula*'s plot points is often repeated by *Ganja & Hess*'s defenders, who regard the film's postproduction fate as a tragedy facilitated by mainstream cinema's inability to assimilate Black subjectivities.[10] As a corollary, it has also been assumed that Kelly enlisted Gunn to make a vampire film specifically to cash in on the box office success of *Blacula*, American International Pictures's Black-cast revision of the Hollywood vampire formula.[11] Yet, *Blacula* was not released until August 1972, *after* filming wrapped on *Ganja & Hess*. For his part, Kelly has claimed that Gunn reached out to *him* soon after their introduction and that it was Gunn who presented the original idea for what would become *Ganja & Hess*.[12]

As with many of the arguments that erupted following *Ganja & Hess*'s disastrous reception, the disagreement over who should receive credit, or take responsibility, for the original idea is a reflection of intrinsic philosophical (and often racially determined) divisions over the balance of power between filmmakers and investors in the commercial cinema. Kelly, of course, has an ulterior motive for suggesting that he and Gunn were on the same page at the outset of their collaboration: to pin the film's *financial* disaster squarely on the director's deviation from the plan Kelly authorized. Gunn, in addition to perhaps mitigating his residual embarrassment over making a vampire movie, wanted to deflect blame for the reedited film's *artistic* disaster. It also remains unclear exactly why Gunn was drafted to make a horror movie when Kelly-Jordan's other Black directors under consideration, Angelou and Baldwin, were allowed to develop more personal "serious" projects.[13] After all, the genre's tropes and conventions seem far removed from the cultured and sophisticated image that both Kelly-Jordan and Gunn himself sought to promote. Perhaps Gunn really was, as Chiz Schultz has speculated, "desperate" for a chance to make another feature, enough so that he would stoop to becoming a horror director.[14] Kelly-Jordan, in turn, possibly rationalized its position through a slight adjustment of its guiding mentality: at least one of its movies needed to generate the revenue that would cover the losses incurred by the nobler failures. Who better to turn to for this hit than the one person in its stable who had actually made a movie? According to Waymon, Kelly believed Gunn had the most box office potential of the company's signed directors because someone, a major studio no less, had already trusted Gunn enough to let him make its film.[15]

Only after accepting this challenge, presumably, did Gunn grasp the vampire tale's relevance within a Black/Afrocentric context, with *blood* supplying the critical metaphor. Gunn would later insist that he used blood only "because I was told to make a movie about a vampire." His preferred reading was that *Ganja & Hess* is about *addiction*, and blood was just an arbitrary vehicle for this message: "I just took a metaphor and . . . in the place of blood it could be anything. It could be drugs. It could be coffee."[16] Gunn's conviction that "addiction" was the true subject of his screenplay was further reflected in its title change, from the straightforward *Blood* to the more evocative citation of the protagonists' first names: street names for marijuana and hashish, respectively. Regardless of these qualifications, "blood" in *Ganja & Hess* is not solely a generic obligation. Privately, Gunn was fond of observing that "the blood of the thing is the truth of the thing," an axiom that respects blood as that which comprises the very substance of any object. ("You *can* get blood from a stone," he told Waymon. "It's whatever the stone is made of.") And whereas white Americans tend to regard blood as abject and associate its ritualistic use with vampirism and the occult, many other cultures, especially marginalized and oppressed societies including American Indians and Australian aborigines, more readily appreciate the symbolic connection of blood to spiritual cleansing.[17]

To make the movie he really wanted to make, Gunn deemed it necessary to employ deception. The initial draft he submitted was, therefore, structured much like a conventional genre narrative in order to receive Kelly-Jordan's blessing. Yet, the lengths to which Gunn went to foster the illusion that he was making a commercial movie are still subject to debate. According to Kelly, the first iteration of Gunn's script, which he approved for production, mixed a horror story with "a sophisticated thirties comic feel." This version involved vampires but also a mummy that is somehow transplanted to Harlem and "ends up walking down 125th Street." This premise is suggestive of the later vampire spoof *Love at First Bite* (1979); indeed, Kelly surmises that a major Madison Avenue agency pilfered Gunn's original idea and, eventually, turned it into the George Hamilton vehicle.[18] Waymon denies, however, that such elements were ever part of *Ganja & Hess*, and no trace of such a scenario exists in Gunn's archived collections.[19]

Nevertheless, at least one of Gunn's early drafts features plot situations and dialogue deliberately inserted by the author to further the impression that *Ganja & Hess* would be a "straight" vampire movie. Gunn remarked in a university lecture in the early eighties that he "peppered his original screenplay with a fair amount of traditional horror-movie subterfuge."[20] He was, subsequently, at liberty to prune this material from his shooting script or during the postproduction phase. Gunn's assertion is corroborated by the earliest accessible (albeit undated) version of the *Ganja & Hess* screenplay, which is liberally sprinkled with references to vampires and vampirism, none of which appear in the shooting script. In the first draft's opening scene, as Hess witnesses an accident victim being wheeled from an ambulance, he speaks in a voice-over: "My name is Hess Greene, and I'm a vampire."[21] Later, Hess hypothesizes that "vampirism as an idea is part of the super culture" of (the fictive) Myrthia, and, were the consumption of blood to proliferate in the modern day, "it would be considered a perversion, and a vampire a degenerate."[22] In Gunn's revised final draft screenplay, dated June 15, 1972, all of these references are modified, with "desire" substituted for "vampirism" and "bloodsucker" for "vampire."[23]

No one speaks the word "vampire" in the finished film either, which complements Gunn's general goal of maximizing narrative ambiguity, allowing the viewer to draw her own conclusions about psychological motivation. In the final cut of *Ganja & Hess*, for example, Hess's revelation to Ganja of the nature of her transformation is not audible; though he clearly speaks to (and quarrels with) her, his dialogue is drowned out by nondiegetic music and a separate voice-over track. In contrast, in the original script his explanation is both perceptible and utterly unambiguous:

> GANJA: WHAT HAVE YOU DONE TO ME? You've got us both on something what is it [sic]. WHAT IS IT?
>
> HESS: I told you!
>
> GANJA: I DON'T BELIEVE YOU! . . . You got me on something that's fucking with my mind . . . goddamn you!
>
> HESS: WE'RE VAMPIRES!
>
> GANJA: Stop It! . . . What is it I'm on . . . What is it I need?
>
> HESS: BLOOD! . . . BLOOD! . . . BLOOD![24]

These glaring signposts did serve their intended purpose, which was to procure funding from Kelly and Jordan. At some point during preproduction, however, the executives read an updated version of the *Ganja & Hess* screenplay and were, as Schultz recalled, "horrified." Gunn and Schultz were summoned to Kelly-Jordan's Manhattan headquarters, where Kelly confronted them over the script's departure from the original premise. When his backer accused him of being "insane," Gunn answered with a melodramatic flourish: "You think this is insane . . . I have more insanity in the top drawer of my bureau than you can imagine!" The director then, allegedly, threw a chair through an office window. If Gunn's unhinged response was calculated to unnerve his employers and discourage them from further interference, it worked marvelously. Neither Kelly nor Jordan visited the production sites, nor did they approve the cast or attend screenings of the dailies.[25] The producers, therefore, had no real understanding of what Gunn was making of their investment until the picture was completed and it was too late to change it back. This degree of detachment lends credence to Waymon's contention that, as he and Gunn instantly intuited, Kelly would not "get" the film because he, like the purveyors of blaxploitation cinema, saw Black people solely "in terms of purchasing power."[26]

Gunn and Waymon's opinion of Kelly-Jordan's motivations as mainly exploitive was seriously challenged, however, by Tim Lucas and David Walker's meticulous appraisal for *Video Watchdog* in 1991, in which the authors argue that Kelly and Jordan were "genuinely interested in cultivating serious Black cinema."[27] David Kalat, writing in the same journal sixteen years later, agrees. In his view, the producers "wanted something more prestigious than the usual blaxploitation product," and the fact that Kelly-Jordan actively solicited the participation of "respected African-American artists and dignitaries" substantiates the firm's artistic pretensions.[28] Walter Metz, writing more recently, finds it implausible that the partners could be "completely blind to the fact that they were assembling highly talented, radical African American artists and material."[29] All of these scholars are correct: providing opportunities for Black intellectuals to make "quality," "artistic" movies was in fact Kelly-Jordan's raison d'être. This does not mean that Gunn's inferences were wrong, just that his conception of what is *possible* in an "art" movie was unconstrained by the models sanctioned by the art movie audience. The scripts for *Georgia, Georgia* and *The Inheritance*, while obviously the work of innovative artists, do not seriously break with the highly conventional properties of the international art cinema. *Ganja & Hess* was much more difficult to decipher by way of traditional art film viewing schemas, as chapter 4 illustrates.

With Kelly and Jordan absent, the role of on-location supervisor nominally fell to Schultz. Schultz unwaveringly supported Gunn and protected the creative team from executive interference, though he, too, was seldom on the set due to irregular financial compensation.[30] As on the simultaneous *Honeybaby, Honeybaby* shoot, payment for *Ganja & Hess*'s crew was often partial and slow to arrive. This situation worsened when production manager Lou Pastore and Schultz's assistant Janus Adams were robbed at gunpoint. The coworkers were transporting the week's payroll from the bank to the filming site when their car was forced to the side of the road by armed bandits. Crew members cynically speculated that the burglary was mob related, because of Pastore's Italian heritage.[31]

Like many of the entries in the Black movie boom, *Ganja & Hess* employed a largely white production team, with one notable exception, associate producer (and future chair of the National Endowment for the Arts) Joan

Shigekawa. The film's technical crew positions, by comparison, were dominated by people of color; according to Victor Kanefsky, Gunn wanted an entirely Black crew but was unable to find a sufficient number of Black personnel to fill every position.[32] Perhaps the key African American participant on the technical side was Hinton, who, thereafter, claimed to be the first Black director of photography on a North American feature film by virtue of his work on this picture.[33] *Ganja & Hess* further supplied motion picture experience for hairstylist Annie DeMille and the sole cinematic credit for costumer Scott Barrie, whose designs were very much in vogue in the seventies. Wardrobe supervisor Celia Bryant and makeup artist Scott Cunningham, both in high demand throughout the boom, lent valuable support as well.

Gunn's commitment to providing opportunities for Black film workers complemented the previous efforts of Schultz and Kanefsky in integrating the industry's technical guilds, which had long colluded to shut out nonwhites. In advance of filming on *The Angel Levine*, Schultz created an apprentice program that groomed young men and women of color for production jobs and successfully pitched it to the Ford Foundation, which had recently begun financing Black-oriented, public affairs television programs, *Soul!* and *Black Journal* among them.[34] The proposal resulted in a $25,000 grant that underwrote the hiring of fifteen trainees who observed and received instruction from professional technicians on the *Angel Levine* set; upon completion of the shoot, the apprentices formed their own production company.[35] No films resulted from this venture, but some trainees went on to play key roles on a number of boom-era movies, including Drake Walker, who wrote the original story for *Buck and the Preacher*, and Lawrence Cook, the lead actor in Ivan Dixon's incendiary narrative of urban revolt, *The Spook Who Sat by the Door*. Three graduates of the Ford Foundation program assumed key positions on *Ganja & Hess*: assistant director Anthony Major, production supervisor Ed Dessisso, and script supervisor Renoir Darrett. Major and Dessisso capitalized on their experience by coproducing *Super Spook* (1975) for independent distributor Levitt-Pickman. Major directed and cowrote the screenplay with Dessisso and two additional *Ganja & Hess* collaborators, actor Leonard Jackson and stuntman Tony King, both of whom also starred in this minor blaxploitation effort.

Kanefsky, meanwhile, had for years been trying to increase the number of African American editors in movies and television. While working for ABC in 1969, he asked an executive producer about the paucity of

Black editors at the network. The executive, evidently unaware of William Greaves, Hugh Robertson, and John Carter, each of whom had cut features by that point, replied that there were not any to recruit. In response, Kanefsky joined the faculty at National Educational Television, where he tutored aspiring editors at *Black Journal* for two years. Upon being hired for *Ganja & Hess*, Kanefsky asked and got approval from Pastore to bring aboard an African American apprentice.[36] Kanefsky requested *Black Journal*'s best candidate, who turned out to be Samuel Pollard. Pollard had just completed the yearlong coursework at National Educational Television yet had been contemplating changing careers owing to a lack of job prospects.[37] *Ganja & Hess* provided the twenty-three-year-old with the first credit of what would become a long and illustrious career, including a partnership with Spike Lee (and an Oscar nomination for coproducing Lee's *4 Little Girls* in 1997) and a teaching position at New York University.

By most accounts, the *Ganja & Hess* shoot was not plagued by the animosities that afflicted other contemporaneous, Black-cast films with integrated crews. Kanefsky claims that some of the whites on the crew (wrongly) believed their technical knowledge of filmmaking to surpass that of their Black coworkers, and they resented being placed in positions subordinate to them.[38] Most of the principals nevertheless agree with Marlene Clark's assessment of the shoot as guided by a generally positive vibe, thanks to Gunn's ability to unite people: "Film crews had been traditionally all-white, yet here was a crew that was totally mixed—and their devotion to Bill, and to what he was trying to say, was really quite impressive."[39] Waymon endorses Clark's view of a collective sense of mission: "Everyone on our crew had been waiting for something like this." Whereas their previous jobs had seldom if ever been a source of professional pride, *Ganja & Hess* "challenged everybody's skills and instincts and craft. We trusted people, and we got the most out of them."[40]

Story of an Obsession: *Ganja & Hess* Scene by Scene

Estimates of the length of the *Ganja & Hess* shoot vary, but everyone agrees that the shooting schedule was extremely condensed. By Klotman's calculations, filming took three to four weeks, whereas Waymon remembers the entire shoot taking sixteen days, with two days cut short by rain.[41] Gunn's production notebook logs the first day of shooting as July 5, 1972, and it details the scenes filmed on (or planned for) each day through the 8th. The remaining shooting days in Gunn's handwritten schedule, running from July 10 to July 24, are simply blank or labeled with the phrase "refer to call sheet."[42]

Regardless of the precise number of days spent on filming, the film's relatively short production schedule guaranteed that each was packed with activity. Shooting days regularly lasted between fourteen and eighteen hours and encompassed many separate setups. Gunn would then go home and spend another three hours agonizing over the following day's scenes. Often this involved rewriting in order to capitalize on the "energy" of his colleagues, especially the actors, who supplied him with endless "food for thought."[43] Gunn drew heavily on his actors' own personalities to flesh out their characters, providing those additions fit within the parameters of the behaviors and motivations detailed in the script. He was also open to creative input on the most crucial production decisions. The following subsections identify the artistic effects resulting from these decisions and the process by which Gunn's prose was so eloquently translated to a cinematic idiom.

Credit Sequence I: Hess (0:00–3:40)

In an influential appreciation of *Ganja & Hess*, in his 1979 book *American Film Now*, James Monaco asserts that, even before the picture's beginning credits conclude, the viewer understands that she is witness to "an extraordinary film."[44] These initial scenes are so rich with poetic imagery and ambiguity that Klotman and Manthia Diawara's groundbreaking analysis of the movie focuses almost entirely on disentangling the narrative and symbolic threads knotted together in the eight-minute opening sequence.

The introductory scenes in the finished film deviate significantly from Gunn's initial conception, and this departure provides immediate confirmation of David Kalat's observation that the traits that make *Ganja & Hess* "truly unique were not written, nor yet hinted" in the script.[45] Originally, the opening was to serve a function similar to the vast majority of narrative film openings: to straightforwardly introduce the protagonist—in this instance, Hess Green, an aloof, wealthy anthropologist and geologist renowned for his research on extinct African cultures—and to provide sufficient exposition and backstory to help the viewer comprehend important details about the setting, the secondary characters, their relationships and motivations, and so on; and to stoke the viewer's curiosity by planting enigmas to be resolved later. Gunn's final draft screenplay begins with a pickup basketball game at a recreation center, which is followed by a friendly conversation between the young referee, Richard, and Dr. Green, who volunteers at the center. Per the script's instructions, the camera then trails Hess through the streets of the city (Harlem in the original script; Spring Valley, New York, in the succeeding draft). He passes a church, from which "revival music pours out," and pauses at the sight of a bloody accident victim being led into a hospital. On the soundtrack, he speaks: "My name is Hess Greene, and I have a taste for blood."[46] Gunn's script fortifies this crucial bit of exposition by introducing a second "narrator": a typewriter that spells out "Part One . . . The Nativity," to which Hess's voice-over adds "The birth. Notebook on the beginning. The Myrthian papers and how I became addicted."[47]

As written, the impending scene begins to relate the ways by which Hess "became addicted." The doctor walks through the sixteenth-century collection at the Metropolitan Museum of Art, accompanied by Jack Sargent, a white archaeologist (played in the movie by John Hoffmeister), to the office of Mr. Wood, an elderly white administrator. After introducing Hess to his new assistant, George Meda (played by Gunn), Wood displays the museum's recent acquisition of relics from the long-defunct civilization of Myrthia. Wood shows Hess a skull fragment joined to a sliver of petrified wood and fashioned in the shape of a dagger. As Hess marvels at the fragment, he explains the circumstances by which the Myrthian culture blossomed "a thousand years before the Egyptians."[48] The culture was eventually destroyed by its queen's and finally its entire population's addiction to human blood, which "was believed to be a substance of the soul . . . Without it one could not enter their comparable kingdom of heaven."[49]

The opening of *Ganja & Hess* the *film*, in contrast, severely disrupts the narrative coherence established within the *script*'s first few pages. The first four images organize details from Salvatore Albano's neoclassical marble sculpture *The Fallen Angels* (1893) housed at the Brooklyn Museum, which replaced the Met as the locale for the meeting between Hess and Jack Sargent (see fig. 3.1). There follows an abrupt switch in location to a church revival in progress, captured in a montage of seemingly "wild" shots. The new setting introduces us to the reverend Luther Williams, a character Gunn added to the story only weeks before production began, appearing for the first time in Gunn's June 15 final script revision.[50] Luther's preaching motivates a transition to footage of the minister at his second job, driver for Hess Green. The chauffeur speaks vaguely of his employer's sickness—"He's an addict. He's not a criminal, he's a victim"—as the subtitle "Part I Victim"

Figure 3.1 *Ganja & Hess*'s title sequence introduces the tale of two fallen angels. *Ganja & Hess* (Blu-ray), Kino Lorber Films.

redundantly flashes on the screen. Hess's observance of a man prone on the street and attended to by paramedics is inserted at *this* point of the film, arresting the present tense of the narration. In addition, Luther's reflection that Hess is "addicted to blood" is undercut by Hess's dispassionate expression. If the doctor has a taste for blood, why no visible hunger pangs?

Credit Sequence II: The Museum (3:40–8:05)

Hess's lack of outward emotion is partly attributable to the understated performance style of actor Duane Jones. Granted, Hess Green is obviously more introspective than the agitated take-charge hero that Jones played in his only previous screen outing, Ben in George Romero's *Night of the Living Dead* (1968). Yet, for much of *Ganja & Hess*'s running time, Jones comes off as a bit diffident, forcing the viewer to deduce the turmoil roiling beneath his placid exterior. This supposed passivity was criticized by several of the picture's original reviewers, who mocked the idea that viewers would invest emotionally in "a dour, laconic type who rates little sympathy."[51]

On the contrary, Jones's artistic choices are strategic; they especially pay off near the film's conclusion, when Hess's spiritual awakening is conveyed through Jones's surprisingly violent physical reactions, which underline the profound break experienced by the character. The role's duality likely appealed greatly to Jones, whom Schultz remembers as conflicted by the divide between the "expressive" and "intellectual" aspects of his being (as ostensibly signified by his two professions: acting and teaching).[52] Uncomfortable with the notoriety bestowed by the Romero classic, Jones shunned movie roles in favor of theatrical performance and direction, often in productions at the Richard Allen Center for Culture and Art in Manhattan. Jones also taught English, and he began a four-year stint as the chair of the literature department at Antioch College immediately after filming *Ganja & Hess*.[53]

In the *Ganja & Hess* screenplay the museum conference is dominated by Hess's disquisition on the "blood society" of ancient Myrthia, a disquisition he continues that evening with Meda at his home.[54] These segments, in which a more loquacious version of Hess lays out the origin story of the cursed dagger, were shot but excluded from Gunn and Kanefsky's final cut. They were reinstated in *Blood Couple*, Fima H. Noveck's reedit of the film for Heritage Enterprises, which retroactively imposes a clearer causal pattern onto Gunn's filmed material and minimizes the ambiguity created by Kanefsky's methods.

Kanefsky joined *Ganja & Hess* after the producers had been unsuccessful in recruiting John Carter. Hearing of Schultz's search, Kanefsky submitted two of his pictures, a boxing documentary cut in "an impressionistic montage style" and a short adaptation of *A Child's Christmas in Wales*, which was broadcast on National Educational Television in 1966. Impressed by *A Child's Christmas*, which "animated" still photographs to bring Dylan Thomas's classic tale to life, Gunn accepted the applicant over the objections of those who doubted that Kanefsky could cut a live-action feature. Because he was on salary from the start of production, Kanefsky was a constant presence at the main shooting site, the Apple Bee Farm Estate in Croton-on-Hudson, New York.[55] He, his assistant Cynthia Castleman, and Pollard set up in a cottage near the main house, where they synced dailies and assembled a rough cut on a flatbed Moviola.[56]

Though Gunn, too, expressed some early reservations about Kanefsky, he soon realized that the latter's input was making the film better.[57] Kanefsky's documentary background instilled in him an approach to editing that deemphasized linearity and causality. He did not even consult shooting scripts when cutting film, a practice that had deeply irritated Hollywood director Christian Nyby, for whom the editor did uncredited work on the 1965 spy picture *Operation C. I. A.*[58] As Kalat notes, Kanefsky was unaccustomed to cutting scenes "in a predetermined pattern to adhere to some pre-existing storyline."[59] Instead, he combined shots in order to evoke ideas on a subtextual level. Gunn was completely amenable to this practice, as Kanefsky quickly inferred. After screening a day's worth of rushes for Gunn for the first time, Kanefsky realized that he had done most of the commenting. On the second night, he simply stated which takes he preferred, and Gunn agreed with his choices. Satisfied that they were on the same wavelength, Gunn never again asked Kanefsky to show him dailies, and he largely stayed out of Kanefsky's way during postproduction, allowing the editor to put together segments on his own and present them every other week for Gunn's approval.[60]

Kanefsky spent a lot of time on *Ganja & Hess*'s opening, linking fragments in sometimes bewildering ways. Following the revelation of Hess's blood addiction, several mysterious shots appear of Meda pacing in an unidentified room and aiming a revolver at his mirror reflection. Luther's voice-over returns, with a thematically resonant reading of the "Bread of Life" sermon from the King James Bible ("Whoso eateth my flesh, and drinketh my blood, hath eternal life; and I will raise him up at the last day," John 6:54–55). But Christ's words are confusingly matched to a shot of Hess and Jack Sargent at the Brooklyn Museum (see fig. 3.2). Two track ins, linked by a dissolve, then bring us a close view of a woman in a billowing white dress, cowering near a tree beneath threatening skies, in Féréol Bonnemaison's 1799 painting *Young Woman Overtaken by a Storm* (see fig. 3.3). Gunn's point in spotlighting this particular work is a bit obscure, although Walter Metz has astutely linked the painting's allegorical suggestion of "a world in crisis in the wake of the French Revolution" to Hess's own "personal and political turmoil."[61] In yet another departure from the script, the film drops the meeting among Hess, Sargent, Meda, and Mr. Wood (who is deleted altogether from the story). In its place, there is merely Sargent's voice-over introducing Hess to "your new assistant" under a brief close-up of Meda puffing on a joint and glaring contemptuously offscreen.

The disjointed sequence of events that opens *Ganja & Hess* employs two additional devices of note, both added in postproduction, that *should* have helped clarify the film's plot. Gunn's execution of these techniques, however, serves to further obfuscate. First, at the behest of the executive producers, a series of explanatory intertitles were added just prior to the *Fallen Angels* montage:

Figure 3.2 Jack Sargent (John Hoffmeister) leads Hess Green (Duane Jones) as they wind their way through the Brooklyn Museum's general collection. *Ganja & Hess* (Blu-ray), Kino Lorber Films.

Figure 3.3 "What's happening over *there* ... in *that* painting": detail from *Young Woman Overtaken by a Storm*. *Ganja & Hess* (Blu-ray), Kino Lorber Films.

> Doctor Hess Green...
> Doctor of anthropology Doctor of geology...
> While studying the ancient Black civilization of Myrthia...
> was stabbed by a stranger three times...
> one for God the Father one for the Son...
> and one for the Holy Ghost...
> stabbed with a dagger, diseased from that ancient culture...
> whereupon he became addicted and could not die...
> nor could he be killed.

This statement establishes certain key details of character and setting, but it also creates a problem of chronology. The incident of Hess's stabbing and his subsequent conversion to the undead do not happen until nearly twenty minutes into the film. Yet, the intertitles' use of the past tense ("was stabbed by a stranger") and the voice-over's use of the present tense ("He's addicted to blood") make it appear that Hess is a vampire even *before* we see him punctured by the Myrthian dagger. Kanefsky later conceded that this confusion of tenses may have simply been a continuity mistake, although this sort of modernist flourish would scarcely have been out of character for either Gunn or himself.[62]

An additional, more imaginative attempt is made in the opening of *Ganja & Hess* to reinsert the backstory that was lost when Gunn cut the scene of Hess narrating to his colleagues the grim legend of the Myrthians' decline. In the film, the responsibility for telling this legend shifts to a nondiegetic vocalist accompanied by a fluttering solo trumpet. The vocalist sings the story of the lost civilization ("By the Christians it is written that in the Black Myrthian age / There existed an addiction to blood among its people") over images of the Albano sculpture, the church service, and, eventually, a protracted Rolls Royce limousine ride from Brooklyn to Westchester County. A good deal of vital information is delivered in Waymon's African-style incantation, which also discloses in advance the resolution to the plot's final major enigma. By referencing the means by which Myrthia's slaves could escape the prison of eternal life, via "an implement of torture touch[ing] their darkened hearts," the song foreshadows Hess's own fate.

Waymon set Hess's scripted monologue to music because he felt, in his own words, that "it was so important that it needed a voice," and he recorded this oratory a cappella because "the audience needed to clearly hear the words."[63] Still, the unconventional presentation of this plot exposition—in song form—arguably decreases the likelihood that the viewer will be able to process that information. For the spectator more attuned to atmosphere and sensuality, however, this song's haunting rendition is just one of many small touches that make *Ganja & Hess* such a richly evocative text.

Meda (8:05–11:45)

Ganja & Hess was not the only early seventies vampire movie shot on location in Westchester County. *House of Dark Shadows* (1970), a feature film spin-off of ABC's cult soap opera *Dark Shadows*, was filmed in the village of Tarrytown, ten miles south of Croton-on-Hudson and a short ride across the Tappan Zee Bridge from Nyack. *House of Dark Shadows* is set mainly at the Lyndhurst Estate, a gaudily Gothic mansion that provides a suitably spooky environment for Barnabas Collins's wicked doings. Like *House of Dark Shadows*, *Ganja & Hess* mostly takes place in a cavernous country manor that exudes faded opulence. These qualities evoke both timeworn Gothic literature formulas and what Carol Clover identifies as the horror cinema trope of the "terrible place," in which the pursued are trapped and victimized by the monster.[64] In most vampire movies, the otherness of the terrible place complements the vampire's own separation from socially sanctioned normality. In *Ganja & Hess*, the setting marks the protagonist as *doubly* estranged. The sole African American resident for miles (or, as he describes himself, "the only colored on the block"), Hess knows that his impeccably managed estate, aristocratic lifestyle, and high-toned friends will not shelter him from scrutiny should a Black corpse turn up on a neighboring property. Simultaneously, Hess's affluence isolates him from the surrounding community of African Americans, who are identified with the grittier spaces of the neighboring city. In these rundown urban settings, Hess is free to prey on the sort of victim whose disappearance will not trouble the local authorities.

The viewer gets a first fleeting glimpse of the mansion's grandeur as Hess's limo rolls up the driveway and Meda's bags are collected by Archie, the butler who "came with the house." In actuality, Hess's domain is the Apple Bee Farm Estate, which was constructed in the twenties by architect William G. Tachau for George W. Naumburg, son of a New York banker (see fig. 3.4). The structure remained in the Naumburg family's possession for decades but had been unoccupied for three years prior to production on *Ganja & Hess* and thus was available to rent for practically nothing. The news that a team of moviemakers had moved in at Apple Bee Farm quickly spread, which resulted in a nerve-shredding visit from a local Teamsters official. The "tough character" showed up unannounced at Schultz's office three

Figure 3.4 Robert Yarnall Richie's photograph of George Washington Naumburg's Apple Bee Farm Estate, Croton-on-Hudson, NY, ca. 1932–1934. DeGolyer Library, Southern Methodist University, Robert Yarnall Richie Photograph Collection.

days before the start of filming to object to the picture's nonunion status. Unmoved by the producer's pleas of poverty, the Teamster offhandedly noted that he had learned "that where you're shooting is all wood . . . and highly flammable." It was not until Schultz mentioned that *Ganja & Hess* was "a Black film" that his uninvited guest lost interest in pressing the matter and left, sparing the production (and the house itself) a shockingly premature demise.[65]

As with the inaugural segment, *Ganja & Hess*'s version of the postsupper conversation between Hess and Meda severely truncates what is called for in the screenplay. In the film, a two-shot pairing covers the transition to the men chatting over coffees served up by the omnipresent Archie. A cutaway to a corner of Hess's parlor allows the viewer a first peek at the meticulous detail of Tom John's production design, represented here by an almond-eyed African statuette, two clay pots, a stone stool on a marble end table, a phonograph, and a copy of Nina Simone's *Gifted & Black* LP (see fig. 3.5).[66] In the shooting script, Meda and Hess fall into deep discussion of the Myrthians and their belief in their desire for blood, and this discussion

Figure 3.5 Gifted and black: Nina Simone makes a cameo appearance amid the curios in Hess Green's living room. *Ganja & Hess* (Blu-ray), Kino Lorber Films.

continues later in Hess's library. During this latter exchange, which Gunn shot but cut from the finished film and Noveck restored, Meda paints a watercolor of a male figure with outstretched arms near a solid red cross (see fig. 3.6). Hess sits at his desk, further examining the wooden dagger and noticing that it also "contains elements of human bone." No sooner has Hess spoken this observation than he pricks his finger with the implement's sharp end, an accident he conceals from his guest.

The resulting implication, that Hess is infected even *before* Meda stabs him with the same dagger later that night, possibly explains why Gunn disposed of the library scene altogether. In its place, he added an unscripted and seemingly tangential monologue for the character he himself plays. As Hess and Meda unwind, the latter shares a humorous story about a film director in Holland who commits an egregious social gaffe by shouting "Cut!" while shooting a street scene, not realizing that the Dutch word "kut" translates in English to "cunt." Meda's long-winded telling of the joke elicits subdued exasperation from Hess; after an elongated silence, Meda shifts the topic of conversation back to the Myrthians. Meda's Holland anecdote bears no relevance to the plot at large, making it all the stranger that Gunn devotes nearly two minutes of screen time to its delivery. Implicitly, however, the story comments on the potential danger awaiting those who naively cross cultures. As one might deduce from the intermingling

Figure 3.6 In a scene cut from *Ganja & Hess*'s original cut but reinserted into *Blood Couple*, Meda (Bill Gunn) paints a watercolor of a crucifixion while Hess holds forth on ancient Myrthia. *Blood Couple*, in *Creatures, Critters, and Crazies* (DVD), Gemstone Entertainment.

of African and European decor in his drawing room, Hess is the target of Meda's warning.

Meda's Crack-Up (11:45–18:50)

His hosting duties finished for the night, Hess retires to bed. He fidgets absentmindedly with the wooden dagger, and there follows a languorous dissolve to a slow-motion procession through an open meadow, through which the Myrthian queen (Mabel King), named in the script as "Helgda," leads two young men. Another dissolve returns the action to the Brooklyn Museum. A shot of Jack Sargent, now wearing a silver mask, extending his hand to Hess is graphically matched to a shot of Helgda making an analogous gesture, figuratively closing the time gap between two forms of cultural vampirism (see fig. 3.7). The surrealism of the dream sequence is underscored by a distorted remix of the Musée de l'Homme's recording of

Figure 3.7 Queen Helgda (Mabel King) beckons Hess from across the Atlantic, and across the centuries. *Ganja & Hess* (Blu-ray), Kino Lorber Films.

"Bungelii Work Song" (or "Bongili Work Song"), from Folkways Records' 1950 release *Music of Equatorial Africa*.[67] Described in the record's liner notes as a tribute to "the delights of beaten out bananas, a variety of food much appreciated by the Bongili," this antiphonic, improvised composition is the film's only featured piece of music not composed or recorded by Waymon, though he is responsible for the song's slowed-down speed and slurred sound effects.[68]

The disquieting and uncanny effect of this scene on film supplants the mood of sheer terror struck in Gunn's script. The May 30 draft version of Hess's dream begins with the doctor in bed, dictating into a tape recorder his imagined re-creation of Myrthia's destruction. The civilization's downfall is triggered by the desertion of the queen by her own army, which has "fallen into a strange religion." As Hess envisions Helgda's cruel revenge on her remaining subjects, the whoosh of a saber pierces the soundtrack. Suddenly bound to a tree, a panicked Hess is overtaken by Helgda and two female disciples. A deep gash opens across his torso and the queen drinks deeply from the wound. Hess then awakens from his nightmare, sweating profusely.[69] One of the most gripping passages in the screenplay, this segment as written was perhaps too expensive to realize. Yet, it is equally likely that Gunn sought to eliminate the most flagrantly horrific moments when translating script to screen, lest the viewer start to suspect that *Ganja & Hess* was "just" a horror movie.

Jarred awake from his blood-curdling hallucination, Hess hears faint strains of classical music coming from the parlor. He investigates, but Meda is nowhere to be found. Searching the manicured grounds of his estate, Hess finds his inebriated assistant perched on a tree branch six feet off the ground, next to a dangling noose. Meda's casual aside, "I tried not to involve you," is icily contested by his host, who confidently predicts that "you can *believe* the authorities will drag me out for questioning" in the event of a guest's suicide. As is so often the case with *Ganja & Hess*, the true "subject" of this scene is clearer on the page. In the script, from the moment Hess discovers Meda on the estate grounds, the latter's emotional state and intentions are obvious: his face is streaked with tears, the noose fitted firmly around his neck. Hess's first inclination in the face of this emergency is to recite from Oscar Wilde's *De Profundis*, in which the incarcerated author writes of his desire "to commit suicide on the very day on which I left prison."[70] But Hess does not quote Wilde in the movie, and his colleague's mental state is a bit more ambiguous: the noose hangs limply from the branch, and Meda's mood is one of detached insouciance rather than emotional ruin (see fig. 3.8).

That Meda's face is not even visible in this scene testifies to the influence of James Hinton. Hinton's compositions throughout *Ganja & Hess* are consistently arresting without appearing overtly arranged or manipulated, a quality developed in his previous career as a photographer and documentarian of the civil rights and Black power movements. Gunn personally recruited Hinton, presumably on the strength of the latter's work for Harlem Audiovisuals Inc., which Hinton cofounded in 1969 with his brother Rufus and Black arts movement advocate Larry Neal, among others.[71] Hinton was primarily responsible for the vibrant yet naturalistic 16 mm cinematography for Amiri Baraka's short documentary on political organization in Newark, *The New-Ark* (1968), and Neal's companion piece *May Be the Last Time* (1969). Hinton's contributions to *May Be the Last Time* illustrate both his photo-realist eye for capturing the quotidian minutiae of urban African American life and an acute appreciation for found symbolism, as seen in the fleeting image of a campaign placard for the Baraka-backed slate of candidates being swept up with the trash following their election losses. *Ganja & Hess* is equally marked by its cinematographer's ability to spot metaphorically rich details within urban (and natural) landscapes.

Figure 3.8 From the depths: Hess talks a distraught Meda down from the gallows tree. *Ganja & Hess* (Blu-ray), Kino Lorber Films.

Though Hinton had never before shot a narrative feature, his authority on the *Ganja & Hess* set was second only to the director's. Hinton had access to Gunn's personally prepared scrapbook brimming with fabrics and magazine clippings of various textures and colors.[72] He became the behind-the-camera surrogate for Gunn, who on set mainly concerned himself with actors' performances.[73] Hinton must have prompted the decision not only to keep Meda's face offscreen during his taut confrontation with Hess but to let it play out in a single master shot, disrupted only by cutaways to the full moon. The high-key luminosity provided by the moonlight, which carves out Hess and the noose from a pitch-black background, creates one of the film's most indelible images. As with many of *Ganja & Hess*'s striking chiaroscuro effects, this setup was probably economically motivated as well. For this scene, in particular, the low-light conditions conceal the fact that the footage was recorded at a different site, a tree on Gunn's own property.[74] Hinton's stylistic flourishes also serve to obfuscate the seriousness of Meda's aims; he comes off as a bit of a crackpot more than a menace to himself or others, which makes his savage outburst in the following sequence all the more shocking.

To further stress Meda's disturbed mindset, Gunn bridges the plot points of Hess's nighttime "rescue" of Meda and Meda's subsequent attack

Figure 3.9 "The murderer let the victim go": Meda acts out a previous suicide attempt. *Ganja & Hess* (Blu-ray), Kino Lorber Films.

on Hess with a brief but pivotal vignette, a monologue that subtly clarifies character intentions yet conveys them via obscure means. Shirtless, with mucous trickling from his nostrils, Meda calmly speaks about the "schizophrenic" nature of suicide. He describes his realization, in the midst of a suicide attempt, that he was acting as both "victim" and "murderer." Grabbing his hair with one hand and brandishing an imaginary knife with the other, Meda acts out both positions simultaneously, demonstrating how "the murderer let the victim go" (see fig. 3.9). In the follow-up scene, murderer and victim finally fulfill their destiny, leaving a similarly divided and doomed successor in their bloody wake.

Murder/Suicide (18:50–27:15)

Many contemporary viewers of *Ganja & Hess* lose the narrative thread around the scene of Meda's death. The sequence in its entirety, which features successful *and* unsuccessful suicide bids in addition to a failed murder attempt, is clearly a major turning point; the movie's opening series of intertitles, in fact, was largely intended to illuminate what happens in this sequence. Of course, those intertitles are necessary precisely because of Kanefsky's elliptical editing, which muddies the causal relations that are fairly self-evident in Gunn's script and Noveck's reedit. *Blood Couple* transfers the opening titles to this section's dramatic climax, at the moment when Hess tries to end his own life, to make it crystal clear that Hess is "addicted [to blood] and could not die . . . / nor could he be killed." Gunn's cut, in contrast, requires the viewer to draw these inferences and make these connections on the basis of indefinite and even conflicting information.

The sequence begins with a handheld track in on Hess asleep in bed. Now acting out the "murderer" side of his fractured personality, Meda wildly brings an ax down onto the headboard, missing Hess by inches. The men wrestle awkwardly about the room as a thunderstorm rages outside, until Meda finally pins his prey to the floor. Seizing the Myrthian dagger from the nightstand, Meda viciously stabs his mentor. (In a remarkable associative edit, Kanefsky cuts away during the attack to a close-up of a photograph of jazz musician Stanley Turrentine eliciting a violent shriek from his tenor sax.) Immediately sensing the gravity of his mad act, Meda collapses in despair on the bed. In the script, Meda takes his own life at this point, but not over remorse. Rather, he is driven to it upon observing the apparent immortality of his victim, who snaps in annoyance at his would-be assassin to yank out the dagger protruding from his heart. Within seconds of the weapon's removal Hess's wound vanishes, as does the blood spattered across his body. Suppressing his own shock, Hess gives his traumatized guest a couple of tranquilizers and escorts him back to his room, all the while reassuring Meda that he hallucinated the entire episode. Once alone, the catatonic Meda shoots himself with a gun from his suitcase.[75]

Ganja & Hess, the film, contains no such motivating action to clarify Meda's suicide. Rather, Gunn directly cuts from Meda writhing in anguish and regret on Hess's bed to a close shot of a calm and focused Meda at Hess's typewriter. Kanefsky felt that the resulting two-minute segment was entirely superfluous, narratively speaking, and the scene was removed prior to the movie's New York premiere, though it remained in the print Gunn took to Cannes.[76] This *plan-séquence* shows Meda putting the finishing touches on a poem addressed to "the Black male children." "Philosophy is a prison," Meda reads back to himself, in that it "disregards the uncustomary things about you." The poem condenses many of Gunn's thematic obsessions into a succinctly worded warning aimed, perhaps, at the director's younger self. As a Black, queer child Gunn had endured psychological harm inflicted by a system of schooling primarily concerned with the social stratification of its pupils. Speaking through Meda, Gunn affirms that education in the abstract has little to offer the Black male child, for the "dreadful need in man to teach . . . destroys the pure instinct to learn." Meda's monotone modulates slightly as the poem reaches its emotional apex: "You are the despised of the earth / That is as if you were water in the desert / To be adored on this planet is to be a symbol of success / And you must not succeed on any terms, because life is endless." The allusion to "endless life" reverberates due to *Ganja & Hess*'s vampirism theme, of course, but it also seems to hint at Gunn's aspiration as a Black artist: to live on through creative achievement.

Consequently, though his character crumples up the typed pages after speaking their words aloud, Gunn himself valued "To the Black Male Children" as an effective statement of artistic purpose. The poem was quoted in full in Janus Adams's interview of Gunn in the June 1973 *Encore*, in which the author supplied a lengthy explication of its verses. The line, "And you must not succeed on any terms," Gunn assured the reader, actually refers to *whites*' "kind of succeeding."[77] He elaborated further on this analysis in a later unpublished piece, possibly used for the introductions of museum and university screenings of *Ganja & Hess*.[78] Gunn, the practicing artist, was not finished with the poem either. Much as he had recycled passages from *All the Rest Have Died* for *Johnnas*, Gunn reused "To the Black Male Children" in an early draft of his play *Black Picture Show*, in which it is credited to the playwright Alexander, another Gunn stand-in.[79] Kanefsky may have believed that the "suicide note" scene did not work because its message so obviously came not from the character but from the filmmaker. But if such a purely autobiographical gesture was acceptable in literature, why not in the so-called author's cinema? Like Alexander, who elsewhere in *Black Picture Show* quips, "Art, devoid of me, is genocide, at best," Gunn was never shy about exercising this prerogative.[80]

After discarding his note, Meda bathes in preparation for death. He picks up his revolver, rises from the tub, and kneels naked before a full-length mirror; a reverse shot conspicuously frames him beside a makeshift cross on the wall (see fig. 3.10). Kanefsky cuts back to Hess in his bedroom, checking his own body in the mirror for signs of a wound. The sound of a gunshot returns us to the bathroom, where Meda's body sprawls amid a spreading pool of blood. Hess rushes in and reflexively dives to the floor, quenching his raging thirst by drinking from Meda's wound. Narrative chaos is complemented by frenetic technique: jittery camerawork, fragmented editing, and amplified, overlapping sound drenched in reverb.

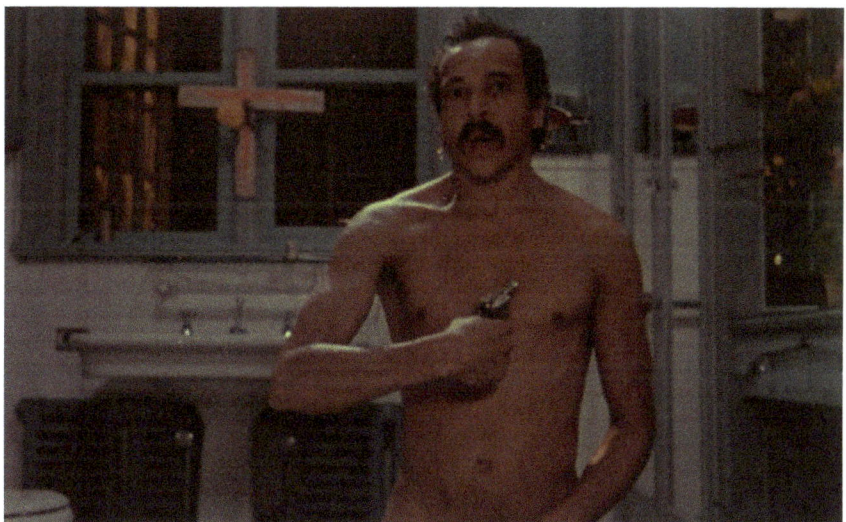

Figure 3.10 "Murderer" finally catches up to "victim": having stabbed his host and typed a farewell poem, Meda shoots himself in Hess's bathroom. *Ganja & Hess* (Blu-ray), Kino Lorber Films.

The hum suddenly cuts out completely, and we see Hess in extreme long shot, striding across an open field, then dropping to his knees to pray (see fig. 3.11). In the script (and in *Blood Couple*), what happens next is unambiguous. After appealing to God to join his Son in "joyful resurrection," Hess shoots himself in the chest. "There is not a wound. He cannot die."[81] Yet, there is no audible gunshot on the film's soundtrack, only Hess's despondent howl. As usual, Gunn eliminates the most salient narrative detail, presuming that the landscape's majestic sweep, set against the shrinking, forlorn figure occupying a sliver of the center frame, is sufficient to articulate that Hess has been cursed with eternal life.

The scene's lyrical effect is further enhanced by means of an extraordinarily fortuitous coincidence. A solar eclipse occurred at the very moment that Hinton photographed Jones kneeling in the field, which fixes the date of filming as July 10, 1972, when a partial solar eclipse was visible throughout the northeastern United States (see fig. 3.12).[82] It is not difficult to interpret the gradual darkening of the image while Hess beseeches God for absolution as an ominous prophecy of his fate. In view of the eclipse's implications within African American history, particularly the February 1831 annular eclipse that convinced Nat Turner of his destiny to command a slave

Figure 3.11 Fleeing to an open meadow, Hess begs God's forgiveness for his impending act. *Ganja & Hess* (Blu-ray), Kino Lorber Films.

Figure 3.12 Seconds later: as Hess prays, his world falls into literal darkness, thanks to the solar eclipse of July 10, 1972. *Ganja & Hess* (Blu-ray), Kino Lorber Films.

Figure 3.13 Nat Turner, 141 years earlier, received a similar sign, as famously interpreted by Bernarda Bryson in her 1934–1935 illustration "Nat Turner profesies [sic] the rebellion which will take place with the eclipse of the moon, or, 'Nat Turner's Rebellion.'" © 2019 The Estate of Bernarda Bryson Shahn / Licensed by VAGA at Artists Rights Society (ARS), New York.

insurrection, perhaps Gunn meant to further imply that Hess's enslavement will, to paraphrase Turner himself, similarly remove the seal and hasten the day of judgment (see fig. 3.13).[83]

Surviving (27:15–31:55)

The *Ganja & Hess* screenplay follows up this ghastly sequence with two short scenes that poke fun at vampire movie conventions, though only the first made it to film. As the words "Part II Survival" appear and a jaunty, upbeat instrumental rendering of Waymon's "You Got to Learn" begins, Hess is shown nonchalantly reclining (and smoking a cigarette) in a doctor's office as a nurse swabs a needle mark on his arm. Left unattended, Hess sets a fire in a wastebasket and slips out of the room; while the staff battles the blaze, he swipes several bags of blood plasma from a refrigerator and quietly leaves the building. The notion of a vampire stealing from a blood bank would become, weirdly enough, one of *Ganja & Hess*'s most highly praised features, with the *New York Times* commending the gag as "a new wrinkle in the genre" and *Variety* identifying it as "a move that Dracula should have thought of."[84] The second segment of comic relief, unfilmed by Gunn but included in Spike Lee's *Ganja & Hess* remake, is set at an afternoon gathering on the grounds of Hess's estate. Hess, moving among the various pairings of guests, is roped into a debate between "Mrs. Tyson" and "Mr. Blair" about how citizens of all classes are "junkies of one sort or another."[85] Mrs. Tyson, intrigued by the bright red concoction in Hess's hand, brazenly snatches the drink and samples it; she then passes it off to Archie as he walks past, instructing him to "put vodka and a little black pepper and a dash of lemon in it."[86]

The movie's version of Hess's garden party dispenses with the obvious joke, instead making a point about the protagonist's European-style decadence through seemingly irrelevant incidents. The scene opens mysteriously on an older white woman, identified as "Poetess" in the credits, ambling along a tree-lined path with an adolescent biracial boy. The soft strains of Bach's "Jesu, Joy of Man's Desiring" are audible in the background. The woman's recitation ("A muse lingers in the room and dangles a melody in the air like a ripe fig") is interrupted when she spots the host. The boy rushes to Hess, who exclaims "Enrico, what a surprise! No one told me you were coming." The fact that Hess has a son, presumably on hiatus from boarding school, is indeed a surprise, as no mention has been made of him in the film's first twenty-eight minutes. Gunn worked out a motive for his unexpected introduction but ultimately withheld it. "We needed a scene that showed that Hess had a son," recalls Waymon. "[Hess is] a man of means . . . not the kind of man who wouldn't have an heir. He wasn't a playboy, but he must have bedded many women," though he never married.[87] Enrico chats, somewhat formally, with his father in French about his lessons, then Hess drops him off at the beverage table before making his way indoors to prepare his "Bloody Mary" in secrecy (see fig. 3.14).

Figure 3.14 Hess catches up with his son Enrico (Enrico Fales), never to be seen nor mentioned again. *Ganja & Hess* (Blu-ray), Kino Lorber Films.

This lengthy dialogue between father and son, recorded in a single take, is of no real narrative importance; accordingly, the son disappears completely from the picture following this scene. Nevertheless, it does add another layer to the protagonist's character. In Gunn's fiction, individual complexity assumes the significance that most Hollywood filmmakers assign to motivation. His characters are frequently upwardly mobile, but even those at the lower end of the economic spectrum still possess (or affect) a worldliness and erudition bordering on alienation. Their acquisition of bourgeois tastes is not necessarily to their advantage, of course, yet these qualities nonetheless constitute a necessary corrective to the constricted range of Black lives on-screen.

The garden party episode also features several cultural notables slumming as unbilled extras, whose presence further establishes the setting's high-class ambience. Gunn's neighbors, the renowned postmodern novelist William Gaddis and his wife Judith Thompson, are among the guests, as are Ulric Haynes, diplomat and future US ambassador to Algeria, and Yolande Toussaint Haynes, a former Miss Haiti. Josephine Premice, the dynamic Haitian American vocalist and stage actor, is also visible as a partygoer. And, in his sole motion picture appearance, Premice's thirteen-year-old son, Enrico Fales, performs flawlessly as Hess's son for nearly two uninterrupted minutes.

The decision to film these festivities (mostly) in a single take was motivated in part by Gunn's desire to capitalize on the so-called golden hour, the short period of time before sunset when daylight is softer and more diffuse. One of many very long takes in *Ganja & Hess*, the shot of Enrico's stroll was perhaps the most difficult for Hinton to realize considering the time constraints, Fales's lack of experience, and the continuous and convoluted series of tracks and pans necessary to keep the actors in frame. The lack of zooming suggests that Hinton was using the fixed-focal-length "prime" lens that he claimed to have utilized on virtually every shot in the film. Though ultimately blown up to 35 mm for theatrical exhibition, *Ganja & Hess* was filmed in Super 16, a modified 16 mm format that widens the film's aspect ratio from 1.37:1 to 1.66:1. Due to the use of this inexpensive format, Hinton was obliged to shoot mainly with a prime lens because of the zoom lens's weakened image resolution. The difference can be understood by comparing the already fairly grainy image of Hess and his son in conversation to the image of Hess walking purposefully back toward the house, for which Hinton switched lenses in order to zoom in slowly on Hess's receding figure. By the end of the latter shot, the picture dissipates into almost total illegibility: an apt visual analog for the ongoing erasure of Hess's sense of self. Hinton confessed that the large number of long takes Gunn requested "unnerved" him.[88] Yet, based on the many dazzling effects resulting from this approach, Gunn's confidence in Hinton's ability was in no way unfounded.

First Prey (31:55–38:45)

His survival now hinging on his access to human blood, Hess resigns himself to making day trips to the inner city for sustenance. His first stop is a seedy dive bar, an actual Nyack business named Chicken Charlie's. The real-life establishment's bartender gets several seconds of screen time, as do various locals who congregate by the men's room and snidely comment on Hess's "slick" attire.[89] A sex worker (Candece Tarpley) and her pimp (Tommy Lane, a stuntman best known for crashing through Richard Roundtree's Times Square office window in *Shaft*), seated at the bar, immediately recognize the doctor as a potential mark. The woman, identified as "Rose" in Gunn's screenplay, sidles over to Hess's table and breaks the ice with a pointless anecdote about her downstairs neighbor, "Dolores Kinkade."

A straight cut relocates the couple to Rose's cramped apartment, where she removes her blonde wig. The return of "Bungelii Work Song" on the soundtrack cues us to Hess's anticipation, which is violently interrupted when the pimp suddenly leaps from a hiding spot. He thrusts a knife into Hess's back, to no avail; nor do the shots from Rose's handgun slow her client's progress. Hess quickly subdues his attackers and sinks his teeth into Rose's neck, then uses a penknife to open her companion's jugular vein, in a highly convincing (and costly) prosthetic makeup effect created by Scott Cunningham. These events are knit together according to a now-familiar pattern of heavy stylization mixed with documentary naturalism. The assault and its aftermath are intercut with flashbacks to Chicken Charlie's and possibly subjective interludes, including mysterious views of Meda aiming his revolver at an offscreen target and a first-person glide down a heretofore unseen corridor, past a masked Jack Sargent. The scene concludes in bleak reality, with Hess vomiting in Rose's dingy bathroom.

This prolonged interaction serves as a good encapsulation of Gunn's willfully perverse tactics of genre subversion. As outlined in the screenplay, the scene is narratively coherent and conventionally suspenseful. In the script, Hess is painfully sensitive to the color red, which underlines his need for blood. The color's every appearance, from Rose's painted nails to a "razor nick on the cheek of the bartender," awakens his sensual craving.[90] Additionally, the screenplay supplies clear justification for Hess's nausea: in the bathroom, he discovers a needle and a spoon, evidence that his victims were junkies. The sequence as scripted resolves with an especially creepy example of the "traditional horror-movie subterfuge" Gunn claimed to have inserted solely to secure financial backing. Sick from opiate-tainted blood, Hess passes out on the bathroom floor and awakens at dawn. He stumbles back toward his victims' bodies, then watches in terror as color slowly returns to their gray faces. The corpses begin gasping for breath. Finally, Rose opens her eyes, and the concurrent sound of her nails clawing at the floor sends Hess into a frenzied sprint for the exit.[91] That the recipient of a vampire bite will eventually rise from the dead herself is not at all hinted in the scene as filmed, maybe because Gunn assumed viewers' familiarity with vampire movie conventions. Or, he wanted to preserve the surprise surrounding the dramatic reanimation at the very end of the picture. Both options indicate that Gunn *did* respect at least some of the narrative pleasures the horror genre has to offer.

Figure 3.15 Rose (Candece Tarpley) opens fire when Hess turns the tables on his attackers; a topsy-turvy David Susskind coolly observes. *Ganja & Hess* (Blu-ray), Kino Lorber Films.

This level of respect might also explain why the fine details that flesh out the Rose character did not survive the transition to film. In the screenplay, Rose is given a backstory: she has an "old man" who has been in prison for two months, and she used to manage a Bickford's Restaurant in Brooklyn. She also speaks in a daffy stream of consciousness that establishes her as a relatively sympathetic character. In the film, these layers are stripped away, downgrading her to the status of generic victim. The sole trace of the quirkier Rose is evidenced by the (fleetingly visible) poster of syndicated talk show host David Susskind that hangs upside down above her bed (see fig. 3.15). The poster's baffling presence is acknowledged in the screenplay, though hardly elucidated. When Hess catches sight of it, he blankly mutters Susskind's name. As if answering an implicit follow-up question, Rose replies: "I can't stand him . . . matter of fact, I hate him. You want some of that Champale?"[92]

Ganja (38:45–45:20)

A few months before joining the *Ganja & Hess* shoot in Croton-on-Hudson, Marlene Clark was approached by a *Playboy* writer for comment on opportunities for African American actors in the New Hollywood. "Blacks still get screwed in movies made by white men" was her curt response.[93] Clark's cynicism was hard earned. In the late sixties, she parlayed a modeling career into some film work, but her debut roles, in *Midnight Cowboy* and *Putney Swope* (1969), were brief, uncredited appearances. Clark had a striking cameo as a go-go dancer in *The Landlord* but did not meet the film's screenwriter until shooting wrapped, when she was introduced to Gunn by her then husband, Billy Dee Williams. As Clark later recalled, the future collaborators "hit it off immediately," and within a half hour of making acquaintance Gunn offered her a part in his next project.[94] Had it come out on schedule, *Stop* might have been Clark's breakthrough; in its absence, her career remained mired in mediocrity. She acted occasionally in low-budget exploitation movies and on television, all the while honing her skills under the tutelage of legendary acting teacher Stella Adler.[95]

Clark's persistence finally paid off when Gunn developed the part of Ganja especially for her. *This* was the role she had been waiting for and, as Waymon recalls, was simultaneously terrified by.[96] Ganja's character is written as astoundingly gorgeous, and, in the screenplay, Hess is so shaken by his first sight of her that he falls into a sort of trance. Poetically, he articulates his astonishment over a freeze-frame of Ganja's luminous face: "It's a shock to any system to see perfection. To have perfection hurled at you in the split second of seeing that woman sitting in my car.... The result of centuries of war and pain. No casual pleasure brought about those features. There was some great loss somewhere. Some great horde of peoples have suffered to bring about that nose arched in such a way as to exert power over my every hidden appetite."[97] The part demanded much more than natural beauty, however. As we learn in the pair's initial telephone conversation, during which she demands to talk to her "freaked out" husband and then insists that Hess provide her with lodging while she awaits his return, Ganja is no empty vessel waiting to be filled through a man's attention. She is a brazen, independent woman with "a tongue like a viper's," who is unafraid to dictate her desires without equivocation.[98] Ganja's beauty justifies Hess's instant attraction to her, but her interiority is what drives the remainder of the narrative.

Ganja and Hess's mutual introductions, originally by phone and then face-to-face in Hess's driveway, were among the earliest scenes filmed by Gunn and his crew.[99] Ganja's initial on-screen appearance was carefully planned to ensure maximum impact. Prefaced by a subtitle announcing, "Part III Letting Go" (the last of three parts), the scene opens on a woman's

Figure 3.16 "Tell your boss I'm here": Ganja (Marlene Clark) contemptuously studies her quarry. *Ganja & Hess* (Blu-ray), Kino Lorber Films.

hand dialing a rotary pay phone with a pen. Our first views of Ganja as she snarls into the receiver are limited to fragments: red lips and fingernails, fur stole, black headwrap, pearl necklace. The strategy bestows an aura of mystery and elegance on the character, not unlike a femme fatale in a forties film noir. We do not get an unobstructed look at Ganja's face until she arrives at the manor and steps from the limousine that Hess dispatched to the airport (see fig. 3.16). The double delay in introducing Ganja, to both Hess and the viewer, establishes and then preserves the subtext of inscrutability that will become so important to her character. Gunn was, therefore, unreceptive to Kanefsky's suggestion of bringing Ganja in at an earlier point in the plot so that she and Meda would be in Hess's house at the same time, unaware of each other's presence. Though the idea intrigued Gunn, ultimately, he decided that Hess probably could not handle such an arrangement "psychologically."[100]

The overwhelming force of Ganja's personality intensifies when the action moves indoors. Ganja, having changed into a beige kaftan, wanders downstairs to the parlor, where Hess reclines on the wooden floor, reading and listening to a record. The song playing, Waymon-Gunn's "March Blues," is performed by Mabel King in the unmistakable style of Bessie Smith, whose life story Gunn was supposed to film for Kelly-Jordan after

Ganja & Hess's completion. Marlo David has perceptively noted the parallels between Smith and Ganja, one actual and one fictional embodiment of the "classic blues woman." Like Smith, who enjoyed dalliances with many women and men outside of her legal and common-law marriages, Ganja is a woman who puts her own sexual gratification before that of her lovers. "What has distinguished these kinds of women in the pantheon of black womanhood," David observes, "is their erotic subjectivity shown by their union of fierce independence with sensual interdependence," a rephrasing of Audre Lorde's influential definition of "the erotic" as "self-connection shared."[101] Gunn's fascination with this personality, a sexually liberated Black woman both "desired and desiring," is manifest in many of the featured female roles in Gunn's narratives.[102] Several of those parts were specifically tailored for actors, from Diana Sands to Clark to Gloria Foster, especially adept at conveying such qualities. In turn, they did some of their best work interpreting his characters.

Gunn's faith in Clark was such that she is the only actor in *Ganja & Hess*, other than Gunn himself, to be entrusted with a lengthy, introspective, seemingly free-form monologue: two of them, in fact. The first puts a period on the protagonists' initial encounter. Lighting up a joint, Ganja laughingly shares a story about her friend, a ballet dancer, who smuggled the very grass she smokes out of Mexico by stuffing it in condoms and inserting them in his rectum. The similarities between Meda's tale and Ganja's are difficult to miss; both relate a humorous episode involving an artist abroad, and both resolve with a profane punch line that elicits no reaction at all from a distracted listener. This uncanny repetition evokes Hess's anxiety about the consequences of having yet another Meda in his house while also preparing the audience for Ganja's upcoming soliloquy, a more somber meditation of far greater psychological significance. Though this particular oration is comparatively madcap, Clark's self-assured delivery signifies that, even in a state of inebriation, Ganja is usually the one in control, no matter the apparent balance of power.

Seduction (45:20–51:25)

Unlike the scripted version of *Ganja & Hess*'s first love scene, in which Ganja acts on her sexual hunger while Hess struggles to repress his literal hunger, the corresponding passages in the film play out in near silence. The sequence is both exemplary and typical of *Ganja & Hess* in its paring of

Figure 3.17 Still life with cigarettes, cheese plate, and Marxist theory. *Ganja & Hess* (Blu-ray), Kino Lorber Films.

verbal *description* in favor of visual *suggestion*. Bearing in mind his irritation at other directors' failure to respect his work as a screenwriter, Gunn's willingness to scrap pages and pages of his own highly literate and often brilliant dialogue is all the more astonishing.[103]

As with many of the film's scenes, the seduction begins and is intercut with static compositions that highlight one or more of the many artifacts and antiques scattered throughout the archeologist's home environment. This technique is usually attributed to Kanefsky, who claims that Gunn did not "think much about things like transitions" because he was far more interested in character.[104] As Hess nervously gulps his wine following Ganja's racy anecdote, Kanefsky enlarges two details within the living room setting. He first cuts away to a close-up of the aforementioned African statuette, flanked by two vases. Then, Hinton's camera elevates for a high-angle still life of a glass tabletop teeming with artfully arranged bric-a-brac, including a cheese plate, a paperback copy of Marxist historian Jean Suret-Canale's sociological study *Afrique Noire: Geographie, Civilisations, Histoire*, and a hatchet with a delicately engraved handle (see fig. 3.17).[105] These objects of the camera's transitory gaze, many of which belonged to the director, are not exactly neutral in their meaning. Though several of the pieces are African in origin, the aesthetic seems to be primarily a European one, possibly augmented during Gunn's time studying art on the continent.[106]

In the screenplay, dialogue creates an amusing counterpoint between the two main characters as they become increasingly stoned. Hess, tortured by his awful predicament, stays riveted to his seat while Ganja dances to a rhythm and blues record. Finally, he rises and announces with grim seriousness, "I have to confess . . . I've killed two people." Ganja retorts, "I hope one of them was George." Ignoring her wisecrack, Hess unburdens his conscience with a soul-baring howl of pain: "I am addicted to blood . . . I am ADDICTED TO BLOOD! WHERE ARE YOU GOD!" "How come every rich man I meet is so fucked up," sighs Ganja, as she kisses him for the first time.[107] The exchange in full sheds light on the motivations deemphasized in the movie: Ganja is enticed by Hess's affluence as well as his physical attractiveness, whereas Hess is drawn to Ganja as a potential blood source—though he fights the temptation.

In the film, pages of scripted speech and exposition are jettisoned and replaced by evocative imagery to underscore the duo's emotional states. Rather than wail in misery, Hess merely lies down on the floor without a word. A cut promptly transports the couple to the bedroom, where an initially responsive Hess abruptly stiffens and flees to the attic, his surging bloodlust cued by the recurrence of the Myrthian field song. As Ganja calls to him, Hess downs a glass of plasma and spreads out on a mattress, the angle of his body captured by Hinton's camera in a daring allusion to the radical foreshortening effect in Andrea Mantegna's fifteenth-century masterpiece, *Lamentation over the Dead Christ* (see fig. 3.18). Ganja suddenly appears by his side, and the two make love in a montage of jump cuts accompanied by the soft chimes of Jewish bells, selected by Waymon to suggest the "electricity" between them.[108] The bells are just one of the many unconventional instruments Waymon employed for the score, in consultation with music supervisor Edward Bland and musician Nadi Qamar, inventor of the Mama-Likembi, an instrument constructed from traditional African thumb pianos. Waymon himself plays an electrified version of Qamar's harp elsewhere on the soundtrack.[109] Additional sound effects, Waymon recalls, were elicited from "pans, knives, forks and the cardboard rolls of paper towels."[110]

As evidenced in this scene, the diverse range and eclecticism of Waymon's musicianship perfectly complemented Gunn's varied objectives for *Ganja & Hess*, though his compositions also certainly stand on their own merit. Despite the film's limited release, the music for *Ganja & Hess* was recognized at the time as a major accomplishment, particularly for a rookie film composer who merely "wanted to prove to [himself]" that he could do

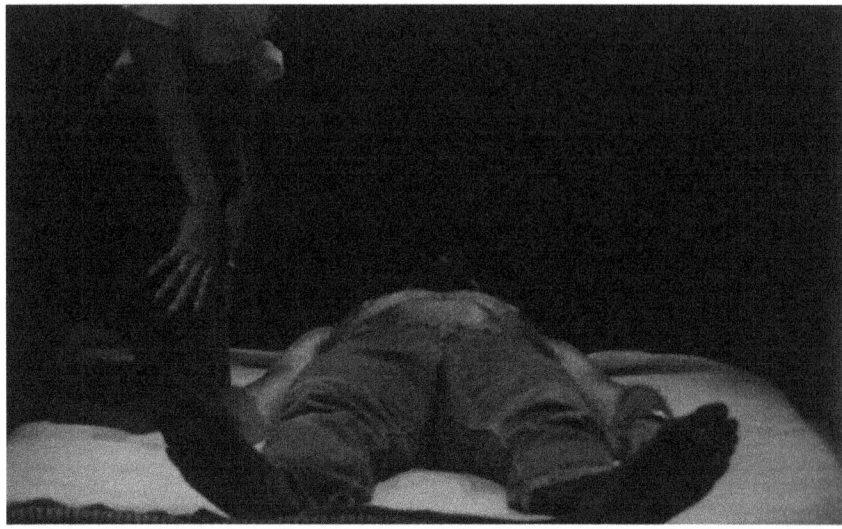

Figure 3.18 Hess's lamentation: Ganja weighs the options for reigniting her lover's dormant passion. *Ganja & Hess* (Blu-ray), Kino Lorber Films.

the job.[111] The *Ganja & Hess* score has acquired many new fans in recent years, in part due to the exposure provided by *Da Sweet Blood of Jesus*, which features an extended performance of "You Got to Learn," and by its repurposing by contemporary hip-hop artists.[112] An even greater appreciation was stymied, nevertheless, for decades, by the lack of an official soundtrack album. After Kelly-Jordan dumped the film, Waymon approached RCA and PolyGram about a *Ganja & Hess* record then tried unsuccessfully to put it out on his own label, Resolution Records.[113] Finally, forty-five years after the movie's public premiere, *Ganja & Hess*'s original soundtrack was issued for the very first time by Strange Disc Records for Record Store Day, April 21, 2018. Appropriately enough, the album was given a vinyl-only release, as it would have received in 1973.

Domestic Bliss, Domestic Violence (51:25–1:03:05)

After they spend the night in the attic, Ganja and Hess's whirlwind courtship continues over breakfast on Hess's terrace overlooking the New Croton Reservoir. Ostensibly, the point of this interlude is to explore the nature of their rapidly progressing infatuation and to further emotionally distance Ganja from her husband. She flatly states that she is mainly motivated by money, though her dreamy stares at Hess betray the depth of her romantic attachment. Ganja engages him in a playful interrogation that David characterizes as "bluesy" in its mimicking of the "give-and-take interaction" of blues performance.[114] The taciturn Hess parries the handful of "impolite questions" Ganja poses about his personal life while simultaneously basking in her intoxicating charm. The establishment of this dynamic is key to understanding what binds the two characters despite significant impediments to their union.

For Gunn, this dynamic was so important that he rejected Kanefsky's proposal to creatively recut the breakfast table exchange so that the lovers would humorously appear to be talking around or past each other, as in a Harold Pinter play. Kanefsky, with the aid of Cindy Castleman, assembled the conversation in this fashion and presented it, triumphantly, for the director's approval. Gunn, who Kanefsky remembers as being normally very "polite and complimentary," qualified his enthusiasm by requesting some minor fix; Kanefsky, sensing Gunn's hesitation, cut him off and admitted that the idea was a "mistake." Relieved, Gunn agreed. These were the terms of the men's working relationship: Gunn was always willing to entertain the suggestions of collaborators, yet he knew how to manipulate them into accepting his own viewpoint as the correct one. Rather than tell a colleague to "do it *this* way," he would simply advise her to "do *something*." Once his colleague's solution matched his own, he implemented it.[115]

The other major theme of the breakfast scene is the development of the acrimony between Ganja and Archie. Archie's ubiquitous presence and unyielding devotion to his employer deeply irritate Ganja, who prods the butler with passive-aggressive taunts and mocks his compromised Blackness by casting doubt on his familiarity with hominy grits (see fig. 3.19). Their awkward interaction allows both Clark and Leonard Jackson, a veteran of stage and screen who reunited with Clark and producer Schultz in 1977 for *The Baron*, the opportunity to exercise their improvisatory skills and comedic timing.

Jackson's achievement here as comic foil, humiliated by both Ganja's acid tongue and his boss's bemused indifference, is all the more impressive given that his head is cut off by the top of the frame throughout the sequence. There are conflicting accounts about the reasons for this. Gunn was fond of claiming, when probed by curious viewers, that Archie's head was cropped out of these compositions because of the cultural irrelevance and interchangeability of domestics in general.[116] Kanefsky maintains that

Figure 3.19 "Do you sometimes feel overworked, Archie?" Ganja toys with the flustered servant (Leonard Jackson), to his master's bemusement. *Ganja & Hess* (Blu-ray), Kino Lorber Films.

Hinton confided to him that Archie's partial exclusion was the result of an issue with the viewfinder for the Super 16 camera, which requires a special frame for the operator to see the image in its entirety. Hinton's miscalculation was not corrected by Gunn because he himself never peered through the viewfinder.[117] Yet, in 1998, Hinton claimed to have purposely tilted the camera down because Jackson was such a strong performer that he would have otherwise dominated the scene.[118] Outtakes from *Ganja & Hess*, later inserted into *Blood Couple*, show that Hinton did film some close-up "singles" of Archie as he reacts, mortified, to Ganja's provocations (see fig. 3.20). Their existence implies that the director of photography was aware of the necessity for reaction shots of Jackson alone, and why: because his face is not visible in the master shots.

After breakfast, Ganja lingers on the veranda while Hess secretly prepares for yet another murderous errand in town. She catches sight of him in conversation with Luther, appearing for the first time in the picture in his position as Hess's stableman. (Footage of Luther singing to himself in the stable appears in *Blood Couple*.) As Hess climbs into his silver Jaguar, Ganja makes clear her intention to stay by soliciting his opinions on dinner and, then, marriage. He deflects both questions, then zooms off in his

Figure 3.20 Archie's missing reaction shot, reinstated for *Blood Couple*. *Blood Couple*, in *Creatures, Critters, and Crazies* (DVD), Gemstone Entertainment.

convertible coupe. Hess's predilection for British luxury sports cars was actually a cost-saving measure for the filmmakers, as both the Jaguar and the Rolls belonged to Waymon. It also represented another poke in the eye of Hollywood convention. In the movies, even a radio disc jockey from Carmel, California, might own a vintage Jaguar XK150, as in Clint Eastwood's *Play Misty for Me* (1971) . . . as long as he is white. Black characters in seventies American cinema, on the other hand, "were *not* supposed to drive Jaguars."[119]

The Jaguar guides Hess into downtown Ossining, the locale used by the filmmakers whenever they needed a "sleazy" cityscape.[120] Here he encounters a white woman with a babe in arms, unsuccessfully beckoning male passersby. Hess walks up, and she smilingly ushers him inside a squalid tenement house. When Kanefsky cuts back to this setting at sequence's end, we are taken inside her dreary single room, dominated by a brass bed and adorned by a couple of naked light bulbs and an incongruously colorful Madonna-and-child portrait. The woman is propped up in bed, wrapped in a bloodstained bedsheet; her baby, at whom Hess shoots a nervous glance

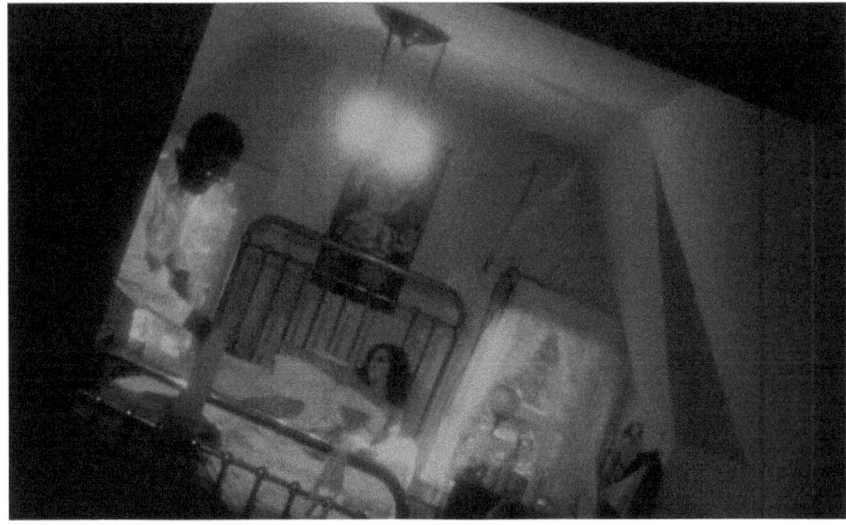

Figure 3.21 Hess dresses hurriedly as his latest victim lies in eternal repose; her child wails from offscreen. *Ganja & Hess* (Blu-ray), Kino Lorber Films.

as he collects his clothes, screams offscreen (see fig. 3.21). As if mimicking a rocking cradle, Hinton's camera chillingly rolls from one Dutch angle to its complement as Hess exits (see fig. 3.22).

Hinton's cinematographic innovations are likewise felt when Gunn crosscuts to Ganja's discovery of her vanished husband's body. The suspenseful buildup to this revelation proceeds as might be expected of any horror movie in which an unsuspecting character blunders across a victim's grisly remains. Searching the cellar for an acceptable cooking wine, Ganja wrenches open the door to a walk-in freezer and is met by the lifeless gaze of Meda, ghostly white and swathed in a plastic sheet resembling an encasement of ice. The sight of the blood-drained carcass completely unnerves the usually self-composed Ganja, who screams uncontrollably.[121] Although Ganja's investigation is endowed with a suitably creepy ambiance, Hinton expressed a far greater sense of pride over the preceding scene. At first blush this scene, of Ganja and Archie squabbling in the kitchen, might strike some as rather blandly composed. Yet Hinton singled it out as evidence of his principal contribution to American cinema: the reconceptualization of, in David's phrasing, "how black bodies were photographed in motion pictures."[122] The kitchen setup captures "the full range of the tonal spectrum," from the "true whites" of the sink, cabinets, cellar door and costumes to

Figure 3.22 Like a pendulum, Hinton's camera slowly swings to the left after Hess's retreat. *Ganja & Hess* (Blu-ray), Kino Lorber Films.

the "true blacks" of the frame's unlit nooks and crannies (see fig. 3.23). Crucially, the image preserves the "diversity of tonality" signified by Clark and Jackson's skin tones, as did earlier shots juxtaposing the light-skinned Gunn and the darker-shaded Jones.[123]

In his recorded commentary for the *Ganja & Hess* DVD, Hinton shares a production memory that is richly expounded on in David's essay, about an assistant's attempt to brighten Jones's skin tone for the camera. Addressing his mentee in private, Hinton repudiated the premise that all Black actors on film must be brightly lit to secure proper exposure. "If a person's skin is dark, or black," Hinton instructed, "let it go black."[124] The movement toward an antiessentialist approach to representing Black subjects, especially with regard to darker tones, was by that point well underway in the field of artistic photography, as seen in the output of Roy DeCarava, whose low-contrast, monochromatic pictures of African American people and environments have been acclaimed as "formal compositions in rich tones of blackness."[125] Hinton studied under DeCarava, and he later acknowledged his teacher as the "first black man who chose by intent . . . to devote serious attention to the black aesthetic as it relates to photography and the black experience in America."[126]

But cinematographers, particularly Hollywood cinematographers, lagged well behind fine artists, and even observational documentary filmmakers and

Figure 3.23 Hinton lets it go "black" as Ganja and Archie squabble over wine. *Ganja & Hess* (Blu-ray), Kino Lorber Films.

photojournalists, in respecting the range of Black skin hues. Gunn averred that the Black actors in his films were not made up and that he preferred to photograph their natural flesh tones precisely because "we're so multi-colored as a people." Actors of African descent, in his view, were traditionally lit and photographed in white-directed movies "like the side of a fence": hard, flat, and in "cartoon colors."[127] In Hollywood's integrated-cast movies up through the sixties, the Black characters, no matter their actual numbers, are cinematographically treated as a single, undifferentiated figure, whereas white characters are individuated pictorially just as they are narratively. *Ganja & Hess*'s recognition of the visual diversity among its subjects, all supposedly the same "color," constituted a defiant rejoinder to Hollywood practice. According to Waymon, *Ganja & Hess* was about "how we looked, the color of our skin. Bill shot us how we are, he got rid of the glaring lights Hollywood usually uses to shoot us. The graininess of the image was *deliberate*."[128]

Clash and Truce (1:03:05–1:11:15)

The sequence in which Ganja confronts Hess over her appalling discovery in the basement and then reconciles with him is one of the film's most innovative, and Gunn obsessed over its execution.[129] In the final draft screenplay

Figure 3.24 Ruined appetites: Hess assiduously avoids Ganja's accusatory gaze at the dinner table. *Ganja & Hess* (Blu-ray), Kino Lorber Films.

it is divisible into two discrete segments. Both segments were filmed, but the second was not included in Gunn's final cut. In its place, he devised two entirely new scenes: each lasting a single shot, each advancing the narrative via the further revelation of character—Ganja's bewitching mercuriality, Hess's resigned stoicism—rather than through straightforward exposition.

The first of the two segments plays out, with minimal cutting, within what Hinton identified as his favorite setup in the film.[130] As the scene begins, the camera zooms out to emphasize the distance between the two characters, positioned at opposite ends of the dining room table, with Ganja in the middle ground glaring at Hess in the foreground (see fig. 3.24). Having just feasted in the previous scene, Hess is not hungry. He half-heartedly apologizes to Ganja, whom Hess assumes made a "special effort" to cook dinner, while avoiding her piercing stare. His placid exterior does not crack even when Ganja gravely utters, "I know you killed my husband"; he merely summons the dumbfounded Archie and asks him to clear the table.

Infuriated by Hess's stony silence, Ganja bolts from the table and walks straight to the far background plane, into the parlor, where she paces and fumes. She then storms back into the dining area as the camera tracks backward on her movement, until finally she plops down on a chair beside Hess, tacitly demanding a full accounting of the circumstances of her husband's untimely demise. Such an accounting is forthcoming in the screenplay, but not in the finished film. The film snips Hess's explanation that Meda's death came by his own hand, caused by the shock of watching his victim's instantaneous recovery from the wounds inflicted by the Myrthian dagger. In the script, Hess further reveals to Ganja his own addiction to blood, noting that he drank not only Meda's blood but that of three other victims and would have taken hers, as well, had he not barricaded himself in the attic the previous evening. Ganja's counterintuitive response to this confession is to ask Hess to marry her. She is not frightened by Hess's story ("I believe my husband committed suicide. What the rest of your game is, I don't know"); the only thing she fears is "being poor."[131]

Even in the writing stage, Gunn must have sensed that this scene was too clear-cut in its illumination of plot points, so he added an(other) element of strangeness to act as a counterpoint. As Hess endeavors to dispel Ganja's confusion, the room goes dark. Archie appears with a candelabra, explaining that the power has gone out, and the lovers' conversation resumes by candlelight. Gunn shot this "blackout" scene, as confirmed by its inclusion in *Blood Couple*, but without most of the screenplay's expository dialogue. In this filmed version, Hess merely verifies that Meda killed himself, and Ganja proposes marriage without explaining her motivation. Yet, even this abridged attempt at clarifying the characters' motives was too conventional for Gunn, who ultimately cut the exchange altogether from the finished film. Instead, the action transitions to a monologue delivered by Ganja, for which there is no scripted equivalent.

For the third time in *Ganja & Hess*, a character delivers a rambling anecdote; for the third time, that anecdote is seemingly improvised by the actor seated in front of Hess's fireplace. Isolated against a black background, Ganja emotionally calls forth the painful memory of a snowball fight she participated in as a child, for which she was harshly disciplined (see fig. 3.25). Returning home after hours of battling with neighborhood kids, Ganja excitedly reported her adventures to her mother, who, in turn, slapped her daughter, branded her "a slut," and accused her of lying about her whereabouts. "That was a very decisive day in my life," Ganja concludes, "because that day I decided that I would provide for Ganja, always. Do whatever had to be done, take whatever steps had to be taken. But always take care of Ganja."

In addition to foregrounding the will to self-preservation as Ganja's most prized trait, this rumination also continues the precedent set by Gunn's own

Figure 3.25 "It was as though I was a disease": Ganja explains herself to Hess during the blackout. *Ganja & Hess* (Blu-ray), Kino Lorber Films.

performance. In retrospect, the central purpose of Meda's peculiar tangent about his friend's faux pas is to model a method of screen performance that complements the elliptical, arbitrary pattern of the film's storytelling. Gunn wrote each character, yet on set he might bypass the script's directives and simply offer up "an idea for the character in a scene, which was then 'filled out' by the actor." For the "snowball fight" scene, Gunn supplied Clark with the "idea": Ganja's poisoned relationship with her mother as a catalyst for her own egotism. In rehearsals, Clark then "filled out" the idea by devising a monologue about an incident from her own life: the snowball fight and her subsequent punishment. Because the event actually happened to her, it was "easy to do."[132] The only line that was transferred directly from Gunn's imagination to Ganja's narrated experience is her mother's complaint, "I came down with Ganja," as if her daughter were a disease with which she was afflicted.[133]

To an extent, this is an exemplary illustration of "emotional memory" as advocated by the Strasberg school of Method acting. Its use in this scene, however, is only partially redolent of its use in Method-associated plays such as *Blues for Mister Charlie* and Tennessee Williams's *Suddenly Last Summer*: two works in which, similarly, "a female character both recounts and, importantly, re-experiences an emotionally heightened event from her

Figure 3.26 As Waymon's pulsing score surges on the soundtrack, Hinton's camera stays fixated on a barren hallway. *Ganja & Hess* (Blu-ray), Kino Lorber Films.

past."[134] The event's disclosure by Ganja is enlightening but not a crucial narrative revelation, and under Gunn's supervision Clark underplays the scene, calmly relaying her childhood remembrance without the dramatics associated with the Method. Like so many of Gunn's psychologically damaged characters, Ganja does not so much *relive* past traumas as *describe* them, sensitively and exhaustively, in order to be understood.

As her story closes the soundtrack unexpectedly erupts with a loud drum fill that leads into a jazzy, midtempo variation on "You Got to Learn," extending this composition's unique function as, in Morgan Woolsey's estimation, "a flexible motif" that recurs "in a variety of affective modes at key moments in the film."[135] An abrupt cut moves us from the granular image of Ganja illuminated by the fireplace, eyes ablaze, to a congruently static shot of an empty hallway some unspecified time later. As Ganja's mirthful shouts mingle with the Waymon song, the protagonists fleetingly pop into the frame only to immediately duck through a doorway or dash past Hinton's camera and out of sight (see fig. 3.26). Finally, having run out of flowers to fling at each other, they stop in the center of the frame to caress each other and catch their breath (see fig. 3.27).[136] This improvised frolic through the house produces a rare instance of unbridled joy, a brief but jubilant

Figure 3.27 After a frenetic chase, the protagonists come to rest front and center, acceding to the camera's stubborn stillness. *Ganja & Hess* (Blu-ray), Kino Lorber Films.

respite for Hess from the torment of his morbid existence. This moment of abandon also helps Gunn bridge a rather daunting narrative gap, its exuberance sufficient to distract the viewer from questioning the implausibly rapid evolution of Ganja's attitude toward her partner, from revulsion to resignation to ecstasy to matrimony.

Interrupted Honeymoon (1:11:15–1:19:15)

The marriage of Ganja and Hess, both in the legal sense and with regard to the groom's initiation of his bride into a deathless and parasitic existence, begins with a blunt cut from the couple's hallway romp to their wedding ceremony beside Hess's sparkling pool. The daytime nuptials are witnessed by a few friends previously seen attending the garden party, namely Bill Gaddis, Judith Thompson, Ulric and Yolande Haynes, Jack Jordan's young daughter, plus Hoffmeister as Jack Sargent, and presided over by Waymon as Luther Williams, who performs the service in jeans (see fig. 3.28). The surreality of the gathering is complemented by the startling (though easy to overlook) apparition of the Myrthian queen, visible in the far background (see fig. 3.29). This much-admired detail was not a last-minute invention, surprisingly; Gunn's final screenplay draft calls for the sudden appearance

Figure 3.28 Unholy matrimony: Luther Williams (Samuel Waymon) marries Ganja and Hess in a poolside ceremony. *Ganja & Hess* (Blu-ray), Kino Lorber Films.

Figure 3.29 An unacknowledged guest watches the proceedings from afar. From left to right: Jones, King, William Gaddis, Clark, Hoffmeister, Waymon. *Ganja & Hess* (Blu-ray), Kino Lorber Films.

of the "Black Queen standing naked beneath a tree," which is explicitly labeled as Hess's "hallucination."[137]

As Luther administers the vows, the film flashes back, or ahead, to a shot of the couple dragging Meda's corpse through an open field at night, presumably to be ditched in the woods. This criminal act more appropriately symbolizes the pair's irrevocable bonding, and its significance is seconded on the soundtrack by the reintroduction of "Jesu, Joy of Man's Desiring" over the dissolve from bright sunshine to evening shade. The link between these rituals is then cemented by the simultaneous addition of "You Got to Learn" to the mix. The layering of two songs on top of each other was an effect suggested by Kanefsky, who recalls being stumped during postproduction by a passage for which the music "wasn't powerful enough." Gunn reacted with skepticism, but Waymon was intrigued enough to request a rough mix, which he loved.[138] Equally impressed, Gunn later ordained the very same effect for a scene in *Black Picture Show*, an early draft of which calls for a comparable "collage of Black music mixed with Bach" following the overture.[139]

In bed that night, Hess further plumbs the motives behind Ganja's readiness to cast her lot with a "psychotic." Gunn's original script, as usual, clarifies her reasons for marrying him: "First because you're good in bed . . . second for your money . . . There ain't enough money in the world to compensate for a tired lay."[140] The filmed version of the script substitutes a different rationale: Ganja believes that Hess's insistence that he is a vampire is actually a freaky sexual fetish. She is not even thrown by Hess's solemn avowal to her: "I *really* want you to live forever."

The image of the couple in a heated embrace dissolves to the same view after some time has passed. Now Hess, completely nude, sits at the foot of the bed as Ganja's bloodstained cadaver lies before him (see fig. 3.30). A second dissolve to the same angle, slightly later, moves Hess to a corner of the room, his body partially occluded by a bizarrely humanoid antique lamp, as he awaits his wife's revival (see fig. 3.31). The latter dissolve was Kanefsky's brainchild, and Gunn surely appreciated the tone of decadent elegance that it bestows on the scene.[141] An alternate resolution to the scene, preserved in an outtake, is borderline nauseating in comparison: a brutal close-up of Ganja's motionless face reveals a string of drool streaming from her mouth to her throat (see fig. 3.32).[142]

Perhaps more than any other sequence in the film, the imagery depicting Ganja's implied resurrection skirts the edge of intelligibility: Ganja, in a

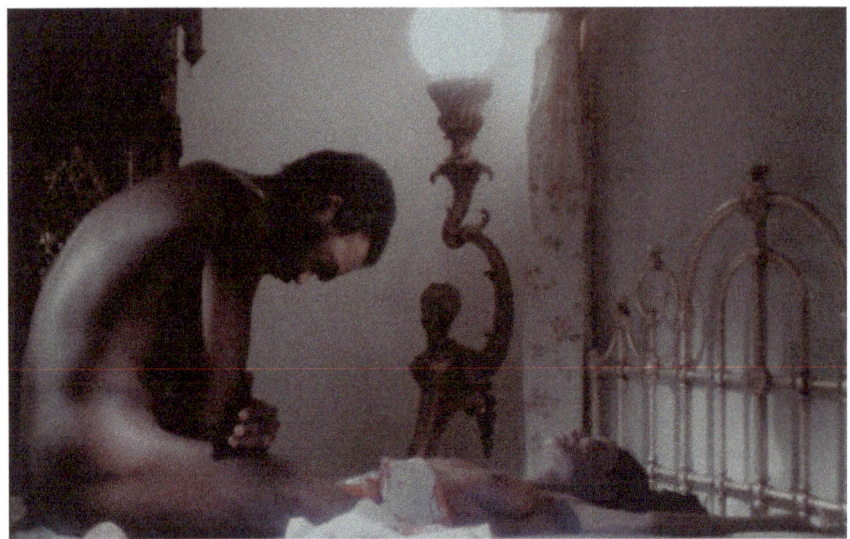

Figure 3.30 "I *really* want you to live forever": Hess makes good on his wedding night promise to his new bride. *Ganja & Hess* (Blu-ray), Kino Lorber Films.

Figure 3.31 Hess waits for Ganja to revive and join him among the living dead. *Ganja & Hess* (Blu-ray), Kino Lorber Films.

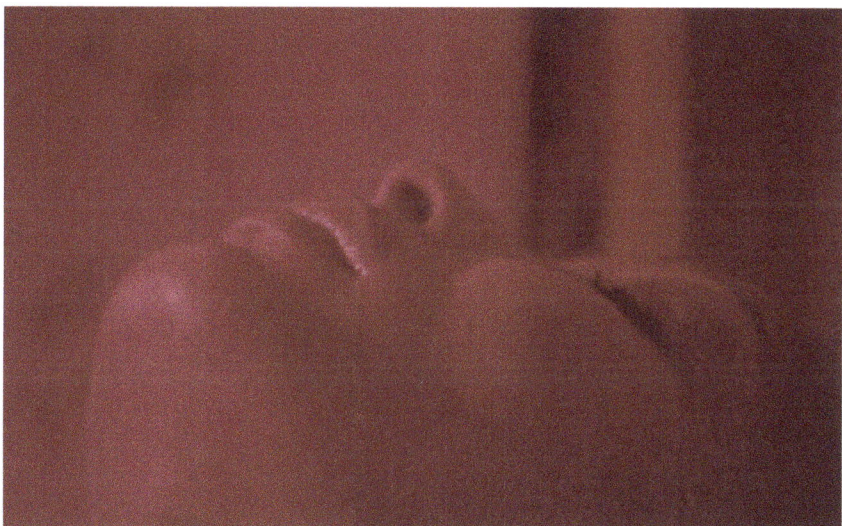

Figure 3.32 In an alternate take, missing from any released version of *Ganja & Hess*, Hinton's camera zooms out from Ganja's (temporarily) lifeless face. Courtesy of James E. Hinton Collection, Harvard Film Archive, Harvard College Library.

diaphanous white gown, runs in slow motion across a lawn; a foot (presumably Hess's) steps over the crosshatched shadow cast by a swinging door; Ganja loses her balance and tumbles to the ground; Hess's feet backtrack through the doorway; Ganja brushes her hair and feverishly rubs her face and throat as she sits before an oval mirror; Ganja lies prone in the grass, gulping from a mud puddle. The fragmented nature of the sequence suggests that we are witnessing a subjective moment, perhaps a nightmare experienced by Ganja as she hovers between mortal and immortal states. (This interpretation is possibly corroborated in the ensuing scene, which includes Ganja's offhand observation, "I had a terrible dream last night.") Per usual, Gunn's screenplay furnishes the narrative coherence missing from the movie. After Ganja awakens in the scene as written, she dresses and walks outside; Hess monitors her from a distance. Unaware that blood is what she craves, she tries to slake her thirst by drinking from a puddle. Her eye is drawn irresistibly to "the brilliance of a blood red rose," into which she sinks her teeth.[143] The script elucidates the film's supposedly random pattern of images as reflecting Ganja's actual experience and not the illogic of a fever dream. The film, in contrast, eschews linearity and motivation in order to evoke rather than explicate.

Hess, finally, takes Ganja for a walk in the garden, where he attempts to explain their mutual condition. Unable to penetrate her intransigence, he impassively produces the Myrthian dagger and stabs his wife in the heart. Hess's reason for this aggression is relatively obvious despite the suppression of the couple's conversation, which is concealed in Gunn's script and muffled in Gunn's film: to show Ganja irrefutable evidence of her own immortality. Yet, this was not obvious enough for Fima Noveck, who added an explanatory voice-over track to his re-creation of the scene for *Blood Couple*. The embarrassingly literal resulting exchange essentially restates the plot of the entire film up to that point:

> GANJA: I had a terrible dream last night. I dreamed you murdered me.
>
> HESS: It wasn't a dream, Ganja. It's a terrible reality.
>
> GANJA: What are you talking about?
>
> HESS: When I told you last night that I wanted you to live forever, I meant it. I want you to live forever just as I will. I love you and I don't want to face losing you, ever. You didn't dream, darling, I really did kill you. I stabbed you three times with the same Myrthian dagger your husband stabbed me with. Without his knowing it he rendered me immortal, and I have rendered you immortal, deliberately. Now we're both condemned to an eternal life on this earth.
>
> GANJA: I don't believe you. You're mad. It's all a lot of nonsense.
>
> HESS: No, it is not. I'll prove it to you once again.

Needless to say, none of these lines (other than the first) are spoken in Gunn's cut. Characteristically, Gunn regarded the "second wedding" scene as another opportunity for privileging lyricism over narrative lucidity and character psychology over exposition. Rather than a summary of story events, Gunn's soundtrack is dominated by Hess's voice bitterly observing that "the only perversions that can be comfortably condemned are the perversions of others. . . . I will persist and survive without God's or society's sanction. . . . I will not be guilty." The scene's leisurely progression allows the viewer's eye to linger on the sun peeking through the trees, the intricate patterning and primary colors on the blankets cloaking the newlyweds, the subtle variations between the repeated shots of Hess ceremoniously lifting the dagger above his head, and the vertiginous camera movements that embody Ganja's collapse.[144]

Gunn, in fact, expected this sequence to stretch on even longer. Hinton's archive contains a rough succession of unused shots, presumably cobbled together to serve as a sort of prologue for the garden walk. This brief montage

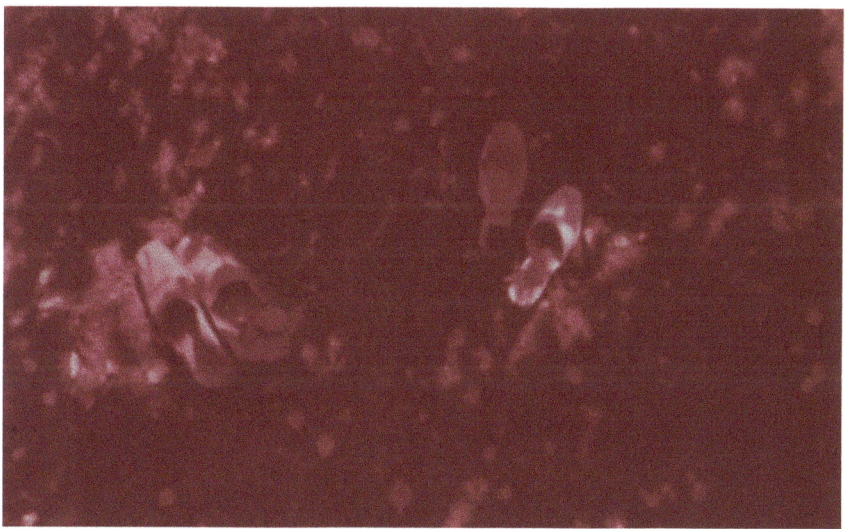

Figure 3.33 The couple's "second wedding" begins with a characteristically enigmatic image, in a sequence dropped from the original cut of *Ganja & Hess*. Courtesy of James E. Hinton Collection, Harvard Film Archive, Harvard College Library.

presents a delicate tableau of two pairs of bedroom slippers placed on the ground and an over-the-shoulder framing of Ganja and Hess seated next to each other on the grass, holding hands (see figs. 3.33 and 3.34).[145] Sadly absent from the final cut, the latter composition is disarming in its quiet affirmation of the genuine affection that exists between the two, despite the obstacles that continually threaten that affection.

Dinner (1:19:15–1:29:15)

As with so many of the outstanding set pieces in *Ganja & Hess*, the details of the picture's most sexually graphic and shockingly violent scene deviate significantly from those proposed at the script stage. In all versions motivation and end point are clear enough: Hess, realizing that his supply of plasma is dangerously low, extends a dinner invitation to Richard, the athletic director from the rec center in the screenplay's opening. (In the film, the question of how Hess knows the nameless guest goes unanswered.) After the meal, Hess excuses himself, leaving Richard and Ganja to pursue their blatant flirtation, and soon the couple is having sex on a bathroom floor. Aroused to a frenzy by the taste of blood drawn by her fingernails,

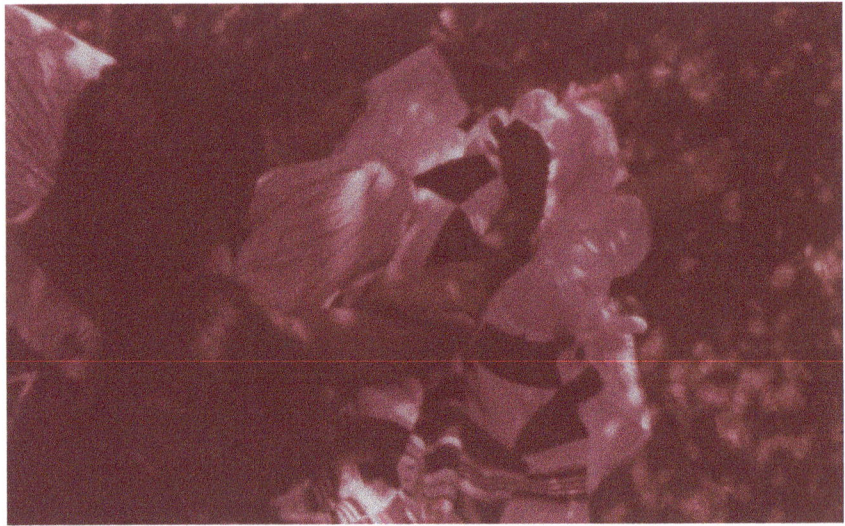

Figure 3.34 Hess comforts Ganja during her torturous transition, in a sequence dropped from the original cut of *Ganja & Hess*. Courtesy of James E. Hinton Collection, Harvard Film Archive, Harvard College Library.

Ganja literally dines on her partner. Aghast, she flees the bathroom, leaving Hess to drain the remaining life fluid from Richard's depleted form.

As this account suggests, the action in and of itself is undeniably potent. Its stylistic representation both complements and complicates the overall emotional affect. By virtue of its surrealistic visuals, droning soundtrack, and abstract editing, the episode strongly evokes its sex scene counterpart in Gunn's previous film, *Stop*. In its new incarnation, however, this psychedelic tapestry of effects is interpretable less as a shared hallucination than as an aesthetic inclination.

The sequence begins on a note of slight absurdity: as Ganja writhes in agony, her husband, dapperly attired and toting a glass of blood, slowly materializes in her room aboard a miniature lift. Ganja accepts the glass and drinks hungrily, her eyes giving away her shame. Hess informs her that he has invited a guest to dinner because she requires a "distraction." There is a dissolve to yet another still life: a reproduction of Andrei Rublev's fifteenth-century icon, *The Trinity* (see fig. 3.35). Kanefsky wittily follows this image with a wide shot of Hess, Richard, and Ganja seated around the dinner table that evening, graphically matched to the three angels who dined with Abraham at the Oak of Mamre (see fig. 3.36). In addition to intimating a mildly

Figure 3.35 Quiet communion: Kanefsky highlights a detail from *The Trinity*, Andrei Rublev's fifteenth century icon. *Ganja & Hess* (Blu-ray), Kino Lorber Films.

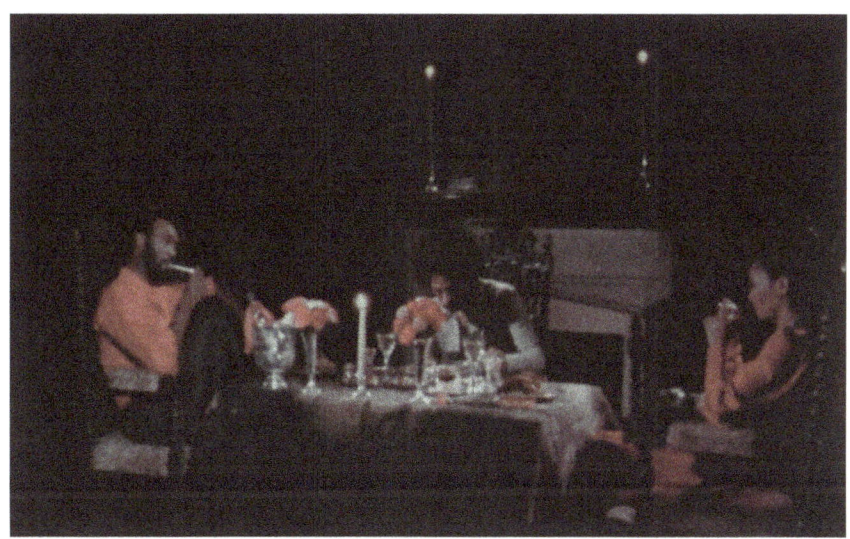

Figure 3.36 Rublev's spirits become Gunn's fallen angels. *Ganja & Hess* (Blu-ray), Kino Lorber Films.

Figure 3.37 Hess leads the lamb, Richard (Richard Harris), to the slaughter, in footage cut from the climactic dinner sequence. Courtesy of James E. Hinton Collection, Harvard Film Archive, Harvard College Library.

blasphemous joke, this particular juxtaposition conceals the elision of a good amount of scripted plot material, much of which was filmed but not used.

Almost all exposition is lopped from the buildup to Ganja and Richard's mutual seduction. In Gunn's final cut, this sequence begins in medias res, with Richard politely engaging in small talk between bites of food. No traces remain in the film of the lengthy preface that Gunn deliberated over for several weeks prior to shooting. In the unused footage, Hess leads Richard into the living room, where both men are taken aback by the stunning woman before them, "dressed in red satin to the floor," whom Hess identifies only as his "house guest" from Holland (see fig. 3.37).[146] The force of impact on the two men is accentuated by an almost 180-degree cut from Hess and Richard, halted in their tracks, to the ravishing Ganja alluringly returning the camera's gaze (see fig. 3.38). Having left her that morning scarcely capable of sitting up, Hess surreptitiously questions Ganja while Richard admires the house's interior design. She hands Hess a chalice filled with cat's blood, the key to her rejuvenation, and leaves to attend to their guest. Realizing that he is losing control over the situation, Hess angrily tosses aside the wildflowers Ganja picked for a table decoration. This excised footage also catches several details of Tom John's impeccably chosen decor and

Figure 3.38 In the succeeding reverse shot, Ganja's magnificence stops her lovers dead in their tracks. Courtesy of James E. Hinton Collection, Harvard Film Archive, Harvard College Library.

props, right down to the dinner plates, which resemble roulette wheels with diamonds and roses in place of numerals (see fig. 3.39).[147]

In Gunn's first pass at writing this scene, Richard is far more loquacious than he will be in later manifestations. Perhaps unsurprisingly, his attitudes and preoccupations reveal him to be a classic Gunn "type": hyperliterate, jaded, race-conscious, and fiercely individualistic. In the original script, Richard has a surname, "Vendémiaire," after the first month of the French Revolutionary calendar.[148] It is a fitting choice, because in this draft Richard is given a wide berth from which to expound on the need for Black liberation, which he considers to be humanity's only hope. "Our revolution rejects every ideology but the one of *total* freedom," he tells his hosts. "White people running back and forth from fascisism [sic] to democracy to communism to socialism . . . there isn't one of these that includes everyone regardless of their individual drive."[149]

As their interjections make clear, both Ganja and Hess are conversant with the subject of Black revolution; Hess, in particular, seems to relish the opportunity to talk racial politics with a stimulating conversationalist. Near the end of their dialogue, however, Richard is tossed a seemingly arbitrary, more existential query:

Figure 3.39 Richard's last supper is appropriately served atop a roulette-wheel design, as documented in an image from the *Ganja & Hess* outtakes. Courtesy of James E. Hinton Collection, Harvard Film Archive, Harvard College Library.

> HESS: How do you feel about the possibility of eternal life?
>
> RICHARD: What has that got to do with me?
>
> HESS: If you were given the secret of eternal life, what would you do with it?
>
> RICHARD: I'd teach it to the children.
>
> HESS: Why?
>
> RICHARD: Because they'll need to be indestructible.[150]

Hess's question, of course, slyly acknowledges why Richard is there in the first place. More broadly, Richard's dialogue, much like Meda's suicide poem, functions to redirect the viewer's interest to larger yet related themes. Yet, since nearly all of the conversation among Richard, Hess, and Ganja was cut from the finished film, perhaps Gunn felt that Meda's poem accomplished this task on its own.

An equally probable motivation for the pruning of Richard's lines has to do with the awkwardness of the person playing the part. Richard Harris was a teacher and a friend of Gunn's with no previous acting experience. The director did his best to prepare the novice performer by extensively rehearsing his scenes prior to the shoot.[151] In the end, however, the only audible lines Harris speaks during the dinner sequence, in which he talks of his job

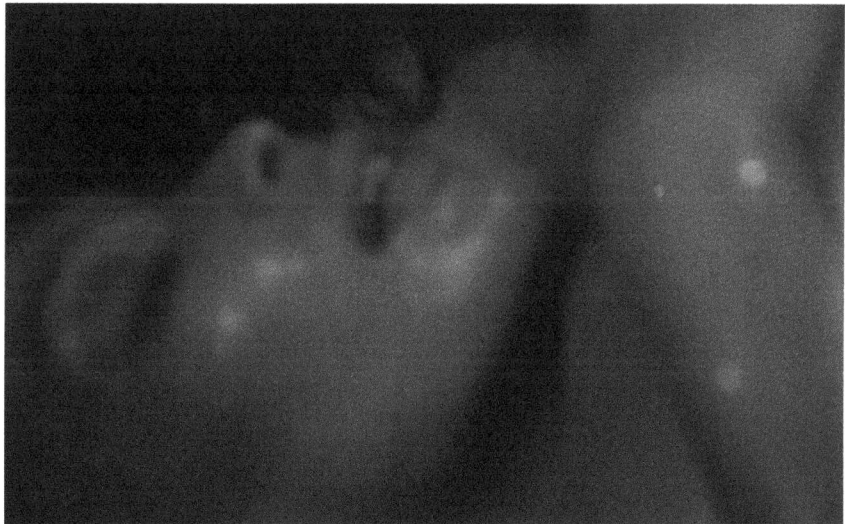

Figure 3.40 Hinton's "haptic" camera pauses on the lovers' sparkling, intertwined bodies. *Ganja & Hess* (Blu-ray), Kino Lorber Films.

in a soft-spoken, no-nonsense manner, were probably improvised. According to Schultz, Harris was mortified by his performance and had his name altered in the credits (to "Richard Harrow") so that no one would know he was in the film.[152] Harris unquestionably possessed the right physical characteristics for the role, as attested to by the extended postdinner seduction scene that he performs with Clark. Unused footage divulges that Gunn also filmed several shots that exploited Harris's physical grace through a funky pas de deux with Clark, presumably danced to one of Ganja's soul LPs.[153]

In the movie, Gunn segues directly from Richard and Ganja exchanging meaningful gazes at the table to the lovers disrobing in the opulently decorated, candlelit bathroom. The montage of their foreplay unfolds similarly to the ménage à trois segment at the end of *Stop*, complete with trippy, throbbing instrumental music and slow dissolves across smoldering glances and intimate touching. Following a lingering French kiss, Richard penetrates Ganja on top of an immaculate white fur rug. Hinton's handheld camera sinuously encircles the couple, paralleling their passionate exploration of each other's bodies, and defocuses to capture the tiny bursts of light reflecting their beads of sweat: glitter, in actuality, that Gunn carefully strewed over the actors' torsos and legs (see fig. 3.40).[154] Clark and Harris's

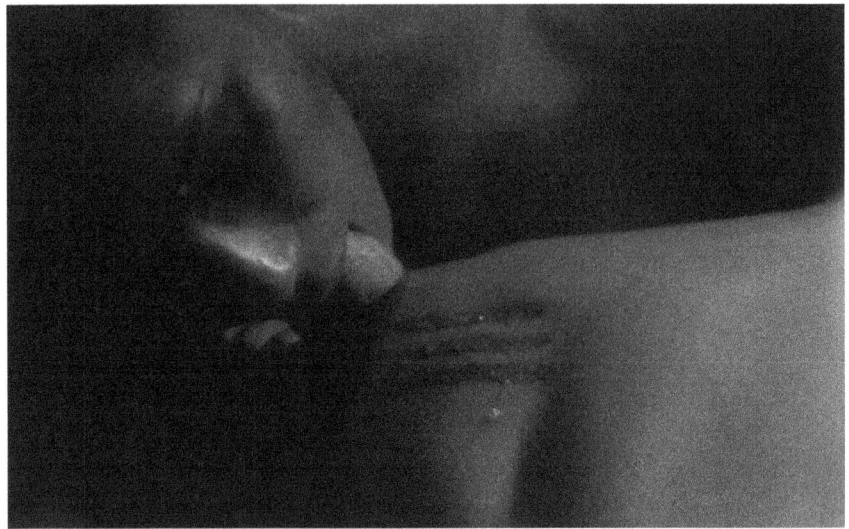

Figure 3.41 In the midst of their impassioned lovemaking, Ganja locates Richard's most vulnerable spot. *Ganja & Hess* (Blu-ray), Kino Lorber Films.

sexual chemistry duplicates the fevered intensity of the annotations in Gunn's script, which calls for Ganja to orgasm "as her nails rip down his back. . . . His sexual promise to her is so devastating that she begins to weep fully."[155] In her elation, Ganja discovers blood trickling from the gashes on Richard's back, which she laps with her tongue (see fig. 3.41). Gunn then cuts to a close shot of Ganja outdoors, nibbling on a flower that leaves behind a residue of red fluid. Originally filmed for the postwedding night sequence, in which Ganja seeks to quench her insatiable thirst, the image in this context becomes purely symbolic. Its lyrical connotations are further multiplied when Kanefsky cuts to a shot of yet another exquisite objet d'art: a blue ceramic face that secretes blood from its eyes and mouth.

The scene returns to Ganja licking Richard's wound, then goes back to Ganja dropping the flower in horror and emitting a piercing scream that is interwoven with the musical drone on the soundtrack. Richard's body, suddenly and improbably drenched in blood, teeters and falls off Ganja's own. As substantiated by *Blood Couple*, the sequence originally ended with a trembling Ganja begging for help from her husband, who indifferently replies, "you save any for me?"[156] *Ganja & Hess* eliminates Hess's line, instead letting Waymon have the last "word." In the fullest expression so far of the composer's "chaotic and disorienting aural aesthetic," the aforementioned drone gradually becomes a cacophony, incorporating fragments of "Bungelii Work Song" and wild animal screeches, that matches the bedlam on the image track.[157] Conceivably, Gunn clipped the spouses' cross talk at the conclusion because it highlights attitudes—Ganja's building ambivalence, Hess's corrupting cynicism—that will soon be reversed. The scene, therefore, resolves wordlessly, though pitched at a level of unrestrained terror.

This deafening climax aside, the sequence's sharpest sting comes at its tail end, amid an environment of serene tranquility. In an extreme long shot, held for a full minute, Ganja and Hess carry Richard's plastic-enfolded figure across a vast field and set it down among the reeds. Ganja kneels next to the body and reaches out to touch Richard's chest. As she realizes that their victim is still breathing, Hess forcibly pulls her away. "He's alive!" she protests, and we are finally reminded of that crucial aspect of the mythology surrounding vampires: their victims become vampires, too. Gunn suppressed our recall of this convention by eliminating the scripted scene in which Rose and her pimp revive from Hess's attack. He also trimmed a truly unsettling vignette that appears late in his revised screenplay. Walking up a street jammed with pedestrians, Hess is stunned to glimpse

> the woman with the baby that he picked up. . . . She walks slowly along, she wears black and carries the child in a sling around her neck to take the weight from her arms. . . . The sling is a black piece of transparent material through which we see the sleeping child.
> It is apparent to Hess that the woman whose eyes stare straight ahead of her like an addict has taken the blood of her own child.
> Hess runs in terror across the street to avoid the terrible sight.[158]

Through expunging these horrifying details, Gunn discourages us from thinking too hard about what happens to the unfortunate souls sacrificed to quench the protagonists' bloodlust. Possibly, he wanted to focus our attention on Ganja and Hess's experience alone, emphasizing their seclusion and their consequent dependence on each other. Nonetheless, the undead status of one of their victims will eventually (and memorably) be revisited.

Pleading the Blood (1:29:15–1:41:50)

Now one final and vital chunk of exposition must be disclosed, and Gunn conveys it as economically as possible. The scene opens on Ganja and Hess huddled in front of the fireplace, shivering and isolated, in an encapsulation of their ennui and despair following the abandonment of Richard's twitching corpse. Hess takes cold comfort in a book on ancient cultures, which he casually describes to Ganja as "a guide to our destruction." Quoting the Myrthian queen Helgda, who has haunted him for nearly the film's entirety, Hess unveils a potential "solution" to their ordeal: their souls may be "released into the bosom of [the] Creator," providing that "the implement by which [their] god was destroyed . . . cast a shadow on the heart." Ganja repeats the passage back to Hess. "If the shadow of the cross is against our heart, it will destroy us?" Hess responds affirmatively, but there is a caveat. The cursed one seeking release must worship God. And so, for the hedonistic man of science to be saved literally, he must first be saved spiritually. His progress from this point can thus be appraised skeptically, as a desperate, eleventh-hour appeal for mercy—a convenient renunciation of his earlier proclamation "I will persist and survive without God's . . . sanction"—or as a sincere, earnest embrace of the Church as savior. (*Gunn's* position on this matter is explored in greater depth in the next chapter.)

The bravura set piece depicting Hess's bid for salvation, through Christian baptism, opens with a Pentecostal church service in progress, the very one glimpsed in fragments in the film's opening, with a choir led by a commanding female vocalist (Betty Barney) performing a gospel rendition of "You Got to Learn." The camera picks out various faces in the entirely Black congregation, including the presiding minister, Luther Williams, seated behind the piano. During a temporary lull in the singing, dancing, and clapping, the minister asks whether anyone present wants to be prayed for. As Luther leads the choir in a stately hymn (another Waymon composition), Hess soberly trudges up the aisle. At the altar he is blessed by his employee, who tells him, "Today is the day that you give your life to Jesus."

Hess's presence supplies a narrative motivation, but that motivation is secondary to the sequence's enthralling effect. Gunn strove to faithfully replicate the feel and atmosphere of this distinctly African American milieu, yet the scene's degree of spontaneity is also by design. In the *Ganja & Hess* screenplay, the church revival is an abstraction: an unidentified preacher simply asks for worshippers "to come forward to testify," and Hess complies.[159] The very thinness of this description verifies that Gunn planned for most of the action to be decided upon on-site. The only particular cinematographic effect called for by the script is a series of near-subliminal images of Hess's victims intercut among shots of the preacher laying hands on the doctor's head. These brief flashbacks do not appear in the director's

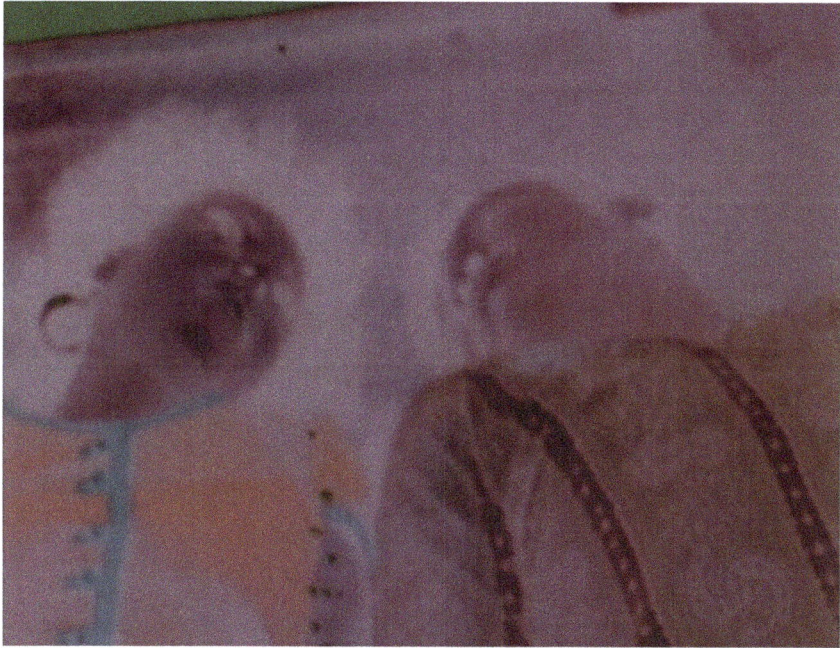

Figure 3.42 During Hess's impromptu baptism, his mind flashes back to memories of his victims, rendered in solarized form in the *Blood Couple* recut. *Blood Couple*, in *Creatures, Critters, and Crazies* (DVD), Gemstone Entertainment.

cut, though they were reinstated (in solarized form) in *Blood Couple* (see fig. 3.42). Perhaps Gunn felt the effect was too intrusive and self-consciously arty, especially in the context of the naturalism and authenticity that his actors and cinematographer worked so hard to evoke in this segment.

With that objective in mind, the production team solicited the participation of a real-life congregation to help them actualize Hess's spiritual awakening. Waymon approached a fellow Nyack resident, Pastor Elizabeth Alston, who ministered at Evangel Revivaltime Church at the corner of Depew Avenue and South Broadway, and asked her for permission to re-create a service on church premises. She agreed, under one condition: they had to wait "until we finish *our* service." Like most of Nyack's African American residents, none of whom had ever before seen "a camera crew shooting a Black film," Alston was fascinated by the production's novelty, and she consented to appear in it as herself. She is visible at Waymon's side throughout this sequence, while several members of her congregation can be seen in fleeting close-ups. Alston's church eventually closed, ending the

Figure 3.43 Evangel Revivaltime Church in 2015, now known as the Nyack Center (exterior). Photograph by author, July 1, 2015.

building's function as a house of worship from the time of its construction in 1839. However, the structure was renovated in the nineties and thrives today as a community center (see figs. 3.43 and 3.44).[160]

The tight shooting schedule at Evangel Revivaltime precluded the possibility of second takes. It thus fell to Hinton and the film's camera and sound recording technicians to surmount the setup's technical complexities and obtain enough usable footage to fill a reel's worth of screen time. To efficiently record his subjects' interactions, Hinton drew on his experience at Harlem Audiovisuals and approached the task as if he were filming "a [cinema] vérité documentary." Only two cameras were used for coverage. The camera responsible for shooting close views was positioned on a baby tripod at ground level to the right of the pews; this angle provided the images of Hess's plodding march to the stage. The second camera was placed in the balcony, at the rear of the room, to take in a wider frontal field of view (see fig. 3.45). In combination, the cameras provided two extremely long master shots, and they were stagger started so that one camera would continue filming while Hinton changed the magazine in the other. Though

Figure 3.44 Evangel Revivaltime Church in 2015, now the Nyack Center (interior). Photograph by author, July 1, 2015.

Figure 3.45 View from the balcony: flanked by the real-life head of Evangel Revivaltime, Pastor Elizabeth Alston, Luther baptizes his wayward friend. *Ganja & Hess* (Blu-ray), Kino Lorber Films.

Figure 3.46 View from the floor: flanked by a misplaced light stand, Hess marches up the aisle to receive salvation. *Ganja & Hess* (Blu-ray), Kino Lorber Films.

he was given only vague instructions to follow the actors' movements and "anticipate what might happen," Hinton nevertheless pulled off the scene without a glitch—save for one clearly visible light stand (see fig. 3.46).[161]

The success of the shoot depended equally on Waymon, who had never acted before and who was initially reluctant to play the part. "What makes you think I can do it?" he asked Gunn, who replied, "You're an actor. You don't know it, but I've seen you onstage. You have an *honesty* about you, you're not one to hide your feelings; they're on your face, in your eyes."[162] Despite Gunn's confidence, Waymon was highly intimidated by the responsibility for carrying one of *Ganja & Hess*'s most important scenes with only ambiguous stage directions to work from. On set, Gunn provided Waymon with an outline of the ceremony and some advice: "Just be yourself. I wouldn't give the scene to you if I didn't think you could do it." "I don't have a clue what I'm going to do," Waymon told Jones just before the cameras began filming. "But just roll with it. We're going to church."[163] Appropriately led by the spirit, the amateur actor delivers a virtuoso performance, moving effortlessly among the minister's varied roles: pianist, choir director, sermonizer ("You know, I'm high right now . . . but I'm high on the Lord"), and saver of souls. According to Schultz, after the day's filming wrapped,

Alston asked Waymon to stay on at Evangel Revivaltime as an assistant pastor, because he had so captivated the congregation with his charisma.[164]

Waymon's proficiency as a stage performer was not the only factor in his casting. Gunn knew that the role of the minister had to be played by someone familiar with the milieu if the details of the service were to be credible. Waymon, the son of preachers, was certainly qualified in that sense. "You understand the power of the church, of blood, of redemption," Gunn told Waymon prior to filming. "You understand the meaning of salvation. You understand *exultation*." These words of encouragement greatly assisted Waymon's characterization, helping him recognize that everything in the scene was about exulting, via the linking of "musical and spiritual glorification." The agnostic Hess is present because, in Waymon's view, he "*wants* to be saved; he understands wanting to be free: free of something he thought was both a blessing *and* a curse."[165]

Hess's actions gesture toward the Christian rite vividly referred to as "pleading the blood." James Baldwin's description of this rite as practiced in his own Pentecostal church, which opens his critical essay on *The Exorcist* (1973) and the sociocultural phenomenon it spawned, offers an indirect endorsement of the Gunn film's superior portrait of authentic Christian rapture:

> When the sinner fell on his face before the altar, the soul of the sinner then found itself locked in battle with Satan: or, in the place of Jacob, wrestling with the angel.... The soul in torment turned this way and that, yearning, equally, for the light and for the darkness: yearning, out of agony, for reconciliation—and for rest: for this agony is compounded by an unimaginable, unprecedented, unspeakable fatigue. Only the saints who had passed through this fire—the incredible horror of the fainting of the spirit—had the power to intercede, to "plead the blood," to bring the embattled and mortally endangered soul "through."[166]

Correspondingly, the true protagonist of *Ganja & Hess*'s "baptism scene" is not the preacher but the supplicant, who does not even appear inside the church until the sequence is nearly five minutes underway. Hess is visibly changed by his encounter with the Holy Spirit, and this change is portrayed with utter conviction by Jones, who convulses in a state of barely contained ecstasy as he walks back up the aisle and out the front doors. Stationed outside the church, Schultz watched as an entranced Jones continued walking for a full block, involuntarily jerking and speaking in tongues until he was restrained by crew members.[167]

Figure 3.47 Delivered from his anguish, Hess runs toward the light... *Ganja & Hess* (Blu-ray), Kino Lorber Films.

After staggering from the church, Hess is next seen running in slow motion through a sun-dappled field, released from his torment, his shirt undone and a smile on his lips (see fig. 3.47). The church choir's harmonies overlap from the previous scene but more softly, reinforcing a mood of quiet acceptance and repose. After an hour and a half of images of Hess in agony, constricted by enclosed settings and tight framings, this caesura beautifully renders his path to transcendence through blissful submission. In the script's alternate version, conversely, Hess's fate is communicated in darker, more foreboding terms, via haiku-like stage directions: "Hess turning in slow motion and walking up the aisle toward the door. / The lights up and blinding, causing everything to go high key. / He moves in slow motion through the door. / It is apparent that he is dying."[168]

Letting Go (1:41:50–1:53:00)

After Hess passes through the meadow oasis, Gunn dissolves to a medium close-up of his protagonist in a familiarly claustrophobic setting of suffering (see fig. 3.48). A cut to a wider framing reveals Hess, in evident distress, sitting before the fireplace in his parlor. Most of the furniture has been cleared away, and dead leaves skitter across the floor. A makeshift

Figure 3.48 . . . and finds himself in the shadow of the cross. *Ganja & Hess* (Blu-ray), Kino Lorber Films.

wooden cross is suspended from the ceiling, and a naked light bulb throws the shadow of the crucifix onto the wall to Hess's left. Ganja stands nearby, nervously surveying this macabre tableau. The scripted exchange between the two makes Hess's suicidal objective explicit; true to form, Gunn boils down their dialogue in the movie to a couple of utterances that distill the characters' fates to their essence. "Come with me," Hess pleads. "Please, *please* come with me." His plea is paralleled on the soundtrack by the sung repetition of the phrase "come and go with me," which accelerates into an agitated chant recalling Waymon's a cappella performance in the opening. With great difficulty Hess rises, his attention riveted to the cross offscreen. He is granted a final poetic reverie in the form of a point-of-view shot, representing his own wandering spirit, darting through a field as if seeking a final resting place. Awed by this vision of "the glory of death," Hess steps into the cross's shadow and lurches forward onto the floor.[169]

As Hess falls, his arm inadvertently knocks the light bulb into a crazy spin. In a striking shot dropped from Gunn's final cut but used in *Blood Couple*, the careening bulb causes the shadow of the cross to "follow" Ganja as she frantically tries to dodge it (see fig. 3.49). Scurrying about the room, clad entirely in black, she eerily resembles an expressionistic monster, such as Count Orlok in Murnau's *Nosferatu* (1922) or The Babadook in Jennifer

Figure 3.49 While Hess embraces his annihilation, Ganja dashes from corner to corner to keep the crucifix's shadow from falling across her own heart, in a shot restored in *Blood Couple*. *Blood Couple*, in *Creatures, Critters, and Crazies* (DVD), Gemstone Entertainment.

Kent's same-titled supernatural chiller from 2014. *Blood Couple* ends with Ganja cowering in the darkness, her fate unresolved. In contrast, *Ganja & Hess* gives her more time to ponder whether to join Hess in the afterworld or to continue stalking this one, which is just long enough for Gunn to deliver a stunning denouement.

The horrific implications of her ultimate decision are foreshadowed by yet another hypnotic sound effect built around a contorted human voice. At the start of Hess's death throes, a harsh wheezing noise displaces the chanting on the soundtrack, its jagged, irregular rhythm suggesting a man straining to catch his breath. When Gunn cuts to Hess lying motionless on the floor, the voice's low rumble erupts into an unearthly, high-pitched yowl intended as a metaphor for "someone losing his soul."[170] To create such a sound, Waymon drew on his experience with primal scream therapy in the early seventies. Developed by psychologist Arthur Janov in

1968, primal scream therapy was a briefly fashionable treatment based in the cathartic purge of repressed trauma, most notoriously via the "primal scream." The act of spontaneous and uncontainable screaming as a means of exhuming long-buried feelings of hurt and rage was a major factor in the treatment's appeal among creative artists like Waymon and John Lennon. Several songs on the latter's solo debut album, *John Lennon/Plastic Ono Band* (1970), incorporated modified primal screams in order to impart painful experiences "outside semantic coherence." For Hess's death scene, Waymon's process closely mirrored what Paul Williams and Brian Edgar identify as "the dramatic form of Janovian therapy—which began with 24 hours of isolation and moved into a three week 'intensive' of almost daily open-ended Primal sessions."[171] Locking himself in his music room (where "they fed me under the door"), Waymon spent almost three days alone, yelling into a Nagra tape recorder until he was satisfied with the results. "I had an out-of-body experience in that room," he later recalled. "When I came out, I was physically spent."[172]

Ganja's rejection of her late husband's example is first signaled on the soundtrack, as the wail of an ambulance's siren fades in nearly a half minute before the scene shifts. In an amusing graphic match, Gunn cuts from Ganja deliberating in front of the homemade cross to a close-up of a cross stenciled onto the ambulance's side window, which then overlays the figure of the dazed widow when the vehicle comes to rest (see fig. 3.50). The paramedics, played by actual first responders from the Westchester Ambulance Company, load Hess's body and drive away as Ganja looks on, seemingly at loose ends.

Gunn authored a few additional scenes that show Ganja as a tad more clearheaded and resolute in the wake of Hess's death. According to the script, she burns all of Hess's personal papers, including "his entire Myrthian file," in the living room fireplace and tosses the petrified wooden dagger into the river.[173] No filmed record of any of these actions exists, but a scene was shot in which Ganja, returning from discarding the dagger, happens across Archie's lifeless body on the pathway back to the manor. In a surviving outtake, she runs shrieking, arms outstretched, away from the cadaver and directly at the camera (see fig. 3.51).[174] None of this appears in the release version of *Ganja & Hess*. Instead, Gunn cuts directly from the ambulance's departure to Ganja at an upstairs window. The ellipsis preserves the ambivalence underlying her feelings, if only momentarily.

Figure 3.50 As the paramedics arrive to spirit Hess away, the cross on the ambulance window is superimposed on his complicit widow. *Ganja & Hess* (Blu-ray), Kino Lorber Films.

Figure 3.51 In an image preserved in Hinton's outtakes, Ganja flees in terror at the sight of Archie's bloody corpse. Courtesy of James E. Hinton Collection, Harvard Film Archive, Harvard College Library.

Figure 3.52 The return of the repressed: Richard emerges from the murky depths of mortality. *Ganja & Hess* (Blu-ray), Kino Lorber Films.

In the story's final moments, Ganja's concentration is seized by what she sees through the window frame. A cut to her point of view, combined with a zoom in, identifies the source of her alarm: someone, or something, emerging from the swimming pool. The interloper peers over the ridge, then dramatically hoists himself out of the water (see fig. 3.52). It is Richard, reanimated, naked as when he was left to die but now cleansed of bloodstains. Returning Ganja's look, he breaks into a full sprint toward the house, accompanied by a manic percussion motif on the soundtrack. His surge is arrested, however, in a freeze-frame at the very moment at which his outstretched body vaults over, in a surprise reveal, Archie's supine form (see fig. 3.53). In the scripted climax, Ganja is terrified by the sight of the valet's blood-drenched corpse, but her fear dissipates when Richard, standing over his fresh kill, smiles at her. At second glance, Ganja smiles back at Richard, who then resumes his charge.[175] The movie condenses her acceptance of Richard's unspoken proposition into three unadorned shots of Ganja at the window, taken from the reverse angle and linked by jump cuts: Ganja looks down with apparent dismay, her gaze shifts toward the viewer, and her sour countenance melts into a wry smile (see fig. 3.54). Although Clark's understated expression sustains the ambiguity surrounding her true motives,

Figure 3.53 A reanimated Richard leaps into the unknown, and Archie's fate is finally verified. *Ganja & Hess* (Blu-ray), Kino Lorber Films.

Figure 3.54 The smile on Ganja's lips in the narrative's final moments gives away her unspoken intentions. *Ganja & Hess* (Blu-ray), Kino Lorber Films.

Figure 3.55 "You got to know when it's all over": Gunn's credit cues the Evangel Revivaltime choir and, in its final reprise, Waymon's theme music. *Ganja & Hess* (Blu-ray), Kino Lorber Films.

the last shot nonetheless confirms her choice to remain within the earthly realm.

Fittingly, for a film that so committedly thwarts expected convention, the end of Ganja and Hess's story is not the end of *Ganja & Hess*. In a brief nondiegetic epilogue added at the last minute, Gunn reintroduces the human voice for the sake of symbolic closure.[176] On the image track, Ganja's hauntingly enigmatic smile is suddenly and improbably replaced by a picture of innocence: a group of children, identified by Schultz as the choir from Evangel Revivaltime Church, lined up in rows before a white panel backdrop (see fig. 3.55).[177] After Gunn's superimposed credit fades out, the children sing, in consecutive alternate takes, the eighteenth-century evangelical hymn "There Is a Fountain Filled with Blood," penned by the English poet and abolitionist William Cowper:

> There is a fountain filled with blood
> Drawn from Emmanuel's veins;
> And sinners, plunged beneath that flood,
> Lose all their guilty stains.

Cowper's poignant lyrics allow Hess to "speak" one last time, in a final plea for forgiveness and redemption. Though the choir sings only the first verse, a familiarized spectator may imagine the hymn's fifth stanza sung by Hess's own "poor lisping, stammering tongue" as he "lies silent in the grave." The Waymon song that returns once again in the movie's final moments and continues long after the end credits run out might then be heard as Ganja's final riposte. She answers her beloved's plaintive refrain with pragmatism and candor, as always: "You got to learn to let it go / You got to know when it's all over."

4

JUDGMENT

The Reception and Revival of *Ganja & Hess*

> They were afraid of its becoming an artistic success.... They really think we're imbeciles. It's no joke. And if you do a piece of work that has any sort of intellectual importance or if it gets any kind of artistic recognition they think the work won't make money because black people won't understand it.
> —Bill Gunn, quoted in C. Taylor, "Bill Gunn," 102.

> [One white] critic [of *Ganja & Hess*] wondered where was the race problem. If he looks closely, he will find it in his own review.[1]
> —Bill Gunn, in Gunn, "To Be a Black Artist," 7.

JUST PRIOR TO ITS OFFICIAL PREMIERE ON APRIL 19, 1973, *Ganja & Hess* was given an unbilled sneak preview in Westport, Connecticut, an affluent, predominantly white New York City exurb. The picture had just started when Gunn overheard one of the audience members sitting behind him. "Oh no," the voice groaned, "not another nigger film."[2] The Westport preview of *Ganja & Hess* was the first of several demoralizing screenings that dogged the filmmakers during the first month of exhibition. The common thread linking these fiascos was a misjudgment of the film's target viewership, particularly with regard to racial demographics and attitudes. Westport, for instance, prided itself for its alleged cultural sophistication yet had also recently become bitterly divided over the transfer of African American children to its schools from nearby Bridgeport, a decaying industrial center transformed by "white flight."[3]

Ganja & Hess's Westport showing was a harbinger of its disappointing Manhattan reception, a reception also directed by white sensibilities. Kelly-Jordan opened the picture at a midtown art house with a mainly Caucasian clientele. The New York daily newspaper and broadcast reviewers, whose dismissive contempt effectively crippled the picture's ability to attract patrons in its original run, were also mostly white. White-controlled institutions with fewer purely commercial motivations, including that spring's Cannes Film Festival, did eventually play a part in *Ganja & Hess*'s resurrection and critical rehabilitation. Most of the heavy lifting, however, was undertaken by the individual viewers, critics, and students of African American cinema who later encountered *Ganja & Hess* via university and film society screenings, museum and repertory theater bookings, and public discourse and word of mouth. They were the first to recognize *Ganja & Hess*'s true significance, and their enthusiasm and devotion helped guarantee the movie's survival, though credit for actually executing its rescue must go chiefly to Pearl Bowser and to Gunn himself.

The reasons behind *Ganja & Hess*'s critical and financial failure in its commercial release and those behind its subsequent reappraisal and endurance are surprisingly congruent. What condemned the picture in the eyes of reviewers and even its own distributors in 1973 is what has intrigued movie lovers and scholars ever since. Indeed, the fascination that contemporary fans invest in the film largely stems from the legend of its initial rejection. Nearly every reference to *Ganja & Hess* in print after 1973 alludes to the infamous story of its premature withdrawal from circulation and its unceremonious dumping into grind house theaters, after being refashioned into a by-the-numbers blaxploitation horror flick. Although this account, especially concerning Fima Noveck's role in the supposedly savage recutting, was challenged and partially rebutted by Tim Lucas and David Walker in *Video Watchdog* three decades ago, it remains the standard narrative of the movie's troubled history.

To clear up the discrepancies in this oft told narrative, this chapter begins with a detailed record of the truncated theatrical distribution of *Ganja & Hess* and its *Blood Couple/Double Possession* offshoots. I then tackle more speculative questions of which of the film's elements contributed to its hostile early reception and why. *Ganja & Hess* blends storytelling characteristics from the European art cinema, plot conventions from the horror genre and vampire subgenre, and copious quantities of blood and nudity from the exploitation flick with an African American cast, iconography, and themes.

White film reviewers accustomed to a certain set of expectations for "quality" Black films proved unable to take seriously one that integrated a variety of modes rather than adopt the social realist model authorized by Hollywood with the "racial problem" picture. *Ganja & Hess*'s inability to find an audience in its theatrical release was primarily due to the critical (and industrial) resistance to its multimodal nature, or to the perceived extremes of the film's unconventional combinations of multiple modes of address. Through close analyses of these modes, I explain how *Ganja & Hess*'s reclamation as a motion picture classic is grounded in a newfound appreciation of those very "excesses."

Blood Sells? The Packaging and Repackaging of *Ganja & Hess*

The gala opening and exclusive first run of *Ganja & Hess*, renamed as such when the title *Blood* was claimed by *Deep Throat*'s Gerard Damiano for his own 1973 horror release, was booked for the 537-seat Playboy Theater at 110 West Fifty-Seventh Street.[4] Today, this space houses the Directors Guild of America's New York screening facility. In the seventies, it was part of Hugh Hefner's media empire, one of a small national chain of upscale movie houses that provided platforms for art films with frank subject matter, notably those backed by Hefner's own fledgling production company. The decision to open *Ganja & Hess* at the Playboy is perhaps indicative of the type of viewership that Kelly-Jordan envisioned for the picture: a "sophisticated" adult audience looking for sex and violence with a veneer of artistic pretension.

Jordan also hoped, as Bowser later recalled, that the publicity from a glitzy premiere in midtown Manhattan might help inoculate *Ganja & Hess* from an expected onslaught of negative reviews from those critics who viewed the film eight days prior.[5] The executives rented limousines and klieg lights and scheduled a champagne reception at Automation House, a brownstone on East Sixty-Eighth Street that housed an institute for innovative art and technology.[6] Chiz Schultz, who felt that *Ganja & Hess* would benefit more from a limited opening befitting an art movie, was encouraged to arrive at the Playboy by limousine but instead walked the mere four blocks from CBS headquarters, his then current workplace. In Schultz's view, Kelly and Jordan saw *Ganja & Hess* as the only one of their projects, many of which had already been suspended or were otherwise in limbo, with a chance to pay off big, and they bet on it accordingly.[7]

Partly due to the clash of wills between *Ganja & Hess*'s creative team and its executive group, opening night provoked a wide range of emotions among the principal collaborators. For Marlene Clark, the premiere was a rare moment of validation from an industry that largely restricted her to degrading secondary roles. On this night, she received full movie star treatment: "There was a splashy party afterward—and being the lead actress, I was pretty much the star of the party! Nothing like that had ever happened to me before. It was wonderful."[8] Schultz's experience was decidedly more taxing. The producer nervously observed the audience's reactions to specific scenes, particularly the moment when a naked Gunn (as Meda) dips a toothbrush into his own dirty bathwater and brushes his teeth. At that point, two viewers rose from their seats, declared it "the most disgusting thing they had ever seen," and left.[9] Kelly had already seen the director's cut at a private advance screening; the Cinerama execs in attendance walked out about a half hour into projection. Convinced the film was a "disaster," Kelly remembers being "sick with anxiety" when the final credits rolled, yet he dutifully called up to the stage Gunn, Clark, and Duane Jones. As he introduced the actors, Kelly's wife Peggy overheard a cutting remark from the balcony, where two men had spent the evening mocking the action onscreen. "Look at that asshole," one quipped, in reference to Kelly. "He thinks he's got something good."[10]

The afterglow did not last long for Clark, who was blindsided by the movie's critical response. The verdict from the reviewers at the major New York dailies was unanimous: *Ganja & Hess* was a flop. The pans from the *Post*'s Archer Winsten, who faulted Gunn for "wast[ing] a lot of time, effort and film on a picture that doesn't amount to much," and *Times* second-stringer A. H. Weiler, who decried the film's "confusingly vague mélange of symbolism, violence and sex," alone might have been sufficient to sink *Ganja & Hess* at the box office.[11] Critics of lesser influence took their swings as well, at the picture's fragmented narrative and supposedly amateur aesthetic. Ann Guarino in her one-star *Daily News* review complained about the "disjointed" story and editing, whereas *Newsday*'s Joseph Gelmis claimed to be unable to determine the film's premise without reading the production notes, a failure that he attributed to the "clumsiness [of Gunn's] story-telling techniques."[12] William Wolf's brutal summation in the arts weekly *Cue* encapsulated the middlebrows' patronizing mindset: "When you stop and think about the story, [*Ganja & Hess*] is really just an anemic time-waster."[13]

Gunn's movie got a more favorable reaction from the alternative press. Reminiscent of the advance media attention for *Stop*, several of the more positive notices for *Ganja & Hess* came from sexploitation publications. Terry Guerin, a regular contributor to *Penthouse*, praised the picture in Andy Warhol's magazine *Interview*, and award-winning dramatist Paul Carter Harrison penned an appreciation for the debut issue of Holloway House's Black-centered erotic monthly, *Players*. Unfortunately, *Players* did not hit the newsstands until nearly six months after *Ganja & Hess*'s disappearance from theaters, and Harrison's review thus functioned more as a postmortem than as a timely recommendation.[14] The same fate awaited James Monaco's evaluation. Monaco shopped his euphoric review to various New York journals: as the author related to Gunn himself, the *Times* "liked the way it was written but intimated that the politics weren't right for them," and Andrew Sarris at the *Village Voice* expressed interest but rejected it due to a lack of space. By January 1974, Monaco was resigned to sending it to the more specialized film quarterlies, "which means," he ruefully (and presciently) observed, that "it would only serve as an obituary."[15]

Monaco aside, Black writers for Black-centered periodicals were the film's most fervent supporters. James Murray, writing in the *Amsterdam News*, recognized *Ganja & Hess* as a "precedent-setting drama" and "the most important Black-produced film since" *Sweet Sweetback's Baadasssss Song*.[16] Yet, Murray's endorsement had minimal impact on tickets sold during the picture's Playboy run. Not only was Fifty-Seventh Street a prohibitive distance from New York's Black neighborhoods, as Gunn pointedly observed, but African Americans were also, according to an informal survey conducted that year, less liable to be swayed in their movie choices by the opinions in Black newspapers (which served an audience considerably older than the population's most frequent filmgoers) than by coverage in the white press or on Black-oriented radio.[17]

Gunn did not suffer his film's detractors gladly. At the probable cost of permanent damage to his relationship with the white reviewing fraternity, he used multiple media as vehicles for a counterattack. In a promotional spot on WCBS-FM (whose own movie critic, Leonard Harris, had panned *Ganja & Hess* weeks earlier) and a follow-up letter to the *Times*, Gunn exposed the critical establishment's systematic bias against Black films.[18] Critics' screenings, he revealed, are almost always "held under white auspices," and African American reviewers are often unaware of or not invited to these previews.[19] Consequently, most of those charged with reviewing

Ganja & Hess lacked the rudimentary understanding of Black experience and knowledge required to evaluate it. "There are times when the white critic must sit down and listen," Gunn admonished. "If he cannot listen and learn, then he must not concern himself with black creativity." At the very least, he continued, the white press must come to terms with its influence over the propagation of African American cinema. "Maybe if the black film craze continues, the white press might even find it necessary to employ black criticism," Gunn acidly concluded. "But if you can stop the craze in its tracks, maybe that won't be necessary."[20]

The fact that most of the mass-market dailies did not even bother to send their first-string reviewers to the critics' screening compounded this neglect, and Gunn did not hesitate to call out this affront, too.[21] Nor did he mince words about the impudence displayed by those at the preview. One critic, unidentified in Gunn's letter, apparently left the theater after watching only twenty minutes of *Ganja & Hess*, then reviewed it anyway. "Three years of three different people's lives," Gunn marveled, "graded in one afternoon by a complete stranger to the artist and to the culture." The director reproached Weiler for misstating plot details, intimating that the *Times* representative might have avoided such errors had he listened to the film "over the sounds of [his] own voice."[22] But Gunn saved his most caustic disdain for the reviewers' "appreciation" of Clark, whom the male critics appraised solely on the basis of her sexual desirability. "Dressed or nude," Weiler writes, "Miss Clark is an arresting presence."[23] Winsten is even cruder: in his estimation, Clark compensated for Jones's "dull, confusing" performance by virtue of being a "brownskin looker."[24] "That kind of disrespect," Gunn remarked, "could not have been cultivated in 110 minutes. It must have taken at least a good 250 years."[25]

Gunn's irritation was further piqued by white critics' silence regarding the most impressive honor bestowed on *Ganja & Hess*, which was announced just prior to its Playboy premiere: its selection by the Association of French Film Critics, from a field of hundreds of entrants, as the sole American picture to be screened during International Critics Week at the Cannes Film Festival.[26] Though this distinction was prominently featured in newspaper advertisements during the film's commercial engagement, Kelly-Jordan declined to provide support, financial or otherwise, for its Cannes exhibition.[27] Knowing that the showing might be canceled unless a member of the production team was present, Gunn sold his tennis court to pay for a solo trip to the festival, where he presented his movie on May 19.[28]

For Gunn, Critics Week was like a coronation. Years later he relished telling the story of encountering a massive crowd outside a screening facility on La Croisette; he assumed they were waiting to see Ingmar Bergman's *Cries and Whispers* (1972), also screening out of competition. A woman told him, "It's for *your* film. Moscowitz [*sic*] reviewed it yesterday."[29] "Moscowitz" was Gene Moskowitz, *Variety*'s movie critic in Paris, and his assessment of Gunn's film "as an original work outside of any conventional category, genre or stereotype" stoked the curiosity of intellectuals alienated by the commercialism of the festival's spotlighted entries.[30] Numerous secondhand accounts affirm that the audience response to *Ganja & Hess*, which was projected several times that week, was nothing short of ecstatic. Monaco reports that, at one screening, "an audience of notoriously cynical film students jumped to their feet applauding even though the film still had half an hour to run." Louis Marcolles, head of the Association of French Film Critics, declared *Ganja & Hess* "the most popular film in the Critic's [*sic*] Week."[31] Feted for days by the French press and paparazzi as well as by those fellow filmmakers able to overcome their envy, Gunn excitedly relayed his adventures back to Sam Waymon in telephone calls that inevitably began, "You won't *believe* this . . ."[32]

Cannes '73 was to have been a coming-out party of sorts for Black American cinema, a testament to its artistic maturation. *Ganja & Hess* was not, however, supposed to be the festival entry heralding this arrival. Columbia's *Wattstax*, a documentary of an all-star concert to benefit the Los Angeles community of Watts, and, especially, Warner Bros.' *Lady Sings the Blues* were the showcase "Black movies" at that year's Cannes. Each was financed by one of the top Black-owned record labels in America, Stax and Motown, respectively, which served to focus attention on these films in tandem.[33] Warner Bros. invited *Amsterdam News* publisher Clarence B. Jones to the studio's fiftieth anniversary celebration at Cannes; reportedly, this was the first time an African American newspaper was represented among the media guests at the festival. In exchange, the *Amsterdam News* ran a piece that praised Hollywood's efforts to promote Black-themed films in overseas markets.[34]

To Gunn and Waymon's delight, *Ganja & Hess* stole some of the thunder implicitly promised to its studio competitors. "The biggest thrill we had," Waymon remembers, "was the fact that the majors couldn't touch us; they had no clue as to what this was all about. They did know we were independent, and how dare we slap them in the face like that, not needing them and upstaging their junkets at Cannes." According to rumor, one of the parties most aggrieved by *Ganja & Hess*'s press attention was *Lady Sings the Blues* star Diana Ross. Ross and her Motown team expected to be showered with praise after *Lady Sings the Blues*'s closing night screening, but the French press was underwhelmed. To add insult to injury, festival attendee Josephine Baker, a contemporary of Billie Holiday, snubbed Ross and attached herself to Gunn.[35] Baker was so blown away by *Ganja & Hess* that she made an impromptu, twenty-five-minute speech to the assembled media, extolling the film and defending it from the attacks of American critics. Baker's fulsome praise capped off one of the most gratifying weeks of Gunn's career. His brainchild had become not just the first independent feature directed by an African American to be screened at Cannes; it had been one of the most enthusiastically received pictures of the festival's sixteen days. Gunn departed France with an international reputation and seemingly limitless potential. And then, as he later told Clyde Taylor, "I came back and it was as though it had never happened."[36]

Just as Gunn was gathering accolades across the Atlantic, *Ganja & Hess* reached the end of its theatrical life, yanked from its Playboy engagement after only two weeks. The reasoning behind this drastic measure is, even now, not entirely understandable. Evidently operating under the assumption that the movie possessed relatively broad-based commercial appeal, Kelly-Jordan pulled *Ganja & Hess* when it failed to accrue substantial revenue in its first two weeks, rather than risk further losses. And yet, considering its decision to initially book the film in a solitary Manhattan art theater rather than in dozens of big-city houses, Kelly and Jordan treated *Ganja & Hess* in some respects as if it was indeed an art film. Given their adherence to certain tenets of art cinema distribution, it is curious that they gave up on the picture after only two weeks, hardly enough time to allow a word-of-mouth campaign to build. The actual attendance figures for *Ganja & Hess*'s run at the Playboy are also, unsurprisingly, a matter of dispute. Waymon remembers the theater being "packed" during those two weeks, whereas Kelly swears that, "after a few days, hardly anyone came to see it."[37] *Variety*'s weekly box office reports suggest a relatively lukewarm reception: a "disappointing" $5,000 in the first week, and a roughly equivalent total in the second week.[38] All things considered, the trade paper's evaluation of the film's opening weeks—"No fires being set here"—is probably fairly accurate.[39]

For a specialized picture with a "small" opening, *Ganja & Hess*'s performance was hardly catastrophic. But the *reviews* were, and, in Kelly's view, that sabotaged any chance of cultivating a buzz around the picture and, thus, enticing the art house crowd to turn out. Kelly-Jordan found itself in a tough situation: it had sunk most of its money into one film and pinned its hopes on it becoming a hit, which would, in turn, generate the income necessary to keep the company's other projects afloat. At a premiere meeting, attended by Bowser at Jordan's invitation, Kelly-Jordan staff brainstormed about "audience development" and lining up "possible nontheatrical outlets" for *Ganja & Hess*.[40] However, the need for a quick payout apparently overruled the adoption of a more bottom-up strategy for nurturing an audience, even though such an approach paid dividends that year for other non-action-oriented Black films. *Five on the Black Hand Side*, for example, steadily built anticipation through special screenings for politicians, educators, and religious groups prior to its national rollout.[41] Kelly-Jordan, however, had its sights set almost solely on commercial venues.

In the end, the receipts from *Ganja & Hess*'s New York run were so meager that, as Kelly claims, "no theater would take it anywhere." A follow-up commitment at the Playboy Theater in Chicago and "a big post-screening event at Hefner's Playboy Club" were canceled. Advised by Saladin Nader that *Ganja & Hess* had "to become a standard horror film" to receive further bookings, Kelly summoned Gunn and Waymon to his Madison Avenue office and told them that the movie had to be recut "because we're losing our shirts." Gunn retorted that no one would alter a single frame and stormed out. To underscore the point, he returned almost immediately to the sixteenth-floor suite, wiped Kelly's desk clean, overturned tables, and threw a water cooler against the office wall.[42] Predictably, the gesture did not win over Kelly, who within weeks sold the property to Heritage Enterprises. Though the reediting of *Ganja & Hess* may have been initiated by Kelly-Jordan to attract prospective buyers, the job was finished under the sponsorship of Heritage president Skip Steloff, an exploitation producer notorious for publicizing the death of a stuntman by shark attack for a film Steloff promptly retitled *Shark!* (1969), which director Samuel Fuller subsequently disowned.[43] Steloff mocked *Ganja & Hess*'s Cannes enthusiasts as "French insiders, effete auteurists, and film cultists" and promised that Heritage would deliver what Kelly-Jordan had supposedly paid for: a "hard, tough, blood and guts, smashing knockout of a horror film."[44]

Judging from this ludicrously hyperbolic pledge, it seems likely that Steloff and Heritage had no idea of what they had to work with. The only way *Ganja & Hess* would be converted into a "hard, tough, blood and guts horror film" was through extensive reshooting, if not a complete remaking. Yet, Steloff believed that such a transformation could be effected through recutting alone. After Victor Kanefsky declined its invitation, Heritage brought aboard Russian-born editor Fima Noveck.[45] Noveck had by this point, in David Walker's phrasing, "established himself as a one-man postproduction house," a film "doctor" called in by independent distributors to salvage allegedly unreleasable acquisitions. Curiously, in view of Steloff's stated intentions for *Ganja & Hess*, Noveck's métier was not exploitation but European imports, like Lina Wertmüller's *Love & Anarchy* (1973), which he "tailor[ed] . . . to suit the American palate."[46]

As the first scholars to closely examine the Heritage reedit, Walker and Tim Lucas scrupulously catalogued the surprisingly varied additions and subtractions undertaken during the movie's second postproduction. Though some of Waymon's score is (perhaps unintentionally) retained in *Blood Couple*, it is largely replaced by what Lucas and Walker aptly classify as "moody, cheap-sounding synthesizer noodlings," supplied by an uncredited composer, and by music in the public domain.[47] "March Blues," for instance, is supplanted by synthesizer music during Meda's suicide and by "Jesu, Joy of Man's Desiring" when Ganja first joins her host in the latter's living room.

To clarify the film's plot, which he found "esoteric for the sake of being esoteric," Noveck chopped almost fifty minutes of footage from the original cut.[48] He worked to make the expository scenes less ambiguous by postponing Gunn's opening intertitle and by eliminating shots of Meda aiming his gun at a mirror. The major story thread, arising from the mystery of the Myrthian dagger and the vampirization of the two leads, is privileged in Noveck's restructuring, whereas passages with only a tangential bearing on that thread, including Hess's walk with his son and Ganja's snowball fight monologue, were removed. Yet, Noveck also drew liberally from Gunn's outtakes in his reconstruction, unwittingly saving from obscurity six nearly intact, self-contained scenes. These added elements provide further narrative clarification, though it is also possible that Noveck rescued these scenes from the cutting room floor mainly because *Blood Couple*, which clocks in at just under eighty minutes, required additional padding to attain feature length.

Perhaps the most striking aspect of the recutting of *Ganja & Hess*, as David Kalat has deftly elucidated, is the degree to which Noveck used Gunn's approved screenplay as a blueprint. "Where Heritage's cut differs from"

Ganja & Hess, Kalat observes, "it tends to mirror the script."[49] In other words, the relatively more coherent structure of *Blood Couple* originates with Gunn himself, whose screenplay more conventionally emphasizes linearity, motivation, and unity than the film he made from it. Gunn did not shoot every scene in the script, but several of the scenes that were shot and discarded from his original cut were reinstated by Noveck, especially those scenes that serve to clarify causal relations and character psychology.

Despite Gunn's obviously significant contribution to its final form, however, *Blood Couple* has traditionally been described in the scholarly literature as a bastardization of Gunn's creation. Lucas and Walker attribute this to the fact that some of the initial writing on *Ganja & Hess* was mistakenly "based on information found only in *Blood Couple*," and, in their zeal to defend Gunn's vision against its desecration, later scholars sometimes exaggerated the extent of the changes imposed by Heritage.[50] Monaco inaccurately reported that Noveck even shot a few entirely new scenes.[51] Critics operating under this false impression no doubt felt confident in proclaiming that *Blood Couple* bore "little" to "no resemblance" to Gunn's original cut, even if they had only seen the latter.[52]

The makers of *Ganja & Hess* naturally regarded even the slightest modification of their efforts as an unforgivable violation of its artistic integrity. Waymon, Schultz, and Gunn walked out of a private screening of Noveck's cut in September 1973, then immediately hired a Manhattan attorney to pressure Kelly-Jordan and Heritage to delete their names from the credits.[53] *Blood Couple*'s script is, therefore, billed to the nonexistent "Hamm Parker" and "Al Condrey," and the actors playing George Meda and Luther Williams go unidentified. Noveck is listed as director, under his birth name, F. H. Novikov. (Director of photography James Hinton and production designer Tom John, whose contributions to *Ganja & Hess* were largely unaffected by the reediting, retained their credits.) Kanefsky also demanded the removal of his credit following the *Blood Couple* preview. Quietly seething over the obliteration of his meticulous craftsmanship, Kanefsky nonetheless stuck it out to the very end of the screening then bolted for the exit; he was followed by Noveck. The two men had known each other, professionally, for a long time; now, the senior editor was brashly seeking validation from the man he replaced. Noveck trailed him all the way to the train until Kanefsky finally "let him have it," excoriating the revised work and warning its overseer that "their professional paths should never cross again." Kanefsky never forgave Noveck for the "butchering" of his signature accomplishment.[54] Noveck, in contrast, simply moved on to his next job. Until Walker contacted him in 1990, he had completely forgotten about *Blood Couple*.⁵⁵ Upon prompting, however, Noveck recalled doing what he could to preserve "the flavor of [Gunn's] storytelling" and claimed, rather improbably, that Gunn himself had complimented his attempts.⁵⁶

Though Heritage had acquired the rights to *Ganja & Hess*, the responsibility for handling its reconstitution remained with its original backer. Following Jordan's departure in the spring of 1974, Kelly returned to the Noveck cut to make one final push for relevance in independent film distribution. His vampire picture now reduced in length to "more exploitable, double-bill proportions," Kelly circulated it on the domestic grind house and drive-in circuits.⁵⁷ But, even in this "more exploitable" version, which debuted in March in select markets, *Blood Couple* performed poorly. In its first-week engagement in downtown Louisville, *Blood Couple* grossed only $3,500, less than reissues of *Coffy* and *The Mack* had pulled in locally over the previous week. A personal appearance by costar Mabel King on opening day did little to boost attendance.⁵⁸

Somehow, even this financial setback did not spell the end of the property's distribution life. Shortly after Noveck applied the finishing touches to *Blood Couple*, the industry was rocked by the seismic success of another religious-themed, viscerally gory horror picture: *The Exorcist*, directed for Warner Bros. by William Friedkin and photographed by Gunn's cinematographer on *Stop*, Owen Roizman. *The Exorcist* spawned innumerable low-budget rip-offs in both the United States and abroad, many of them rushed into production in the early months of 1974. Some were so close in story line to the original *Exorcist* that they practically qualified as unsanctioned remakes; Warner Bros. successfully brought legal action against a handful of these, including *Beyond the Door* (1974) and American International Pictures's Black-cast *Abby* (1974). Some independents sought to cash in on *Exorcist*-mania through cheaper tactics. As Lucas writes in his authoritative study of exploitation maestro Mario Bava, "a number of unscrupulous, low-end film distributors seized the opportunity to repackage some older, unprofitable imports with new monikers" that called to mind the Friedkin hit, including Bava's *Lisa and the Devil* (1974), which was padded with new footage and repackaged by its producers as *House of Exorcism*.⁵⁹

In light of the staggering popularity of *The Exorcist* with African American viewers, Kelly tested "a new exorcism-pitched" campaign in the spring of 1974, though another year would pass before it was executed.⁶⁰

Figure 4.1 Kelly-Jordan takes another stab at the exploitation market with the trailer for *Double Possession*, the second title for the Heritage Enterprises recut of *Ganja & Hess*. Courtesy of James E. Hinton Collection, Harvard Film Archive, Harvard College Library.

When *Blood Couple* resurfaced in 1975 for downtown showings in Washington, DC, Chicago, and Atlanta, no further alterations had been made to the picture itself, but the title had been changed to *Double Possession*. The extant trailer for *Double Possession*, likely the only one created for the movie in any of its forms until 2018, conveys how the distributors endeavored, with debatable results, to manufacture the illusion of content related to demonic possession (see fig. 4.1). Over a montage of violent and ominous images culled from the Heritage cut, a portentous voice reads aloud the introductory intertitles from the source text; the film's title then appears in superimposition, accompanied by a thunderclap sound effect. A series of spoken non-sequiturs ensues, matched with recurring shots of Hess drawing his dagger on Ganja in the garden: "What happens when the devil wants to possess a woman's soul? What happens when one soul is not enough? . . . The devil took a woman's soul, and then the woman took a man. A horrifying story of a man and woman possessed by the devil!"[61]

The trailer provides no actual evidence of an exorcism plotline; that connection was instead forged through print publicity. According to a synopsis reproduced in the *Amsterdam News*, the protagonist of *Double Possession* is "exorcised of his demons in one of the most forceful sequences ever filmed inside a Black church."[62] Noveck had, in fact, substantially trimmed the scene of the church service, but he fortuitously left intact Luther's baptizing of Hess. This baptism was passed off as an exorcism in the film's promotion; the one-sheet used for the *Double Possession* advertising campaign features a small photographic portrait of the minister, identified as "The Exorcist" (see fig. 4.2).[63]

Unfortunately, for Kelly, the American filmgoer's appetite for all things exorcism-related had abated by this point, and theatrical bookings for *Double Possession* slowed to a trickle. In the eighties, the Noveck version returned with a vengeance, this time using home video as a distribution vehicle. Debuting, in 1985, under the Video Gems label, the Heritage recut was circulated on VHS under a variety of Afrocentric titles (and sometimes accompanied by explicitly racist cover art), including *Black Vampire, Black Evil, Black Out: The Moment of Terror*, and the "original," *Blood Couple*.[64] The latter title is the one used for the recent Gemstone Entertainment DVD release, on which it is arbitrarily packaged with *White Zombie* (1932) and *How Awful about Allan* (1970).

The Multimodal Text: *Ganja & Hess* . . .

Despite the various amputations inflicted on Gunn's movie after it was taken from him, it is possible (thanks to home video) to view the "same" text today as one might theoretically have seen in 1973. What has changed are the cultural and aesthetic contexts in which that text is received. Although *Ganja & Hess*'s critical reevaluation in America was initiated only months after its ignominious withdrawal, its reevaluation as a major work of cinematic art began in earnest in the late eighties and early nineties. This period coincides with a surge of interest within academia and critical communities in the practice that Jeffrey Sconce terms "paracinema," which he defines as "a particular reading protocol, a counter-aesthetic turned subcultural sensibility devoted to all manner of cultural detritus." Although the growing appreciation of *Ganja & Hess* as a landmark independent African American film might have taken place even without this particular "realignment on the social terrain of taste," it is difficult to imagine its

Figure 4.2 Devil in the details: exorcising the artistry from *Ganja & Hess* in *Double Possession*'s print campaign. Courtesy Black Film Center/Archive, Indiana University, Bloomington, Indiana.

revival generating the same degree of enthusiasm without the endorsement of paracinematic entities.[65] The attention of *Video Watchdog*, which published three major essays on the film and was tangentially involved in the DVD release through the participation of Kalat, a frequent contributor, has been especially significant.

In the remainder of this chapter, I argue that *Ganja & Hess*'s multimodal status helps explain both the picture's initial rejection *and* its eventual acceptance during a period of transformation for taste cultures. My conceptualization of the multimodal text is akin to Kevin Heffernan's definition of the "hybrid film" text in his study of the American reaction to *I Am Curious (Yellow)* (1967), a Swedish import that mixed "elements of the art film, the exploitation film, and the general release motion picture."[66] *I Am Curious*'s amalgamation of these aspects, along with hints of softcore pornography, proved to be amazingly lucrative from a financial standpoint. *Ganja & Hess* similarly fused a variety of modes and genre appeals that, in certain combinations (e.g., blaxploitation, sexploitation, art house horror, Black-themed horror), performed splendidly at the box office. Some of its juxtapositions, on the other hand, proved to be indigestible even for critics of the time, let alone audiences.

Ganja & Hess's twisting of convention *within* any single one of the categories or modes that Gunn mobilized was likewise faulted by reviewers, typically on the grounds of extremity or excess. Sconce identifies "excess" as an essential feature of the paracinema fanatic's enjoyment of the paracinematic text.[67] In the context of its original release, however, the excessive qualities of *Ganja & Hess* merely confounded those who had grown accustomed to movies deviating from Hollywood practice only in conventionalized ways. The most common (albeit implicit) refrain voiced in the initial reviews for *Ganja & Hess* was that the movie was too much: too *bloody*, too *sexual*, too *arty*, and too *Black*. It would take years for each of these alleged vices to be reclaimed in bourgeois cultural discourse as virtues.

As "Horror Show"

In his review of *Ganja & Hess*'s Blu-ray edition, horror scholar Kim Newman proclaims the film to be "at once an important work of African-American cinema *and* a major vampire movie" and notes that it has "suffered" because of this dual classification.[68] Gunn himself was conflicted by this apparent incompatibility. He was adamant that his objective had always been "to make a film about cultural displacement—*not* vampirism" and that making a vampire picture was "the last thing I want[ed] to do."[69] Though he had been enthralled by monster movies in his youth, Gunn lost interest once he realized they were about sexual repression; from that point on, he claimed, "I couldn't care less." To sustain his interest while writing *Ganja & Hess*, Gunn conceived of his protagonist as "trapped in a vampire movie. . . . trying to find his way out." That is what the story is "really all about," he remarked, in 1975, "It's [about] a much more interesting character who is trapped into a trivial situation."[70]

Ganja & Hess's early advocates adopted Gunn's disparaging attitude toward the horror genre to promote his film as an individual accomplishment that simply borrowed the vampire tale framework as a springboard for a wholly distinct exploration of more serious themes.[71] Even Kalat, a longtime champion of paracinematic texts, has defended *Ganja & Hess* by denigrating the supposedly exploitive horror flicks that it superficially resembles. *Blacula* "is a straight-forward genre piece," Kalat contends, but "*Ganja & Hess* is as singular and unique a movie as you will ever see." Though it employs the vampire picture's familiar narrative structure, that structure "*merely* provides a medium to convey the allegory about drug abuse and addiction."[72]

Gunn performed his variation on the genre at a time when the industrial mainstreaming and critical reconsideration of the American horror film had yet to be fully implemented. It took the record-shattering performance of *The Exorcist* to persuade major studios to invest in a series of high-profile horror projects, many of them remakes of established classics or adaptations of best-selling novels, including Universal's *Jaws* (1975) and *Dracula* (1979), United Artists' *Carrie* (1976) and *Invasion of the Body Snatchers* (1978), Twentieth Century-Fox's *The Omen* (1976), *Alien* (1979), and *Nosferatu the Vampyre* (1979), and Warner Bros.' *The Shining* (1980). None of these pictures received unanimously positive reviews, yet all were treated by mass media critics with a degree of respect that was mostly absent from their evaluations of low-budget independent horror. The latter type of movie, whether gritty and graphic like *The Last House on the Left* (1972) or florid and flamboyant like Terence Fisher's entries in Hammer's *Dracula* and *Frankenstein* series, was regularly categorized as "exploitation" and summarily dismissed. Critical manifestos that lauded no-frills exploitation horror, most notably Robin Wood's groundbreaking essays, and "trash" cinema aesthetics would eventually determine the direction of horror scholarship and connoisseurship. Yet, this wave arrived too late to influence *Ganja & Hess*'s initial critical reaction.

To understand the critical prejudice that greeted *Ganja & Hess*, it is instructive to compare its reception to that conferred on *Night of the Living Dead*, one of the few exploitation horror films of the time to garner moderate critical appreciation upon release.[73] Both the Gunn and Romero pictures would ultimately be acclaimed for their use of allegory, but the allegorical dimension in *Night of the Living Dead* was easier for progressive critics to recognize early on. *Night of the Living Dead*'s apocalyptic tenor resonated especially forcefully for those interested in reading Vietnam War–era popular texts for signs of pervasive and "universal" fragmentation and social dissolution.

The most concrete point of overlap, of course, between the films is the casting of Duane Jones. Quite possibly, Gunn deliberately exploited Jones's presence in order to play on the expectations of the horror-savvy viewer. The script's depiction of a mortified Hess reacting with revulsion as his first victims revive seems to directly allude to the sequence in *Night of the Living Dead* in which Jones's character, Ben, watches in disbelief as the corpses of Helen and Harry Cooper reanimate. Ben quickly composes himself and shoots them both, in accordance with his macho objective of eradicating as many of the marauding ghouls as necessary. In contrast, Hess, himself already one of the "infected," runs away in panic from a mess of his own making. Gunn's appreciation of the intertextual associations attached to Jones suggests that the filmmaker was more attuned to the genre's potential enchantments than he willingly acknowledged. Actually, Gunn engaged with horror conventions and premises across his career. *Stop*, like *Ganja & Hess*, draws on elements of the Gothic or haunted house subgenre, and additional classic horror elements are explored in two of Gunn's unpublished eighties projects: the Egyptology-centered thriller novel *Egyptian Murals* and the "Grand Guignol"–style, voodoo-themed play *Family Employment*.[74]

Gunn's sly tweak of vampire tropes in the scene of Hess's blood bank robbery also evinces an awareness of contemporary developments in the subgenre. *Ganja & Hess* was one of several early seventies pictures to probe an anachronistic vampire protagonist's efforts to adapt to the modern urban world, along with American International Pictures's *Count Yorga, Vampire* (1970) and *Old Dracula* (1974) and Hammer's *Dracula A.D. 1972* (1972).[75] Newman situates *Ganja & Hess* within even more specific trends, such as the tendency to spotlight "civilised vampires procuring their nourishment under cover of medical institutions," and credits Gunn with innovating the exceedingly ugly, deglamorized depiction of the vampire's addiction later seen in Paul Morrissey's *Blood for Dracula* (1974) and Romero's *Martin* (1978).[76] Many noteworthy postseventies vampire films, from Tony Scott's *The Hunger* (1983) to Guillermo del Toro's *Cronos* (1993) to Park Chan-wook's *Thirst* (2009), also owe something to Gunn's grim vision of the vampire-addict's day-to-day existence.[77]

Additionally, Gunn was possibly affected by the ongoing breaching of the lines that traditionally separated genre cinema and art cinema—as well as national and global cinemas, and "'auteur' and 'trash' cinemas"—across the Atlantic.[78] Present-day scholars have argued that both postwar European art cinema and postwar European horror are unstable, hybrid forms that "favor loosely structured plots and intense psychological subjectivity, . . . push the envelope of what was then considered acceptable with regard to the onscreen depiction of sex and violence," and "share a tendency toward bold experimentation with design, color, lighting, camerawork, editing, and sound."[79] Ian Olney and Adam Lowenstein posit that horror and art film practices developed in response to the same cultural stimuli: World War II, the Holocaust, and related large-scale historical traumas.[80] Indeed, *Ganja & Hess* could have served as a case study in Lowenstein's *Shocking Representation*. As with that book's primary examples, like Georges Franju's *Eyes without a Face* (1960), Gunn's synthesis of modernism and realism holds the unique ability "of making trauma matter to those beyond its immediate point of impact."[81] The particular historical trauma interrogated by *Ganja & Hess* goes back much further than World War II, however. Along with William Crain, Gunn was one of the first American filmmakers to fully grasp the vampire myth's relevance within Afrocentric contexts of colonialism and enslavement. He was thus among the first, as Harry Benshoff affirms, to metaphorically equate vampirism with slavery's enduring legacy.[82]

In related ways, *Blacula* and *Ganja & Hess* demonstrate that a Black "version" of a mainstream film genre is not merely an act of "poaching," to borrow Robin R. Means Coleman's term.[83] One could make a case that the seemingly uncomplicated act of changing a genre's racial context, of "Blackening" a familiar genre trope or formula, *necessarily* produces a degree of ideological (self-) critique. Citing *Blacula* for support, George Lipsitz has shown that the racial specificity of Black-themed genre pictures, particularly those produced during periods of intensified social anxiety, transforms the relevant genre's conventions and challenges its inherent conservatism. In *Blacula*'s precredits prologue, set in 1780, the African prince Mamuwalde and his bride Luva visit Dracula's castle to negotiate a cessation of the European slave trade. There, the bigoted count attacks and entombs the prince, whom he curses with an eternal, unslakable thirst for blood. Lipsitz infers from this scene that "connecting the count's power to white supremacist beliefs makes the victimization of the prince and princess all the more terrifying. . . . Accustomed to thinking of Dracula as European, watching this film makes us think of him as white."[84] Unlike Mamuwalde, Hess Green is no avenger-hero. Yet, in Benshoff's valuation, *Ganja & Hess* participates as does *Blacula* in the exploding of "generic parameters by blurring the oppositions between normality and monsters."[85]

That said, of the two, only the former resists the impulse toward "demonization" inherited from "both the horror film and the culture at large."[86] For Benshoff, *Ganja & Hess* effectively challenges the casual employment of misogynistic and homophobic attitudes in seventies African American horror. Even in "progressive" texts such as *Blacula*, gender and sexual difference often displace the central monster as the narrative's true source of threat. Gunn's movie refuses to accede to this convention, mechanically imported to the blaxploitation-horror cycle from the broader genre and fortified by the presence of "expert" characters. There are no "brave vampire hunters" to be found in *Ganja & Hess*, no secondary figure who steps forward to "issue nationalist, masculinist, and heterosexist punishments on the unruly bodies" of their bloodsucking adversaries.[87] Rather than mobilize familiarly gendered relations among monsters, victims, and experts to preserve a hypermasculine social order, Gunn seizes on those horror icons and customs that, in a different racialized context, promote a reexamination of the value of adhering to such restraints.

The vampire picture's very particular conceptualization of *blood* supplied Gunn with his prime metaphor. Blood often figures thematically in African American fiction to suggest continuity across generations of Black people, a continuity rooted in but not limited to biology. A representative example of just such a treatment can be found in August Wilson's conception of "blood memory," which functions in his plays, according to Harry Justin Elam, "as a metaphor for [Wilson's] central idea of reimagining history and for appreciating how the African and African American past is implicated in the present."[88] *Ganja & Hess* uses blood for similarly allegorical purposes, but we might more profitably consider this use in conjunction with the term "blood politics" and the meaning of *mixture*. For John Edgar Browning, the notion of blood politics relates to who among the probable targets in a classic vampire narrative is permitted "the *privilege* of being 'turned'" rather than elided and discarded, and this privilege is often determined by "markers of race, class, and sex."[89] As the vampire's victimizing of social and economic Others became more commonplace in sixties and seventies horror cinema, the threat posed by the mixing of blood became more urgent.

Within the culture in which *Ganja & Hess*'s characters dwell, blood mixing in any form is understood as contamination. Hess initially refuses to recognize contamination as a danger. In the screenplay, he answers Meda's query about the morality of consuming blood with the observation, "I suppose it would be less of a sacrilege to drink blood than to spill it."[90] The punishment Hess suffers upon his "turning" thus represents a cruel and cosmic retribution: he is forced to both spill and drink the blood of others, infecting even the woman he loves. At the risk of exhausting the metaphor, perhaps it can be said that Gunn himself suffered for his embrace of contamination and impurity as *formal* principles, as substantiated by *Ganja & Hess*'s financial and critical failure.

Current-day scholars, however, have proven far more receptive to "contaminated" and "impure" forms than the discursive communities that first encountered *Ganja & Hess*. Recent essays by Dale Hudson and Harrison Sherrod emphasize the film's horror status because its foregrounding of the vampire mythos, which "emerges from colonial exchanges" between Eastern and Western Europeans in the nineteenth century, is just as crucial to its hybrid and impure essence as Gunn's blending of modes and styles.[91] *Ganja & Hess* is a quintessential "transnational" horror text in Hudson's view because the contamination embodied by the vampire of color is linked to both the figurative "unending co-contamination" of multiculturalism and the "generic impurity" of the hybrid text.[92] Sherrod highlights several of Gunn's formal techniques because they provide fitting visual correlatives for the vampire tale's objectification of its protagonist, which corresponds to the historical objectification and demonization of Black bodies. Noting that "the practice of collecting is at the forefront" of the film, Sherrod regards the seemingly arbitrary cutaways to Hess's decorative curios as uncanny reminders of their owner's apparent deficit of humanity, their purpose to elicit a "contrast between person and thing."[93]

Hess's transformation into a monster therefore renders him doubly victimized because he is doubly objectified, as Sherrod argues. Whether as

Black man or as vampire, he is merely a thing in the eyes of modern Western society, lacking the agency attributed to "normal" people. By virtue of being a horror film in which whiteness is the norm under constant threat, *Ganja & Hess* enabled Gunn to address the objectification and dehumanization of Black people without actually dramatizing interracial conflict.

As "Sexplicity Pic"

Sherrod's analysis exemplifies the newfound respect for *Ganja & Hess*'s achievement in the context of its genre roots rather than in spite of them. The movie's rehabilitation as a "sexplicity pic," to use *Variety*'s demeaning designation, has been slower to come.[94] The "sex film" label was often applied by the industry trades in the early CARA era to discredit independent productions. As noted in Christine Milliken's study of the press attacks on *The Killing of Sister George* (1968), the industry's demonization of flagrant or "perverse" sexual content was enthusiastically carried out by the conservative critical establishment.[95] Although *Ganja & Hess* received an "R" rating rather than the dreaded "X," its undeniable sexual explicitness functioned to Kelly-Jordan's detriment.

Gunn clearly put a lot of thought into the staging and editing of *Ganja & Hess*'s most graphic sexual encounters, and this careful reflection yielded many memorable details, including the body glitter and what Waymon evocatively describes as the "erotic exchange" of Marlene Clark placing a ring on Richard Harris's toe.[96] Almost none of *Ganja & Hess*'s early reviewers, however, were inclined to assess such frankness as a legitimate aesthetic strategy. For these critics, every flash of nudity and every suggestion of coupling marked the picture as "dirty." To bolster their case, many reviewers greatly exaggerated the volume of sex and nudity in the movie. Robe in *Variety* sneeringly demoted *Ganja & Hess* to the status of "a sex film" and bemoaned that "what might have been a 'different' version of the vampire story winds up as, basically, a horror film in which most of the principals spend more time out of their clothing than in them."[97] Winsten and Weiler, their lust for Clark momentarily harnessed, rebuked *Ganja & Hess* for "hover[ing] on the verge of pornography" and ineptly applying a patina of artistic pretension "to conceal [its] accent on blood and nudity."[98] Alone among the 1973 pundits, Harrison in *Players* defended the sex in Gunn's film as "beatific" and favorably compared its representation to the "insipid titillation" and "masturbatory indulgences" in a trio of then current European pictures—*A Clockwork Orange* (1971), *Last Tango in Paris* (1972), and *Cries and Whispers*—all of which won acclaim for their supposed advancements in honestly portraying sex on-screen.[99]

Gunn's attackers were perhaps fatigued by a then recent cycle of highly sexualized *Dracula* knockoffs, later classified by Newman as "vampire porno."[100] This trend, which dominated the subgenre in the early seventies, produced some of the period's more distinctive vampire pictures, including *The Velvet Vampire* (1971) and the Belgian import *Daughters of Darkness* (1971), the latter of which was recut by Fima Noveck for US release. Yet, American reviewers for mass-market publications rarely excused overt manifestations of sexuality in genre films. Studio productions were given more leeway, of course. But, for an independent horror film to be taken seriously rather than dismissed as exploitive, the sex had to be rendered as covertly as the violence (or, perhaps, as Harrison implies, to be de rigueur for art cinema, the sex had to be rendered *as* violence). On-screen nudity and fornication, like on-screen gore, were almost always regarded by mainstream critics as gratuitous and, thus, irredeemable.

As with exploitation horror, it would take several years before the "dirty movies" of the sixties and seventies would become acceptable objects of study. Contemporary historians have now begun a comprehensive inquiry into the industrial, aesthetic, and social changes of the immediate postcode era that inspired such texts. Technically speaking, *Ganja & Hess* is not a sexploitation film. It was not specifically marketed as an "adults only" attraction solely of interest to prurient tastes, like the work of softcore auteurs Russ Meyer, Radley Metzger, and Doris Wishman, nor does its plot function merely "to present the maximum nudity and sexual content" allowed, as stipulated by Elena Gorfinkel's definition.[101] Still, *Ganja & Hess*'s sexual dynamics are indisputably integral to the whole. Specifically, the picture's focus on nonnormative sexuality brings it in line with the "'queering' veins of resistance, opposition, and challenge" that Hudson identifies as fundamental to so many postcolonial vampire movies.[102]

Ganja & Hess's queer dimensions further help explain both the film's initial critical dismissal and its academic reclamation. Superficially, the plot deals solely with heterosexual forms of desire. Yet, because of Hess's identity at the outset as a guarded intellectual, unmarried, and seemingly without aspirations of heterosexual romance, the question of his sexual orientation is a relatively open one. As a wealthy, potentially queer African American man who is also a vampire, Hess is multiply "closeted." As illustrated by

Figure 4.3 Hess, slumming in Ossining, cruising Chicken Charlie's. *Ganja & Hess* (Blu-ray), Kino Lorber Films.

his awkwardness at Chicken Charlie's, he struggles to convincingly pass as "authentically" Black in lower- and working-class Black milieus, nor does he quite come off as "authentically" straight in his interaction with Rose (see fig. 4.3). Hess implicitly seems drawn to the possibility of intimacy with other men, and the desire he appears to harbor for many of the secondary male characters (Meda, Luther, and Richard) is but another explosive secret that he must conceal from the outside world, if not from himself. Vampirism is not just a metaphor for whiteness in this equation; it is also a metaphor for homosexuality, which the era's "racialist discourse . . . 'theorized' as a 'white disease' that had 'infected' the black community.'"[103]

Although Gunn's screenplay insists that Hess's attraction to Ganja is deep and instantaneous, it also leaves open the possibility that Hess becomes involved with Meda's widow because he views her as a proxy for her deceased husband. Hess had, after all, been violently penetrated by Meda with a phallic dagger at the climax of a whirlwind, one-night "tryst," following an extended tussle between the half-naked duo. Hess's "possession" by Meda on his own bed is then reciprocated when he drinks deeply from Meda's nude body on the bathroom floor. Hess later manipulates Ganja in an explicit act of sexual surrogacy. In seducing the dinner guest, Ganja stands in for Hess himself, until he suddenly materializes at the end of the sequence, ready to pick up where Ganja leaves off. His desire for Luther, in comparison, is most provocatively visualized during the baptism scene, in which the sensuality of the interplay between the preacher and his supplicant is accentuated by the close proximity of Hess's head, which jerks spasmodically, to the minister's groin.

The moments of physical contact that Hess shares with other men release from him a carnal energy that is seldom present elsewhere in the film, even in his clinches with Ganja. Yet the main heterosexual romance itself is also endowed with powerful connotations of nonnormative sexuality. In a reflexive moment, Ganja rationalizes Hess's avowed bloodlust and fear of damnation as some sort of sexual role-play. "Everybody's some kind of freak," she observes. "Everybody I know is into something, you know. You're into horror movies. I can dig it." Ganja is willing to indulge her groom's monstrous perversions in exchange for a life of material comfort. Almost immediately, however, the conditions of their arrangement are altered without her consent. She ends up serving Hess as both beard and procurer, providing the bait of polyamorous enticement to lure virile young men to their doom.

As Marlo David details in her 2011 essay, Ganja herself is a queer figure no less than her husbands. David likens Ganja to a "classic blues woman" like Bessie Smith, whose creativity Gunn conjures via the soundalike music that accompanies Ganja's initial exploration of the Green mansion.[104] Ganja's directness and will to self-preservation likely stem from her adolescent reaction to being branded "a liar and a slut" by her own mother, the one person who reasonably could be expected to defend her against such a misogynistic accusation. Thus, resolved to give the world "a full case of" the disease she supposedly carries, Ganja infiltrates that world and forces it to adapt to her own material, psychic, and sexual needs. Even her involuntary conversion to the ranks of the undead only momentarily deters—and eventually enhances—her quest for erotic self-fulfillment. Unlike Hess, she is not tormented by her vampiric status; ultimately, she embraces it.[105]

Drawing on bell hooks's theoretical formulation of the resistance tactics historically employed by Black women both *in* (as characters) and *at* (as spectators) the movies, David finds evidence of Ganja's autonomy in the confrontational and unapologetically direct looks she exchanges with men. Rebutting Diawara and Klotman's implication that Ganja's "potential sexual pleasure and control" are not fully acknowledged until the film's concluding moments, David locates just such a contemplation in Ganja's very first in-person interaction with Hess, whom she studies with a long discomfiting look of contempt.[106] Ganja's penetrating, interrogating gaze subsequently returns at moments of seduction. Her interlocked glances with Richard, especially, become so intense that Hess imperceptibly drops out of the narrative, and the newly joined couple move wordlessly from the dinner table to the bathroom, where Ganja calls the shots.

The early critical objections to the erotic overtones and undertones in *Ganja & Hess* seem, in part, to be coded responses to the perceived moral danger posed by its queer energy, whether represented by a straight yet sexually liberated blues woman or through the subversive potential of the male lead's homoerotic desire. Reviewers attempted to neutralize the former threat by condemning the on-screen representation of Ganja's sexual emancipation as merely smutty. The picture's gay nuances, in contrast, did not even register on the critics' consciousness, beyond Winsten's arch insinuation that the concluding image of Richard sprinting through Ganja's backyard could "be considered remarkable" if Gunn's intentions were not so transparently pornographic.[107] David, writing nearly four decades later, characterizes the director's handling of that same moment as "far from exploitative . . . offer[ing] an organic, natural, tender portrayal of black male full frontal nudity."[108] The increasing recognition of and sensitivity to Black female and queer subjectivities, so clearly delineated in the gap between Winsten and David's evaluative sensibilities, has unquestionably contributed to the building appreciation of *Ganja & Hess*, in particular, and Gunn's work, in general.

As "Doggedly Artsy"

In her pioneering essay on the "oppositional gaze," hooks forges a theory of resistant spectatorship through the prism of her personal moviegoing history. Awakened at an early age to the American cinema's ignorance and misrepresentation of Black women, as exemplified by the shabby treatment of Peola, the "tragic mulatta" played by Fredi Washington in *Imitation of Life* (1934), hooks initially fought back against Hollywood's hegemony by forsaking the movies altogether. When she returned to the cinema as a young woman, hooks tried to interest her female friends in European films, noting that "they did not have in their deep structure a subtext reproducing the narrative of white supremacy. . . . The lives they depicted seemed less rooted in fantasies of escape."[109] Yet her efforts at conversion were not often successful, perhaps because these films' typically all-white milieus appear to replicate the whiteness of the American screen.

One suspects, however, that hooks's rationalization of her friends' disinterest in European cinema is incomplete. These pictures are not just white; they are also, in the eyes of many, pretentious. The relatively difficult, demanding form of art cinema in its postwar heyday discourages viewers' identification with characters and absorption in story worlds, whereas the classical Hollywood form seduces and encourages spectators to indulge in such pleasures in a comparatively uncomplicated fashion. Further, the classical storytelling model is *so* pervasive that any conscious deviation from it is destined to attract accusations of inflated self-importance and willful obscurantism.

As a film that brazenly announces its deviance right from its opening moments, *Ganja & Hess*'s critical reception was shaped by each individual reviewer's tolerance for European-style ambiguity. The line separating the defenders of formal ambiguity from its decriers did not necessarily reflect a racial divide. James Murray's critique in the *Amsterdam News*, for example, assumes the rhetoric of the art cinema enthusiast. *Ganja & Hess* "certainly marks the first time that a film geared for the Black audience has ever approached its subject matter with an appeal and message geared toward the intellect," Murray effuses; "for an *attentive* viewer, [Gunn's] style and message will be unmistakable and refreshing."[110] Conversely, Gunn's cerebral approach was the root cause of Donald Bogle's annoyance with both the movie and its supporters. Bogle mocked the "black intellectuals" who championed the film's distinctiveness by overestimating its artistry. *Ganja & Hess* is "doggedly artsy . . . an intellectual's dream," he contends. Its refusal to provide clear motivation or resolve enigmas shifts the responsibility for meaning-making to the critic, reducing it to "an open vessel into which one can pour his or her point of view."[111] This position aligned Bogle, a founding scholar of Black cinema studies, with mass media reviewers like Joseph Gelmis, who maligned *Ganja & Hess* for its "muddled" technique and for straining to construct a metaphorical "commentary on blood lust" rather than "to entertain."[112]

That Gunn should extensively draw on foreign art cinema conventions of narrative and style is not particularly surprising, given his pancultural aesthetic. Though he only occasionally publicized it, his collaborators have verified that Gunn "admired the European filmmakers."[113] The two never explicitly discussed other directors' styles, but Kanefsky believes that Gunn was conceivably influenced by the French modernist Alain Resnais, whose nonlinear and disjointed conception of time and space is palpable throughout *Ganja & Hess*.[114] Kanefsky is more certain about Gunn's affinity for Ingmar Bergman. Gunn was fond of citing a (possibly apocryphal) Bergman quotation about symbolism: when pressed on the meaning of "the clock running down the street" in one of his movies, the Swedish maestro reportedly responded that it meant "whatever you want it to mean."[115] Gunn similarly declared that (almost) all critical interpretations of his films' symbolic content were valid. He was not above teasing viewers for their impulse to interpret; Gunn delighted in fabricating rationales for particularly perplexing techniques, such as the cropping of Archie's head during the scene of Ganja and Hess's breakfast on the terrace. Nonetheless, Gunn's commitment to encouraging figurative readings was generally as unwavering as that of his European contemporaries. This commitment resulted in, to borrow Samuel Pollard's classification, "the only African American film that's also a European art film," one whose creators were more interested in "creating a feeling, an impressionistic feel" than adhering to "a linear story line."[116]

"If I were white, I would probably be called 'fresh and different.' If I were European, 'Ganja and Hess' might be 'that little film you must see.'"[117] As his letter to the *New York Times* attests, Gunn understood that his preferred methods *usually* elicited praise from critics, providing that they were applied in movies that dealt with "universal" (i.e., white) subject matter. *Ganja & Hess* was almost never discursively positioned as part of the so-called American Film Renaissance, or the wave of European-inspired auteur pictures that proliferated in the late sixties and early seventies. Though it also employs loosened causality, unmotivated actions, shifting character goals, story irresolution, and various tools of genre deconstruction, *Ganja & Hess* has seldom attracted critical comparisons with Renaissance milestones like *Bonnie and Clyde* (1967), *The Graduate* (1967), *Easy Rider* (1969), *The Godfather* (1972), and *Nashville* (1975). If at all, Gunn's film is discussed in the context of blaxploitation horror movies, most of which utilize far more commercially oriented storytelling devices.[118]

Ganja & Hess is rarely scrutinized in tandem even with those Renaissance films with which it outwardly shares modes of production and address. *Wanda* (1970), Barbara Loden's sole theatrical feature, makes for an especially intriguing comparison. Both pictures were independently produced on small budgets and shot in 16 mm. Like *Ganja & Hess*, *Wanda* was a European festival favorite that showcases a memorably inscrutable performance by its stage-trained writer-director. Both films also draw on the formal conventions of art cinema by way of episodic, leisurely paced stories and a long-take visual aesthetic that frames characters against vast, outdoor panoramas. Yet, though it, too, flopped in its own limited run in a single Manhattan theater, *Wanda* still attracted serious critical attention from specialized film journals and even some mainstream press organs. *Ganja & Hess* was not afforded a comparable measure of respect. For middlebrow reviewers, any Black genre movie adopting an "elliptical approach" to storytelling and combining "odd camera angles, fantasy scenes, slow motion sequences and choppy editing" could only result, seemingly, in "a confused hodge-podge."[119]

Tempting as it may be to dismiss *Ganja & Hess*'s first wave of reviewers as philistines, they are not entirely off base in implying that Gunn's rule breaking is excessive, even for an "art movie." Style and narration in *Ganja & Hess* do not quite function as they normally do in postwar art cinema.[120] Although Gunn does use many of the art cinema's "standard" techniques of deviation, he implements those techniques in especially unpredictable and atypical ways, so much so that some commentators have acknowledged the inadequacy of objective description in accounting for the film's effects. Lucas and Walker stress *Ganja & Hess*'s ineffable and "sorcerous" qualities, the product of "the way its camera is freed to be distracted from its characters by what's happening over *there* in *that* field or in *that* painting."[121] Monaco acknowledges the insufficiency of plot summary in conveying the picture's brilliance, instead appealing to descriptions of the film's "voice," its "flavor and mystery."[122] Reaching for traditional terms of evaluation, many of the film's earliest backers found even those specially reserved for art film effects to be useless.

The stylistic strategies featured in *Ganja & Hess* are astonishingly eclectic, incorporating "straight documentary, high melodrama, dark ritual, and cool realism," in Monaco's estimation.[123] The film's formal design accordingly resembles a collage or assemblage, in the vein of Marxist political modernist benchmarks like Tomás Gutiérrez Alea's *Memories of Underdevelopment* (1968) and Dušan Makavejev's *W. R.: Mysteries of the Organism* (1971). As previously detailed, Gunn and Hinton's assimilation of the observational documentary style is evidenced by the church revival scene, which depends on a skillful interweaving of footage from multiple cameras and direct sound. Elsewhere, Gunn appropriates Brechtian distanciation

Figure 4.4 Archie gapes at Ganja, fuming in the extreme background; Hess impatiently clinks his wine glass in the foreground. *Ganja & Hess* (Blu-ray), Kino Lorber Films.

as filtered through the sixties oeuvres of Jean-Luc Godard and Andy Warhol, courtesy of the ostensibly improvised autobiographical monologues directed toward an offscreen listener. The altercation between Ganja and Hess at the dinner table, climaxing with her furious stride back toward the fireplace in the adjacent room, paraphrases the deep-space layering of activity and extreme long-take style of realism advocated by film theorist André Bazin and famously practiced in Orson Welles's early Hollywood productions (see fig. 4.4). Finally, the poetic symbolism associated with the artisan directors of the Romantic avant-garde cinema is manifest in several of *Ganja & Hess*'s abstract cutaways, such as the image of Ganja biting down on a flower, inserted at the moment of her fatal assault on Richard (see fig. 4.5).

In addition to this promiscuous mix of stylistic modes, Gunn's paring down of exposition, character psychology, and causality goes far beyond what most sixties and seventies European art house imports were offering. The opening sequence's fragmenting of action and jumble of tenses pose significant problems for narrative comprehension, and successive sequences sustain these ambiguities rather than clear them up. Seldom does the plot provide a definitive answer to an enigma posed earlier in the story. Character motivations are extremely obscure throughout, notably with regard to

Figure 4.5 Drawn irresistibly to the color red, Ganja nibbles a flower in a misplaced attempt to satiate her hunger. *Ganja & Hess* (Blu-ray), Kino Lorber Films.

Meda's murderous attack on his employer and Ganja's quick absolution of Hess for her husband's death. Because the movie lacks those properties that supply the art film devotee with the means to solve the narrative's puzzles, the *Ganja & Hess* viewer must search elsewhere for equivalent delights. Perhaps, as Diawara and Klotman propose, she might find them outside the realm of story altogether, in the patterns formed and associations evoked by "objects and gestures that either repeat or contrast with elements of each other, depicted in linear or circular relations."[124] Or, she might follow Brad Stevens's advice and focus her attention on the digressions that appear to delay the main story action yet are actually "of greater consequence than the main narrative path."[125]

Based on a comparison of the film's numerous "drafts," armed with the knowledge that Noveck used Gunn's screenplay as a guide, one could argue that Heritage's alleged butchering of *Ganja & Hess* constituted an attempt not to make the film narratively and generically conventional, as is commonly assumed, but to make it conform to the criteria of "acceptable" art cinema narration. *Blood Couple* is just as much an "art film" as *Ganja & Hess*: it just manipulates style and narration in ways that are more palatable to the average art house aficionado. *This* is the type of art film that Kelly-Jordan had expected, the type that Stig Björkman had delivered with *Georgia, Georgia*: serious, adult, and faithful to the imperatives of social realism. Perhaps the only commercially successful entry in the Black movie boom that approximates *Ganja & Hess*'s modernist approach is *Sweet Sweetback's Baadasssss Song*, which combines radical politics with a complex amalgamation of staged material, documentary footage, optical effects, and elliptical editing. Unlike *Ganja & Hess*, however, *Sweetback* is structured around a heroic odyssey, within which correct and incorrect ideological values are clearly demarcated (along racial lines). Those generic storytelling conventions made the Melvin Van Peebles film acceptable to a relatively broad yet overwhelmingly Black audience, though the film's reception by reviewers, even within Black critical communities, was bitterly divided.[126]

The expectations established for African American commercial cinema by the early seventies, even the action-oriented examples, mandated the use of socially conscious yet straightforwardly realist modes of storytelling and style. Art films of the period, marketed on the promise of freedom from aesthetic restrictions, were *expected* to deviate from the norms of classical form . . . but within prescribed limits. *Ganja & Hess* violated both of these specifications. It functions, therefore, within the context of the postwar art cinema much like the Myrthian dagger relates to the Brooklyn Museum's general collection: as an artifact that resists assimilation into a larger neocolonialist institution. Arguably, its severest transgression lies in its attempt to mix multiple modes. Just as "turning" the conventional movie vampire Black serves to make the viewer uncomfortably aware that Dracula is not just European but white, the excessive use of ambiguity and irresolution in *Ganja & Hess* serve to make the viewer uncomfortably aware that the same is true of art cinema itself.

As "Race Picture"

Most critics in 1973 agreed that *Ganja & Hess* was, or attempted to be, an "art film." More obliquely, the question addressed in their reviews was: is it a "Black film" (or, in Winsten's phrasing, a "race picture")?[127] Furthermore, can a film truly be a "Black film" without *white* faces? Countless mass media critical appraisals of Black movies during the boom years imply that, for a film to "say something" about Blackness, it had to tackle issues related to *inter*racial conflict and, ultimately, denounce acts of racism on "both sides," particularly if its story was set in the present day. To the bafflement of white reviewers, *Ganja & Hess* was not directly about interracial conflict. In fact, apart from the very minor roles of Jack Sargent and the "Poetess," there are no white speaking parts in the picture.

Winsten's fruitless search for the "race problem," alluded to in this chapter's epigraph, illustrates one of the predominant means of devaluing the creative output of Gunn and comparably attuned Black artists. Neither mainstream film reviewers nor art house patrons proved capable of negotiating a narrative that revolved around bourgeois African Americans seemingly unaffected by the "race problem." Though they regularly scorned blaxploitation, white critics were perversely reassured by the ubiquitous presence of the "get Whitey" revenge scenario in those pictures, precisely because it reified their own positions of privilege. The ferocity with which the blaxploitation hero struggles against the white power structure, in other words, corroborates the durability and inevitability of that structure.

Certainly, the actions of *Ganja & Hess*'s major characters, excluding Ganja herself, are bounded by the racial otherness imposed on them by white society. Yet, these characters actively battle their psychological colonization by *whiteness* rather than take up arms against individual oppressors. The struggle is especially acute for Meda, but also, crucially, for Hess, who is initially portrayed as "numbed by the weight of his *European* possessions," in Gunn's assessment: "When he has let go, then there is a deep-gut desire within him to exist, create, and survive on his own. That's why the *true black* story is not concerned with the *ancient white* problem of racism, which we see as an aging white indulgence ... which we can no longer support as artists or as a people."[128] *Ganja & Hess*'s surface conflict is more *intra*racial, with the rupture located along the axis of class. There are no concessions made to the white viewer conditioned to seeing himself at the center of the world, even a "Black" world. Unable to glimpse themselves in the film, white critics, therefore, had very little to say about it. In a maddening paradox, *Ganja & Hess* was considered not Black *enough* by virtue of its neglect of white fantasies ... which is also what makes it *too* Black.

As suggested above, *Ganja & Hess* was judged to be insufficiently "Black," not only because of its rarefied milieu but because of its arty trappings, which appear borrowed from the largely white domain of European art cinema. Many armchair sociologists rationalized the relative failure of "quality" Black-centered pictures during the boom by positing that African American filmgoers were simply not interested in art. Working-class Black filmgoers were presumed to only want tales of Black masculinist warriors violently triumphing over white devils. As *Ebony*'s B. J. Mason lamented in 1972, the African American audience "cares less at this point whether a film costs *one* dollar or one *million* to make—as long as its cool black hero somehow sticks it to 'The Man.'"[129] Yet, even a "black professional" could be susceptible to these films' unequivocal celebrations of Black victory. This much is suggested in Terry Guerin's *Interview* review, in which he relates an anecdote about a buttoned-down Black physician who departs a screening of *Ganja & Hess* complaining that it was "too out there for me. I like films that are straight up and down, shoot 'em up, cops and robbers, know what I mean?"[130]

Ultimately, both the supporters and the opponents of blaxploitation subscribed on some level to the "positive images" line that initially dominated criticism of the cinematic representation of marginalized groups, exemplified by books such as Bogle's *Toms, Coons, Mulattoes, Mammies, and Bucks: An Interpretive History of Blacks in American Films* (1973), Molly Haskell's *From Reverence to Rape: The Treatment of Women in the Movies* (1974), and Vito Russo's *The Celluloid Closet: Homosexuality in the Movies* (1981). For those who hailed the new Black action films, Sweetback, Shaft, and *Super Fly*'s Youngblood Priest were positive representations, because they were winners. For those inclined to campaign for more movies resembling *Sounder*, positivity in representation was grounded in universal humanism more so than in the vanquishing of enemies. From this latter perspective, only the realist style of what Larry Neal disparagingly referred to as "social uplift," with its greater emphasis on naturalistic accuracy and "authenticity," allowed for truly positive representations.[131] Seventies Black films that did not aspire to the status of "positive representation," that rejected both the winner-take-all mentality and the social realist imperative, were unassimilable and, correspondingly, stigmatized. As Michael Boyce Gillespie notes in his acclaimed study of "the idea of Black film," such movies, including *Ganja & Hess*, *The Spook Who Sat by the Door*, and Ralph Bakshi's hugely controversial *Coonskin* (1975), "exceeded what the industry, critics, and moviegoing public expected" and were thus deemed to be of minimal importance.[132]

In several interviews following *Ganja & Hess*'s completion, Gunn condemned the false choice between commercial exploitation and social uplift that had been forced on Hollywood's few Black directors. He denounced the ease with which movies like the *Shaft* and *Super Fly* series secured financing. "Black people making films are chosen by Whites," he sardonically observed. "And the overwhelming drive of the films these White people are producing is to get Whitey. It is all very flattering." Gunn dismissed the notion that Black viewers *need* Black screen "heroes," calling this unspoken requirement "another form of censorship." Yet even the supposedly more dignified Black films, in Gunn's eyes, presuppose an audience of fools because they "spell things out too much."[133] Gunn reserved special animus for *Sounder* on these grounds, repeatedly singling it out for criticism: "They took a children's book and made it into a film for Black audiences. So that shows you what they think of us."[134] Film and television narratives about "the slave situation," notably *The Autobiography of Miss Jane Pittman* (1974) and *Roots* (1977), supplied further proof of the media's condescension toward the Black audience: "They will not show us in charge of ourselves." The purpose of the continued prevalence of the slave narrative, Gunn argued, is to preserve "the slave mentality" and "to convince us that they are *in* control, and that we should really *be* controlled."[135]

Gunn used his press platform to promote his own eclectic approach as particularly suitable for African American viewers. Unlike the white filmgoer, who frequents the cinema mainly as a diversion from boredom, the Black filmgoer might be at the movies to better "understand his reality," a reality that is "much more sophisticated" than his white counterpart's.[136] There is, consequently, a social necessity for a Black cinema that is just as demanding as the European art cinema, which obliges its audience to "think" and to engage with "complex ideas." Black artists must cease "flatten[ing] out" disturbing complexities. "I want hallways, crevices, ditches, hills and valleys," Gunn said in 1982. "I want the people to travel through my piece of work so when they get out, they will have thought their way through something."[137]

Ganja & Hess's harshest critics took offense at Gunn's implicit demand to "think their way through" it. Such a directive was acceptable when the movie in question tracked the progress of characters in the white world, the privileged locale of most art films and even many Black-themed realist pictures. Gunn's transgression was his alleged appropriation of "white" aristocratic lifestyles and "white" cinematic language for a Black story. Yet, not only does *Ganja & Hess* implement tropes of formal complexity in ways that exceed conventional art movie signification; that implementation shares just as much in common with twentieth-century African American literature as with Anglo-American modernism. Indeed, Gunn's advocates have long pointed out *Ganja & Hess*'s kinship to certain Black-authored

Figure 4.6 One of Gunn and Victor Kanefsky's most enigmatic still lifes: a ceramic icon weeps blood as Ganja drains away Richard's life. *Ganja & Hess* (Blu-ray), Kino Lorber Films.

novels. Monaco, for example, identifies the movie's most obvious literary precursors as Jean Toomer's *Cane*, an equally "rare work of art cut whole from the rich fabric of Black culture, with magnificently deep ethnological roots," and Ralph Ellison's *Invisible Man*.[138]

When Gunn turned his attention to filmmaking, he could look to few Black independent pictures for aesthetic inspiration, one possible exception being Spencer Williams's allegorical religious melodrama, *The Blood of Jesus*, one of the most successful "race pictures" of the forties. (Certain compositions in *Ganja & Hess* seem to allude to Williams's striking symbolic images, such as that of an icon "crying" blood [see fig. 4.6].) One of the only Black independent filmmakers prior to 1973 to do something analogous, aesthetically speaking, to what Gunn attempted with *Ganja & Hess* was Van Peebles, whose French-produced debut feature, *The Story of a Three-Day Pass* (1967), famously adapted techniques characteristic of the early French New Wave (and similarly flummoxed American reviewers). In academic discourse, *Sweetback* is, of course, the Van Peebles film most often linked to *Ganja & Hess*. Yet, those who draw the comparison also take pains to problematize it in order to reflect the directors' competing objectives. In his analysis of their significance as "paradigms of black cinema aesthetics," Manthia Diawara notes that both movies "defamiliariz[e] classical film language." Nevertheless, vital distinctions exist: *Sweetback* is linear and modernist; *Ganja & Hess* is "cyclical" and postmodernist. Van Peebles's more dichotomous "aesthetic draws on the logic of Black nationalism as the basis of value judgment, and defines itself by positioning the spectator to identify with the Black male hero of the film," whereas Gunn "aestheticizes the Black imaginary by placing the spectator on the same side as the Black church."[139]

Extrapolating from the progressive reassessment of *Ganja & Hess*, and of other "excessive" Black-centered movies of the period, academics today are receptive to the notion of formal hybridity and multimodality as essential components of the "Black film." They are, at least, increasingly evaluated as more essential than the cultivation of a surface-level naturalism. Mixing modes, generic appeals, and stylistic approaches are embraced as strategies by which Black filmmakers can disrupt established film practice and thereby counteract, as Gillespie encourages, "the fidelity considerations of black film."[140] In a related manner, this reorientation releases Black creators from the forced acceptance of racial difference as primary subject and theme of their art. These shifting perspectives have even started to exert influence on popular perceptions of African American cinema, as captured by Racquel Gates's 2020 *New York Times* editorial on the circulation of "anti-racist" movie guides following that summer's social unrest, which pronounces, "The very idea that Black film's greatest purpose is to be an educational primer on race in America is a notion that we need to lay to rest."[141]

Current sentiments aside, theorists have long argued for the usefulness of particular methods of storytelling to a Black film aesthetic, and *Ganja & Hess* has helped them make their case. Diawara's 1993 study of the "new realism" in African American cinema is heavily informed by Gunn's use of "spatial narration" in *Ganja & Hess*. Spatial narration, to Diawara, is fundamental to a rich strain of Black independent film practice, further illustrated by milestones including *Killer of Sheep*, *Losing Ground*, and *Daughters of the Dust*:

> Their narratives contain rhythmic and repetitious shots, going back and forth between the past and the present. Their themes involve Black folklore, religion, and the oral traditions which link Black Americans to the African diaspora.... Through the repetition of these Black times in [*Ganja & Hess*], Bill Gunn defines a Black aesthetic that puts in the same space African spirituality, European vampire stories, the Black church, addiction to drugs, and liberated

feminist desires.... Black films use spatial narration as a way of revealing and linking Black spaces that have been separated and suppressed by White times, and as a means of validating Black culture.[142]

The value of "space-based" narration for Black filmmakers has been investigated more recently by Allyson Nadia Field, who detects a productive example in Haile Gerima's *Sankofa* (1993). *Sankofa* presents the story of Mona, an African American model in Ghana. Upon entering the dungeon at Cape Coast Castle, used by merchants of the transatlantic slave trade as a holding cell for captured natives, Mona is instantaneously transported back to the previous century and into the body of an enslaved African woman. *Ganja & Hess* is less didactic than the Gerima film, but Gunn's parallel application of what Field labels "overlapping diegeses" indicates a shared intent. At crucial moments, *Ganja & Hess*—as does *Sankofa*, as does *Daughters of the Dust* via the embodiment of a yet-to-be-born narrator—literalizes Diawara's call to put different temporalities "in the same space," as when the Myrthian queen appears in the background as the titular leads recite their marriage vows. The simultaneous occupation of the same frame by characters from different story times is not, of course, the only means by which "Black spaces" may be linked; intercutting among the various diegeses is a more common practice in each of the aforementioned films. Yet, both iterations confirm Gunn's own "investment in reimagining film language to speak to the African American experience and reflect cultural memory and its value as a tool of transformation."[143]

As these examples attest, deviant and excessive style is an indispensable tool in the aesthetic arsenal of the "space-based" Black independents. In terms of content, their pictures reject liberal-humanist assumptions about the universality of love, family, religion, work, and death; instead, all are positioned and explored within a specifically Black context. Still, this attitude is easier to recognize in *Daughters of the Dust*, a film about the migration of Gullah islanders to the US mainland in 1902. Not only is Gunn (unlike Julie Dash) working within and around the perimeter of a traditional genre but his movie focuses on the Black bourgeoisie, and thus its characters interact within environments and adopt viewpoints more typically associated with white figures in American films. Accordingly, *Ganja & Hess*, like much of Gunn's art, was derided by some for not being Black enough because it was not exclusively populated by the poor of the inner city or the rural backwater.[144]

Because of the emphasis he places on the mutability of racial (and sexual, and class) identity, Gunn today might be characterized as a "post-Black" author. The concept of post-Blackness, the meaning and merits of which have been widely debated in the two decades since its popularization by Thelma Golden, chief curator for Harlem's Studio Museum, is generally appreciated to have informed much of the cutting-edge African American art of the post–civil rights generation. In *Queering Post-Black Art*, Derek Conrad Murray attributes its ascendance to "the necessity for many artists and intellectuals to resist the stifling dictates of racial obligation, and its attendant socio-political dogmas."[145] Post-Blackness speaks to a desire by Black artists to step beyond the accepted "regime of representation" supposedly enforced by the venerated elders of the nationalist Black arts movement, who in theory and practice privileged "images depicting black men in the throes of collective resistance" and, thus, downplayed conceptions of Blackness that stressed complexity and multiplicity. Though Gunn was, in fact, older than most of the key Black arts movement figures, like Neal and Amiri Baraka, his rejection of racial essentialism (and "black hyper-masculinity" and heterosexism) aligns him with this more contemporary artistic worldview.[146] Gunn has, thus, begun to be seen by some as an important progenitor of post-Black art, and *Ganja & Hess* has correspondingly entered the canon of post-Black masterworks. Michele Prettyman lists *Ganja & Hess* as the earliest entry in her "post-black cinema archive," as it satisfies the same elemental criteria that she locates in her case study, *Losing Ground*, among them the refusal "to center blackness and racial identity as the subject and object of the film" and the articulation of "an expanded universe of intellectual, cultural, and psychic influences on the narrative and characters and on the aesthetic possibilities of the film itself."[147]

Gunn steadfastly refused the constraints pushed on Black storytellers employed by white-run media entities, almost all of whom were hired for their presumed expertise in "writing Race" rather than the inclination or capacity to tackle other kinds of subject matter. Throughout his career, Gunn unapologetically crafted narratives centered on white characters: *Marcus in the High Grass*, "The Bedlamite," *The Angel Levine*, *The Landlord*, *Stop*, *Territory*. But even those texts that feature Black main characters tend to express a profound distrust of identity politics, a Baldwinian suspicion that "races, social classes, [and] metaphors such as masculinity," as Ed Pavlić explains, were, in fact, "designed to confine, to stop the wheel and thwart the living disturbances of actual human encounters."[148] In Gunn's work, these (proto-post-Black) views are occasionally declaimed with blunt force, as when Johnnas's mother Hilly upbraids her son's teacher for relegating his individualities to the standing of "qualities ascribed to certain groups":

> Why do you need him? To liberate? I liberated my son when I gave him life, and it killed me to see them waiting with their ready-made labels and their pigeon holes ready to stuff him in ... race ... Negro. ... When he was born his hair was the warmest color of brown; they wrote: hair black. His eyes were big, the color of new green; eyes brown, they wrote. ... I said "Look at my child, look at him." They never looked at him. Why can't you look at him?[149]

The sentiments underlying Hilly's outburst are multiplied throughout *All the Rest Have Died*, an ideological companion piece to *Johnnas*. Barney similarly protests that he is not as he is branded: he is not Black but rather "a unique color of almond mixed from a secret formula known only to myself and God, with greens derived from the black of my mother's hair, orange from the brown of my father's skin, and white, which is all colors together, gathered from my enemies and my friends."[150] In its entirety, the novel provides a context for its bohemian protagonist's entreaties to be considered as something other than a "Black artist." When Barney is roped into a dispute about "the Negroes' expression in art" and whether it must be "purely racial," he pleads for the opportunity to decide what is necessary to his art, an option which is granted without question to white creators.[151]

Ironically, the more overt denunciations of racial categorization in *All the Rest Have Died* were taken as evidence of the author's supposed indifference to the authentic suffering of his people. Because Gunn's early literary efforts did not acknowledge interracial conflict as *the* defining characteristic of Black life, some critics proclaimed him out of step in an era in which political and cultural separatism was gaining favor. Noel Schraufnagel's analysis of *All the Rest Have Died* is revealing in its bewilderment at the book's apparent disinterest in censuring racism. He characterizes *All the Rest Have Died* as an "accommodationist" piece, as its "racial materials ... are mere comments on a social situation rather than an integral part of the book."[152] In comparable fashion, Ilona Leki foregrounds the novel's debt to European philosophy, as suggested by its focus on "man's existential crisis, rather than with a black man's racial crisis."[153]

Leki also finds evidence of an ideological evolution in Gunn's art after the publication of his first book, a gradual move away from what she judges to be a conservative, accommodationist stance. The turning point for Leki is the 1964 *Variety* profile in which Gunn vents about Hollywood's discrimination against African American actors.[154] Over the next decade-plus, Gunn's public statements reflect, for Leki, a budding racial awareness. Though he continued to express ambivalence about racial classification and separatism, Gunn also volunteered that "being black" was the "most interesting thing in my life," adding that "I don't believe white artists can see the future that clearly. Part of the future is *not* being white."[155] In a self-tagged "personal statement" on *Ganja & Hess*, Gunn expanded on Meda's edict to "not succeed" by white standards and redirected it toward Black artists in particular. "It is a terrible and wonderful thing to be a black artist in this country," Gunn cautioned, imploring his audience to no longer be "distracted from ourselves. . . . We have been caught up in a cold maze of Oscars and Emmys, and Tonys . . . rewards for penetrating the white conscience. That is not the purpose of art. That is not the purpose of life."[156]

The small handful of midseventies critics familiar with Gunn's early work took note of this seeming alteration in temperament. *Newsweek*'s Jack Kroll regarded this shift as a surrender on Gunn's part to the alleged fashion for "anti-white" narratives. Reviewing *Black Picture Show* in 1975, Kroll unfavorably compared its embittered Black leads to the writer-hero of *All the Rest Have Died*. "Maybe Gunn's consciousness has been raised," Kroll sarcastically postulated, "but I think Barney's words," particularly the monologues in which he rejects racial definition, "represent Gunn's real feeling as a writer."[157] *Ganja & Hess*'s initial reviewers did not, by and large, engage with the movie's subtle inquiry into the legacy of white cultural imperialism, but later scholars have paid closer attention to those aspects that supposedly disclose just such an interrogation, as signaled by the allusion in Meda's suicide note to the title of Frantz Fanon's landmark study of colonialism, *The Wretched of the Earth*.[158] These allusions do suggest, at the least, Gunn's acknowledgment of the rise of revolutionary, anticolonialist politics and rhetoric across the Black diaspora.

Yet, while Gunn's condemnations of white racism may have become more vociferous in the seventies, that does not mean he suddenly became "race-conscious." Race consciousness is evident throughout his entire body of work. Gunn in the sixties well understood that the color line cannot simply be ignored out of existence. It must be confronted because its enforcement is what structures social hierarchies in American life, and even the "freest" Americans cannot transgress it as easily as they might transgress class or even gender and sexual boundaries. In Gunn's view, the seventies

Black artist must first reclaim the ability to self-segregate to then be able to refuse race as the major determinant of her identity. Gunn agreed with Janus Adams's contention that the overarching goal of African Americans should be liberation rather than assimilation or separation, the latter of which presumes the inevitability of white control over the world. At the same time, he repudiated Baraka's dictum that Black art "*must* speak of the people's struggle." Art, Gunn retorted, "can't be touched. It can't be tied down." Because "artists are the only people who seem compelled to be free," they are obligated only to make art that reflects the "truth of [their own] experience."[159]

Ganja & Hess stages the confrontation between Blackness and whiteness in ways that mediate the attitudes expressed in *All the Rest Have Died* and *Black Picture Show*. Whereas the former text might strike today's reader as naively color-blind and the latter as stridently color-conscious, *Ganja & Hess* upholds both as well as many adjacent positions, affirming them as not at all philosophically incompatible. The fascination elicited by the film derives in part from its simultaneous advocacy for and challenging of a range of ideologies. The figure of Meda, in particular, illustrates this duality. Meda's suicide poem, in which he warns "the Black male children" that philosophy "disregards the uncustomary things about you," expresses an individualist credo strongly reminiscent of that of Barney Gifford. But Meda is also a victim of racial politics, driven to self-destruction by his obsession with "the problem of identity."[160] In Gunn's first-draft screenplay, he informs Hess that the source of his torment is *specifically* racial: "I don't give a good Goddamn anymore . . . because I decided that I as a black man will have nothing to do with a system that was and still is designed to enslave me. . . . Because I have been allowed . . . Goddamn, *allowed* . . . to operate the machine that has been used to castrate me."[161] Conceivably, for Gunn, the contradiction that Meda embodies is neutralized by the movie's tacit admission, echoing W. E. B. Du Bois's theory of "double consciousness," that Black people can never *only* be individuals within a system built on their collective "Othering" and exclusion.

Gunn's readiness to question orthodoxies extends to his ambivalence about the role of the church in Black America. Christianity is a major theme of *Ganja & Hess*, yet commentators are split over whether Gunn is condemning its effects or promoting it as an antidote to spiritual deprivation. Several analyses of *Ganja & Hess* supply a detailed rationale for the former position, based in the assumption that Christianity is inherently a white

Western practice and thus incompatible with expressions of African forms of piety. Diawara and Klotman, in fact, attribute the film's disjointed narration to the fact that each of its "narrators" (Luther, Meda, and Ganja) are struggling to impose on the story his or her own conception of the sacred. Because his telling is designed to exhort his followers to embrace Christ and reject pre-Christian gods, the minister's "narrative" is structured according to Christianity's "teleological notion of history." Thus, his featured segments, owing to their documentary-like style, strictly observe temporal and spatial continuity.[162] Alan Stanbrook similarly contends that the film's very form is encoded with anti-Christian bias. In his account, the central thematic conflict of *Ganja & Hess*, that of "the Gospel at war with a suppressed African heritage," is artfully evoked by the aural conflict between "revivalist spiritual" sound and "African atavist" sound.[163]

Under such an interpretation, the matter of whether Hess achieves "true" deliverance in the film's penultimate scene is in serious doubt. Hess's Christian salvation comes at the expense of his immortality, which Lucas and Walker characterize as "African-imbued."[164] Likewise, Benshoff sees Gunn as proposing an equivalence between vampirism and Afrocentrism, which, consequently, implies that Hess, "when he succumbs to Western Christian morality" (and mortality), is, in fact, "denying his African heritage."[165] And, according to Sherrod's reading, immortality in this context is a projection of the Christian church, which is historically "complicit in proselytizing [the] germ rhetoric" that justified the vampiric project of slavery in the first place. Gunn can, thus, be understood as prodding the viewer to question the view that "disease and undeath can only be vanquished through martyrdom," given that the church helped define "disease and undeath" as synonymous with competing systems of religious belief.[166]

These defenses granted, the conclusion that *Ganja & Hess* is unmistakably an "anti-Christian" film, as labeled by some of its early champions, may not hold up to scrutiny.[167] One could just as well assert that the Black church positively influenced Gunn's aesthetic, because it provided him with a model for how Afrocentric forms and traditions might redeem a repressive, Eurocentric structure of belief and communication. *Ganja & Hess*'s sensitivity to Black people's use of Christianity as both a tool of resistance and a means of cultural preservation was recognized immediately by Paul Carter Harrison, who praised the "provocative metaphor" that organizes the film for its attention to "the cosmic sensibility of black life, its spirituality, that hidden layer of potency often inscrutable to the 'plantation bosses.'"[168]

As per usual, James Baldwin's articulation of this principle provides us with the canniest verbalization of what Gunn's cinema visualizes. "The blacks did not so much use Christian symbols as recognize them," Baldwin writes, "for what they were before the Christians came along—and, thus, reinvested these symbols with their original energy." It is only "through the creation [and continuation] of the black church" that the Christian subject recognizes "that your life does not belong to you: nothing belongs to you. This will not sound like freedom to Western ears, since the Western world pivots on the infantile, and, in action, criminal delusions of possession, and of property."[169] Hess's final surrendering of his own worldly possessions signifies that his death is, in fact, a salvation. More accurately, it is a liberation from the simultaneous blessing and curse that eternal life represents.

As All (or None) of the Above

Because of the period's unique industrial and cultural circumstances, the early seventies would have seemed to provide the most hospitable conditions for a film like *Ganja & Hess* to find success. During this optimistic phase of the Black movie boom, when it appeared as if both African American movie attendance and the range of Black film subject matter would expand exponentially, numerous filmmakers and film companies (notably, Kelly-Jordan Enterprises) wagered that a "quality" Black cinema was both possible and profitable. The fate awaiting *Ganja & Hess* thus had the effect of fortifying the systemic race-based discrimination long enforced by the American movie business, and the film's daring deployment of conflicting methods of narration and generic codes provided the industry with the alibi for its containment.

David Kalat has argued that the story of *Ganja & Hess* is the story of its three "versions": "the movie [Bill] Gunn made, the movie that was made from it, and the movie Gunn set out to make."[170] Yet, Gunn's final cut by itself occupies several modes simultaneously: it is an art film, a horror/vampire film, a(n) (s)exploitation film, and a "Black film," among other things. Taken individually, each of these types of movies drew sizable audiences in the recessionary early seventies. Even certain hybrid forms that mixed at least two of these four modes attracted a healthy viewership. By 1973, niche audiences had been identified and profitably targeted with Black exploitation films, European art house horror, and Black-themed horror. Furthermore, the exploitation elements of gore and frank sexuality were now crucial to the appeal of both the horror genre and the art cinema. Although the stratification of distribution and exhibition in the United States discouraged the marketing of certain combinations, some hybrids did find an audience. But the one combination that proved untenable, according to conventional wisdom, was "art cinema" mixed with "Black cinema," or the juxtaposition of Black casts and content with obscure stylistic and storytelling strategies indicative of European modernism. As illustrated by the commercial and critical rejection of Wendell B. Harris's unclassifiable *Chameleon Street* eighteen years later, this disdain continued well past the blaxploitation period and into the second Black movie boom of the late eighties and early nineties. A comic character study about an incorrigible social-climbing con artist, *Chameleon Street* similarly failed, as Gillespie observes, "to be appreciated or understood as an art film, independent film, American film, or black film. Moreover it suffered for being all these things at once, if not more."[171]

Conventional wisdom's hypothesis went largely untested during the early seventies, however. *Ganja & Hess* was perhaps fated to be a box office disappointment due to its formal radicalism; regardless, it was also denied any real opportunity to identify and develop a fan base. By the time of *Ganja & Hess*'s premiere, Kelly-Jordan's economic model had been readjusted, such that the company required immediate and constant revenue streams to compensate for a reduced production slate. By giving up almost instantly on its film's prospects, after just two mediocre weeks at a single ill-chosen venue, Kelly-Jordan reversed its founding, guiding philosophy. *Ganja & Hess*'s production may have been enabled by a desire to create artistic motion pictures, but its suppression signified a capitulation to the lowest common denominator. Kelly-Jordan's eventual failure, and the failure of many of the independents that dabbled in Black "quality" moviemaking in the twentieth century, should thus be understood as a consequence of conflating a film's artistic value with its economic function.

5

RESURRECTION

Ganja & Hess's *Life after Death*

> The character [of Hess] for me was a Black man in America who had achieved everything... and then suddenly in front of him is the future; it is about the future.[1]
>
> —Bill Gunn, quoted in Anderson, "Seminar for Black and Third World Filmmakers."

Though awareness of *Ganja & Hess* has yet to penetrate mainstream consciousness, its reputation has steadily and stealthily risen over the course of nearly five decades. Across that time span, the film has been "lost," recovered, preserved, recirculated, and reclaimed as one of the great works of African American cinema, independent cinema, and horror cinema. This chapter (and the Conclusion) survey the various mileposts along its journey to recognition: the screening and eventual deposit of a 35 mm copy of the director's cut at MoMA in the midseventies; the preservation and frequent exhibition of a 16 mm print in the early eighties; the publication of Gunn's screenplay in 1991; the film's initial release on DVD in 1998; the 2014 remake; and the 2018 theatrical rerelease.

Gunn continued to produce accomplished art after *Ganja & Hess*, mainly as a playwright, but he never directed another feature film and rarely acted on-screen. Though he continued to write screenplays and teleplays on commission, Gunn was blackballed by the major studios after his acrimonious departure from *The Greatest*.[2] Thereafter, he spent a significant amount of energy, right up until his death, drafting original scripts for his own purposes. These projects further elaborated on his career-long contemplation of social, artistic, and familial estrangement, although these themes took on added significance for Gunn in the wake of his clashes with movie bosses over creative control. Much of this chapter, in fact, analyzes the central impact of Gunn's tribulations with *Ganja & Hess* (and *Stop* and *The Greatest*) on his later artistic output. His bitterness over demeaning treatment on these ventures was most obviously channeled into *Black Picture Show* and *Rhinestone Sharecropping*, both of which chronicle the misfortunes of an underemployed Black filmmaker and his manipulation by his supposed benefactors.

Gunn's disenchantment with the movie business was indirectly articulated in several additional late-career ventures as well. The theme of the Black artist's exploitation by the white culture industry is obliquely interrogated in *Territory*, an acerbic satire that marked Gunn's final attempt to direct a commercial feature. His last completed visual narrative, *Personal Problems, Volumes 1* and *2*, represented a rebuke of Hollywood simply through the audacity of its conception and production. The nearly unanimous critical praise garnered by *Personal Problems* during its recent limited release obscures how the serial was widely ignored during its initial circulation, despite pockets of promotion in the African American press, and even rejected for exhibition on public television. That this nearly three-hour-long, loosely structured, and partially improvised soap opera, shot on low-resolution videotape, became one of the major critical hits of 2018 is proof positive of an ongoing Bill Gunn renaissance.

This chapter, then, traces two simultaneous yet opposing trajectories: the steady acceleration of interest in *Ganja & Hess* since its preliminary withdrawal, and the arrested development of Gunn's post–*Ganja & Hess* career. Furthermore, by exploring the recuperation of *Ganja & Hess* for Black cinema history, this account opens a window on the picture's (and Gunn's) considerable influence on Black auteurs, ranging from contemporaries to currently active filmmakers. Appropriately, the conclusion privileges one of the few figures who qualifies under both of those categories: Spike Lee, the most recognizable African American movie director and the driving force behind the *Ganja & Hess* remake.

The Restoration Era: *Ganja & Hess* on Tour

The transferal of *Ganja & Hess*'s ownership from Kelly-Jordan to Heritage Enterprises also altered the picture's economic position. Conceived and executed as an art object with the potential for ongoing profitability, Gunn's work was suddenly converted into an exploitation property with an abridged commercial life span. Under pressure to reshape this footage into a form suitable for drive-in and grind house engagements, Fima Noveck was under no obligation to consider the film's long-term prospects. *Ganja & Hess*'s negative was thus cavalierly destroyed in the course of its transformation into *Blood Couple*. Compounding this atrocity, the few prints of Gunn's cut still floating around were called in by Heritage president Skip Steloff for a "giant bonfire."[3] At least two nearly intact 35 mm prints slipped through Steloff's dragnet, however, and wound up in the possession of the film's original creative team. Kanefsky managed to acquire one during the distributors' negotiations, which he kept concealed for years.[4] The other was obtained by Gunn, who stored it in a vault at MoMA; this copy could be exhibited or rented only with Gunn's permission.[5]

The rescue of *Ganja & Hess* from cinematic purgatory was underway within months of its sale to Heritage, thanks to the imprimatur of MoMA. MoMA may not have been the first venue to screen Gunn's print following the film's disappearance from commercial theaters; reportedly, *Ganja & Hess* was shown to an admiring crowd at the University of Pennsylvania in the fall of 1973.[6] But MoMA's status as standard bearer of American high art supplied the cultural cachet necessary to initiate the film's reclamation. *Ganja & Hess* was first screened at the museum in December 1973 as part of a program of movies duplicating the lineup from Critics Week at that spring's Cannes Film Festival. The first showing, on December 20, was exactly the sort of "premiere" that *Ganja & Hess* deserved in the first place, as opposed to the desultory affair at the Playboy the previous April. The auditorium was packed not only with the director's colleagues and friends but with many luminaries from the New York community of Black filmmakers, who gave the film a rousing reception.[7]

Contrary to the *Amsterdam News*'s ominous description of this event as the "final" showing of *Ganja & Hess* "in its original version," the MoMA screening was intended to serve as a kickoff for a possible rerelease.[8] Adrienne Mancia, associate curator of MoMA's Department of Film, favorably compared the response to *Ganja & Hess*'s December shows to the enthusiasm that greeted the museum's sneak previews of *Easy Rider* and *Sweet Sweetback's Baadasssss Song*, which for her confirmed the Gunn film's strong "commercial potential."[9] In 1974, Gunn himself implied that *Ganja & Hess* was destined for "general release" as soon as Heritage's recut was pulled from distribution.[10] This plan never panned out, but MoMA's 35 mm copy quickly became a hugely popular stock title, attracting sizable crowds every time it was shown at the museum.[11]

Gunn's donated print would also become one of the most frequently rented films in MoMA's collection. This version traveled extensively across the continent in 1974, playing museums in Brooklyn and Philadelphia and a film festival in Mexico City.[12] *Ganja & Hess* was particularly in demand throughout the seventies for Black film series at African American colleges. These bookings routinely included commentary by Black cinema scholars, such as Clayton Riley, who hosted a special presentation at the Black Film Institute at the University of the District of Columbia, and Oliver Franklin, founder of the Newark Black Film Festival, who took Gunn's movie to Talladega College in Alabama.[13] News of the director's cut's resurrection and newfound cult started to spread. Marlene Clark learned of the revived interest in *Ganja & Hess* from a UCLA professor in the midseventies; she then began appearing at Los Angeles screenings on a semiregular basis.[14] Samuel Pollard was not fully cognizant of the film's reach until he attended a showing around the same time at a Harlem theater, during which he was amazed by the enthusiasm of the audience.[15] James Monaco also took note of the movie's "extraordinary reputation, especially among Black filmmakers." Though only "a few thousand people" had seen *Ganja & Hess* by the end of the decade, it signified "a valuable secret those who have seen it are eager to share with those who haven't."[16]

Ganja & Hess was included as part of the Obeah Communication Collective's prestigious series on "Third World Involvement in Film" at the Studio Museum of Harlem and Countee Cullen Library in February 1975. The four-day event featured a lecture by Donald Bogle on Oscar Micheaux and screenings of movies by the pioneering Senegalese director Ousmane Sembene and the Cuban period drama *Lucia* (1968), the latter of which was debated by a panel of filmmakers including St. Clair Bourne and Kathleen Collins.[17] A contemporaneous *Amsterdam News* report suggests that the *Ganja & Hess* screening had to be canceled at the last minute due to the lack of a 35 mm projector, disappointing an overflow crowd along with Gunn himself.[18] The film's presence in this series is nevertheless highly significant, as it marks one of the first efforts by programmers to contextualize *Ganja & Hess* as part of a global tradition of oppositional Black cinematic practice.

Gunn's participation in a similar yet more expansive event five years later was even more important for establishing an international reputation for his movie and strengthening connections with a community of ascendant Black filmmakers and historians. The two-week Festival of Independent Black American Cinema, curated by Catherine Arnaud and Catherine Ruelle in consultation with Pearl Bowser, opened on October 20, 1980, at the Forum des Halles in Paris. Gunn brought his print of *Ganja & Hess*, and, based on lingering memories of the film's Cannes glory seven years prior, its exhibition was highly anticipated and enthusiastically received.[19] Apart from a handful of "race movies" from the twenties, such as works by Micheaux and Richard Maurice, the program was dominated by recent offerings by African American directors.[20] Several of these directors were in attendance, and they took part in roundtable discussions of their films and on the state of Black cinema in general. Among them were other members of the heterogeneous East Coast scene of Black independents: William Greaves, Michelle Parkerson, Jacqueline Shearer, Warrington Hudlin, Collins, and Bowser herself.[21] Aside from the fifty-four-year-old Greaves, Gunn was the elder statesman of this seasoned group.

The Festival of Independent Black American Cinema is perhaps best remembered today for "put[ting] L. A. Rebellion filmmakers in dialogue with Black independent filmmakers in other parts of the country."[22] The LA rebellion was a loose confederation of filmmakers of color who enrolled in production programs at UCLA starting in the late sixties and produced major work throughout the seventies. Inspired by a diverse set of counterhegemonic cultural influences, from Micheaux and Italian neorealism to the Black arts movement and "Third Cinema" theory and practice, the class-conscious rebellion filmmakers "worked with a common purpose to create a new Black cinema characterized by innovative, meaningful reflection on past and present lives and the concerns of Black communities in the U. S. and across the African diaspora."[23] *Ganja & Hess* is not as overtly didactic as some of the better-known rebellion pictures nor does it make the lives of working-class African Americans its main subject. Yet, it does share thematic preoccupations that Allyson Nadia Field, Jan-Christopher Horak, and Jacqueline Stewart have attributed to the rebellion movies en masse, including drug abuse, class exploitation, and cultural imperialism. Additionally, its blending of narrative, documentary, and avant-garde formal techniques anticipates rebellion filmmaker Ben Caldwell's own strategies for "develop[ing] a new film language" in *I & I: An African Allegory* (1979), another festival feature.[24] Given his like-minded artistic objectives, Gunn's acceptance by the rebellion cohort and his inclusion in the gathering at the

Forum des Halles was entirely fitting, as was *Ganja & Hess*'s inclusion in the package of festival films, compiled by Bowser, that toured New York state the following spring.[25]

Gunn's triumphant return to France fortified his bond with Bowser, who would become such an important figure in *Ganja & Hess*'s safeguarding that Gunn referred to her as his "fairy Godmother."[26] In the early seventies, Bowser served as associate director of Third World Newsreel; in that position, she helped oversee the distribution of dozens of independent African American movies. *Ganja & Hess* made an indelible impression on her, and she subsequently championed (and programmed) Gunn's movie at every chance. It was Bowser who, around the time of the Paris retrospective, informed Gunn of the damage incurred by the MoMA copy of *Ganja & Hess* after years of constant projection at festivals, colleges, and museums. The destruction of the film's negatives precluded a full restoration, as did issues of rights ownership. Therefore, Bowser proposed to withdraw the distribution print once enough money could be obtained to strike a 16 mm internegative. Under her supervision, $10,000 was raised in less than a year through numerous special screenings and direct appeals by Gunn, who dutifully traveled with the movie almost wherever and whenever it was shown.[27]

Ganja & Hess was back in circulation in a new preservation copy in 1982, and Gunn resumed his hectic schedule of screenings, sometimes accompanied by Bowser, Sam Waymon, or both.[28] Even without Gunn's guaranteed presence, *Ganja & Hess* remained a popular film rental for Third World Newsreel throughout the decade. Yet, it remained relatively difficult to see in its original form because of its absence from the home video market. Whereas the Heritage recut was ubiquitous on VHS in the eighties, Third World restricted the sale of videotapes of *Ganja & Hess* to schools, libraries, and museums, and this arrangement continued after Gunn's death in 1989.[29] Third World's distribution agreement with Gunn, as renegotiated after Bowser left the company in 1987, prioritized the 16 mm rental market. Gunn was recognized as the work's producer in possession of all necessary consents and licenses, and Third World promised to strike new prints for circulation once Gunn secured ownership of the copyright.[30] In 1988, *Ganja & Hess* headlined Bowser's film series at the Brooklyn Museum on independent Black American directors, and its inclusion in a film festival in Umeå, Sweden, prompted a belated rave review in the British cinema journal *Films and Filming*.[31]

Figure 5.1 Bill Gunn and Kathleen Collins, friends and collaborators on set and in the classroom, at the Black Film Center/Archive Festival/Workshop in 1983. Courtesy Black Film Center/Archive, Indiana University, Bloomington, Indiana.

Gunn's picture also continued to amass a devoted following within academia. Third World Newsreel's statement of royalty payments for the year after Gunn's death indicates that most rentals were collected from university screenings.[32] Gunn, in the eighties, developed close ties with one university in particular: Indiana University, the home institution of Phyllis Klotman, a pioneering scholar of African American cinema. Klotman's impassioned advocacy for *Ganja & Hess* predates the analysis she coauthored with Manthia Diawara, an early draft of which Gunn read and complimented.[33] According to Waymon, Klotman invited the two men to speak at Indiana University, Gunn to film students and Waymon to musicologists, after *Ganja & Hess* was first released.[34] When Klotman founded the Black Film Center/Archive in Indiana University's Department of Afro-American Studies, Gunn was one of many notables who signed on as a sponsor and sat for a videotaped interview.[35] Both Gunn and Collins were involved in the inaugural Black Film Center/Archive film festival in 1983 (see fig. 5.1). Soon thereafter, they joined the faculty of Afro-American Studies for a semester, joint-teaching a class titled "Exploring the Black Aesthetic."[36]

College film series and symposia in the decade's latter half increasingly linked Gunn's picture to recent waves of Black filmmaking rather than to the reviled blaxploitation trend. At a 1984 UCLA conference, *Ganja & Hess* shared the bill with several LA rebellion movies, including works by Charles Burnett, Haile Gerima, and Billy Woodberry, and also with *Joe's Bed-Stuy Barbershop: We Cut Heads* (1983), a New York University thesis film that had charmed many viewers at the Lincoln Center's New Directors/New Films Festival.[37] This would not be the final time that Bill Gunn and Spike Lee shared space on a festival schedule. In 1986, the Blacklight Festival of Black International Cinema in Chicago hosted projections of *Ganja & Hess*, promoted as a "cult favorite," and Lee's groundbreaking feature, *She's Gotta Have It*, in its American premiere.[38] Thanks to just the sort of gradual, art house–focused buildup that Kelly-Jordan failed to deliver for *Ganja & Hess* thirteen years prior, *She's Gotta Have It* became a sleeper hit and jump-started a demand for Black films and directors not seen in Hollywood since the early seventies. This second Black movie boom would, in turn, furnish Lee with the cultural capital necessary to reanimate his predecessor's astonishing vision, a quarter-century later.

Writing *about* the Screen: Gunn's Black Picture Shows

As Gerald R. Butters observes in his book on Black film exhibition in Chicago in the seventies, a consensus has emerged over the causes of the Black movie boom's expiration.[39] Cinema historians most frequently point to industrial incentives: namely, the shift in Hollywood practice away from the targeting of niche audiences and toward a renewed concentration on the big-budget box office spectacular that ostensibly appeals to all demographics, African Americans included. During the early seventies, the key to the Black-themed picture's success had been its low production costs. According to James Murray, the average cost of a blaxploitation film made between 1970 and 1973 was just $700,000, whereas the average Hollywood budget of the time exceeded $1 million.[40] Keeping expenses to a bare minimum guaranteed the producers of Black-oriented movies a consistent return on investment: modest, to be sure, but one that generated steady, predictable profits.

Such a mode of production had no place in the New Hollywood of the post-*Jaws*, post-*Star Wars* (1977) era. The studios' new policy was to increase budgets while decreasing the number of films produced annually, counting on the bigger stars and more astounding special effects financed by the added expenditure to push grosses to record heights, and movies that could only be expected to bring in minimal rentals were deprioritized. Perhaps the phenomenal profits accrued by *Sweetback* and *Super Fly* discouraged the majors from improving the production values of their Black-centered product, as the precedent established by these two pictures promised millions in return for a risk of practically nothing. During the summer of 1972, smack in the middle of the boom, orders were given to studio teams working on Black film projects to, in Murray's words, "tighten tight budgets and shorten short production schedules." Even the budget of Motown's prestigious *Lady Sings the Blues* was trimmed from $5 million to $3 million.[41] After the perceived box office failure of *The Wiz* in 1978, budgeted at $23 million, Black movies were anathema in Hollywood. The dubious notion, as expressed by Bogle, that "no one was interested in seeing black movies" persisted for nearly a decade.[42]

In the absence of industrial support for Black cinema, the "crossover" film soared to a position of prominence. The rise of the crossover film, which "recouped commercial cinema's star system by relying on a few, isolated, big-name black stars for their box-office draw," and its supplanting of the blaxploitation film can be traced to two discoveries by the Hollywood studios about their audience: (1) whites do not patronize "Black" films, and (2) Blacks *do* readily attend "non-Black" films.[43] Specifically, *Variety*'s revelation that Black filmgoers accounted for 35 percent of the tickets sold for *The Godfather* and *The Exorcist* was, as Nelson George notes, an important milestone signifying Hollywood's heightening awareness of the crossover potential of "universal" genre pictures.[44] The success of these and other box office champs with the African American audience affirmed that the all-Black cast was not an essential ingredient for tapping the Black market.

"Cleola and me had just heard," Sam Dodd remarks at the beginning of *Rhinestone Sharecropping*, "that B. C. Pictures and five other major studios announced mainly through the columns that they were not planning to produce any more Black Pictures. . . . The industry will of course continue its effort to integrate what has unfortunately been referred to as the white film until an acceptable racial balance has been achieved to the satisfaction of the community at large. 'In other words, we're out of work,' I said to Cleola, who had just ordered a new top for her Mercedes."[45] The very real slump in the number of "Black Pictures" and opportunities for nonwhite film personnel, well underway by 1977 when *Rhinestone Sharecropping* is set, continued for several years beyond its 1981 publication date.⁴⁶ In this climate, Gunn was forced to redirect his creative talents to other media, though he doggedly continued until his death to seek backing for his own movies. Gunn's artistic projects after 1973, whether fully realized or merely theorized, verify that the cinema and his own stunted filmmaking career were never far from his thoughts. In fact, the author's first major undertaking after *Ganja & Hess*'s aborted distribution was a direct by-product of that very debacle.

Black Picture Show

Black Picture Show was made possible by the relationship its author had forged with Joseph Papp, the legendary founder of both the NYSF and the Public Theater. This mentorship paid artistic dividends in the seventies and eighties, when Papp produced two Gunn originals, *Black Picture Show* and *Rhinestone*, and directed a third, *The Forbidden City* (1989). One of the few New York stage producers willing to take a chance on edgy material from unheralded "ethnic" and women writers, Papp vowed to retain his commitment to diversity and social engagement when he was named head of theater at Lincoln Center in 1973.⁴⁷ Determined to attract younger and more racially integrated audiences, even at the risk of alienating the center's traditional base of subscribers, Papp solicited work from Ron Milner, Anne Burr, Ed Bullins, Gunn, and other innovative artists who specialized in what he referred to as "hunchbacked" plays: superficially flawed creations that nonetheless "address themselves to the major psychological problems of our times."⁴⁸ Like the 1974–1975 season opener, Burr's *Mert and Phil*, a tragicomedy about a failing working-class marriage, *Black Picture Show* was conceived as a provocation. Given the makeup of *Black Picture Show*'s audience, which one attendee conservatively estimated as seven-eighths white, it was, perhaps, inevitable that the result of this provocation was outrage from the paying customers rather than self-reflection.⁴⁹

Gunn completed *Black Picture Show* in a single month, though the idea behind it had been gestating for nearly ten years.⁵⁰ A brief rehearsal period commenced in early 1974, with roles for Edward Bell and *Super Fly*'s Ron O'Neal under the direction of Gilbert Moses; Max Roach was enlisted to write the score.⁵¹ By the time of the preview bookings at Philadelphia's Annenberg Center in late December, Gunn had taken over as director and Waymon as composer, and Dick Anthony Williams had been cast in the lead.⁵² *Black Picture Show* opened in January 1975, roughly one year into the reappraisal of

Ganja & Hess. Those New Yorkers who had caught Gunn's movie at MoMA or read about it in the *Village Voice* likely interpreted the play as a parable of the author's own misadventures in the movie business. Quentin Kelly's secretary, as well, assumed that the obnoxious movie producer character was a caricature of her boss; she advised Kelly to skip the play.[53]

Broadly speaking, *Black Picture Show* divides neatly into two nearly self-contained, highly disparate blocks of narrative. The protagonist's son, J.D., provides a general frame of reference at the start: speaking directly to the spectator, he relates the story behind his father's recent untimely death. As he begins, Waymon (on piano) and an onstage five-piece band perform the first of fourteen songs. The bandleader and sidemen, who are occasionally acknowledged by the characters, embody Gunn's commitment to an antinaturalist style, one that moves African American art beyond "the spectacularly popular dynamics of urban guerilla warfare and the Street Life as exclusive theoretical references," as Clayton Riley enthused.[54]

Black Picture Show's first act is a loose rewrite of "The Bedlamite," which borrows the short story's melancholy mood and its fixation on the enduring effects of domestic trauma. Again, the lead character is an aging widower named Alexander, whose failing memory prevents him from fully comprehending the reasons behind his current institutionalization and from meaningfully connecting with his only son. Yet, rather than a rest home, the Alexander of *Black Picture Show* resides in a mental hospital, a detail he himself does not grasp until the end of act 1. After the prologue, Alexander appears and flashes back to 1951, to a conversation with his mother, Lilly. When her husband returns to the house after a rendezvous with his lover, Lilly calmly shoots him and then overdoses on pills and gin. In the present, J.D. arrives for a visit. The son is also a filmmaker but a more commercially successful one, and the pair's mutual jealousies incite fierce bickering and attempted one-upmanship. Eventually, J.D. breaks it to his horrified father that he resides in an asylum, and the act ends with Alexander forced into a straitjacket by two attendants.

Act 1 foregrounds acts of homicide, suicide, and insanity, all in the course of establishing a general atmosphere of foreboding complemented by a suitably noir-like staging. In contrast, act 2 plays like a vicious comedy of manners, similar to Gunn's savage portrayal of the *haute bourgeoisie* in *The Landlord*, but with sights set squarely on Hollywood's cultural barbarism, as epitomized by those white studio power brokers who procure genuine talent for the express purpose of throwing it away. The action commences with the entrance of Rita, Alexander's young status-seeking second wife. She is the principal host for a dinner for Philippe de Valois, a sleazy film producer whom she hopes to persuade to give her husband a writing job, and his daft wife Jane, who spews inanities like "Black people are so fantastic. They're really what's happening. White people are so boring. I hope you take over. Everybody'll have fun."[55] The party's fifth wheel is J.D., who curtly asks the producer why his father is only worthy of hiring for a "colored picture."[56] In private, Alexander pleads with his son to quit interfering with his "hustle": "You're an ant fighting a landslide. You're a dog ripping a cat to pieces. It's all part of nothing! I need the money! Without the money I'm sport! Keep throwing the dog meat and he won't eat you!"[57] After J.D. leaves in disgust, Alexander completely surrenders his dignity. Taunted by Philippe, who lobs several thousand-dollar bills onto the floor, Alexander strips naked, revealing (in Gunn's original staging) a spangled codpiece.[58] He signs a contract, and the asylum attendants reappear; they tie up Alexander and Rita, who are promptly executed by their guests. The de Valoises place rhinestone masks on the corpses and exit.

A close reading of *Black Picture Show* suggests that the author's chief inspiration might have been his disastrous association with Warner Bros., more so than his recent liaison with Kelly-Jordan. Regardless of his secretary's suspicions, Kelly is probably only one of several models for the Philippe character. Another potential candidate is the executive from Warner Bros. who dropped by Gunn's office on the studio lot during *Stop*'s preproduction. Offering his encouragement, the man told Gunn, in a sentence reproduced almost verbatim in *Black Picture Show*, that, if *Stop* were a hit, he would never have to write another word. For Gunn, it was as if the interloper had delivered "a death threat."[59]

Black Picture Show contains a sprinkling of allusions to the *Ganja & Hess* saga, in particular, including a casual reference to Andy Warhol's *Interview*, one of the few periodicals to positively review Gunn's picture.[60] Most intriguingly, Gunn planned, up until a month before previews, to integrate actual scenes from *Ganja & Hess* into *Black Picture Show*. The playscript calls for a film to be projected at Rita and Alexander's soiree for the amusement of the de Valoises. Attributed to J.D., the movie is described in the stage directions as "a slow-motion film of hundreds of naked men, Black and White, being herded by armed guards."[61] Into this sequence, or possibly in its place, Gunn wanted to edit footage from *Ganja & Hess*, presumably to reinforce his identification with the character of J.D., the Black artist who quietly affirms his commitment to the "counter-revolution."[62] Although Kelly-Jordan Enterprises was contacted about rights authorization, no print of *Ganja & Hess* was ever used during *Black Picture Show*'s Lincoln Center run, perhaps due to excessive rental, projection, and duplication costs.[63] Still, Gunn's efforts to incorporate it indicate the film's significance to him as a real-world manifestation of *Black Picture Show*'s cautionary tale.

Unlike *Ganja & Hess*, *Black Picture Show* did receive solid reviews in the *Times* and the *Post*, and, eventually, it earned Audelco Awards for Best Play and Playwright and Tony nominations for Featured Actor (Williams) and Featured Actress (Linda Miller as Jane).[64] These accolades notwithstanding, some front-rank drama critics panned it on the grounds of "reverse racism." The *Time* reviewer objected to the farcically broad characterization of the de Valoises, as did *New York*'s John Simon, who despised "the obligatory white-hating scene . . . in which a bestial Hollywood producer and his whacked-out wife come to dinner and humiliate their black hosts while making white pigs of themselves."[65] Simon, among others, took exception to the insinuation that anyone other than Alexander was to blame for selling out his talents. Weary of this allegedly hackneyed trope, Brendan Gill in the *New Yorker* wondered: "Why is it worse for a black to sell out to a white than for a white to sell out to a white, or, for that matter, for a black to sell out to a black? Except on grounds of racial snobbery, with its implication that all blacks ought to be able to be counted on to behave more honorably than all whites, why should the question of color arise?"[66]

A brief pointed passage in *Black Picture Show* illustrates Gunn's own understanding of the changing stakes for African American artists amid the growing obsolescence of "race-neutral" attitudes. During the play's first act, Alexander recalls an excursion to a Harlem theater to see "a play I'd written when I was in revolt against a world I thought that I could change. And the play had come back at me again like my own voice crying Mother . . . Mother. . . . A young black woman thanked me [afterward] and said 'Because of you I no longer feel guilty because I am light-skinned.' And all I could say was beware."[67] The explicitness of the metaphor here, that years of regret have stripped *both* Alexander and Gunn himself of their remaining illusions about social progress, was precisely the problem for *Newsweek*'s Jack Kroll. "Gunn's mistake," he concludes, "was his attempt to write a 'black' play." Whereas Kroll, seemingly the only mass-market critic familiar with Gunn's previous publications, found a unique authorial voice at play in *All the Rest Have Died,* courtesy of its "raceless" monologues, *Black Picture Show* frustrated because it lazily rehashes nationalist platitudes. To Kroll, Alexander's caustic observation that "white heaven is colored hell" sounded like a playwright desperate to establish his radical bona fides, by way of "racial polemics," rather than uphold the standards of good dramaturgy.[68]

In light of Kroll's assertion, it is worth revisiting the microaggression that actually incites Alexander's rejoinder about "colored hell." "I'm sticking my neck out for you, you know," Philippe reminds his less-than-grateful subordinate:

> If you want to know the truth, my big money people don't want a Black writer.... The studio is a little worried that you might get too arty... this is a business [and] they want a fast moving script with lots of action. A beginning, a middle, and an end. And we want a Black script... down Black humor. Don't be afraid. Remember, in this case the Black is the rule, the White is the exception to the rule... nice, huh? You gotta create a fantasy world where Black is the driving force.[69]

Philippe's instructions underscore the preposterousness of the scenario that Alexander's script must follow. Such a world is unthinkable; it could *only* exist in the movies. Its very impossibility, in fact, is what endows Philippe and his industry coconspirators with their positions and their extravagances, which are maintained via the power to solicit and sell fantasies designed to pacify their publics. There are "no such things as Black films," J.D. insists.[70] More implicitly, Gunn argues that the adjective "Black" should be applied with extreme discretion, if at all, to mass-marketed texts like Hollywood movies (and Broadway plays), for which Black artists are always subject to financial and ideological constraints enforced by their corporate masters. Even in the best of circumstances, Black artists are still shut out of "the interlocking white worlds where money and decisions are made."[71]

Unsurprisingly, not even the eminence of Joe Papp could ensure continued exposure for underrepresented playwrights at Lincoln Center. Papp's initial stance as head of theater had been, as the *Times* reported, one of defiance: "If subscribers objected to his choice of plays... he would not change the plays, but he would change the subscribers." Two years later, following the hostile reaction (even from within the Lincoln Center administration) to *Black Picture Show,* Papp suddenly "renounce[d] his policy of presenting new American plays" in favor of a greater emphasis on "revivals of classics with guest stars."⁷² In June 1975, Papp quit his position altogether and returned to the Public Theater. "There's a reason why you don't see any serious Black plays," Riley angrily remarked after Papp's capitulation. "White people want Blacks to entertain and then go back home, they would prefer not to know the truth. As the ancient Roman messenger was killed for bringing bad news, they kill off serious Black playwrights like Bill Gunn ... because they don't like the news he brings."⁷³ The negative fallout from Gunn's prestigious "Black play" precisely proved its narrative point. Too much was at stake, the Philippe de Valoises of the world had too much to lose, for Papp to be allowed to follow through on his original vow.

Rhinestone, *Rhinestone Sharecropping*, and *The Forbidden City*

In an equally impudent response to *Black Picture Show*'s detractors, Gunn returned to nearly identical subject matter in his follow-up play, originally titled *Games*. This time out, a fresh encounter with movie industry toxicity served as Gunn's catalyst. *Games* is set mainly during a Hollywood script conference in which a Black screenwriter, tapped to adapt the life story of a Black football star, sees his work mangled beyond recognition by the biopic's duplicitous producer and a monstrous studio executive. In a plot twist that would be clipped from the final version, it is eventually revealed that Sam, the screenwriter, is in cahoots with the producer's Black mistress; together, they have been plotting to blackmail her lover. The writer ultimately realizes, however, that his determination to play both "games" simultaneously, flattering his white superiors while secretly undermining them, does not make him any less complicit with the system.⁷⁴

Before its arrival as a stage production, *Games* appeared in the form of a roman à clef under the title *Rhinestone Sharecropping*, which was issued in 1981 by Ishmael Reed's imprint I. Reed Books. Gunn viewed *Rhinestone Sharecropping* as a companion piece to *Black Picture Show*, the main distinction being that the play depicted the writer-hero "at home" whereas the novel shows him "at work."⁷⁵ The career humiliation that inspired *Rhinestone Sharecropping* had yet to occur when *Black Picture Show* debuted, but the play displays remarkable prescience about Gunn's immediate future when Alexander complains, "I have to write this very ... dangerous ... vile movie for a lot of money ... Cause I'm broke."⁷⁶ The "vile movie" that would derail Gunn's own Hollywood comeback was *The Greatest*, the film version of Muhammad Ali's ghostwritten autobiography, starring Ali as himself. Gunn was signed in late 1975 to adapt the recent best seller, following a vetting by the Nation of Islam and a trip to its headquarters in Chicago. Ali also gave his personal blessing after visiting Gunn and Waymon's house in West Nyack, though he retained rights of final approval over the screenplay.[77]

Within months of his abrupt firing from *The Greatest* in 1976, Gunn began converting the details of his unsavory experience into fiction, albeit fiction that stayed "very close to the truth of what happened" on the Ali project.[78] Several of the real-world influences on *Rhinestone Sharecropping* are only barely disguised in the novel. Like Gunn himself, Sam Dodd is hired to tell the life story of a major sports star, in this case "Big Mike" Rambow, gridiron legend. Dodd accepts the job reluctantly due to the miniscule offer from "B. C. Pictures"; he is paid $30,000 (and, providing that he is credited in the final cut, "a small percentage" of the net), a ridiculously low figure given that "the running rate for white writers of my caliber, more or less, is at least two hundred and fifty thousand or more."[79] Dodd subsequently elicits the ire of his producer, Cubby Steinbeck—a British transplant, just like *The Greatest* producer John Marshall—and the studio executives by submitting abnormally long scripts. (Gunn's own drafts of the Ali biopic ran to 262, 220, and 149 pages.)[80] "A hundred and fifty page script is just asking not to make the movie!" the studio boss seethes. "Who wants to sit through two and a half hours of Black bullshit."[81] Ultimately, Steinbeck, the film's director, and two studio executives "negotiate" a plethora of cuts to Dodd's script to ensure the movie comes in under budget.

In the end Dodd is fired by B. C. Pictures in favor of a "name" white writer, just as Gunn was thrown off *The Greatest* and replaced by Ring Lardner Jr., who received sole writing credit. The finished film's script was largely unchanged from Gunn's final revision, although Lardner, director Tom Gries, and/or Monte Hellman, who stepped in when Gries died of a heart attack during postproduction, ironed out the complex flashback structure that Gunn had employed.[82] Dodd is likewise forced to accept a deal that will net him merely $10,000, whereas his replacement receives a $450,000 payday, despite the fact that the final draft revises less than 30 percent of Dodd's prose.[83] "We were fighting for our dignity and self-respect," Waymon recalls of Gunn's impasse with Columbia. "It's the *subtleties* of racism that really get you: the invisible knives and guns. You can't see them, but they're slicing you up. It makes some people so angry and bitter that they never overcome it."[84]

Rechristened as *Rhinestone*, the story of Sam Dodd also served as the basis of a stage musical, in accordance with Gunn's original conception. Directed by the author and featuring a Waymon score, *Rhinestone* premiered in November 1982 at the Richard Allen Center on West Sixty-Second Street. The center, under the leadership of founder Hazel J. Bryant, was an important sponsor of the late-career theatrical endeavors of Gunn and his friends Kathleen Collins and Duane Jones. *Rhinestone*, which Bryant personally produced, was generally commended for its "technically superior" presentation on a middling budget; its first half, in particular, drew applause from the *Village Voice* for its effervescent choreography and vocal performances from cast members Joe Morton, Joe Seneca, and Jackée Harry.[85] But whereas some mainstream reviewers had grudgingly admired the bruising repartee in *Black Picture Show*, most seemed to resent having to sit through the torrent of abuse and "grievance-venting" supposedly flung about in the newer work, which the *Times*'s Frank Rich likened to "spending nearly three hours staring into a gaping wound."[86] Following the conclusion of *Rhinestone*'s "limited showcase" at the Allen center, Waymon's production company unsuccessfully sought partners to help finance a longer off-Broadway run and a potential soundtrack album.[87] Investors were possibly put off, however, by the subject matter, which, by 1983, must have seemed outdated, given the play's promotion as an examination of "the true meaning of 'blaxploitation' in the entertainment industry."[88]

The balance of Gunn's playwriting efforts in the eighties steered clear of the scathing film-industrial critique at the center of both *Black Picture Show* and *Rhinestone*, concentrating instead on troubled family histories. *Family Employment* was submitted to Papp in 1985 with Gunn's handwritten addendum: "Is there such a thing as a comedy-, murder-, drama-horror play?"[89] The synopsis, prepared by the NYSF, suggests a return to the bloodletting that pervades *Ganja & Hess*, elevated to delirious heights reminiscent of Mario Bava's protoslasher epic *A Bay of Blood* (1971): "the family of a successful Negro American journalist commits mayhem and murder on a voodoo-soaked Caribbean island. By the end of the play, the only survivor is the single granddaughter: her uncle has killed her grandfather and her mother, her mother has killed the grandfather's new wife, and uncle and mother have earlier killed (intending to kill their father) their father's secretary (male)."[90] *Family Employment* was scheduled for production at the Public Theater following Gunn's death, but this plan was shelved after

Papp's own passing in 1991.[91] Nor did anything become of *Renaissance*, also completed in 1985. Like *Black Picture Show*, *Renaissance* is about a father and son in show business; like *Rhinestone*, it surveys the milieu of African American popular culture in the early twentieth century, in this instance the Harlem Renaissance of the twenties.[92] In its period detail and its focus on intergenerational relationships and the lives of artist-protagonists, this unproduced script represented something of a dress rehearsal for Gunn's final publicly exhibited work.

Opening at the Public Theater the day after the playwright's death, *The Forbidden City* provoked one final round of vituperation from the mainstream critical establishment, which recycled many of the complaints that it had lodged against Gunn's writing for three decades. *The Forbidden City*, the story of a maladjusted middle-class Black family in 1936 Philadelphia and the abuse inflicted by the matriarch, played by Gloria Foster in an Obie-winning performance, on her sensitive son, was predictably denigrated as "all too obviously a playwright's revenge *in excelsis* on Mom."[93] Its excessive psychologizing made it appear overly derivative of Tennessee Williams, whom critics had accused Gunn of ripping off since *Marcus in the High Grass*.[94] Tellingly, white reviewers also regarded *The Forbidden City*'s premise as totally implausible. John Simon, then embroiled in controversy for his quixotic crusade against color-blind casting in the New York theater, registered disbelief that *any* African American family might have lived comfortably during the depths of the Great Depression.[95]

Certainly, Michael Feingold assured his *Voice* readers, had Gunn not been seriously ill during *The Forbidden City*'s development, he would have cleared up the play's many "undigested ambiguities." It seems rather more likely that Gunn reveled in its surrealistic touches, such as the frequent quoting, by all characters in every imaginable context, of the verse of African American poet Paul Laurence Dunbar. The second act climaxes in a crescendo of absurdity, via the sudden revelation of the son as "a literary genius, an advanced drinker, and a sexual prodigy" and a closing soliloquy spoken by the fully grown ghost of a brother who died in infancy.[96] For the entirety of his creative life, Gunn had battled against the preconceived notions of (white) self-appointed authorities on how his (Black) creations would and should behave, in all manner of dramatic situations. Though *The Forbidden City* was not intended to be his swan song, Gunn must have relished this final opportunity to needle the guardians of proper art making and standards of imaginative expression.

Writing (and Acting) *for* the Screen: Gunn's Last Picture Shows

If playwriting afforded Gunn the ability to flex his creative muscles after *Ganja & Hess*, writing for television provided a way of paying the bills. The various teleplay assignments that Gunn was offered almost invariably required Black protagonists; they also tended to conceptualize Blackness as something reducible to the status of a social problem, to be neutralized to soothe white anxieties. Though these commissions need not be condemned out of hand as instances of Gunn cynically "writing Race for money," as Sam Dodd might have characterized them, Gunn seemingly put little of his own artistic personality into these scripts. One possible exception to this rule was "Sojourner," a fictionalized biography of Sojourner Truth. The subject of this well-received telecast, which aired in March 1975 as part of the second season of CBS's Bicentennial-themed anthology show, *The American Parade*, may have resonated deeply with Gunn, as his mother had acted in a radio play about the beloved abolitionist when he was a boy.[97]

In the seventies, Gunn mostly scripted single episodes of established or anticipated shows rather than develop his own series ideas. Typically, the anticipated shows never came to fruition. One that did was *Watch Your Mouth!* a National Educational Television–produced series for PBS, which was funded by a grant from the Department of Health, Education, and Welfare. Gunn was one of six writers contracted to supply scripts for this "comedy-drama on language usage," set in a racially and ethnically mixed high school classroom supervised by an English teacher played by Joe Morton.[98] Gunn accepted purely commercial bids from television producers into the next decade, the most ambitious of which was a ten-hour miniseries about African American troops in World War I. At the time of his death, Gunn had finished a research "bible" and four of six installments of *Men of Bronze*, which was ultimately abandoned.[99] The same destiny awaited *The Lena Horne Show*, a proposed showcase for the iconic entertainer, developed by Bill Cosby and *The Cosby Show* executive producers Marcy Carsey and Tom Werner. Gunn was hired as head writer for *The Lena Horne Show*, which Werner promised would, like the smash hit *Cosby Show*, "celebrate the small moments of life" while simultaneously capitalizing on its star's larger-than-life magnetism.[100] The participation of Horne, playing herself, signified a return to a milieu Gunn knew well but that was almost entirely absent from broadcast television: the world of the Black bourgeoisie, of those who, like Hess Green, "know about old furniture, azaleas, and . . . can order their wine in French."[101] Unfortunately, the series never reached the production stage.

As noted in previous chapters, several Gunn narratives are built around the subjectivity of what Marlo David calls a "blues woman" character, an independent, sexually emancipated woman whose desires are foregrounded. Marlene Clark's roles in *Stop* and, especially, *Ganja & Hess* exemplify this persona within Gunn's original works. The author also explored more literal embodiments of the blues woman in narratives based on the lives of Black female performing artists, including his projected Bessie Smith biopic and, to a lesser degree, *The Lena Horne Show*. Not all of his subjects were famous, and, perhaps as a consequence, Gunn found no takers for his screenplay *Jeanne Duval*, the story of the Haitian-born dancer who was Charles Baudelaire's longtime partner, nor was he able to sell PBS's *American Playhouse* on his treatment about Elizabeth Cotten, a ninety-three-year-old folk-blues guitarist.[102] One of these scripts did get made, reportedly: a documentary on the life of jazz singer Alberta Hunter. Gunn is credited by some as director and producer on the BBC's five-part documentary *The Alberta Hunter Story 1900–1950* (1982), but whether he did anything other than cowrite each episode (with Chris Albertson) is uncertain.[103]

Personal Problems, Volumes 1 and *2*

Gunn's major television initiative of the eighties was executed under conditions that could scarcely have been more different from those that (almost) birthed *The Lena Horne Show*. Granted, *Personal Problems* was also a "commission" of sorts. Its basic premise, story elements, lead characters, and even some of the dialogue had been worked out prior to Gunn's association. Its formal qualities, particularly its editing rhythms and narrative ambiguities, confirm the input of its director, to be sure. Yet, the form of *Personal Problems* also implies a readiness on Gunn's part to relinquish some of the hard-earned creative control to which he had become accustomed. In part, this alteration of his established methods and preoccupations was prompted by the technical drawbacks of shooting on video in the late seventies and early eighties. More pertinently, it was mandated by the serial's very conception as a communal enterprise and its consequent dependence on a partnership grounded in trust among equals.

The primary force behind *Personal Problems* was Ishmael Reed, the acclaimed poet and novelist. Reed, Steve Cannon, and Joe Johnson, compatriots within the Umbra collective of Black New York writers, cofounded a publishing house specializing in works by nonwhite authors; *Black Picture Show* had been one of its first releases. Inspired by various artist friends who kept phoning him to vent their daily aggravations, Reed pitched to Cannon an idea for a Black-acted, Black-produced soap opera, to be set amid New York's working-class African American population.[104] In keeping with the melodramatic traditions of the soap format, *Personal Problems* would chronicle the day-to-day interactions of its subjects. However, Reed refused to dwell on the racial indignities his characters might conceivably endure, as he objected to the prevalence of such conceptions of African American life in the mass media. "The kind of thing that is acceptable to the media these days," he vented, "is for blacks to write about how much they suffer." Echoing Gunn's public statements about the limitations imposed on Black filmmakers by the social uplift model, Reed reminded his readers that pain "isn't the *only* emotion available to people. There's no need to glorify it."[105]

Even before Gunn joined the project, a preliminary version was produced in another medium: radio. This audio-only edition of *Personal Problems* was developed by Reed, Cannon, and a cast of three: playwright Walter Cotton, who doubled as producer; Vertamae Grosvenor, best known as the author of *Vibration Cooking: Or, the Travel Notes of a Geechee Girl*, a classic of African American culinary anthropology; and veteran actor James Wright, whose career highlights included minor parts in the legendary "Voodoo *Macbeth*," Orson Welles's 1936 Black-cast staging of the Shakespeare classic at Harlem's Lafayette Theatre, and the lead role in *Souls of Sin* (1949), one of the last "race movies." Working from a rough treatment of Reed's devising, Grosvenor, Cotton, and Wright structured their characters—Johnnie Mae Brown, her husband Charles Brown, and Father Brown, respectively—through improvised dialogues; these recorded conversations were then "transcribed, edited and re-performed."[106] The audio episodes were disseminated on cassette tapes by Reed, Cannon, and Johnson Communications, but most listeners would have heard them broadcast over the airwaves in New York on Cannon's regular program on WBAI or in the San Francisco Bay area on KQED.[107]

Using a $4,000 grant from the National Endowment for the Arts in 1978, Reed and Cannon took the first steps toward translating their vision of "diversity within the working poor" to the small screen.[108] They hired Gunn, who expanded the first radio episode of *Personal Problems*, a short vignette set at the Browns' breakfast table, into a forty-minute video. This "rough video draft" was shot on three-quarter-inch U-matic tape, edited, and then shopped to PBS; it was also shown at the San Jose Film Festival and in arts venues in or near New York state, including Reed's temporary home base of Dartmouth College.[109] PBS was not interested, no doubt partly because of the format's inherent technical weaknesses, circa 1979. The pilot's sound mix is fairly haphazard, and its images often appear to "smear" on figure movement and lighting adjustments. The analog tapes also proved highly susceptible to distortion, and they decayed with the passage of time. Gunn had strong reservations about video for these reasons, yet, in the end, he found ways to adapt his visual aesthetic to the medium's technological limitations, forging an analogy between "the granular, slightly soiled quality of the video image," as described by Howard Hampton, and "the degradation and constraints of particular domestic spaces."[110]

Like Reed, Gunn gradually embraced the democratizing aspects of video and what that meant for African American filmmakers who wanted to produce art independent of capitalist control. The National Endowment for the Arts sanctioned this objective as well, and, in the fall of 1980, the agency kicked in funds for a further augmentation of Gunn's "first draft," which would become known as *Personal Problems, Volume 1*.[111] The cast and crew reconvened in 1981 to make *Volume 2*, without Wright, who passed away in the interim; the resultant death of his character became a major story point of the second and final installment.

Equipped with a projected budget of $30,000 for *Volume 1*, the producers increased staff to around thirty people.[112] Robert Polidori, an avant-garde filmmaker and fine arts photographer, joined the production as director of photography, and Carman Moore further elaborated on the original score he composed for the pilot. Writing and editing duties were shared by multiple cast and crew members; new actors, many of whom worked for scale, were brought in to invent or flesh out story lines.[113] As typical for a Gunn picture, the cast reflected a broad range of professional know-how. Seasoned performers such as Waymon, Leonard Jackson, and Gunn share the screen with novices like Michele Wallace, the Black feminist critic, and Reed himself, who has a memorable cameo as a Republican businessman who verbally spars with a condescending white radical (see fig. 5.2). Gunn gave even the amateur actors considerable freedom in creating their characters, trusting them to "build their own backstories and develop dialogue on the set" as Polidori let the camera run.[114] Cotton appreciated Gunn's effortless capacity

Figure 5.2 In a cameo as the mysterious "Mr. Damien," Gunn mingles with quarreling lovers Raymon (Sam Waymon) and Johnnie Mae (Vertamae Grosvenor) at a hotel room party. *Personal Problems* (DVD), Kino Lorber Films.

to "reassure the crew and the actors with his humor when they encountered the usual problems associated with a small-budget production."[115]

The reviews welcoming *Personal Problems*'s recent rerelease frequently comment on the meandering quality of its plot and its numerous *temps morts*. Contrary to fashion, whether of 1980 or 2018 vintage, both episodes are saturated with tender moments of solo character introspection as well as utterly banal household and workplace activities. Thus, in its storytelling strategies, the serial outwardly appears to lack discipline. Yet, a comparison of the project's successive drafts substantiates that Gunn did impart greater clarity and focus to the narrative. This was a crucial objective, given the multiple lines of action and dozens of characters juggled across *Volumes 1* and *2*.

The aforementioned breakfast table exchange among Johnnie Mae, Charles, and Father Brown makes for an instructive example. The original radio version, developed by Reed and the actors from their improvisations, established the scene's basic narrative components: Johnnie Mae cooks breakfast for Charles; he grills her about her late night out; she informs her husband and his father that her ne'er-do-well brother Bubba and his wife are coming to stay with them indefinitely; Charles loses his temper. Comic relief is provided by the characters' tangential banter about old movies. Charles remarks that, while waiting up for his wife, he fell asleep watching *The Guns of Navarone* (1961), prompting Johnnie Mae to inquire why that film always seems to be on TV. When Charles shifts topics to an investment opportunity, Johnnie Mae strains to recall the Sidney Poitier movie with a plotline concerning a shady financial arrangement. She finally remembers the title, *A Raisin in the Sun* (1961), only to be contradicted by Father Brown, who misidentifies the film as *Cabin in the Sky* (1943), which he obliviously refers to as "Tavern in the Sky."

All of these details are present in the radio pilot, the "rough video draft," and *Personal Problems, Volume 1*. Yet, the evolution of their presentation suggests much reflection on Gunn's part on how best to translate this material to a visual medium. The audio-only draft comes off as effortlessly naturalistic, with the actors' understated performances nicely complementing their characters' rambling conversation styles and techniques of subtle deflection. The middle draft deviates very little from the radio prototype, narratively speaking, but the performances are marred by an overreliance on shouting to underline the major points of exposition, perhaps in a concession to the primitive sound recording setup. The polished final draft indicates that Gunn learned from and took steps to correct the second version's shortcomings and heighten the viewer's empathy for the characters. Extraneous detail is trimmed, and the couple's back-and-forth quarreling is delivered with more nuance. Moreover, *Volume 1*'s breakfast scene does not take place until an hour into the ninety-minute episode, following a lengthy sequence that establishes the Johnnie Mae character as a complex protagonist with a many-sided personality: she is, we learn, a South Carolina native, a poet, a nurse who works long hours at Harlem Hospital, and a woman discontented with her life and marriage, who seeks solace in an affair with Raymon, a slick-talking musician. By the time Johnnie Mae and Charles finally share their first long scene together, we have a firm understanding of her frustrations, and the suspense surrounding the implied questions about the spouses' future is enhanced.

Despite the narrative economy present *within* individual scenes in *Personal Problems*, Gunn elsewhere applies his editorial sensibilities in ways that flout standard storytelling goals. The spatial and temporal relationships *between* scenes in the sixty minutes leading up to the breakfast are as enigmatic as those found in any stretch of *Ganja & Hess*. Gunn cuts freely among documentary-style interviews of Johnnie Mae by an unidentified offscreen interrogator, ambient shots of Manhattan streets and lyrical glimpses of the scenery off the Taconic State Parkway, a song performed for Johnnie Mae by Raymon, and several unmotivated flashbacks and flash-forwards. *Volume II* carries over many of the ambiguous techniques of *Volume I* and even resurrects some of the *same* ambiguities, including a brief scene in which Johnnie Mae discovers Charles in bed with his lover; the incident appears in both episodes, but its status as objective or subjective is never cleared up. Inserts that verge on poetic abstraction are interspersed throughout both volumes, also, as exemplified by the close-up of multihued flowers that closes *Volume I*, which evokes a line from Johnnie Mae's poem about a "blazing field of colors running amok, dancing."

"From moments where people walk across screen with a hazy, almost apparition-like softness, to the use of music, Gunn's film looks incredibly strange to the 2018 eye, sans powerful iPhone cameras or superficial Snapchat filters."[116] Joshua Brunsting's contemporary impressions encapsulate the alien otherworldliness of *Personal Problems*'s style, the product of both antique technology and an aesthetic that privileges not just ambiguity but polyphony (see fig. 5.3). The independent "race cinema" of the twenties and thirties is, perhaps, the most appropriate referent. (Indeed, Wright's casting was a conscious means of cultivating this association, as Reed later verified.)[117] *Personal Problems*'s "home movie" aesthetic recalls the freewheeling visual and aural practices of Oscar Micheaux's first talkies: hybrid works, produced during a moment of technological upheaval, that explore new storytelling possibilities while simultaneously observing the established conventions of the domestic melodrama genre. Furthermore, like Micheaux's surviving silent films, *Personal Problems* highlights an impressively diverse range of personalities from the broader Black community, or what Pearl Bowser and Louise Spence refer to as the "heterogeneous ensemble" with regard to Micheaux's fiction. Neither of these pioneers, Gunn nor Micheaux, were content to stock their movies with characters who simply fulfilled the mandate for "positive images."[118]

As Nicholas Forster notes, the early distribution history of *Personal Problems* further calls to mind Micheaux, who personally transported his films all around the country, often reworking and revising them to fit the upcoming exhibition situation.[119] These tactics became necessary for Reed

Figure 5.3 The bustling cityscape smears surrealistically across the video frame as Johnnie Mae's brother Bubba (Thommie Blackwell) departs the train station. *Personal Problems* (DVD), Kino Lorber Films.

as well, owing to the disinterest of national networks and cable channels in airing a Black-cast soap opera. PBS was the most logical platform for *Personal Problems*, based on the connotations of high art and diverse representation attached to the project. But Reed was informed by public television executives that PBS already "had enough films of such nature already," though in his opinion the network's commitment to Black-centered programming was evident solely in its endless recycling of specials about crack addiction.[120]

Undaunted, Reed traversed the nation for the remainder of the eighties, showing one or both volumes of *Personal Problems* at any venue that would accept it. Following a world premiere at the Centre Georges Pompidou in Paris in November 1980, *Volume 1* had its domestic unveiling a few weeks later at the New School's Parsons School of Design before a sold-out crowd populated by New York's "Black artistic and intellectual elite."[121] Though some in attendance were "baffled" by the episode's experimental structure, an *Amsterdam News* critic proclaimed the work to be "a powerful and historic statement," one that "ought to be preserved in libraries as a milestone in the effort of Black people to project a truer version of our own image via the video media."[122] Audiences at subsequent screenings agreed. "We have received many comments from the audiences who've listened to or viewed the 'Personal Problems' series," Reed documented in an early press release, "the most persistent of which seems to be that until 'Personal Problems' these audiences had never seen black people as they really are" in film or commercial television.[123]

Such responses certified that an audience hungry for more "authentic" representations existed, and Reed exhausted every option to locate that viewership. *Personal Problems* was shown at museums, festivals, universities, academic conferences and video centers, and on local TV stations, even a few PBS affiliates. (Reed's publishing imprint also marketed videocassettes of *Personal Problems* for home consumption.) Yet, without the involvement of a major distribution network, the producer's reach only extended so far. At the start of his odyssey, Reed expressed cautious optimism for the future of Black image-making, positing video as the instrument that could circumvent "the strangle-hold major communications networks have on the means to free expression."[124] The technology was quickly revealed to be a double-edged sword, however. Although video enabled more minority voices to be heard, its rapid degradation required long-term investment for continued maintenance and upgrading to new formats. Accordingly, when *Personal Problems*'s exhibition prospects dried up in the late eighties, the tapes were left to languish. Almost no one saw Gunn's final work for the screen for nearly three decades.

Losing Ground and *Territory*

After completing *Personal Problems, Volume 2*, Gunn told Reed, "Now I know that I can do my own movies."[125] Gunn was energized by the project and took pride in its completion, certainly, but he had never really doubted his ability to make films, with or without the assistance of the studios or the major independents. He had continued to field outside offers in the decade following *Ganja & Hess*'s withdrawal, starting with *The Afrikan Sun*, an Afrofuturist sci-fi thriller about a sixteenth-century West African king who is reborn in the present day as "a Black Messiah who will lead the descendants of his tribes [sic] people back to their rightful home."[126] Gunn's exploration in *Ganja & Hess* of the continuities between the early modern slave trade and present-day neocolonialism perhaps convinced *The Afrikan Sun*'s neophyte producers of his suitability for this tantalizing albeit unmade project. More typically, Gunn was approached to write and/or direct biographies of Black historical figures. In addition to *The Greatest*, Gunn was linked to both a proposed film about the spiritual leader Father Divine (for Warner Bros., no less) and a Marian Anderson biopic to be produced by Edward Bell.[127]

With many of his post–*Ganja & Hess* film projects stalled in development, Gunn made an unheralded return to the cinema as an actor in Kathleen Collins's independent feature debut. *Losing Ground* constituted the first official screen partnership between the longtime friends and neighbors following several theatrical collaborations: Collins had served as assistant director on *Black Picture Show*, and Gunn acted, alongside his *Losing Ground* costars Seret Scott and Duane Jones, in Collins's 1982 off-Broadway play *The Brothers*.[128] *Losing Ground* tracks the personal journey of Sara (played by Scott), a straitlaced philosophy professor who seeks out the nature of ecstatic experience. Sara's painter husband, Victor, cajoles her into joining him for a month-long retreat in an upstate New York bedroom community, where he spends his days sketching, drinking wine, and flirting with the local Puerto Rican women. Though he himself enjoys a fling with a young artist's model, Victor is incensed when Sara invites to their summer rental an eccentric unemployed actor (Jones), her colleague in a student film in which she has impulsively agreed to appear. *Losing Ground*'s talented cast, which also includes Billie Allen, Gunn's costar from the 1954 special "Carmen in Harlem," is uniformly terrific but Gunn's performance stands out. As Victor, Gunn naturally projects the air of careless relaxation assumed by male artists as a birthright. Yet, while Victor disgraces himself through his petulant immaturity and shabby treatment of his wife, his irrepressibility is also manifest in more constructive ways, as evidenced by his sporadic and joyful bursts of dancing. These multiple dimensions make for both a challenging obstacle to Sara's self-discovery and a rewarding character study on their own terms. Perhaps owing to such complexity, in addition to the foregrounding of its female subject's "interiority" (a constant preoccupation across Collins's filmic and literary output, as numerous scholars have theorized), *Losing Ground* did not receive national circulation nor substantive attention until its 2015 restoration by Milestone Film and Video.[129]

Collins and Gunn must have seemed to some as an unlikely duo on the surface, given their dissimilar backgrounds. Collins, who was Gunn's junior by thirteen years, grew up in a religious household and studied religion and philosophy at Skidmore College. A civil rights activist, she demonstrated no real interest in the cinema until she discovered the French New Wave while studying at the Sorbonne in the midsixties. When she met Gunn, Collins had established herself as one of the few African American film editors in New York and would soon take a job at City College teaching screenwriting and film history.[130] Despite their divergent career paths, Gunn and Collins shared many affinities as artists, including a digressive approach to storytelling. As recounted by Reed, one of the PBS staff directors who rejected *Personal Problems* derogatively categorized the two filmmakers as students of "the Hudson River school of cinematography, because of their cinematic style—a style that took its time to linger over a flower, a body of water, some interesting light, a walk through the woods, a camera that moseyed over elegant dinner scenes, or paused on a piece of sculpture."[131] The pair also bonded over their interest in African American representations that confounded Hollywood stereotypes. *Losing Ground*'s milieu is a world of artists and intellectuals, of existentialist debate and bohemian flights of fancy. This reorientation made the story almost indecipherable to white audiences and critics, a phenomenon Gunn had previously experienced with *Ganja & Hess*. He later divulged an infuriating yet illustrative anecdote about a white woman who withdrew her offer of a shooting location for *Losing Ground* after reading Collins's script. "Well Kathy, I'm confused," the woman confessed. "These people aren't black."[132]

The persistence of such attitudes steeled Gunn's commitment to making his own films without input from white-controlled channels of financing. In one particularly ambitious scheme, Gunn explored the possibility of forming a production company to make a picture titled *Friendly Warning*. Gunn, Waymon, and Kanefsky were to serve as chairman of the board, president, and secretary, respectively, while several affluent African Americans, including Max Roach and disc jockey Eddie O'Jay, would be investors.[133] Kanefsky recalls being the sole white person present at a Brooklyn meeting for potential stakeholders, all of whom were staunchly militant Black nationalists despite their wealth.[134] In 1982, Waymon pitched *Friendly Warning* to Chiz Schultz, proposing a budget of $250,000 and confirming the participation of cinematographer Ed Lachman and soul music legend Gil Scott-Heron, who promised to contribute a theme song.[135]

Another of Gunn's original screenplays, *Territory*, came much closer to realization than *Friendly Warning*. *Territory* was not supposed to be a capstone or a summary statement of artistic purpose, though it did revisit the interracial subject matter and satirical brashness of Gunn's first screenplays. In fact, the earliest surviving version of *Territory*, titled *The Rain Forest*, was probably written around 1968. The social milieu of the story is that of protest during the late sixties, of Black Panther marches and New Left demonstrations against the Vietnam War policies of Lyndon Johnson and Dean Rusk. Various hip, sixties-era Manhattan hotspots, including Arthur, the discotheque, and Paraphernalia, the boutique, are also referenced in this initial draft.[136]

Gunn's script also features a number of soundtrack and editing directions that call to mind the freewheeling New Wave–influenced strategies favored by New Hollywood filmmakers like Hal Ashby, who generously employs such devices in *The Landlord*. Among the unmotivated and ostentatious techniques sprinkled throughout *The Rain Forest* are nonsimultaneous voice-over narration, incongruous nondiegetic music, freeze-frames, direct address to the camera, and alternating color and black-and-white film stocks. Appropriately, the story's white protagonist, Max, is an experimental filmmaker assembling, as he vaguely describes to his well-heeled parents, "some non-objective . . . film. I don't know what it'll be yet. . . . I don't know . . . It's very important . . . to me." "Is it something new wave . . . one of those subway films?" his mother asks nervously.[137] Upon reworking *The Rain Forest* in the early seventies, Gunn prefaced his amended script with an evocative excerpt from Richard Schickel's *Life* magazine review of Arthur Penn's *Alice's Restaurant* (1969): "It is important not to go to the New American Movie expecting to see the Old American Movie. What is happening is something like what happens in a piece of jazz music. The plot functions rather like the melody in jazz . . . It is less important than the improvisatory flights it suggests and encourages."[138] This epigraph implicitly advances two important pleas to the script's reader: to accept *The Rain Forest*'s episodic structure as a legitimate artistic method, no less than the guiding principles behind free-form jazz; and, more important, to recognize that this method had already been legitimated by mainstream reviewers, when applied to specifically white stories.

The early seventies revision of Gunn's story, retitled *Territory*, necessarily dropped the late sixties signifiers, such as the demonstrations and militant meetings, and reduced the number of Vietnam references. The protagonists themselves have not changed that much, however, which makes them already seem poignantly anachronistic, like casualties of the sixties trying to come to terms with recent cultural convulsions. Psychologically speaking, the main characters are ciphers, though in this updated draft their detachment functions like a mechanism of self-preservation. Max is now identified as a multimedia installation artist who labors tirelessly on his impending solo exhibition (at a thinly disguised MoMA). Like the Caucasian antihero of *Stop*, Max is the central variable in an interlocking network of intra- and interracial romantic couples. An additional parallel can be drawn with Gunn's characterization of Elgar Enders in *The Landlord* in that Max, like Elgar, has clearly "grown up casual." Yet *Territory*'s investigation of its protagonist's unexamined privilege is not nearly as gentle as the corresponding investigation in *The Landlord*. The serrated edge applied by Gunn to this later revision makes *Territory*, as declared in an NYSF reader report, a more penetrating commentary on "me decade" ennui and alienation, a "devastating portrait of the upper- and middle-class people of contemporary America: affluent, casually jaded, unable to find any meaning in their lives and not really attempting to search very hard."[139]

Territory is primarily concerned with Max's relationships with other whites. Maggie, his spoiled mistress, refuses to leave her husband, whom she regards with open contempt. She eventually decides that she has little use for Max either and abandons him at a discotheque, leaving with a man she meets on the dance floor.[140] Max is occasionally obliged to indulge his parents, particularly his self-centered mother, by dining with them at the tony Colony Club in Midtown or, in the surreally derisive opening scene, accompanying them to an equine mating exhibition at a private stable.[141] Max's only apparent friend, his gallery assistant Duff, is a barely functioning stoner who coasts through life without consequences for his bad choices, whether spiking the hors d'oeuvres with hashish at Max's MoMA opening or allowing his precocious eight-year-old daughter to burn his marriage license, in tribute to Isadora Duncan.[142]

The display of Gunn's characteristic verbal brilliance in these sections partially conceals the deeply pessimistic undercurrent that propels the screenplay's secondary, "Black" story line. This line is built around the story of Pierre, a reluctant hitman for an underground revolutionary organization, and his live-in girlfriend Ina, an actor and former lover of Max. Though Max is the disaffected artist-protagonist of this particular Gunn text, Pierre is clearly its author-surrogate: a moody intellectual who hauls around a copy of Camus's *The Fall*, an important intertext for Gunn's fiction.[143] At a meeting with his contact in a Central Park café, Pierre is informed that he has been selected to carry out an immediate political assassination. Robotically, he heads for the men's room at the Central Park Zoo, where he shoots a Black congressional candidate, a "James Farmer type," and flees.[144] The likelihood that Pierre is, in fact, a sketch of the author during the late sixties is raised by Gunn's subsequent acknowledgment that he found himself "heavily into this activism thing" for about a year, but that his involvement only led to paralysis: "I couldn't do anything; I had to withdraw."[145] Pierre, too, makes a vague commitment to the "revolution" but discovers he cannot in good conscience surrender his individual identity for the sake of a collective political program. Gunn was able to walk back from the brink, but Pierre gives in to fate; he is shot down in the street when he ignores a police officer's command to halt for questioning.

As with so many Gunn scripts, *Territory* neglects to expose the causes underlying crucial effects, thereby making character motives highly enigmatic. In *The Rain Forest*, Pierre's contact provides an explicit justification for his deadly assignment. "Every dope peddler...whoremaster...pimp... phoney black puppet politician the machine sends up here to keep the black people in line," he snarls, have "all got to go."[146] In the rewrite, no reason is given for the assassination that precipitates Pierre's existential crisis; rather, the act's very meaninglessness is foregrounded. Similarly, though Max and Pierre seem to be old friends, the circumstances through which they met are never explained. Possibly, they know each other through Ina, whose bed Max cynically returns to after Pierre's death.

The ambiguity surrounding the origins of their acquaintance is complicated by Max's eventual appropriation of Pierre's memory for use in a trendy art object. Pierre's first appearance in *Territory* comes when he unsuccessfully attempts to hail a taxi. As the image zooms in, Pierre argues with a cabbie stopped at a red light; when the light changes, the vehicle zips away, leaving the Black man caught in the middle of the street, surrounded by streaming traffic and unable to return to the sidewalk. A cut then reveals that Max has been filming the entire encounter from a nearby office building.[147] Later, when he learns of Pierre's death, Max obsessively replays his footage of the incident, freezing repeatedly on Pierre's look of resignation and juxtaposing it with "the fearful expression of the cab driver."[148] The resulting loop ends up as one of the dozens of modules in his sprawling museum piece, vividly described by Gunn as a "maze of neon constructions" and "moveable sculpture" projecting a "kaleidoscope of moving flesh," a hideous monstrosity that captivates the artist's obscenely wealthy patrons even as it assaults their senses.[149]

The feebleness of Max's attempt at memorializing his friend, which is understandably lost in this cacophony of sound and image, perhaps signifies a painful self-recognition on Gunn's part. The constituency of white "sophisticates" and intellectuals that disproportionately comprised Gunn's audience, who publicly supported institutions like MoMA and Lincoln Center, could really only relate to Black bodies and minds reduced to states of degradation. The endless repetition of Pierre's humiliation, captured without his consent as he stands trapped on a busy street, in close proximity to where he will be gunned down only days later, is a familiar exploitation of Black pain for the entertainment of a privileged white spectator. Max's repackaging and commodifying of Pierre's suffering for touristic consumption evokes J.D.'s carnivalesque introduction of his father's story in *Black Picture Show*: "For your use, your criticism and your perversion, I give you the last day of his life for your diversion!"[150] Yet, J.D. speaks with a heavy irony that masks the bitterness of experience. Max, who has a lifetime exemption from such experience, regards Black victimization as a career opportunity.

Though Joseph Papp expressed interest in doing *Territory* as "a TV play" in the midseventies, the property lay dormant for another decade.[151] When Gunn revived it once again, another round of modifications was due. According to a synopsis, the final iteration of *Territory* is set in the late seventies, after "the love generation has gone back to their Highballs." Max now runs the Film Department at MoMA and plans a retrospective of "video portraits of 'New York Life on Full Screen.'" One of his portrait subjects is the bullet-riddled body of Pierre, who Max photographs in the morgue, now identified as "what's left of the Black Revolution's foot soldiers."[152] In March 1985, this script was purportedly ready to film. Waymon invited Schultz to serve as line producer, having by that point received written commitments from a formidable lineup of actors: Keir Dullea, Joe Morton, Lonette McKee (later replaced by Carole Cole), Dorothy Tristan, and Geraldine Page, with whom Gunn had been friends since they performed together in *The Immoralist* in 1954. Waymon, serving as executive producer in order to avoid a repeat of the fractured relationship with upper management that plagued *Ganja & Hess*, notified Schultz that he was already entertaining offers from various distributors, including Paramount, Columbia, MGM/UA Home Video, Republic, Motown, and HBO.[153]

By October, it appeared as if an original Bill Gunn screenplay was about to go before the camera for the first time in thirteen years. *Variety* reported that preproduction was about to officially begin on Gunn's "romantic mystery-thriller." *Territory* would shoot for two weeks in New York and four in Canada on a budget of $1.5 million: a million less than Waymon's opening estimate, but nearly five times what was allocated for *Ganja & Hess*. Key technical and creative positions were filled: Lachman was to be director of photography, Isaac Hayes signed on to compose the score, and Nina Simone agreed to contribute a song.[154] Although preproduction stretched on for almost two years, Waymon maintains that *Territory* would have been made and, subsequently, distributed by New World Pictures if not for the unexpected death of Page, who improbably had become the package's most bankable actor thanks to her Oscar win for *The Trip to Bountiful* (1985).[155] With Page's death, *Territory* was consigned to the long regrettable list of abandoned Gunn movie ventures.

Territory's cancellation was a significant loss for an American "indie" cinema that was starting to come into its own but would, ultimately, prove to be nearly as exclusionary in its policies toward minority artists and audiences as the New Hollywood had been. It was, consequently, a sadly fitting end for a project that analogized Gunn's frustrations as a Black filmmaker in postsixties America, many of which stemmed from the limits imposed on both his audience and his funding bases. When the vogue for Black-themed pictures ended in the late seventies, as Gunn noted with dismay, many African American filmgoers supported the "racist movies" that Hollywood produced in their place, thereby removing the incentive for the studios to make Black films or hire Black creative personnel.[156] In this climate, Black independents could not count on white investment because their movies were generally not built around stereotypical depictions of African Americans. ("Nothing scares White Americans more than a complicated Negro.")[157] A few rich whites might put some money into noncommercial Black art, Gunn realized, but on the condition that "we stay submerged intellectually as a people." In marked contrast, no comparable restrictions were placed on the mostly white artists who benefited from the many "crazy white millionaires" willing to bankroll offbeat or unconventional cinema. Blacks with money, in the director's opinion, were of no use at all, because their inherent conservatism precluded their support of Black cultural production. Due to their self-segregation from Black creativity, Gunn warned, the Black American bourgeoisie was "calling down something on the heads of black people that is irrevocable. . . . I don't know how they talked themselves into the self-destructive stupidity they're wrapped up in."[158]

Judging by his late-career pronouncements on the state of the film business, Gunn surely had been worn down by the persistent grind of hustling for money. Yet, while his eighties interviews are loaded with skepticism, they are also punctuated by hopeful projections of what he still intended to achieve. ("I can make fifteen movies with a million dollars," he vowed after his *Personal Problems* experience.[159]) Though he harbored no delusions about the prospects for a new business model for African American cinema, Gunn occasionally sounded notes of wild optimism. In terms that come close to evoking the utopian vision laid out in James Murray's "A Futuristic Fable," Gunn foresaw progress to be made for the establishment of a Black-controlled motion picture industry, even though, as intimated by his chosen metaphor, it would require an almost superhuman level of commitment:

> I once believed—and I still believe it—that we are the 21st century people. . . . It's as though we have been given the potential, but that's all we have. . . . The thing I was saying about the Christ is that Jesus had the potential to become the Christ, so therefore it was already there. . . . The trip was already there but he just decided to take it. He was a man, just like you; it could have been anybody. . . . He said, "I have that potential and I'm going to fulfill that potential." And that's what I think we, as a people, have to do. But it's a terrible, terrible journey. It's not easy. You got to climb the seven moneyed medias. But it's there. It's there for you to do.[160]

CONCLUSION

Ganja & Hess *after Gunn,*
Gunn after Ganja & Hess

> I'm racking my brain.
> What was it James Baldwin said?
> When you finish crying, then what you gonna do? Get up. Get up.[1]
>
> —Bill Gunn, *Rhinestone Sharecropping*, 193.

IN THE FINAL TWELVE MONTHS OF HIS LIFE, Bill Gunn was haunted by premonitions of his own mortality. In July 1988, his longtime friend and collaborator Duane Jones died of cardiac arrest. Having acted in only three pictures (*Night of the Living Dead*, *Ganja & Hess*, and *Losing Ground*) in the first decade and a half of his screen career, Jones had just recently begun to accept movie roles again, mainly in low-budget, independent horror films. Yet, his focus remained the stage. During his lengthy tenure as artistic director of the Richard Allen Center for Culture and Art, Jones directed more than twenty plays, including revivals of *Black Picture Show* and Kathleen Collins's *The Brothers*.[2]

Just two months later, Collins herself passed away from breast cancer, after keeping her diagnosis a secret from even her children for nearly a year.[3] In the months before Collins's unexpected passing, she and Gunn had been mentoring a book project by his childhood friend and "spiritual sister," Jean Love Robinson, who lived across the street from the Gunns in West Philadelphia. As Robinson later recorded in correspondence with Chiz Schultz, Gunn was devastated by Collins's death, yet, "thru [sic] his tears he pleaded with me not to give up on our unfinished work."[4] Robinson's autobiographical novel, *How to Survive in Spite of Your Family*, was published in 1996 and is dedicated to the memories of Collins and Gunn. Of the latter, Robinson gratefully recalled his "last words on the phone to me from his hospital bed... 'Never give up, Jean. You can do it.'"[5]

When his father died, Gunn confided to scholar John Williams that he felt he, too, would not live much longer, even though Bill Sr. had reached the robust age of 98.[6] (Louise Gunn would outlive her son by six years.) By the time the Public Theater was readying *The Forbidden City* for its world premiere, Gunn was being treated for meningitis at Nyack Hospital. Schultz recalls that his friend's final illness was "very sudden, and it worsened quickly," and that Gunn was "furious that he was so sick," given all that he still wanted to accomplish.[7]

Bill Gunn passed away from encephalitis on April 5, 1989, three months before his sixtieth birthday. The memorial service was held twelve days later at Palisades Presbyterian Church, just a few miles from his Tappan residence. Max Roach performed, John Hoffmeister delivered the eulogy and Sam Waymon, the summation, and additional friends and loved ones read and offered testaments.[8] The portrait of Gunn printed on the service program had been originally snapped at a publicity photograph session for *Ganja & Hess*. Whereas Jones, Marlene Clark, and Richard Harris appear costumed in character in these oft reprinted stills, Gunn is decked out in a jean jacket and a wide-brimmed hat, smiling boyishly, looking more like a ranch hand than a movie director.

Writing in the *Village Voice* two weeks after Gunn's death, Greg Tate recounted the many efforts undertaken across two decades to deprive Gunn of the opportunity to make films at all. "The attempt to bury Bill Gunn," he reckoned, "began in his life." Referencing Gunn's late-career struggles, Tate explained the artist's inability after *Ganja & Hess* to obtain financial support by asking a pointed question: "What choice would a darkly brilliant Afrocentric gay aesthete empowered by the Hollywood director's chair have but to take all of us way, way, way the fuck on out?"[9] This was, needless to say, a journey that Hollywood did not wish to embark on, especially once the major studios began to reestablish control over production in the late seventies. Signs of Gunn's impact on commercial filmmakers are, therefore, difficult to discern outside of the innovations *Ganja & Hess* bequeathed to the vampire subgenre.

Gunn's significance as a model for Black independent filmmakers is decidedly more concrete, and it stands to increase in tandem with the renewed availability of his movies. As detailed previously, Manthia Diawara, in 1993, positioned *Ganja & Hess* as a paradigm of one strain of the post-sixties Black film aesthetic. The linear, heroic strain exemplified by *Sweet*

Sweetback's Baadasssss Song spawned countless "existentialist performances of Black people against policing, racism, and genocide," spanning from blaxploitation to the "hood" cycle of the nineties. Conversely, *Ganja & Hess*'s preoccupation "with the specificity of identity, the empowerment of Black people through mise-en-scène, and the rewriting of American history," was reflected in the cyclical narration and symbolism of *Killer of Sheep, Losing Ground,* and *Daughters of the Dust,* the latter of which even "quotes" the image of Meda in his tree perch in Hess's backyard.[10]

Gunn's influence also extends to numerous filmmakers whose highly idiosyncratic creations typically escape the notice of casual cinephiles. These artists value *Ganja & Hess* for its indifference to custom. Dennis Leroy Kangalee, for instance, identifies as part of "a legion of underground and avant-garde painters and dramatists" whom Gunn inspired "to be as strange as they actually were." Kangalee, whose long-delayed movie project *Octavia: Elegy for a Vampire* bears an obvious debt to *Ganja & Hess,* credits Gunn's example for his conviction that art should "eschew rules" and be "informed by a multitude of things."[11] Others, including Ayoka Chenzira, more specifically appreciate Gunn's resistance to predetermined essentialist conceptions of the "Blackness" of Black film. Chenzira, who directed, in 1984, the landmark experimental short *Hair Piece: A Film for Nappyheaded People,* regards her early exposure to *Ganja & Hess* as an event that transformed her understanding of Black cinema: "It's one of the first films that I saw where I felt that the filmmaker had a real freedom and commitment to talk about anything he wanted to talk about in any way that he wanted to talk about it. There were no boundaries around what 'black' was, or is, or what it could be, or what it should be."[12]

With a few exceptions, including *Daughters of the Dust,* Gunn's disciples have chosen not to acknowledge his importance in their movies through direct allusion or citation. *Ganja & Hess*'s influence is most keenly felt in the deep structure of its heirs rather than paraded about at the surface level. Black independent filmmakers have long considered *Ganja & Hess*'s very *making,* the improbability of its very *existence,* as a source of pride and encouragement. To Waymon, this had been the intention all along. Speaking of the warm welcome that he and Gunn received from aspiring directors following *Ganja & Hess*'s Cannes showing, Waymon recalls that "everyone was so proud of us; would-be filmmakers were so inspired. We *wanted* to inspire them." At Cannes, powerful industry reps were envious over how Gunn's low-budget indie flick seized the imaginations of its viewers, whereas their own movies did not. *Ganja & Hess* "gave hope to independent filmmakers," Waymon maintains. "*Lady Sings the Blues* didn't give anybody hope."[13]

Ganja & Hess Revamped: *Da Sweet Blood of Jesus*

One of the up-and-coming Black directors to whom *Ganja & Hess* gave hope was Spike Lee, whose swift career ascent in the mid- and late eighties overlapped Gunn's slow fade. Although Diawara intriguingly classifies Lee's breakout hit *She's Gotta Have It* as part of the aesthetic tradition that *Ganja & Hess* symbolically inaugurated, Lee's initial popular success owes more of a debt to *Sweetback*'s nationalist viewpoint and enthusiastic adoption of violent genre tropes. Lee's ability to attract a broad-based viewership is a reflection of his savvy business sense and eagerness to work within the system, theoretically to subvert it from the inside. Lee's endgame notwithstanding, many advocates for a counterhegemonic Black independent cinema viewed his film practice as complicit with consumer capitalism. Toni Cade Bambara, for one, held up Lee as a negative example for his perpetuation of the "basically reactionary sensibility (homophobic/misogynistic/patriarchal) that audiences have been trained by the industry and its support institutions to accept as norm, as pleasurable, inevitable."[14] To his critics Lee's movies commodify social relevance, co-opting "race and difference . . . into the cultural products of Hollywood."[15] A truly oppositional African American cinema can only thrive, by this logic, when produced by Black artists working in near-total independence, like Oscar Micheaux, Melvin Van Peebles, or Julie Dash.

Gunn himself knew as much as any Black filmmaker in the eighties about the hidden cost of compromise with movie executives and producers, having paid that price for close to two decades. He was convinced that a separate industry was necessary for Black film to survive and flourish, a goal he believed was "not impossible" to attain: "We should have died in the beginning, but we are still here."[16] Yet, Gunn's commitment to independence was, perhaps, more of an imposition than a choice, born of economic necessity rather than separatist fervor. He had willingly traveled the same route that Lee later navigated; indeed, Gunn *began* his screenwriting and directing careers with projects backed by conglomerate-owned major studios. Unlike his more militant contemporaries, he was not opposed to capitalism. "I mean, I love three-piece suits and I love economics and I think people should be millionaires and have a lot of money," he conceded in 1982. "But I do not believe that people should be stupid."[17]

Gunn never commented publicly on *She's Gotta Have It* nor on Lee's provocative follow-up, *School Daze* (1988), nor did he weigh in on the immense significance of Lee's rapid rise within the industry. The distribution deal that Lee struck with Columbia prior to *School Daze*'s release heralded the first New Wave of African American directors working in Hollywood since the early seventies. Gunn did not quite live long enough to witness the second Black movie boom. Presumably, the intense competition among studios and minimajors for the services of unproven Black directors would have left Gunn both bemused and, seeing the astonishing youth of these new recruits, all the more uncertain about his own directing future. Several of these first-time filmmakers, including John Singleton, Matty Rich, and the Hughes Brothers, were Gunn's juniors by four decades, and some were barely out of high school. Furthermore, the films they made, namely *Boyz n the Hood* (1991), *Straight Out of Brooklyn* (1991), and *Menace II Society* (1993), could not have been less similar in subject matter, setting, or tone to something like *Territory*. Had Gunn lived, perhaps the best he could have hoped for was ceremonial status within the burgeoning movement, as a respected elder statesman whose signature achievement, though frequently name-checked by emerging talents, would mean little to investors seeking a sure bet.

Regardless of whether Gunn, as he struggled to patch together the resources for a comeback, gave much thought to the upstart director then storming Hollywood's gates, the veteran filmmaker was certainly on Lee's mind for much of the decade and beyond. Lee first saw *Ganja & Hess* in the early eighties when he was an MFA student at the Tisch School of the Arts at New York University, and he met its director at a lecture at the Film Forum.[18] Lee strongly identified with Gunn due to *Ganja & Hess*'s beleaguered production history, at least as it has been traditionally represented. "He was getting money to make a film and the people who gave it to him, the people who financed it, they really just wanted to cash in on the black exploitation craze," Lee avowed in 2014. "Bill Gunn, was like okie-doke, you wanna give me money, okay. They think they're going to get this but I'm going to slip something in—more than a little something."[19] Lee came to regard *Ganja & Hess* as one of the films that changed African American cinema, and he struck up an acquaintance with Schultz, who invited Lee to guest lecture at Montclair State University in 2011.[20] A couple of years later, on the heels

Figure C.1 Ganja (Zaraah Abrahams) consoles Hess (Stephen Tyrone Williams) and keeps a wary eye on the cross in Spike Lee's 2014 remake. *Da Sweet Blood of Jesus* (DVD), Anchor Bay Entertainment.

of the negative response to his recent movies, the microbudgeted *Red Hook Summer* (2012) and an ill-conceived remake of the South Korean cult noir *Oldboy* (2013), Lee decided to direct a faithful adaptation of Gunn's *Ganja & Hess* shooting script, with Schultz serving as coproducer.

Lee's use of *Ganja & Hess* as his new movie's source material remained a secret right up until its premiere, though rumors proliferated from the moment he announced, in July 2013, a Kickstarter campaign to raise $1.25 million to pay for "the newest hottest Spike Lee joint." (The final total raised was $1.42 million: still less than the original's production budget, adjusted for inflation.) The film, eventually titled *Da Sweet Blood of Jesus*, would, Lee promised, tell "a new kind of love story" about "human beings who are addicted to Blood."[21] Mostly lesser-known actors made up the cast, headed by Stephen Tyrone Williams, Zaraah Abrahams, Elvis Nolasco, and future Oscar winner Rami Malek, and the story's main locales were switched from Westchester County to Martha's Vineyard and from downtown Ossining to Red Hook, Brooklyn (see fig. C.1). Schultz was the only representative from the original *Ganja & Hess* production team to actively participate in the remake. (He also appears in a brief cameo as Hess's physician.) Victor Kanefsky was not approached, and Sam Pollard, Lee's collaborator on six features during the nineties, was unavailable to serve as editor, though his son was briefly in the running for the position.[22] Remarkably, Marlene Clark did not even learn of the remake's existence until months after its premiere.[23]

Waymon did not provide any new music for *Da Sweet Blood of Jesus*, but Lee did obtain his permission to use "You Got to Learn" for the church revival sequence, and he invited the composer to watch its filming from the vantage point of a back pew. Waymon's presence on the set of the Lil' Piece of Heaven Baptist Church seemed to slightly unnerve the filmmaker, who was embarrassed by the sluggishness of his cast during the choir's run-through. Lee shot Waymon a disgusted look following each mediocre take; after three such attempts "he blew up at the actors and told the preacher to do it right, because the man who originally played his character and wrote the song is sitting in the back." (The very next take, Waymon reports, "was the one used in the film.") Lee repeatedly solicited Waymon's blessing over the course of the daylong shoot, asking whether or not Gunn would be "proud of his version." When Waymon answered in the affirmative, a grateful Lee hugged him.[24]

Lee's yearning for the validation of his forebears may come as a shock to those who recall his well-publicized feud with Amiri Baraka and other revered Black artists of previous generations over Lee's depiction of Malcolm X in his controversial 1992 biopic. The filmmaker's transformation of *Malcolm X*'s source material is, in fact, strikingly analogous to his approach to adapting the *Ganja & Hess* script. Lee's epic portrait of the legendary activist is less a version of Alex Haley's celebrated "autobiography" than a revision of James Baldwin's initial adaptation for Columbia. Baldwin's screenplay was revised without his consent by a white writer, Arnold Perl; the resulting draft was then rewritten by Lee, after many years, with an eye toward commercial acceptance. Lee's *Malcolm X* preserves much of the dialogue and a decent amount of plot material from the original draft, as would be the case with *Da Sweet Blood of Jesus*. Indeed, *Da Sweet Blood of Jesus* is far more faithful to Gunn's script than Gunn's own film is (or, for that matter, Fima Noveck's "remake").

Lee also made a few crucial modifications to Baldwin's work, such as amplifying his subject's violent criminal background while downplaying his psychological complexity. Some Baldwin scholars contend that these modifications subverted the writer's intentions. D. Quentin Miller's objections to Lee's supposed violation of the spirit of Baldwin's *Malcolm X* script, which is highly fragmented and deeply personal, could conceivably apply to Lee's overhauling of Gunn's *Ganja & Hess* screenplay as well: "Even though Lee reads the *Autobiography* through the lens of Baldwin's script, he loses something crucial in the process: the subtlety of Baldwin's tender rendition of Malcolm X's life is eclipsed by Lee's polemical excesses.... The end product is not a groundbreaking film befitting its radical subject or the inventive experiment that Baldwin had envisioned, and Lee's emphasis is excessively on the action/adventure staple of the film industry which had been imposed on the script by Perl to Baldwin's dismay."[25]

Of course, Gunn himself (albeit ordained by Kelly-Jordan) was responsible for introducing to *Ganja & Hess* the genre elements that Miller disparages. Unlike Lee, however, Gunn deglamorizes those elements. The bloodshed in *Ganja & Hess*, though revolting at times, never overwhelms the human drama, nor are the perpetrators allowed to escape its serious consequences. In contrast, the hyperrealistic gore and the ferocity of the (often sexualized) violence in *Da Sweet Blood of Jesus* seem like indulgences, so much so as to elicit groans from viewers at its world premiere at the American Black Film Festival in New York.[26] Waymon has similarly expressed disapproval of "the use of blood in several scenes" in the Lee film, and, though he notes that "Bill would have been flattered by the remake," he feels that Gunn would have likely objected to those sequences, too.[27]

The intensification of carnage, like the addition of hip-hop music on the soundtrack in Lee's reimagining of *Ganja & Hess*, is, of course, in part a concession to current tastes. Yet, the inclusion of graphic violence in *Da Sweet Blood of Jesus* also functions to allow Lee to assert "ownership" over the movie, given that such violence has long been a staple of his work. Lee approached the project with the stated goal of maintaining strict fidelity to a shooting script that had first been filmed forty years prior. Perhaps, inevitably, he proved unable or unwilling to wholly conceal his authorial signature. As a result, *Da Sweet Blood of Jesus* is an awkward amalgamation of Gunn's ideas and Lee's directorial tics, incorporating random references to the New York Knicks and the use of a backtracking camera to follow a seemingly levitating male protagonist. Such deviations are largely cosmetic, but their familiarity serves to bring *Da Sweet Blood of Jesus* somewhat closer to the status of a bona fide "Spike Lee Joint" despite the story's basis as a Bill Gunn creation.

Lee also implemented two more substantial changes to the Gunn screenplay, possibly in order to preempt a renewal of the accusations of misogyny that have infused the feminist reception of his work since *She's Gotta Have It*. First, Lee rewrote Ganja's "snowball fight" monologue. In Lee's revision, Ganja recalls her childhood abuse at the hands of her brother, not her

Figure C.2 Ganja contemplates the alluringly unadorned neck of Tangier Chancellor (Naté Bova). *Da Sweet Blood of Jesus* (DVD), Anchor Bay Entertainment.

mother. Devastated, the girl seeks solace from her father, who warns her that the world "is a harsh place, especially for a Black woman.... Ganja has got to take care of Ganja." *Da Sweet Blood of Jesus* thus supplies Ganja with a more explicit incentive for her fiercely guarded independence: as a Black woman she is doomed to callous mistreatment from whites *and* from men in general, and, consequently, she must protect her interests at all costs. The second major variation insinuates that it is, in fact, men whom she regards as her primary enemy. In *Da Sweet Blood of Jesus*, the "dinner guest" becomes a woman named Tangier, a biracial and bisexual former lover of Hess (see fig. C.2). As before, Ganja kills her guest as they have sex on the bathroom floor, only to be reunited with her undead partner in the film's denouement. Yet, whereas Gunn resurrects the ravenous, hypermasculine Richard, whose final mad dash toward Ganja conveys his desperation to either violently possess her or act as her slave, the remake presents her with an implicitly superior option: the calming, restorative, "womanly companionship" of an independent equal rather than a servant or master.

It is on the strength of these changes that Lee could justifiably refer to *Da Sweet Blood of Jesus* as a "reinterpretation" rather than a remake, as the former term suggests more agency on the part of the interpreter. His relationship to the Gunn text was, as he phrased it in promotional interviews, "just a matter of respecting the source, and then trying to make your own film, and trying not to be inhibited by being so beholden to every single thing."[28] At the same time, Lee refused to talk in depth about these changes, ostensibly to refrain from revealing the picture's ending. He, therefore, was never pressed to follow through on the ideological implications of his major plot amendments; he offered no explanation for how the rewriting of Ganja's childhood realization—now, in Lee's version, instilled in her by a man—functioned specifically to make her "the strongest black woman possible," nor did he satisfactorily defend the protracted, titillating depiction of Ganja and Tangier's rough intercourse, with its lingering focus on Tangier's nude body.[29]

Due to his desire to affirm yet not actually discuss his film's differences from the Gunn script and the meaning of those alterations, Lee's public statements on *Da Sweet Blood of Jesus* replicated, with unintentional irony, Gunn's original rhetoric about *Ganja & Hess*'s "message." *Da Sweet Blood of Jesus* was *not*, Lee stressed, a vampire film; rather, it was a serious treatment of *addiction*. "I'm really just repeating what Bill Gunn said," Lee told one interviewer, "which I believe, that the blood addiction in this film is like in the original."[30] But for many Black cinema connoisseurs, "repeating what Bill Gunn said" was not a compelling enough reason for Lee to remake *Ganja & Hess* in the first place. The mainly lukewarm reviews of *Da Sweet Blood of Jesus* highlighted this lack of clear purpose as a serious obstacle for the knowledgeable viewer. The most thoughtful articulation of this opinion was delineated in Kangalee's essay, originally published in *Indiewire*, in which he condemns Lee's hubris:

> Instead of remaking a haunting delicate film into a virtuosic, ironic "art film," why not simply acknowledge the original? Is a remake necessary? Spike Lee would have done us all a favor if he had simply written a monograph on "Ganja & Hess" and called it a day. The world needs to know more about Bill Gunn. And if artists want to pay homage to the masters, we should express what we know about life as opposed to cinema—and that would be enough. . . . All the great masters express and teach us what they themselves know about life. And that's what Gunn did.[31]

The inability to answer such questions perhaps explains the near-total lack of consumer interest in *Da Sweet Blood of Jesus*, despite the publicity surrounding both its crowdfunding campaign and its (novel, at the time) pretheatrical distribution through Vimeo On Demand. Its limited release to a handful of theaters in February 2015 yielded a gross that was arguably less impressive than the return on investment generated by *Ganja & Hess*'s two-week run at the Playboy Theater. Lee's losing streak at the box office would not be broken until the remarkable success of *BlacKkKlansman* in 2018, a movie that, for audiences and critics alike, marked its director's return to surer thematic and generic footing.

The New Millennium

When Gunn died, much of his completed work was inaccessible or had been mostly forgotten. Almost immediately, many of those whose lives he had touched, from his closest confidants to fans he never knew, set out to remind the world of his achievements and advance his reputation as a great American artist. The first retrospective of Gunn's screen efforts was organized one year after his death for the New American Film and Video Series at the Whitney Museum. The festival, which ran from June 19 to July 8, 1990, was curated by Ishmael Reed, who also gave a gallery talk on Gunn's career, with the assistance of John Williams and the participation of Hoffmeister (the executor of Gunn's estate), Waymon, Schultz, and James Hinton.[32] The Warner Bros. cut of *Stop* had its long-delayed premiere, and Reed showed four hours of *Personal Problems*. Despite being on hiatus, the movie lab technicians at MoMA struck a duplicate 35 mm print of *Ganja & Hess*, especially for the Whitney series, to honor Gunn, who "was a special favorite of the Department of Film."[33]

MoMA's print also served as a key source for the picture's release on home video, after it was discovered that Gunn's donated copy had not deteriorated as badly as previously assumed. The first (1998) edition of *Ganja & Hess* in the brand-new DVD format was coordinated by David Kalat for All Day Entertainment with the blessing of Schultz, who acquired the copyright for the original *Ganja & Hess* upon Gunn's death.[34] Kanefsky's privately acquired 35 mm print was the primary source for the transfer, but his copy lacked the scene of Meda reading, "To the Black Male Children." Meda's monologue does not, therefore, appear in the initial home video release of *Ganja & Hess* and would not be reinstated until 2004, when Image Entertainment issued All Day's "Complete Edition," following the scene's recovery from MoMA's 16 mm reduction print.[35] MoMA eventually became even more directly involved in *Ganja & Hess*'s preservation and dissemination, through its supervision of the movie's restoration for Blu-ray release by Kino Lorber in 2012 and the London-based distributor Eureka Entertainment in 2015.

Though there has been no single decisive turning point in the reevaluation of Bill Gunn's artistic legacy, the 2010s will be remembered as the period in which the world finally began to catch up. *Da Sweet Blood of Jesus*, despite its quick disappearance, raised the profile of the original and brought it to the attention of many future converts. Lee's respect for and endorsement of Gunn's original work were undoubtedly factors in *Ganja & Hess*'s theatrical rerelease a few years later. That said, the return of the "first" *Ganja & Hess* to movie theaters was not even the era's most significant Gunn-related rediscovery. The art house revivals of *Losing Ground*, in 2015, and *Personal Problems*, in 2018, bred volumes of publicity, the likes of which Gunn never experienced in his lifetime. *Personal Problems*, especially, was rapturously received during its limited run, with numerous reviewers seconding Howard Hampton's appraisal of the refurbished serial as a "sui generis" masterwork akin to "some mythic Black Arts grail that the protagonist in a Paul Beatty or Percival Everett novel would search the secret archives of the FBI or PBS for."[36]

The seeds of *Personal Problems*'s unlikely rematerializing were planted by two major New York film retrospectives, both curated by Jacob Perlin: BAMcinématek's "The Groundbreaking Bill Gunn," in 2010, and the Film Society of Lincoln Center's "Tell It Like It Is: Black Independents in New York, 1968–1986," in 2015. Encouraged by the positive feedback engendered by *Personal Problems*'s showing at BAMcinématek, despite the decrepit state of the exhibited videocassettes, Perlin began to digitize the vast assortment of video and audio elements that Reed had been storing for nearly a quarter century. For the 2015 series, which also spotlighted the independent film and video work of several of Gunn's East Coast contemporaries, Reed, Perlin, and coprogrammer Michelle Materre invited living cast and crew members to attend the screening of *Personal Problems* and a follow-up discussion led by Reed and Waymon. Shortly thereafter, Bret Wood at Kino Lorber began work on the video's meticulous restoration, which culminated in its theatrical premiere in March 2018 at Metrograph in Manhattan.[37]

A featured attraction at both of these retrospectives, the MoMA print of *Ganja & Hess* continued to be shown with regularity well into the teens. The gradual replacement of 35 mm prints from American movie theaters by "virtual" digital prints, however, necessitated yet another transfer of formats. The 2018 nationwide rerelease of *Ganja & Hess* (kicked off, as well, at Metrograph) debuted a newly remastered digital version that enabled the film to travel to venues that otherwise would have no opportunity to project it. Not for the first nor, surely, the last time, *Ganja & Hess*'s extinction had been deferred and its life span extended via a technological update. As long as its preservation keeps up with the pace of technological change, *Ganja & Hess* stands to inspire movie buffs and media scholars for generations to come.

In this, it will help fulfill the prophecy implied by Sam Dodd's not-so-offhand remark to his Hollywood tormentors in *Rhinestone Sharecropping*, an aside that could easily double as its creator's epitaph: "To remember a man's name is to give him eternal life."[38]

NOTES

Introduction

1. This introduction's epigraph is a Gunn quote from 1982, which originally appeared in C. Taylor, "Bill Gunn."
2. The results of this survey, covering the years 1968 to 1977 and initially published in the July 1978 issue of *Take One*, are reprinted in Monaco, *American Film Now*, 415–419.
3. The Diawara and Klotman piece, first drafted in 1983, was originally printed in the April 1990 issue of *Jump Cut*. Lucas and Walker's essay has received considerable exposure due to its circulation as a special feature on DVD and Blu-ray releases of *Ganja & Hess*.
4. Nicholas Forster's not-yet-published (as of this writing) biography will, undoubtedly, provide the most thorough account to date of Gunn's life and career.
5. Tate, "Bill Gunn, 1934-89," 98 (emphasis in original).
6. Kendrick, "Phantom Cinema," 64.
7. Kendrick, "Phantom Cinema," 66.
8. Kendrick, "Phantom Cinema," 71.
9. Field, *Uplift Cinema*, 25. Also see Bowser and Spence, *Writing Himself into History*; Petersen, "The 'Reol' Story."
10. Kendrick, "Phantom Cinema," 72.
11. Wall and Martin, *Politics and Poetics of Black Film*; Martin, Wall, and Yaquinto, *Race and the Revolutionary Impulse*; Martin and Wall, *From Street to Screen*.

Chapter 1

1. This chapter's epigraph is quoted from J. Murray's 1973 "Futuristic Fable."
2. The phrase is borrowed from a pair of early mass media discussions of the surging popularity of films with mainly Black casts for mainly Black audiences, "The Black Movie Boom" and "Black Movie Boom—Good or Bad?"
3. "NAACP Blasts 'Super-Nigger' Trend," 2. For a detailed account of the contemporaneous debate over blaxploitation, especially among African American critics, see Kenna, "Making Exploitation Black," 201–224.
4. Butters, *From* Sweetback *to* Super Fly, 51.
5. J. Murray, "Futuristic Fable."
6. Jackson, quoted in King, "'Bus' Is Stalled."
7. J. Murray, *To Find an Image*, 122–123, 172; King, "'Bus' Is Stalled."
8. Franklin, quoted in Franklin and Davis, *Wendell Franklin*, 116.
9. "Black Still Times Square Beautiful," 8, 16; Wise, "'Black' and 'Other Action' Rule Loop."
10. J. Murray, *To Find an Image*, 111, 113.
11. Cohn, "Black Pic Employment Still Lags," 32. Also see Verrill, "Black Film Explosion."
12. Pierson, "Blaxploitation, Quick and Dirty," 127, 133.

13. Brown, "Film as a Tool for Liberation?" 37. Also see Green, "Black Man as Movie Hero."
14. J. Murray, *To Find an Image*, 133; Murphy, "50 More Potential Black Theme Films," 20.
15. Michener, "Black Movies," 80.
16. "Black Market"; J. Murray, *To Find an Image*, 134. The latter project was, of course, scuttled by the nearly simultaneous announcement of preproduction on *Lady Sings the Blues* by Motown Productions, a Black-led start-up with powerful industry connections.
17. Kelly, interview; Howard Sanders Advertising, "'Georgia, Georgia' Production Information"; "'L. S. Fields' ('Derby') Really Quentin Kelly," 1, 31.
18. Leeming, *James Baldwin*, 244.
19. Baker and Chase, *Josephine*, 369, 436–437; Jules-Rosette, *Josephine Baker in Art and Life*, 235.
20. "Buys Rights to Film 'Blues for Mr. Charlie'"; Leeming, *James Baldwin*, 248, 251.
21. "'L. S. Fields' ('Derby') Really Quentin Kelly," 1.
22. Kelly, interview.
23. The inconsistencies among press accounts of the size of the African American film audience in this period are discussed in Sieving, *Soul Searching*, 84–85.
24. West, "Makers of Black Films," 18.
25. Angelus, "Black Film Explosion Uncovers," 52.
26. Kelly, interview.
27. Segers, "Quent Kelly Enterprises Succeeds," 3.
28. Kostrzewa, "Secrets of the Tower." I am indebted to Steve Ryfle for bringing this article to my attention.
29. Kelly, interview.
30. Segers, "Quent Kelly Enterprises Succeeds," 3.
31. Gent, "Black Films Are In."
32. "Black Academy N.Y. Fest & 'Oscars'?"; Jordan, quoted in J. Murray, *To Find an Image*, 138.
33. Kelly-Jordan Enterprises Inc., "An EAGER New Audience..."
34. Kelly, interview.
35. Kelly-Jordan Enterprises Inc., invitation to *Georgia, Georgia* premiere.
36. The few contemporary scholars who have given the film detailed attention have focused on *Georgia, Georgia*'s treatment of Black female subjectivity. See Ryfle, "Georgia, Georgia on My Mind"; Poggiali, "Roundtable Discussion."
37. Kelly, interview.
38. Björkman, email message to author; Björkman, audio commentary.
39. [Björkman], *Georgia, Georgia*, treatment.
40. Angelou, quoted in Howard Sanders Advertising, "'Georgia, Georgia' Production Information."
41. Kelly, interview.
42. In the revised treatment, it is noted that "years ago [Georgia] asked for and received a divorce from the 'cullid people.'" Angelou, "*Georgia*," 2.
43. Kelly, interview; Feder, "Deserters in Sweden."
44. Björkman, audio commentary. Angelou was accompanied by her friend Vertamae Grosvenor, who planned to write a book about the making of the picture. Björkman, email message to author.
45. Björkman, audio commentary.
46. Peterson, "Diana Diana," 72; Ryfle, audio commentary. Also see Sloan, "Keeping the Black Woman in Her Place," 31; Bailey, "Black Woman with White Fever."

47. Kelly-Jordan Enterprises Inc., "Summer Is Already Here!"; Kelly-Jordan Enterprises Inc., "Congratulations Diana Sands."

48. This turnout was likely motivated by a rave *Today Show* review from Judith Crist, *Georgia, Georgia*'s most enthusiastic defender in the mainstream media. "Cinerama Releasing 10 by Fall"; Crist, "'Georgia' on Her Mind," 66–67.

49. Weiler, "Forever 'Fantasticks,'" D13, D22; Kelly-Jordan Enterprises Inc., "An EAGER New Audience..."

50. Kelly-Jordan Enterprises Inc., "An EAGER New Audience..."

51. Gunn, quoted in Peterson, "Interview with Bill Gunn," 27.

52. Gunn, quoted in Lino and Bryan, "Interview with Bill Gunn," 46.

53. Kelly, interview.

54. Leeming, *James Baldwin*, 316.

55. Leeming, *James Baldwin*, 248.

56. Baldwin, quoted in Goodman, "For James Baldwin, a Rap on Baldwin."

57. Kelly, interview; "James Baldwin to Try Movies"; Kelly-Jordan Enterprises Inc., "*The Inheritance*." A copy of Baldwin's revised script, titled *In the Cross, a Trembling Soul: The Inheritance*, is held by the Harvard Film Archive. For additional information on this ill-fated project, see O'Malley, "Another Cinema."

58. Weatherby, *James Baldwin*, 315.

59. Kelly, interview.

60. Leeming, *James Baldwin*, 317.

61. Kelly, interview.

62. "Rights to Biopic of Bessie Smith," 1.

63. "New York Sound Track," July 11, 1973; "Rival Bessies."

64. Wilcox to Gunn. *Bessie* was finally realized in 2015 in the form of HBO's production for television, directed and cowritten by Dee Rees.

65. Angelou, quoted in Weller, "Work in Progress," 13.

66. Handsaker, "Finally, a Black Woman Movie Director."

67. Jordan to Angelou.

68. Kostrzewa, "Secrets of the Tower."

69. Segers, "Quent Kelly Enterprises Succeeds," 22; Kelly, interview.

70. Kelly, interview.

71. Ryfle, "Uplifting Black Film," 33.

72. Kelly, interview.

73. Sege, "*Honeybaby, Honeybaby*."

74. Segers, "Quent Kelly Enterprises Succeeds," 3.

75. "Kelly-Jordan to Release Three Films"; Kelly, interview. Also see "Harold S. Lager Named V.P. Sales."

76. "Kelly-Jordan Has Zaire Bout"; Segers, "Quent Kelly Enterprises Succeeds," 3; Kelly, interview.

77. Baker and Chase, *Josephine*, 463.

78. Kelly, interview.

79. Jordan, quoted in Baker and Chase, *Josephine*, 473. In Stockholm, Jordan sunk $200,000 into a new restaurant, "The Best of Harlem"; it failed within three months. Asante, *African American People*, 340.

80. Kelly, interview.

81. "Our Company."

82. Kelly, interview.
83. Sands, quoted in Peterson, "Diana Diana," 72.
84. Moore, "Actress Discusses Her Goals and Roles."
85. R. Taylor, "Biracial Film Company Debuts."
86. Peterson, "Flood of Black Films."

Chapter 2

1. This chapter's epigraph originally appeared, circa 1975, in Gunn, "I Deal Only in Abstractions" (emphasis in original).
2. Baldwin, *Devil Finds Work*, 564.
3. Pavlić, *Who Can Afford to Improvise?* 90 (emphasis in original).
4. Gunn, quoted in Gelmis, "Trying to Overturn the Racial Cliches" (emphasis added).
5. Gunn, *All the Rest Have Died*, 21. The line is also spoken by the title character in Gunn, "Johnnas," 128.
6. Tate, "Bill Gunn, 1934–89," 98.
7. Reed, "Bill Gunn: Director," 118; Fraser, "Bill Gunn, Playwright and Actor."
8. Schultz, interview.
9. C. Taylor, "Bill Gunn," 100.
10. C. Frederick, "Bill Gunn."
11. Steve Ryfle seconds this contention in his insightful review of Gunn's career. Ryfle, "Eclipsed Visions," 26.
12. Gunn, *Rhinestone Sharecropping*, 49.
13. Gunn, "Philadelphia Conspiricy [sic]."
14. "Homegoing Service of William Harrison Gunn."
15. Gunn, "Philadelphia Conspiricy [sic]"; Splawn, "Bill Gunn (1934–1989)," 192; Countryman, *Up South*, 24.
16. Hunter, *Black Citymakers*, 73–74; Wolfinger, *Philadelphia Divided*, 12.
17. C. Taylor, "Bill Gunn," 99.
18. Gunn, quoted in Euvrard, "Bill Gunn," 161.
19. Lino and Bryan, "Interview with Bill Gunn," 15–16.
20. Gunn, quoted in Adams, "Bill Gunn," 56; Euvrard, "Bill Gunn," 161; Lino and Bryan, "Interview with Bill Gunn," 45.
21. Gunn, *All the Rest Have Died*, 14.
22. Gunn, *All the Rest Have Died*, 17–21; Gunn, "Johnnas," 126–128.
23. Gunn, "Johnnas," 137.
24. Gunn, "Johnnas," 138.
25. As Johnnas explains to his white English teacher, "toasty" "means you think maybe you're white and the boys don't like that, they think it's stuck up." Gunn, "Johnnas," 134. Also see Gunn, "Philadelphia Conspiricy [sic]."
26. Gunn, "Johnnas," 133. The protagonist of *All the Rest Have Died* also mentions being "raised on [his] father's Horatio Alger books," as Gunn himself had been. Gunn, *All the Rest Have Died*, 95; Lino and Bryan, "Interview with Bill Gunn," 15.
27. Gunn, "Johnnas," 134.
28. Stockton, *Queer Child*, 6.

29. Moon, *Small Boy and Others*, 3.
30. Gunn, quoted in Peterson, "Interview with Bill Gunn," 96; Moon, "'Gentle Boy from the Dangerous Classes,'" 38. P. Jane Splawn's linking of *Johnnas* to Langston Hughes's poem "Genius Child" is doubly evocative given Hughes's own coding of gay experience in his work. Splawn, "Bill Gunn (1934-1989)," 195.
31. Gunn, "*Johnnas*," 137.
32. C. Taylor, "Bill Gunn," 99.
33. Lucas and Walker, "Savaging and Salvaging," 39-40.
34. Gunn, "*Johnnas*," 135.
35. Gunn, quoted in Adams, "Bill Gunn," 55.
36. Gunn, "Philadelphia Conspiricy [sic]."
37. Euvrard, "Bill Gunn," 161; Stuart, "Bill Gunn's Play a 'Mental Trip.'"
38. Gunn, quoted in Molleson, "Real-Life Struggle of the 'One in Ten,'" 1.
39. Gunn, quoted in Adams, "Bill Gunn," 56.
40. Euvrard, "Bill Gunn," 161.
41. Gunn, *All the Rest Have Died*, 50.
42. Gunn, *All the Rest Have Died*, 124-127.
43. Hyams and Hyams, *James Dean*, 62; Dalton, *James Dean*, 143.
44. Hyams and Hyams, *James Dean*, 256.
45. Gunn, *All the Rest Have Died*, 29.
46. Gunn, quoted in Dalton, *James Dean*, 327.
47. Gunn, *All the Rest Have Died*, 83.
48. Atkinson, "Theatre."
49. Gunn, quoted in R. Frederick, "If Poitier Can't Do It," 17.
50. Gilroy, "Berlin Observes Culture of U.S."
51. "Who's Who in the Cast"; "A 'Different' Television Drama." Also in 1954, Gunn played a boxer on an episode of the DuMont Network's *The Stranger*; a surviving Kinescope of this telecast is held at the UCLA Film and Television Archive and is available to view at https://www.youtube.com/watch?v=5tJzgxTL6jY.
52. Gould, "TV: Church Segregation"; "15 to Spout 'Verses.'"
53. Gunn, quoted in Euvrard, "Bill Gunn," 161. Gunn's only film performances prior to *Ganja & Hess* were in *The Sound and the Fury*, *The Interns* (unbilled; 1962), the Natalie Wood vehicle *Penelope* (1966), and *The Spy with My Face* (1965), which recycles footage of his guest role in *The Man from U. N. C. L. E.* A 1962 profile in the *New York Amsterdam News* tantalizingly notes, without elaboration, that Gunn was offered a starring role in a picture by legendary French director Jean Renoir. "Only 2 Films, But He's Known."
54. Hopper, quoted in Shafrazi, "Dennis Hopper, 1999."
55. Ryfle, "Eclipsed Visions," 27; Bosworth, *Montgomery Clift*, 284.
56. Reed, "Bill Gunn: Director," 113.
57. Kouvaros, *Famous Faces Yet Not Themselves*, 49; Wexman, "Masculinity in Crisis," 128.
58. Atkinson, "Theatre."
59. Wexman, "Masculinity in Crisis," 131 (emphasis added).
60. Enelow, *Method Acting and Its Discontents*, 69, 73.
61. "How Negro Fares in Field of Arts."
62. Molleson, "Real-Life Struggle of the 'One in Ten,'" 1.
63. Gunn, quoted in R. Frederick, "If Poitier Can't Do It," 2, 17.

64. M. Robinson, "Negro Actors Resent His Success"; Landry, "Black Pix," 5.
65. Reed, "Bill Gunn: Director," 114.
66. "The Author."
67. Gunn, "The Bedlamite," 45–46, 67–70.
68. Euvrard, "Bill Gunn," 161; Doul, "Stock Reviews." Also see Gunn, *Marcus in the High Grass*.
69. See Gelb, "'Marcus in the High Grass' Has Debut."
70. Gunn, *The Owllight*.
71. Calta, "Chelsea Theater Center to Open."
72. J. Williams, "Bill Gunn (1929–1989): A Checklist," 786.
73. R. Frederick, "Belafonte's 'Comeback' Film," 5.
74. Euvrard, "Bill Gunn," 161. A detailed analysis of Gunn's various script drafts for *The Landlord* can be found in Sieving, *Soul Searching*, 174–184.
75. Mishkin, "On the Set with 'The Landlord.'"
76. Sweeney, "On Location in Lindsayland."
77. "'Friends' 1st on U Slate."
78. Gunn to Zeitlin.
79. "Gunn 'Moon' Scripter"; Gunn, *Fame Game*. Around this time, Gunn was asked by producer Jay Weston to adapt *Lady Sings the Blues*, but Gunn passed because Weston's final bid was only half of what he was earning on his current freelance assignment. Weston, "Tortured Incubation of a Hit."
80. Schultz, interview.
81. R. Frederick, "Belafonte's 'Comeback' Film," 5.
82. Schultz, interview.
83. Schultz to Belafonte.
84. Schultz to Merrick.
85. DWP to Schultz.
86. Schultz, interview.
87. Peterson, "Interview with Bill Gunn," 27.
88. Brewer, "Private Retreats," 93, 95.
89. Waymon, interview.
90. Batson, "Nyack Sketch Log: Sam Waymon Lived Here."
91. Schultz, interview.
92. Weiler, "Bill Gunn, Actor and Playwright."
93. Gunn, quoted in Lino and Bryan, "Interview with Bill Gunn," 15–16.
94. Gunn, quoted in Adams, "Bill Gunn," 57.
95. Gunn, *Rhinestone Sharecropping*, 41, 48.
96. Byron, "Ducks Stars and 'Best Sellers,'" 26.
97. Byron, "Kinney, W7 Owners Approve Merger," 3; Verrill, "Pledges Kinney."
98. The preproduction and production phases of *Stop* were later repurposed as part of the protagonist's backstory in *Rhinestone Sharecropping*. As usual with Gunn, the fictionalization and its real-world antecedent appear to match up very closely. See Gunn, *Rhinestone Sharecropping*, 82–90.
99. Gunn, quoted in Euvrard, "Bill Gunn," 162.
100. Gunn, quoted in Euvrard, "Bill Gunn," 162.
101. Heller, quoted in Weiler, "Bill Gunn, Actor and Playwright."

102. Euvrard, "Bill Gunn," 162.
103. Gunn, *Stop*, 53.
104. Gunn, *Stop*, 55.
105. Gunn, *Mandala*, 49.
106. Ryfle, "Glorious Ganja," 29.
107. Gunn, quoted in Underhill, "Action...," 22.
108. Gunn, *Stop*, 76.
109. Gunn, *Stop*, 81.
110. Gunn, *Stop*, 83–84.
111. Heller, quoted in Underhill, "Action...," 7 (emphasis in original).
112. Euvrard, "Bill Gunn," 162. Gunn's edit equally impressed the producers of MGM's *Shaft*, then in preproduction. On the basis of *Stop*'s original cut, they asked Gunn to join their project as director, but he declined. Monaco, "Lost Films."
113. Monaco, "Lost Films."
114. Lor, "Archive Film Review: *Stop*."
115. Royalton, "Re: *Stop* (Bill Gunn, 1970)."
116. Warner Bros., "Warner Bros. Presents the Future," 7–10.
117. Church, *Disposable Passions*, 69.
118. "*Stop!*" *Adam Film World*, 80–89; "*Stop!*" *Knight*, 68–73. Much of the text and many of the images from these pieces are reprinted in Poggiali, "Endangered List."
119. Church, *Disposable Passions*, 72.
120. "*Stop!*" *Adam Film World*, 84.
121. "*Stop!*" *Knight*, 68.
122. J. Lewis, "Presumed Effects of Erotica," 12.
123. Simon, quoted in Benshoff, "Beyond the Valley," 93.
124. Benshoff, "Beyond the Valley," 94.
125. David, "'Let It Go Black,'" 41.
126. David, "'Let It Go Black,'" 42.
127. Euvrard, "Bill Gunn," 162.
128. Gunn, *Mandala*, 79.
129. Gunn, *Stop*, 41.
130. Gunn, *Stop*, 43–44.
131. Gunn, quoted in Euvrard, "Bill Gunn," 162.
132. Royalton, "Re: *Stop* (Bill Gunn, 1970)"; Corson, *Trying to Get Over*, 8.
133. Warner Bros., "Fall 1972," *Film Bulletin*, 26. I am indebted to Jonathan Hertzberg for bringing this advertisement to my attention.
134. Monaco, *American Film Now*, 205; Verrill, "TV-Bearish WB Cupboard," 3.
135. J. Williams, "Bill Gunn (1929–1989): Black Independent Filmmaker," 119.
136. "Bill Gunn's Controversial, Underseen 'Stop.'"
137. Gunn, quoted in C. Taylor, "Bill Gunn," 100.

Chapter 3

1. This chapter's epigraphs were originally spoken by Sam Waymon, in an interview in 2015 with the author, and by Gunn, in 1973, quoted in Peterson, "Interview with Bill Gunn."

2. "Plan 'Partisan' Pic."
3. "Harlem, Frisco, No. Africa Locations for 'Partisan'"; Waymon, interview. In 1973, Gunn avowed that *The Partisan* was still in the works and that it would complete a "trilogy" begun by his previous two features. Adams, "Bill Gunn," 54.
4. "Film Notes: New York"; Peterson, "Interview with Bill Gunn," 96.
5. Collins, quoted in Nicholson, "Commitment to Writing," 10.
6. Kelly-Jordan Enterprises Inc., *Georgia, Georgia*.
7. Weiler, "Forever 'Fantasticks,'" D22; Thompson, "New York Beat."
8. Kalat, "In Search of *Ganja & Hess*," 22; Gunn, "*Ganja & Hess*: Film by Bill Gunn," 18.
9. Forster and Prettyman, "Close-Up," 62.
10. For examples, see Monaco, "Blood & Blackness"; J. Williams, "Bill Gunn: Portrait of the Artist," 12; Diawara and Klotman, "*Ganja and Hess*," 299; Kalat, "*Ganja & Hess* Undead," 26; C. Taylor, "Bill Gunn," 101.
11. Sherrod, "Blood of the Thing," 103; Macfarlane, "Corrupted Affections," 22.
12. Kelly, interview.
13. That said, both *Caged Bird* and *The Inheritance* were stalled in preproduction limbo at the time of *Ganja & Hess*'s release. Gunn possibly had these delayed projects in mind when he noted, while introducing his film at Cannes in May 1973, "We're not yet allowed to make personal films—so I was offered a vampire movie to do instead. When they came back, this is what they found." Gunn, quoted in Rosenbaum, "Two Weeks in Another Town."
14. Schultz, interview.
15. Waymon, interview.
16. Gunn, quoted in C. Taylor, "Bill Gunn," 101.
17. Waymon, interview.
18. Kelly, interview.
19. Waymon, interview.
20. Lucas and Walker, "Savaging and Salvaging," 50.
21. Gunn, *Ganja & Hess (Formerly, "Blood")*, 1. In all of the *Ganja & Hess* script drafts, Hess's last name is spelled as "Greene." The final "e" is dropped, however, when the surname appears in titles and credits. Unless I quote directly from one of Gunn's screenplays, I will refer to the character by the variant used in the movie.
22. Gunn, *Ganja & Hess (Formerly, "Blood")*, 11.
23. Gunn, "*Ganja & Hess*: Film by Bill Gunn," 25–26. Gunn's June 15 draft is more or less identical to the May 30 draft later published in Phyllis Klotman's anthology, the major exception being the addition of the Luther Williams character.
24. Gunn, *Ganja & Hess (Formerly, "Blood")*, 92–93.
25. Schultz, interview; Kanefsky, interview. Kelly claims that Gunn banned him from the set at the start of filming because the presence of a white man made the actors "uncomfortable." Kelly, interview.
26. Waymon, interview.
27. Lucas and Walker, "Savaging and Salvaging," 41.
28. Kalat, "In Search of *Ganja & Hess*," 22. Also see Kalat, "*Ganja & Hess* Undead," 25–26.
29. Metz, "From Harlem to Hollywood," 229.
30. Kanefsky, interview.
31. Schultz, interview. Gunn's fictionalized depiction of the incident in *Rhinestone Sharecropping* indulges in conjecture on the heist as an inside job, for which insurance quickly and conveniently covers the losses as to not "mess up the books." Gunn, *Rhinestone Sharecropping*, 112.

32. Kanefsky, interview.
33. Hinton, audio commentary. Chuck Jackson qualifies Hinton's contention, without nullifying it, in Jackson, "Touch of the 'First' Black Cinematographer," 69.
34. Heitner, *Black Power TV*, 15–16.
35. "Ford Foundation's $25,000"; "Belafonte Plays Angel," 77.
36. Kanefsky, interview.
37. Pollard, interview.
38. Kanefsky, interview.
39. Poggiali, "Slinking through the Seventies."
40. Waymon, interview.
41. Klotman in Gunn, "*Ganja & Hess*: Film by Bill Gunn," 19; Waymon, interview.
42. Gunn, *Ganja & Hess* production notebook.
43. Waymon, audio commentary.
44. Monaco, *American Film Now*, 205.
45. Kalat, "In Search of *Ganja & Hess*," 22.
46. Gunn, "*Ganja & Hess*: Film by Bill Gunn," 20.
47. Gunn, "*Ganja & Hess*: Film by Bill Gunn," 21.
48. Gunn, "*Ganja & Hess*: Film by Bill Gunn," 22.
49. Gunn, "*Ganja & Hess*: Film by Bill Gunn," 23.
50. Gunn, *Ganja and Hess*, 34–35.
51. Weiler, "*Ganja and Hess*." Also see Robe, "*Ganja and Hess*," 32; Winsten, "'Ganja and Hess' Opens."
52. Schultz, audio commentary.
53. Fraser, "Duane L. Jones"; "Obituaries: Duane Jones."
54. Gunn, "*Ganja & Hess*: Film by Bill Gunn," 26.
55. Kanefsky, interview.
56. Pollard, interview; Hinton, audio commentary.
57. Schultz, interview.
58. Kanefsky, interview.
59. Kalat, "In Search of *Ganja & Hess*," 23.
60. Kanefsky, interview.
61. Metz, "*Ganja and Hess*."
62. Kanefsky further claims that the shot of Hess's car pulling up to the Brooklyn Museum was *repeated*, without motivation, in his original cut only to later be "fixed" without his knowing. Kanefsky, interview.
63. Waymon, interview.
64. Clover, "Her Body, Himself," 78.
65. Schultz, interview.
66. John, an award-winning art director with extensive credits in television and theater, found and brought in many of the antiques and artworks that are sprinkled throughout Hess's home. The balance of these artifacts was imported mainly from Gunn and Waymon's personal collection. Schultz, audio commentary.
67. Forster, "*Ganja & Hess*."
68. Rouget, "Notes on the Recordings"; Waymon, interview. The original recording of "Bongili Work Song" can be heard at https://www.youtube.com/watch?v=sz51ItZKNxg&index=9&list=OLAK5uy_lD4brVhTSwbUnOQOcOnqvyx5dSy4oaAyo.
69. Gunn, "*Ganja & Hess*: Film by Bill Gunn," 27–28.
70. Wilde, quoted in Gunn, "*Ganja & Hess*: Film by Bill Gunn," 30.

71. Lierow, "'Black Man's Vision of the World,'" 8. Also see Strub, "Archival Spotlight." Hinton continued to work primarily in documentary production for the balance of his career. After *Ganja & Hess*, he quickly transitioned to directing a documentary on sickle cell anemia for the Department of Labor. "Film Notes: New York."

72. Schultz, interview.
73. Hinton, audio commentary.
74. Schultz, interview.
75. Gunn, "*Ganja & Hess*: Film by Bill Gunn," 34–36.
76. Kanefsky and Kalat, audio commentary.
77. Adams, "Bill Gunn," 55.
78. Gunn, "I Deal Only in Abstractions."
79. Gunn, *Black Picture Show* (play draft), 44A.
80. Gunn, *Black Picture Show*, 82.
81. Gunn, "*Ganja & Hess*: Film by Bill Gunn," 37.
82. Hinton, audio commentary.
83. Allmendinger, *Nat Turner and the Rising in Southampton County*, 21.
84. Weiler, "*Ganja and Hess*"; Robe, "*Ganja and Hess*," 32. Also see Wolf, "Films"; Bartholomew, "*Double Possession*."
85. Gunn, "*Ganja & Hess*: Film by Bill Gunn," 39.
86. Gunn, "*Ganja & Hess*: Film by Bill Gunn," 40.
87. Waymon, interview. In *Blood Couple*, Hess identifies himself as a widower.
88. Hinton, audio commentary.
89. Schultz, audio commentary.
90. Gunn, "*Ganja & Hess*: Film by Bill Gunn," 43.
91. Gunn, "*Ganja & Hess*: Film by Bill Gunn," 47–48.
92. Gunn, "*Ganja & Hess*: Film by Bill Gunn," 45.
93. M. Clark, quoted in Darrach, "Hollywood's Second Coming," 227.
94. M. Clark, interview; Ryfle, "Glorious Ganja," 29.
95. Poggiali, "Slinking through the Seventies."
96. Waymon, interview.
97. Gunn, "*Ganja & Hess*: Film by Bill Gunn," 51. This contemplation does not appear in *Ganja & Hess*, but Jones's reading underlies images of the two lovers in postcoital repose in *Blood Couple*.
98. Waymon, interview.
99. Gunn, *Ganja & Hess* production notebook.
100. Kanefsky, interview.
101. David, "'Let It Go Black,'" 33–34; Lorde, "Uses of the Erotic," 57.
102. David, "'Let It Go Black,'" 34.
103. Gussow, "Film Festival Contracts."
104. Kanefsky, interview.
105. In an outtake preserved in Hinton's collection, Hess nonchalantly fiddles with this hatchet while Ganja makes herself at home, echoing Meda's portentous handling of the Myrthian dagger in an alternate take used in *Blood Couple*. *Ganja & Hess* outtakes, Reel 2.
106. Waymon, interview; Peterson, "Interview with Bill Gunn," 27.
107. Gunn, "*Ganja & Hess*: Film by Bill Gunn," 54–55.
108. Waymon, audio commentary.

109. Waymon, interview. Sadly, the names of the score's additional performers are lost to history, as Waymon no longer possesses documentation of the recording.
110. Waymon, quoted in Forster, "*Ganja & Hess*."
111. According to Waymon, jazz titan Max Roach told him "I wish *I* had written that score." Waymon, interview (emphasis speaker's).
112. Mephisto Odyssey's "Some Kinda Freak" (2000), for instance, extensively samples Ganja's wedding night speech. More recently, Clipping's 2019 track "Blood of the Fang" builds on snippets from "The Blood of the Thing (Part 2)," which plays during *Ganja & Hess*'s opening credits; the album on which it appears, *There Existed an Addiction to Blood*, takes its title directly from Waymon's lyric.
113. Waymon, interview.
114. David, "'Let It Go Black,'" 34.
115. Kanefsky, interview (emphasis speaker's).
116. Kalat, "In Search of *Ganja & Hess*," 24.
117. Kanefsky, interview.
118. Hinton, audio commentary.
119. Waymon, interview (emphasis speaker's).
120. Schultz, audio commentary.
121. An outtake in Hinton's collection captures Ganja's reaction to this gruesome spectacle with a pulsating zoom in and zoom out on her wide-open eyes, a crude technique unrepresentative of the film's stylistic design as a whole. *Ganja & Hess* outtakes, Reel 1.
122. David, "'Let It Go Black,'" 31.
123. Hinton, audio commentary.
124. Hinton, audio commentary.
125. Godfrey, "Notes on Black Abstraction," 159.
126. Hinton, quoted in Duganne, "Transcending the Fixity of Race," 187.
127. Gunn, quoted in C. Taylor, "Bill Gunn," 102.
128. Waymon, interview (emphasis speaker's).
129. Gunn carefully worked out the staging and filming of this sequence in his production journal; these pages supply instructions on the configuration and actions of the characters within the frame, rendered in broadly sketched panels. Gunn, *Ganja & Hess* production notebook.
130. Hinton, audio commentary.
131. Gunn, "*Ganja & Hess*: Film by Bill Gunn," 64.
132. M. Clark, interview.
133. Gunn, "*Ganja & Hess*: Film by Bill Gunn," 53.
134. Enelow, *Method Acting and Its Discontents*, 15.
135. Woolsey, "Hearing and Feeling the Black Vampire," 22.
136. Hinton later admitted that he had no idea how to shoot the actors gamboling from one room to another, so he simply set the camera on a tripod and told Jones and Clark to "play in and out of the scene." Hinton, audio commentary.
137. Gunn, *Ganja and Hess*, 74.
138. Kanefsky, interview.
139. Gunn, *Black Picture Show* (play draft), 2.
140. Gunn, *Ganja & Hess (Formerly, "Blood")*, 84.
141. Schultz, audio commentary.

142. *Ganja & Hess* outtakes, Reel 2.
143. Gunn, "*Ganja & Hess*: Film by Bill Gunn," 66–68.
144. The repetition of Hess raising the dagger was added by Kanefsky, who felt that the scene required some "theatricality." Curiously, the entire "second wedding" sequence was missing from the 35 mm copy that Kanefsky covertly acquired when ownership of *Ganja & Hess* passed from Kelly-Jordan to Heritage Enterprises. That absence eventually necessitated Schultz's negotiation with MoMA for the use of its more complete print when *Ganja & Hess* was transferred to DVD. Kanefsky, interview; Kalat, "*Ganja & Hess* Undead," 28.
145. *Ganja & Hess* outtakes, Reel 3.
146. Gunn, "*Ganja & Hess*: Film by Bill Gunn," 72.
147. *Ganja & Hess* outtakes, Reel 1. This design motif is literalized by the large glass diamond Ganja compulsively twirls in her hands throughout the scene, which is barely visible in the film.
148. Gunn, *Ganja & Hess (Formerly, "Blood")*, 96.
149. Gunn, *Ganja & Hess (Formerly, "Blood")*, 99 (emphasis in original).
150. Gunn, "*Ganja & Hess*: Film by Bill Gunn," 74.
151. Schultz, interview; Gunn, *Ganja & Hess* production notebook. Harris died in 1994 and is buried in Pineville, Louisiana.
152. Schultz, interview.
153. *Ganja & Hess* outtakes, Reel 1.
154. Waymon, audio commentary. Chuck Jackson cites these moments as evidence of the film's "haptic visuality," a concept he borrows from Laura U. Marks, noting that Hinton's camera "tends to move over the surface of its object rather than to plunge into illusionistic depth, not to distinguish form so much as to discern texture. It is more inclined to move than to focus, to graze than gaze." Marks, quoted in Jackson, "Touch of the 'First' Black Cinematographer," 78.
155. Gunn, "*Ganja & Hess*: Film by Bill Gunn," 77.
156. Gunn, "*Ganja & Hess*: Film by Bill Gunn," 79.
157. Woolsey, "Hearing and Feeling the Black Vampire," 21.
158. Gunn, "*Ganja & Hess*: Film by Bill Gunn," 81.
159. Gunn, "*Ganja & Hess*: Film by Bill Gunn," 82.
160. Waymon, interview (emphasis speaker's); Batson, "Nyack Sketch Log: Support Nyack's Center." Apostle Alston remained active in Nyack as the Presiding Prelate of St. John Deliverance Tabernacle Inc. until her death in 2019.
161. Hinton, audio commentary.
162. Waymon, interview (emphasis speaker's).
163. Waymon, interview.
164. Schultz, audio commentary.
165. Waymon, interview (emphasis speaker's).
166. Baldwin, *Devil Finds Work*, 565.
167. Schultz, audio commentary.
168. Gunn, "*Ganja & Hess*: Film by Bill Gunn," 83.
169. Gunn, "*Ganja & Hess*: Film by Bill Gunn," 86.
170. Waymon, interview.
171. P. Williams and Edgar, "Up against the Wall."
172. Waymon, interview.

173. Gunn, "*Ganja & Hess*: Film by Bill Gunn," 87.
174. *Ganja & Hess* outtakes, Reel 3.
175. Gunn, "*Ganja & Hess*: Film by Bill Gunn," 88.
176. Gunn, *Ganja and Hess*, 104.
177. Schultz, interview.

Chapter 4

1. This chapter's epigraphs originally appeared with Gunn, in 1982, quoted in C. Taylor, "Bill Gunn," and, in 1973, in Gunn, "To Be a Black Artist."
2. Kanefsky, interview.
3. Klein, *Westport, Connecticut*, 278–279.
4. "Rights to Biopic of Bessie Smith," 69; "N. Y. Rolls (Also Lays) Easter Eggs," 12. Gunn later claimed that Kelly-Jordan's investors had wanted to change the picture's title to *Bad Blood*, an option he despised. The phrase was eventually used for the tagline on *Ganja & Hess*'s poster, "Bad blood runs between them." See "Bill Gunn on WCBS-FM"; Kelly-Jordan Enterprises Inc., "*Ganja & Hess*," April 19, 1973.
5. Bowser, "Possibilities," 12; Robe, "*Ganja and Hess*," 30.
6. Kelly-Jordan Enterprises Inc. and Federation of Addiction Agencies, *Ganja & Hess* program.
7. Schultz, audio commentary; Schultz, interview. Appropriately, given the film's thematic underpinnings, proceeds from the screening and buffet reception benefited a Brooklyn-based network of facilities dedicated to treating drug addicts and reintegrating them into their communities. Kelly-Jordan Enterprises Inc. and Federation of Addiction Agencies, *Ganja & Hess* program.
8. M. Clark, quoted in Poggiali, "Slinking through the Seventies."
9. Schultz, interview.
10. Kelly, interview.
11. Winsten, "'Ganja and Hess' Opens"; Weiler, "*Ganja and Hess*."
12. Guarino, "Demitasse of Blood Anyone?"; Gelmis, "Tired Blood Lust."
13. Wolf, "Films."
14. Gifford, "'Harvard in Hell,'" 113.
15. Monaco to Gunn. Sarris eventually reversed course and accepted the piece for publication two months later. See Monaco, "Blood & Blackness."
16. J. Murray, "Reel Images." Also see Kelly-Jordan Enterprises Inc., "*Ganja & Hess*," April 23, 1973.
17. Lino and Bryan, "Interview with Bill Gunn," 47; "Black Radio, White Press Checked."
18. "N. Y. Critics' Opinions."
19. "Bill Gunn on WCBS-FM."
20. Gunn, "To Be a Black Artist," 7, 30. Paul Carter Harrison's review is also devoted to rebutting the more egregious misrepresentations by Gunn's white critics. Harrison, "Feature Review."
21. "Bill Gunn on WCBS-FM."
22. Gunn, "To Be a Black Artist," 7.
23. Weiler, "*Ganja and Hess*."

24. Winsten, "'Ganja and Hess' Opens."
25. Gunn, "To Be a Black Artist," 7. Blatant sexism also marred one of the picture's few unqualified raves: Terry Guerin's review, in which the author rhapsodizes about Clark's "perfectly accessible breasts." Guerin, "*Ganja and Hess.*"
26. "New York Sound Track," April 18, 1973. Also see "Yank Presence at Cannes," 3.
27. Kelly-Jordan Enterprises Inc., "*Ganja & Hess,*" April 19, 1973; Kelly-Jordan Enterprises Inc., "*Ganja & Hess,*" April 21, 1973; Lucas and Walker, "Savaging and Salvaging," 42; Tate, "Bill Gunn, 1934–89," 98.
28. C. Taylor, "Bill Gunn," 101. Gunn's experience of Cannes in 1973, right down to the tennis court sale, is faithfully recounted, albeit attributed to his fictional alter ego, in Gunn, *Rhinestone Sharecropping*, 40.
29. Gunn, quoted in C. Taylor, "Bill Gunn," 101 (emphasis in original).
30. Moskowitz, quoted in Museum of Modern Art, "New Films from Seven Countries."
31. Monaco, "Blood & Blackness." Also see Diawara, "Black American Cinema," 10; Lucas and Walker, "Savaging and Salvaging," 42.
32. Waymon, interview (emphasis speaker's).
33. See J. Murray, "Black Movies and Music in Harmony."
34. "Black Films Come to the Front."
35. Waymon, interview.
36. Gunn, quoted in C. Taylor, "Bill Gunn," 101.
37. Waymon, audio commentary; Kelly, interview.
38. "N. Y. Rolls (Also Lays) Easter Eggs," 12.
39. "N. Y. Easter Joy Gone," 20.
40. Bowser, "Possibilities," 12.
41. "United Artists 'Black Hand Side,'" 5.
42. Kelly, interview.
43. Waymon, interview; Dombrowski, *Films of Samuel Fuller*, 177.
44. Steloff, quoted in Monaco, "Blood & Blackness."
45. Kanefsky, interview.
46. D. Walker, "Fima Noveck," 50.
47. Lucas and Walker, "Savaging and Salvaging," 44.
48. Noveck, quoted in D. Walker, "Fima Noveck," 52; Lucas and Walker, "Savaging and Salvaging," 50.
49. Kalat, "In Search of *Ganja & Hess*," 23.
50. Lucas and Walker, "Savaging and Salvaging," 43. The veracity of this claim—that critics of the time were unable to distinguish between the original and its revision—is challenged by David Bartholomew's capsule review of *Blood Couple* (a.k.a. *Double Possession*) for *Cinefantastique*. Bartholomew is completely cognizant of the fact that Gunn's film had been "viciously re-edited" and that, consequently, every scene now needed to be evaluated on its own merits. Bartholomew, "*Double Possession.*"
51. Monaco, "Blood & Blackness"; Monaco, *American Film Now*, 207.
52. Leki, "Bill Gunn," 113; Diawara and Klotman, "Ganja and Hess," 314n1.
53. Dumler to Waymon, Gunn, and Schultz.
54. Kanefsky, interview.
55. D. Walker, "Fima Noveck," 50.
56. Noveck, quoted in D. Walker, "Fima Noveck," 53.

57. Lucas and Walker, "Savaging and Salvaging," 42. Also see "Three Kelly-Jordan Films Ready."
58. "'Liberty' Lively $14,000," 12.
59. Lucas, *Mario Bava*, 926.
60. "3 Kelly-Jordan Pix."
61. *Double Possession* trailer, HFA.
62. "Kelly-Jordan to Release Three Films."
63. Kelly-Jordan Enterprises Inc., *Double Possession* (pressbook). Also see Kelly-Jordan Enterprises Inc., "*Double Possession*," March 3, 1975 and September 14, 1975.
64. Lucas and Walker, "Savaging and Salvaging," 54.
65. Sconce, "'Trashing' the Academy," 372, 373.
66. Heffernan, "Prurient (Dis)Interest," 115.
67. Sconce, "'Trashing' the Academy," 386.
68. Newman, "*Ganja & Hess*," 48 (emphasis added).
69. Lucas and Walker, "Savaging and Salvaging," 50–51 (emphasis added); Gunn, quoted by Schultz in Kalat, "In Search of *Ganja & Hess*," 22.
70. Lino and Bryan, "Interview with Bill Gunn," 49.
71. See Diawara and Klotman, "*Ganja and Hess*," 302.
72. Kalat, "*Ganja & Hess* Undead," 26 (emphasis added).
73. Joseph Gelmis explicitly draws such a connection in his unfavorable comparison of *Ganja & Hess* to both *Night of the Living Dead* and Leonard Kastle's lurid crime drama *The Honeymoon Killers* (1970), a pair of "pictures whose amateur look gave them added impact because they looked like documentaries instead of horror shows." Gelmis, "Tired Blood Lust."
74. Gunn, *Egyptian Murals*; Berry, "*Family Employment*." Furthermore, as noted in *Variety*'s for-the-record review, *Stop* strongly resembles Stephen King's *The Shining* in both "structure and subplot." Lor, "Archive Film Review: *Stop*."
75. Lucas, *Mario Bava*, 872. Also see Tudor, *Monsters and Mad Scientists*, 65.
76. Newman, *Nightmare Movies*, 28; Newman, "*Ganja & Hess*," 50.
77. As Lauren Berg theorizes, all three of these pictures allegorize "economically driven neocolonialism" through signifying "the figural bleeding dry of less dominant cultural and economic forces under globalization." Whereas classic vampires are infiltrators of normality, the postseventies vampire is, like Gunn's antique-collecting archaeologist, more of an "importer" representing "the global presence that exists in every localized community." Berg, "Globalization and the Modern Vampire," 10.
78. Hudson, "Vampires and Transnational Horror," 465.
79. Olney, *Euro Horror*, 8.
80. Olney, *Euro Horror*, 7.
81. Lowenstein, *Shocking Representation*, 5.
82. Benshoff, "Blaxploitation Horror Films," 38.
83. Coleman, *Horror Noire*, 119.
84. Lipsitz, "Genre Anxiety and Racial Representation," 218.
85. Benshoff, "Blaxploitation Horror Films," 43.
86. Benshoff, "Blaxploitation Horror Films," 31.
87. Hudson, "Vampires and Transnational Horror," 463.
88. Elam, *Past as Present*, xviii.

89. Browning, "Classical Hollywood Horror," 229 (emphasis added).
90. Gunn, "*Ganja & Hess*: Film by Bill Gunn," 33.
91. Hudson, "Vampires and Transnational Horror," 463.
92. Hudson, *Vampires, Race, and Transnational Hollywoods*, 136; Hudson, "Vampires and Transnational Horror," 466.
93. Sherrod, "Blood of the Thing," 108.
94. "N. Y. Easter Joy Gone," 20.
95. Milliken, "Rate It X?" 36.
96. Waymon, audio commentary. The sex scene between Ganja and Richard is so intense that Noveck actually pared it down for *Blood Couple*, supposedly the more salacious version of *Ganja & Hess*.
97. Robe, "Ganja and Hess," 30, 32.
98. Weiler, "*Ganja and Hess*"; Winsten, "'Ganja and Hess' Opens."
99. Harrison, "Feature Review," 16.
100. Newman, *Nightmare Movies*, 28.
101. Gorfinkel, *Lewd Looks*, 7.
102. Hudson, "Vampires and Transnational Horror," 464.
103. Johnson and Henderson, "Introduction," 4.
104. David, "'Let It Go Black,'" 33.
105. David, "'Let It Go Black,'" 36.
106. Diawara and Klotman, "*Ganja and Hess*," 314; David, "'Let It Go Black,'" 37.
107. Winsten, "'Ganja and Hess' Opens."
108. David, "'Let It Go Black,'" 37.
109. hooks, "Oppositional Gaze," 203–204, 209.
110. J. Murray, "Reel Images" (emphasis added).
111. Bogle, *Blacks in American Films and Television*, 87–88.
112. Gelmis, "Tired Blood Lust."
113. Reed, "Bill Gunn: Director," 116. In his *Impressions* interview, Gunn professes his admiration for Jean Cocteau, the "most adventurous" French director, and for Gillo Pontecorvo's *The Battle of Algiers* (1966), which for Gunn succeeds as both a "personal" and a "political" film. Gunn, quoted in Lino and Bryan, "Interview with Bill Gunn," 47, 61.
114. There is an explicit allusion to Resnais in *Ganja and Hess*'s sex scenes: the glitter sprinkled on the bodies strongly resembles the pulsating beads of sweat on the ash-covered lovers in the famous opening of *Hiroshima mon amour* (1959).
115. Kanefsky, interview.
116. Pollard, interview.
117. Gunn, "'To Be a Black Artist,'" 7, 30.
118. Metz makes a similar point in "From Harlem to Hollywood," 226–227.
119. Weiler, "*Ganja and Hess*"; Guarino, "Demitasse of Blood Anyone?"
120. For an exhaustive catalog of the postwar art film's formal criteria, see Bordwell, "Art Cinema" and Staiger, "With the Compliments of the Auteur."
121. Lucas and Walker, "Savaging and Salvaging," 41, 56 (emphasis in original).
122. Monaco, "Blood & Blackness."
123. Monaco, "Blood & Blackness."
124. Diawara and Klotman, "*Ganja and Hess*," 302.
125. Stevens, "Bodies Off."

126. See Hartmann, "Trope of Blaxploitation."
127. Winsten, "'Ganja and Hess' Opens."
128. Gunn, "I Deal Only in Abstractions" (emphasis in original).
129. Mason, "New Films," 62 (emphasis in original).
130. Guerin, *Ganja and Hess.*
131. Neal, quoted in West, "Makers of Black Films," 67.
132. Gillespie, *Film Blackness*, 36.
133. Gunn, quoted in Adams, "Bill Gunn," 55.
134. Gunn, quoted in Adams, "Bill Gunn," 57. Also see Peterson, "Interview with Bill Gunn," 27; Stuart, "Bill Gunn's Play a 'Mental Trip.'"
135. Gunn, quoted in C. Taylor, "Bill Gunn," 102, 103 (emphasis added).
136. Gunn, quoted in Adams, "Bill Gunn," 55.
137. Gunn, quoted in C. Taylor, "Bill Gunn," 105.
138. Monaco, "Lost Films"; Monaco, *American Film Now*, 205.
139. Diawara, "Black American Cinema," 9–11. This distinction expands on Monaco's abbreviated metaphor: if *Ganja & Hess* is *Invisible Man*, *Sweetback* is *Native Son*. Monaco, *American Film Now*, 205.
140. Gillespie, *Film Blackness*, 2.
141. Gates, "Problem with 'Anti-Racist' Movie Lists."
142. Diawara, "Black American Cinema," 10, 11, 13.
143. Field, "To Journey Imperfectly," 175.
144. Gunn witheringly comments on this phenomenon in *Rhinestone Sharecropping*, in which the protagonist, Sam Dodd, recalls the critiques of his first produced play: "I wrote what I felt, which always lacked the signposts that lead the average man to the ghetto. Critics wrote: 'Mr. Dodd lacks the quality of his people.' I knew what he felt. Like being sealed in a Black tunnel with a Nigger who moves on cat feet. We need to hear the popping of chicken fat to tell where I was, or it was no play." Gunn, *Rhinestone Sharecropping*, 83.
145. D. Murray, *Queering Post-Black Art*, 2.
146. D. Murray, *Queering Post-Black Art*, 4–5. The notion that the Black arts movement and post-Blackness are antithetical in their objectives and practices has recently been challenged by Margo Natalie Crawford, who uncovers proto-post-Black impulses in the earlier movement's second wave. Crawford, *Black Post-Blackness*.
147. Prettyman (Beverly), "Phenomenal Bodies," 17n36, 61.
148. Pavlić, *Who Can Afford to Improvise?* 104.
149. Gunn, "Johnnas," 135, 136.
150. Gunn, *All the Rest Have Died*, 82.
151. Gunn, *All the Rest Have Died*, 155.
152. Schraufnagel, *From Apology to Protest*, 125. Also see Splawn, "Bill Gunn (1934–1989)," 196.
153. Leki, "Bill Gunn," 111.
154. Leki, "Bill Gunn," 112.
155. Gunn, quoted in Smith, "Major Plays Will Come from Blacks" (emphasis in original).
156. Gunn, "I Deal Only in Abstractions."
157. Kroll, "Black-and-White Picture."
158. Metz, "From Harlem to Hollywood," 232.
159. Gunn, quoted in Adams, "Bill Gunn," 55, 56 (emphasis added).

160. Diawara and Klotman, "*Ganja and Hess*," 308.
161. Gunn, *Ganja & Hess (Formerly, "Blood")*, 22 (emphasis in original).
162. Diawara and Klotman, "*Ganja and Hess*," 307.
163. Stanbrook, "*Ganja and Hess*."
164. Lucas and Walker, "Savaging and Salvaging," 41.
165. Benshoff, "Blaxploitation Horror Films," 44.
166. Sherrod, "Blood of the Thing," 109–110.
167. Tate, "Bill Gunn, 1934–89," 98; Bambara, "Reading the Signs, Empowering the Eye," 138.
168. Harrison, "Feature Review," 12.
169. Baldwin, *Devil Finds Work*, 566.
170. Kalat, "In Search of *Ganja & Hess*," 21.
171. Gillespie, *Film Blackness*, 36.

Chapter 5

1. This chapter's epigraph is excerpted from Gunn, in 1975, quoted in Anderson, "Seminar for Black and Third World Filmmakers."
2. Helm, "Ishmael Reed," 147.
3. Monaco, "Blood & Blackness."
4. Kalat, "*Ganja & Hess* Undead," 28.
5. Bowser, "Possibilities," 12.
6. "MOMA Sets Screening of 'Ganja and Hess.'"
7. Monaco, *American Film Now*, 207; Museum of Modern Art, "New Films from Seven Countries." In a 2018 interview, Ayoka Chenzira recalled seeing a 35 mm print of *Ganja & Hess* at an invitation-only screening, along with many other Black filmmakers of New York; quite possibly, she attended MoMA's December 20 premiere. Prettyman, "Close-Up," 72.
8. "MOMA Sets Screening of 'Ganja and Hess.'"
9. Monaco, "Blood & Blackness."
10. Stuart, "Bill Gunn's Play a 'Mental Trip.'"
11. Bowser, "Possibilities," 12.
12. "Biographical Data"; "Theatrical Spotlight."
13. "Film File"; "Talladega College Celebrates the Black Arts."
14. M. Clark, interview.
15. Pollard, interview.
16. Monaco, *American Film Now*, 205.
17. "Entertainment or Revolution?"
18. Guillaume, "Black History in New York State." This report is contradicted by Gunn in a 1975 interview in which he references seeing *Ganja & Hess* at Cullen Library and taking questions afterward. Lino and Bryan, "Interview with Bill Gunn," 49.
19. C. Taylor, "Bill Gunn," 101.
20. "Les Films Noirs Américains," 201; Field, Horak, and Stewart, "Introduction," 30.
21. Bowser and Harris, "Independent Black American Cinema"; "International Sound Track."
22. Field, Horak, and Stewart, "Introduction," 31.

23. Field, Horak, and Stewart, "Introduction," 2. Several key rebellion directors presented their films at the retrospective and took part in discussions, including Charles Burnett (who showed *Killer of Sheep*), Larry Clark, and Ben Caldwell. Bowser and Harris, "Independent Black American Cinema."

24. Field, Horak, and Stewart, "Introduction," 20–21, 28–29.
25. Bowser to Gunn.
26. Bowser, "Possibilities," 12.
27. Bowser, "Possibilities," 17; Lucas and Walker, "Savaging and Salvaging," 55.
28. In 1982 alone, Gunn and his film opened an Independent Filmmakers Series at the Rockland Center for the Arts in West Nyack and graced showcases for Black or postcolonial cinema at the Massachusetts College of Art in Boston, the Collective for Living Cinema in Lower Manhattan, and the Harlem Branch YMCA. "Filmmakers Festival to Open"; Boston Film/Video Foundation, "Calendar: April 82"; "New York Sound Track," April 21, 1982; "Black Images on Film."
29. Griffin to Hoffmeister.
30. Camera News Distribution Agreement; Gunn to Griffin; Griffin to Gunn.
31. Yarrow, "Brooklyn Series to Study Black Images"; "Umea Fest Skeds Kumel"; Stanbrook, "*Ganja and Hess*."
32. Griffin to Hoffmeister.
33. Klotman to Gunn.
34. Waymon, interview.
35. The Criterion Channel made this 1983 interview available to stream in the summer of 2020, coinciding with a three-film Gunn retrospective.
36. "In Memoriam"; Freydberg to Gunn.
37. "Hollywood Soundtrack."
38. Segers, "5th Blacklight Fest."
39. Butters, *From* Sweetback *to* Super Fly, 201.
40. J. Murray, "The Subject Is Money," 253.
41. J. Murray, *To Find an Image*, 170–171.
42. Bogle, *Toms, Coons, Mulattoes, Mammies, and Bucks* (1994), 266. For an incisive analysis of the broader industrial implications of *The Wiz*'s "racialized media reception," see Martin, "Blackbusting Hollywood."
43. Guerrero, *Framing Blackness*, 110.
44. George, *Blackface*, 56.
45. Gunn, *Rhinestone Sharecropping*, 17.
46. See Dempsey and Gupta, "Hollywood's Color Problem"; Cohn, "Black Pic Employment Still Lags."
47. Waymon, interview.
48. Papp, quoted in Gussow, "Classics, Lincoln Center and Papp."
49. O'Farrow, "A Letter."
50. Stuart, "Bill Gunn's Play a 'Mental Trip.'"
51. "BPS"; Kamlot to Moses; Papp to Roach.
52. "'Black Picture Show' 2d Shakespeare Entry."
53. Kelly, interview.
54. Riley, "*Black Picture Show*."
55. Gunn, *Black Picture Show*, 110–111.

56. Gunn, *Black Picture Show*, 99.
57. Gunn, *Black Picture Show*, 105.
58. "Show Out of Town," 58.
59. Schultz, interview; Gunn, *Black Picture Show*, 102.
60. Gunn, *Black Picture Show*, 33.
61. Gunn, *Black Picture Show*, 82.
62. Gunn, *Black Picture Show*, 37.
63. Abbott to Papp, October 28, 1974; Abbott to Papp, November 1, 1974.
64. "*Black Picture Show*"; Leki, "Bill Gunn," 113.
65. T. E. K., "The Blame Game"; Simon, "Music of the Squares."
66. Gill, "Writing about Writing," 61.
67. Gunn, *Black Picture Show*, 30–31.
68. Kroll, "Black-and-White Picture." Gunn's sly allusion to "A White Man's Heaven Is a Black Man's Hell," a song composed by the minister Louis Farrakhan, surely contributed to the play's enthusiastic reception in the Nation of Islam's official journal, *Muhammad Speaks*. J. Walker, "'Black Picture Show.'"
69. Gunn, *Black Picture Show*, 114–115.
70. Gunn, *Black Picture Show*, 96.
71. Riley, "*Black Picture Show*."
72. Gussow, "Classics, Lincoln Center and Papp."
73. Riley, quoted in B. Lewis, "Black Critic."
74. Lynn to Papp.
75. Gunn, quoted in C. Taylor, "Bill Gunn," 101.
76. Gunn, *Black Picture Show*, 44.
77. Batson, "Nyack Sketch Log: Sam Waymon Lived Here"; Harwood, "Modest Assessment from Muhammad Ali."
78. Waymon, interview.
79. Gunn, *Rhinestone Sharecropping*, 22.
80. Gunn, *Rhinestone Sharecropping*, 146; Gunn to Veitch.
81. Gunn, *Rhinestone Sharecropping*, 161.
82. See Gunn, *I Am the Greatest*.
83. Gunn, *Rhinestone Sharecropping*, 176, 191.
84. Waymon, interview (emphasis speaker's).
85. Mitchell, "Bill Gunn's 'Rhinestone' Shines Brilliantly"; Stone, "All That Glitters."
86. Stone, "All That Glitters"; Rich, "Theater: 'Rhinestone.'"
87. Valkhn Communications, "*Rhinestone*."
88. Richard Allen Center for Culture and Art, "*Rhinestone*." As Barbara Cady notes in her *Los Angeles Times* review, this very phrase was used to promote *Rhinestone Sharecropping* as well. Cady, "Playing by the Enemy's Rules."
89. Gunn, *Family Employment*.
90. Berry, "*Family Employment*."
91. Klotman, in Gunn, "*Ganja & Hess*: Film by Bill Gunn," 16.
92. See Gunn, *Renaissance*.
93. Feingold, "Gloria in Excelsis," 98 (emphasis in original). Because Gunn was, according to Schultz's recollection, "terrified" that his mother would see *The Forbidden City*, there is perhaps a sliver of truth to Feingold's opinion. Schultz, interview.

94. Gussow, "A Mother Only a Son Could Love." The Williams influence is more positively framed in Sinclair, "'Forbidden City' Season's Best."
95. Simon, "Myself When Young, Twice," 80; Massa, "Sightlines," 97.
96. Feingold, "Gloria in Excelsis," 98.
97. "Bill Gun [sic]"; "Television Review."
98. Fraser, "'Watch Your Mouth!' on WNET." At least two episodes of *Watch Your Mouth!* were Gunn originals: "Bringing It All Home" and "The Caftan Caper."
99. Archerd, "Just for Variety"; Arnold to Hoffmeister.
100. Werner, quoted in Kleiman, "'Cosby' Producers Plan 2 Similar TV Series."
101. Reed, "Bill Gunn: Director," 116. Following *The Lena Horne Show*'s termination, Cosby hired Gunn for a guest spot on his top-rated sitcom. In his final screen appearances, Gunn performed as one of the card-playing buddies of Cliff Huxtable's father in "The Card Game" and "War Stories."
102. Landis to Gunn.
103. J. Williams, "Bill Gunn: Portrait of the Artist," 12; Lucas and Walker, "Savaging and Salvaging," 55.
104. As phrased by Carolina Ritter in a 1980 profile, *Personal Problems* differs "from the average White soap opera in more ways than one. For example, the characters talk about money like it's money, if you know what I mean." Ritter, "Soap to Alter TV's Complexion."
105. Helm, "Ishmael Reed," 147 (emphasis in original).
106. Reed, *Personal Problems*; Forster, "'Improvisational Jamming.'"
107. Forster, "'Improvisational Jamming.'"
108. Reed, quoted in Wilderson, "Video Tape Soap Operas," 191; Forster, "'New Form of Black Genre Communication.'"
109. Reed, *Personal Problems*.
110. Hampton, "Careworn Chronicles," 56.
111. Forster, "'Improvisational Jamming.'"
112. Korwin-Pawlowska, "'Personal Problems.'"
113. Kernan, "Ishmael Reed's Video Voodoo."
114. Forster, "'Improvisational Jamming.'"
115. Cotton, quoted in Reed, "Bill Gunn: Director," 118. Grosvenor responded so well to Gunn's direction that she asked him to supervise a radio adaptation of John Langston Gwaltney's book *Drylongso: A Self Portrait of Black America*, which she hoped to produce. Chadwick to Gunn.
116. Brunsting, "Joshua Reviews Bill Gunn's *Personal Problems*."
117. Reed, "Black Artist Money Couldn't Buy."
118. Bowser and Spence, *Writing Himself into History*, 132.
119. Forster, "'Improvisational Jamming.'"
120. Wilderson, "Video Tape Soap Operas," 192.
121. Reed, *Personal Problems*.
122. Reed, "Black Artist Money Couldn't Buy"; Mitchell, "Busy Weekend."
123. Reed, *Personal Problems*.
124. Wilderson, "Video Tape Soap Operas," 191–192.
125. Gunn, quoted in Reed, "Bill Gunn: Director," 117.
126. Rising Sun Productions, *The Afrikan Sun*.
127. "Diller Wants Assured Flow"; Bell to Gunn.

128. J. Williams, "Bill Gunn (1929–1989): Black Independent Filmmaker," 139.
129. See Stallings, "'Redemptive Softness,'"; Prettyman (Beverly), "Phenomenal Bodies," 39–97; O'Malley, "Art on Her Mind."
130. A. Clark, "Making Ground"; "Kathleen Collins"; O'Malley, "Art on Her Mind," 82–83.
131. Reed, "Bill Gunn: Director," 115, 116.
132. Gunn, quoted in C. Taylor, "Bill Gunn," 102.
133. "Delphic Corporation."
134. Kanefsky, interview.
135. Waymon to Schultz, March 2, 1982.
136. Gunn, *Rain Forest*, 1–2, 45.
137. Gunn, *Rain Forest*, 26–27. Max's mother humorously botches the designation "underground film," a catch-all term widely applied to noncommercial cinema in the late sixties.
138. Schickel, quoted in Gunn, *Territory*.
139. Zvi, "NYSF Play Report."
140. Gunn, *Territory*, 44.
141. Gunn, *Territory*, 1–2.
142. Gunn, *Territory*, 60, 63.
143. Gunn, *Territory*, 10.
144. Gunn, *Territory*, 16.
145. Gunn, quoted in Adams, "Bill Gunn," 56.
146. Gunn, *Rain Forest*, 42.
147. Gunn, *Territory*, 8.
148. Gunn, *Territory*, 58.
149. Gunn, *Territory*, 62.
150. Gunn, *Black Picture Show*, 3.
151. Zvi, "NYSF Play Report."
152. Crystal Falls Films Inc., "*Territory*."
153. Waymon to Schultz, March 20, 1985.
154. "'Territory' Gearing Up for N. Y., Canada Shoot," 85, 229.
155. Klotman, in Gunn, "*Ganja & Hess*: Film by Bill Gunn," 16.
156. Gunn, quoted in C. Taylor, "Bill Gunn," 104.
157. Gunn, quoted in Euvrard, "Bill Gunn," 163.
158. Gunn, quoted in C. Taylor, "Bill Gunn," 104–105.
159. Gunn, quoted in Euvrard, "Bill Gunn," 163.
160. Gunn, quoted in C. Taylor, "Bill Gunn," 103.

Conclusion

1. This chapter's epigraph originally appeared in 1981 in Gunn's *Rhinestone Sharecropping*.
2. "Obituaries: Duane Jones"; Fraser, "Duane L. Jones."
3. "Kathleen Collins."
4. J. Robinson to Schultz.
5. J. Robinson, *Survive in Spite of Your Family*, xii.
6. J. Williams to Gunn. It is possible that by this point Gunn had contracted AIDS, which was then ravaging creative communities worldwide. Some recent writing on Gunn

identifies AIDS as a contributing factor in the artist's death; Hilton Als was among the first to publicly share this information. Als, "Year in Theatre."
    7. Schultz, interview.
    8. "Bill Gunn Memorial Service."
    9. Tate, "Bill Gunn, 1934–89," 98.
    10. Diawara, "Black American Cinema," 10, 13. In her own words, Julie Dash "bit off a piece" of *Ganja & Hess* in her staging of the scene in which Eula receives sympathetic counsel from her husband's cousin Yellow Mary, as the latter "sits idly in the crook of an oak tree." Dash's citation of Gunn (and James Hinton) was itself reproduced, famously, in Beyoncé's universally acclaimed visual album *Lemonade* (2016). Prettyman, "Close-Up," 73. Also see Rogers, "Diasporic Communion and Textual Exchange," 149.
    11. Kangalee, "Flowers for Bill Gunn."
    12. Chenzira, quoted in Prettyman, "Close-Up," 73.
    13. Waymon, interview (emphasis speaker's).
    14. Bambara, "Reading the Signs, Empowering the Eye," 137.
    15. Bartling, "Intentions and Mass Culture," 122.
    16. Gunn, quoted in Euvrard, "Bill Gunn," 163.
    17. Gunn, quoted in C. Taylor, "Bill Gunn," 104.
    18. Waymon, interview.
    19. Lee, quoted in Harris, "Spike Lee Discusses New Film."
    20. Schultz, interview.
    21. Prospective investors were assured, however, that Lee's movie was "not a remake of 'Blacula.'" "Newest Hottest Spike Lee Joint."
    22. Pollard, interview.
    23. M. Clark, interview.
    24. Waymon, interview.
    25. Miller, "Lost and . . . Found?" 673–674.
    26. Harris, "Spike Lee Discusses New Film."
    27. Waymon, interview.
    28. Lee, quoted in Blay, "Interview." Also see Harris, "Spike Lee Discusses New Film."
    29. Lee, quoted in Juzwiak, "How to Not Make a Vampire Movie."
    30. Lee, quoted in Harris, "Spike Lee Discusses New Film."
    31. Kangalee, "Flowers for Bill Gunn."
    32. J. Williams to Schultz; Waymon to Schultz, May 14, 1990. Reed later revised his talk and included it in his essay collection *Airing Dirty Laundry*.
    33. Morra to Waymon.
    34. Kalat, "*Ganja & Hess* Undead," 28.
    35. Kalat, "In Search of *Ganja & Hess*," 24.
    36. Hampton, "Careworn Chronicles," 55.
    37. Forster, "'Improvisational Jamming.'" In the summer of 2021, Perlin, in collaboration with Hilton Als and the Lower Manhattan gallery Artists Space, organized "Till They Listen: Bill Gunn Directs America," a comprehensive multimedia exhibition and series of public programs, which featured screenings of *Ganja & Hess* and *Personal Problems*, a staged reading of *Black Picture Show*, and a live concert by Sam Waymon. ("Till They Listen.")
    38. Gunn, *Rhinestone Sharecropping*, 143.

BIBLIOGRAPHY

Abbreviations for Archival Sources

HFA: Harvard Film Archive, Harvard College Library, Harvard University, Cambridge, Massachusetts.
MHL: Department of Special Collections, Margaret Herrick Library, Beverly Hills, California.
NYSF: New York Shakespeare Festival Records, Billy Rose Theatre Division, New York Public Library for the Performing Arts, New York City, New York.
SCR: Manuscripts, Archives and Rare Books Division, Schomburg Center for Research in Black Culture, New York Public Library, New York City, New York.
WFU: Special Collections & Archives, Z. Smith Reynolds Library, Wake Forest University, Winston-Salem, North Carolina.

Sources

Abbott, Ron, to Joseph Papp, October 28, 1974. "Series II: Play Department," NYSF.
Abbott, Ron, to Joseph Papp, November 1, 1974. "Series II: Play Department," NYSF.
Adams, Janus Ingrid. "Bill Gunn: We Should Burn All the Books and Start All Over Again." *Encore*, June 1973, 54–57.
Allmendinger, David F., Jr. *Nat Turner and the Rising in Southampton County*. Baltimore, MD: Johns Hopkins University Press, 2014.
Als, Hilton. "The Year in Theatre and Farewell to a Friend." *New Yorker*, January 2, 2016. https://www.newyorker.com/culture/culture-desk/the-year-in-theatre-and-farewell-to-a-friend.
Anderson, Madeline. "Seminar for Black and Third World Filmmakers." *News from International Film Seminars*, n.d. Bill Gunn Papers, SCR.
Angelou, Maya. "*Georgia*: A Screen Treatment by Maya Angelou," n.d., 1–40. Maya Angelou Film and Theater Collection, WFU.
Angelus, Ted. "Black Film Explosion Uncovers an Untapped, Rich Market." *Advertising Age*, July 24, 1972, 51–52.
Archerd, Army. "Just for Variety." *Daily Variety*, February 5, 1987, 3.
Arnold, Danny, to John Hoffmeister, May 10, 1991. Bill Gunn Papers, SCR.
Asante, Molefi Kete. *The African American People: A Global History*. New York: Routledge, 2012.
Atkinson, Brooks. "Theatre: 'Take a Giant Step' Gets Second Chance." *New York Times*, September 26, 1956, 30.
"The Author," n.d. Bill Gunn Papers, SCR.
Bailey, Peter. "A Black Woman with White Fever." *New York Times*, March 26, 1972, D13.
Baker, Jean-Claude, and Chris Chase. *Josephine: The Hungry Heart*. New York: Random House, 1993.

Baldwin, James. *The Devil Finds Work*. In *Collected Essays*, 477–572. New York: Library of America, 1998.

———. *In the Cross, a Trembling Soul: The Inheritance* (screenplay), n.d., 1–128. Dick Fontaine Collection, HFA.

Bambara, Toni Cade. "Reading the Signs, Empowering the Eye: *Daughters of the Dust* and the Black Independent Cinema Movement." In *Black American Cinema*, edited by Manthia Diawara, 118–144. New York: Routledge, 1993.

Bartholomew, David. *"Double Possession"* (review). *Cinefantastique* 5, no. 1 (Spring 1976): 30.

Bartling, Hugh. "Intentions and Mass Culture: Oscar Micheaux, Identity, and Authorship." In *Authorship and Film*, edited by David A. Gerstner and Janet Staiger, 119–136. New York: Routledge, 2003.

Batson, Bill. "Nyack Sketch Log: Sam Waymon Lived Here." *Nyack News and Views*, February 12, 2013. http://www.nyacknewsandviews.com/2013/02/bb_samwaymon/.

———. "Nyack Sketch Log: Support Nyack's Center." *Nyack News and Views*, December 3, 2013. http://www.nyacknewsandviews.com/2013/12/nsl119_support-nyacks-center/.

"Belafonte Plays Angel on and off the Screen." *Ebony*, October 1969, 76–82.

Bell, Edward, to Bill Gunn, March 4, 1979. Bill Gunn Papers, SCR.

Benshoff, Harry M. "Beyond the Valley of the Classical Hollywood Cinema: Rethinking the 'Loathsome Film' of 1970." In *The Shifting Definitions of Genre: Essays on Labeling Films, Television Shows and Media*, edited by Lincoln Geraghty and Mark Jancovich, 92–109. Jefferson, NC: McFarland, 2008.

———. "Blaxploitation Horror Films: Generic Reappropriation or Reinscription?" *Cinema Journal* 39, no. 2 (Winter 2000): 31–50.

Berg, Lauren. "Globalization and the Modern Vampire." *Film Matters* 2, no. 3 (Fall 2011): 8–12.

Berry, David. *"Family Employment*, by Bill Gunn" (reader report), October 11, 1985. "Series II: Play Department," NYSF.

"Bill Gun [sic]: Knowledge Gained at Mother's Knee." *Philadelphia Tribune*, March 29, 1975, n.p. Bill Gunn Papers, SCR.

"Bill Gunn Memorial Service" (program), April 17, 1989. Bill Gunn Papers, SCR.

"Bill Gunn on WCBS-FM Builds 'Bias' Case." *Variety*, May 9, 1973, 2.

"Bill Gunn's Controversial, Underseen 'Stop' Will Finally See the Light of Day (Once Some Minor Problems Are Cleared)." *Shadow and Act*, June 24, 2014. https://shadowandact.com/bill-gunns-controversial-underseen-stop-will-finally-see-the-light-of-day-once-some-minor-problems-are-cleared.

"Biographical Data," n.d. Bill Gunn Papers, SCR.

Björkman, Stig. Audio commentary. *Georgia, Georgia*, DVD. Scorpion Releasing, 1972; 2012.

———. Email message to author, September 17, 2016.

[Björkman, Stig]. *Georgia, Georgia*, treatment, n.d. Maya Angelou Film and Theater Collection, WFU.

"Black Academy N. Y. Fest & 'Oscars'?" *Variety*, April 11, 1973, 3.

"Black Films Come to the Front at Cannes International Film Festival." *New York Amsterdam News*, May 26, 1973, D1.

"Black Images on Film: Music as a Language of Politics and Culture" (advertisement), n.d. Charles H. "Chiz" Schultz/Fireside Productions Collection, SCR.

"Black Market." *Time*, April 10, 1972, 53.

"The Black Movie Boom." *Newsweek*, September 6, 1971, 66.

"Black Movie Boom—Good or Bad?" *New York Times*, December 17, 1972, D3, D19.
"*Black Picture Show*" (advertisement). *New York Times*, January 19, 1975, 109.
"'Black Picture Show' 2d Shakespeare Entry." *Variety*, November 20, 1974, 57.
"Black Radio, White Press Checked as Best Come-On for Black Fans; Race's Own Papers Poor to Loews." *Variety*, February 6, 1974, 5.
"Black Still Times Square Beautiful." *Variety*, September 13, 1972, 8, 16.
Blay, Zeba. "Interview: Investigating 'Da Sweet Blood of Jesus' w/Spike Lee + Lead Actors Zaraah Abrahams and Stephen Tyrone Williams." *Shadow and Act*, June 26, 2014. https://shadowandact.com/interview-investigating-da-sweet-blood-of-jesus-w-spike-lee-lead-actors-zaraah-abrahams-and-stephen-tyrone-williams.
Bogle, Donald. *Blacks in American Films and Television: An Encyclopedia*. New York: Fireside Books, 1988.
———. *Toms, Coons, Mulattoes, Mammies, and Bucks: An Interpretive History of Blacks in American Films*. 1st ed. New York: Viking Press, 1973.
———. *Toms, Coons, Mulattoes, Mammies, and Bucks: An Interpretive History of Blacks in American Films*. 3rd ed. New York: Continuum, 1994.
Bordwell, David. "The Art Cinema as a Mode of Film Practice." In *Film Theory and Criticism: Introductory Readings*, 5th ed., edited by Leo Braudy and Marshall Cohen, 716–724. New York: Oxford University Press, 1999.
Boston Film/Video Foundation. "Calendar: April 82," 1982. Bill Gunn Papers, SCR.
Bosworth, Patricia. *Montgomery Clift: A Biography*. New York: Harcourt Brace Jovanovich, 1978.
Bowser, Pearl. "Possibilities That Might Have Been . . . ." *Black Film Review* 5, no. 2 (Spring 1989): 12, 17.
Bowser, Pearl, and Valerie Harris. "Independent Black American Cinema 1920–1980" (booklet), February 1981. Bill Gunn Papers, SCR.
Bowser, Pearl, and Louise Spence. *Writing Himself into History: Oscar Micheaux, His Silent Films, and His Audiences*. New Brunswick, NJ: Rutgers University Press, 2000.
Bowser, Pearl, to Bill Gunn et al., n.d. Bill Gunn Papers, SCR.
"BPS," n.d. "Series V: General," NYSF.
Brewer, Sherry. "Private Retreats: The Sleeping Rooms of Three Noted Men." *Essence*, February 1978, 93–95.
Brown, Roscoe C., Jr. "Film as a Tool for Liberation?" *Black Creation* 4, no. 2 (Winter 1973): 36–37.
Browning, John Edgar. "Classical Hollywood Horror." In *A Companion to the Horror Film*, edited by Harry M. Benshoff, 225–236. Chichester, UK: John Wiley, 2014.
Brunsting, Joshua. "Joshua Reviews Bill Gunn's *Personal Problems*." *CriterionCast* (blog), March 30, 2018. https://criterioncast.com/reviews/theatrical/joshua-reviews-bill-gunns-personal-problems-theatrical-review.
Butters, Gerald R., Jr. *From* Sweetback *to* Super Fly: *Race and Film Audiences in Chicago's Loop*. Columbia: University of Missouri Press, 2015.
"Buys Rights to Film 'Blues for Mr. Charlie.'" *Jet*, October 29, 1964, 59.
Byron, Stuart. "Ducks Stars & 'Best Sellers.'" *Variety*, February 19, 1969, 3, 26.
———. "Kinney, W7 Owners Approve Merger; Medium-Cost Pix, TV Hype Pledged; Execs to Keep 'Hands Off' Ashley." *Variety*, June 11, 1969, 3, 46.
Cady, Barbara. "Playing by the Enemy's Rules" (book review). *Los Angeles Times*, May 9, 1982, Calendar section, 10.

Calta, Louis. "Chelsea Theater Center to Open in Landmark Church Tomorrow." *New York Times*, March 5, 1966, 14.
Camera News Distribution Agreement, n.d. Bill Gunn Papers, SCR.
Chadwick, Alex, to Bill Gunn, December 10, 1980. Bill Gunn Papers, SCR.
Church, David. *Disposable Passions: Vintage Pornography and the Material Legacies of Adult Cinema*. New York: Bloomsbury, 2016.
"Cinerama Releasing 10 by Fall." *Variety*, April 12, 1972, 24.
Clark, Ashley. "Making Ground: Remembering Kathleen Collins." *Sight & Sound*, January 5, 2021. https://www.bfi.org.uk/sight-and-sound/features/making-ground-remembering-kathleen-collins.
Clark, Marlene. Interview with the author by telephone, August 12, 2014.
Clover, Carol J. "Her Body, Himself: Gender in the Slasher Film." In *The Dread of Difference: Gender and the Horror Film*, edited by Barry Keith Grant, 66–113. Austin: University of Texas Press, 1996.
Cohn, Lawrence. "Black Pic Employment Still Lags." *Variety*, December 1, 1982, 1, 32.
Coleman, Robin R. Means. *Horror Noire: Blacks in American Horror Films from the 1890s to Present*. New York: Routledge, 2011.
Corson, Keith. *Trying to Get Over: African American Directors after Blaxploitation, 1977–1986*. Austin: University of Texas Press, 2016.
Countryman, Matthew J. *Up South: Civil Rights and Black Power in Philadelphia*. Philadelphia: University of Pennsylvania Press, 2006.
Crawford, Margo Natalie. *Black Post-Blackness: The Black Arts Movement and Twenty-First-Century Aesthetics*. Urbana: University of Illinois Press, 2017.
Crist, Judith. "'Georgia' on Her Mind." *New York*, March 13, 1972, 66–67.
Crystal Falls Films Inc. "*Territory*" (synopsis), n.d. Charles H. "Chiz" Schultz/Fireside Productions Collection, SCR.
Dalton, David. *James Dean: The Mutant King*. New York: St. Martin's, 1974.
Darrach, Brad. "Hollywood's Second Coming." *Playboy*, June 1972, 115–124, 216–230.
David, Marlo D. "'Let It Go Black': Desire and the Erotic Subject in the Films of Bill Gunn." *Black Camera* 2, no. 2 (Spring 2011): 26–46.
"The Delphic Corporation," n.d. Bill Gunn Papers, SCR.
Dempsey, Michael, and Udayan Gupta. "Hollywood's Color Problem." *American Film*, April 1982, 66–70.
Diawara, Manthia. "Black American Cinema: The New Realism." In *Black American Cinema*, edited by Diawara, 3–25. New York: Routledge, 1993.
Diawara, Manthia, and Phyllis R. Klotman. "*Ganja and Hess*: Vampires, Sex, and Addictions." *Black American Literature Forum* 25, no. 2 (Summer 1991): 299–314.
"A 'Different' Television Drama: 'Carmen in Harlem.'" *New York Times*, April 11, 1954, X13.
"Diller Wants Assured Flow; Picker with Par, as also WB." *Variety*, July 9, 1975, 3.
Dombrowski, Lisa. *The Films of Samuel Fuller: If You Die, I'll Kill You!* Middletown, CT: Wesleyan University Press, 2008.
Double Possession trailer, n.d. HFA item #16703. James E. Hinton Collection, HFA.
Doul. "Stock Reviews: *Marcus in High Grass*." *Variety*, September 9, 1959, 57.
Duganne, Erina. "Transcending the Fixity of Race: The Kamoinge Workshop and the Question of a 'Black Aesthetic' in Photography." In *New Thoughts on the Black Arts Movement*, edited by Lisa Gail Collins and Margo Natalie Crawford, 187–209. New Brunswick, NJ: Rutgers University Press, 2006.

Dumler, Egon, to Sam Waymon, William Gunn, and Chiz Schultz, September 26, 1973. Charles H. "Chiz" Schultz/Fireside Productions Collection, SCR.
DWP to Chiz Schultz, July 14, 1969. Charles H. "Chiz" Schultz/Fireside Productions Collection, SCR.
Elam, Harry Justin. *The Past as Present in the Drama of August Wilson*. Ann Arbor: University of Michigan Press, 2004.
Enelow, Shonni. *Method Acting and Its Discontents: On American Psycho-Drama*. Evanston, IL: Northwestern University Press, 2015.
"Entertainment or Revolution? The History & Evolution of Black Filmmaking," n.d. Bill Gunn Papers, SCR.
Euvrard, Janine. "Bill Gunn: Créer Une Industrie Noire du Cinéma" [To Create a Black Film Industry]. *CinémAction*, no. 46 (January 1988): 160–163. Translated for this book by Irene Xia, June 5, 2015.
Feder, Barnaby J. "Deserters in Sweden: An Odd Little 'V. F. W' Post." *New York Times*, June 17, 1985, A2.
Feingold, Michael. "Gloria in Excelsis" (review). *Village Voice*, April 18, 1989, 97–98.
Field, Allyson Nadia. "To Journey Imperfectly: Black Cinema Aesthetics and the Filmic Language of *Sankofa*." *Framework* 55, no. 2 (Fall 2014): 171–190.
———. *Uplift Cinema: The Emergence of African American Film and the Possibility of Black Modernity*. Durham, NC: Duke University Press, 2015.
Field, Allyson Nadia, Jan-Christopher Horak, and Jacqueline Najuma Stewart. "Introduction Emancipating the Image." In *L.A. Rebellion: Creating a New Black Cinema*, edited by Field, Horak and Stewart, 1–53. Oakland: University of California Press, 2015.
"15 to Spout 'Verses.'" *Daily Variety*, July 23, 1962, 8.
"Film File." *Washington Post*, February 17, 1978, WK17.
"Filmmakers Festival to Open at Arts Center," March 21, 1982, n.p. Bill Gunn Papers, SCR.
"Film Notes: New York." *Chamba Notes* 2, no. 2 (Spring–Summer 1973): 2.
"Les Films Noirs Américains Présentés dans des Festivals Français." *CinémAction*, no. 46 (January 1988): 199–204.
"Ford Foundation's $25,000 Pays Costs of Blacks 'Filming.'" *Variety*, April 9, 1969, 9.
Forster, Nicholas. "*Ganja & Hess*" (LP liner notes). *Ganja & Hess: Original 1973 Motion Picture Soundtrack by Sam Waymon*. Strange Disc Records, 2018.
———. "'Improvisational Jamming': The Process and Production of Personal Problems." *Metrograph*, March 29, 2018. https://metrograph.com/improvisational-jamming-the-process-and-production-of-personal-problems/.
———. "'A New Form of Black Genre Communication': Bill Gunn, *Personal Problems*, and the Afterlives of Production," March 22, 2017. Society for Cinema and Media Studies Conference, Chicago, IL.
Forster, Nicholas, and Michele Prettyman. "Close-Up: The New York Scene: Introduction: A Scene of New Worlds." *Black Camera* 10, no. 2 (Spring 2019): 52–68.
Franklin, Wendell, and Zeinabu Davis. *Wendell Franklin*. Los Angeles: Directors Guild of America, 1995.
Fraser, C. Gerald. "Bill Gunn, Playwright and Actor, Dies at 54 on Eve of Play Premiere." *New York Times*, April 7, 1989, D20.
———. "Duane L. Jones, 51, Actor and Director of Stage Works, Dies." *New York Times*, July 28, 1988, A24.

———. "'Watch Your Mouth!' on WNET Explains English to Teen-Agers." *New York Times*, March 25, 1978, 37.
Frederick, Candice. "Bill Gunn: An Unsung Hero of Black Filmmaking." *New York Public Library*, April 28, 2016. https://www.nypl.org/blog/2016/04/28/gunn-unsung-hero.
Frederick, Robert B. "Belafonte's 'Comeback' Film." *Variety*, December 18, 1968, 5, 18.
———. "If Poitier Can't Do It They Rewrite for a White Actor: Bill Gunn's Beef." *Variety*, November 4, 1964, 2, 17.
Freydberg, Elizabeth Hadley, to Bill Gunn, January 30, 1984. Bill Gunn Papers, SCR.
"'Friends' 1st on U Slate of Zeitlin." *Daily Variety*, April 30, 1968, 3.
Ganja & Hess outtakes, n.d. HFA item #16718. James E. Hinton Collection, HFA.
Gates, Racquel. "The Problem with 'Anti-Racist' Movie Lists." *New York Times*, July 17, 2020. https://www.nytimes.com/2020/07/17/opinion/sunday/black-film-movies-racism.html.
Gelb, Arthur. "'Marcus in the High Grass' Has Debut." *New York Times*, November 22, 1960, 38.
Gelmis, Joseph. "Tired Blood Lust." *Newsday*, April 20, 1973, 7A.
———. "Trying to Overturn the Racial Cliches." *Newsday*, n.d., n.p. Hal Ashby Collection, MHL.
Gent, George. "Black Films Are In, So Are Profits." *New York Times*, July 18, 1972, 22.
George, Nelson. *Blackface: Reflections on African-Americans and the Movies*. New York: HarperCollins, 1994.
Gifford, Justin D. "'Harvard in Hell': Holloway House, *Players Magazine*, and the Invention of Black Mass-Market Erotica—Interviews with Wanda Coleman and Emory 'Butch' Holmes II." *MELUS: Multi-Ethnic Literature of the U. S.* 35, no. 4 (Winter 2010): 111–137.
Gill, Brendan. "Writing about Writing" (review). *New Yorker*, January 20, 1975, 61–62.
Gillespie, Michael Boyce. *Film Blackness: American Cinema and the Idea of Black Film*. Durham, NC: Duke University Press, 2016.
Gilroy, Harry. "Berlin Observes Culture of U. S." *New York Times*, September 29, 1957, 85.
Godfrey, Mark. "Notes on Black Abstraction." In *Soul of a Nation: Art in the Age of Black Power*, edited by Godfrey and Zoé Whitley, 147–190. London: Tate, 2017.
Goodman, George, Jr. "For James Baldwin, a Rap on Baldwin." *New York Times*, June 26, 1972, 38.
Gorfinkel, Elana. *Lewd Looks: American Sexploitation Cinema in the 1960s*. Minneapolis: University of Minnesota Press, 2017.
Gould, Jack. "TV: Church Segregation." *New York Times*, July 22, 1957, 39.
Green, Theophilus. "The Black Man as Movie Hero: New Films Offer a Different Male Image." *Ebony*, August 1972, 144–148.
Griffin, Ada Day, to Bill Gunn, July 10, 1987. Bill Gunn Papers, SCR.
Griffin, Ada Day, to Jack Hoffmeister, December 9, 1990. Bill Gunn Papers, SCR.
Guarino, Ann. "Demitasse of Blood Anyone?" *New York Daily News*, April 20, 1973, 56.
Guerin, Terry. "*Ganja and Hess*" (review). *Interview*, May 1973, 38.
Guerrero, Ed. *Framing Blackness: The African American Image in Film*. Philadelphia: Temple University Press, 1993.
Guillaume, Nandi. "Black History in New York State." *New York Amsterdam News*, February 22, 1975, B3.
Gunn, Bill. *All the Rest Have Died*. New York: Delacorte, 1964.
———. "The Bedlamite" (short story). *Swank*, October 1967, 45–46, 67–70.

———. *Black Picture Show*. Berkeley, CA: Reed, Cannon, and Johnson Communications, 1975.
———. *Black Picture Show* (play draft), October 21, 1974. "Series III: Scripts," NYSF.
———. *Egyptian Murals* (unpublished novel), n.d. Bill Gunn Papers, SCR.
———. *The Fame Game* (screenplay), February 1971. "Series III: Scripts," NYSF.
———. *Family Employment*, "Version A" (play), January 16, 1985. "Series III: Scripts," NYSF.
———. "*Ganja & Hess*: A Film by Bill Gunn" (second draft screenplay, dated May 30, 1972). In *Screenplays of the African American Experience*, edited by Phyllis Rauch Klotman, 11–90. Bloomington: Indiana University Press, 1991.
———. *Ganja & Hess (Formerly, "Blood")* (first draft screenplay), n.d. "Series III: Scripts," NYSF.
———. *Ganja & Hess* production notebook, n.d. Bill Gunn Papers, SCR.
———. *Ganja and Hess* (third draft screenplay), June 15, 1972. "Series III: Scripts," NYSF.
———. *I Am the Greatest* (screenplay), n.d. Bill Gunn Papers, SCR.
———. "I deal only in abstractions," n.d. Bill Gunn Papers, SCR.
———. "Johnnas" (play). *Drama Review: TDR* 12, no. 4 (Summer 1968): 126–138.
———. *Mandala* (screenplay), November 10, 1969. "Series III: Scripts," NYSF.
———. *Marcus in the High Grass* (play), October 1959. Bill Gunn Papers, SCR.
———. *The Owllight* (play), n.d. "Series III: Scripts," NYSF.
———. "The Philadelphia Conspiricy [sic]," n.d. Bill Gunn Papers, SCR.
———. *The Rain Forest* (screenplay), n.d. "Series III: Scripts," NYSF.
———. *Renaissance* (play), 1985. "Series III: Scripts," NYSF.
———. *Rhinestone Sharecropping*. New York: I. Reed Books, 1981.
———. *Stop* (screenplay), December 6, 1969. Bill Gunn Papers, SCR.
———. *Territory* (screenplay), n.d. "Series III: Scripts," NYSF.
———. "To Be a Black Artist" (letter). *New York Times*, May 13, 1973, 7, 30.
Gunn, Bill, to Ada Day Griffin, September 7, 1987. Bill Gunn Papers, SCR.
Gunn, Bill, to John Veitch, April 2, 1976. Bill Gunn Papers, SCR.
Gunn, Bill, to David Zeitlin, n.d. Bill Gunn Papers, SCR.
"Gunn 'Moon' Scripter." *Daily Variety*, March 3, 1969, 3.
Gussow, Mel. "The Classics, Lincoln Center and Papp." *New York Times*, March 17, 1975, 36.
———. "Film Festival Contracts—and Thrives." *New York Times*, October 6, 1971, 38.
———. "A Mother Only a Son Could Love" (review). *New York Times*, April 7, 1989, C3.
Hampton, Howard. "Careworn Chronicles." *Film Comment*, March–April 2018, 54–57.
Handsaker, Gene. "Finally, a Black Woman Movie Director." *San Francisco Examiner*, November 6, 1971, 7.
"Harlem, Frisco, No. Africa Locations for 'Partisan.'" *Variety*, October 7, 1970, 21.
"Harold S. Lager Named V.P. Sales, for Kelly-Jordan." *Boxoffice*, July 29, 1974, 10.
Harris, Brandon. "Spike Lee Discusses His New Film and Making Movies for 30 Years: 'The Black Audience Is Not Monolithic.'" *IndieWire*, June 27, 2014. https://www.indiewire.com/2014/06/spike-lee-discusses-his-new-film-and-making-movies-for-30-years-the-black-audience-is-not-monolithic-24814/.
Harrison, Paul Carter. "Feature Review: 'Ganja and Hess.'" *Players*, November 1973, 12, 16.
Hartmann, Jon. "The Trope of Blaxploitation in Critical Responses to *Sweetback*." *Film History* 6, no. 3 (1994): 382–404.
Harwood, Jim. "A Modest Assessment from Muhammad Ali: This Pic'll Be Great 'Cause It's All About Me." *Daily Variety*, November 6, 1975, 1.

Haskell, Molly. *From Reverence to Rape: The Treatment of Women in the Movies*. 1st ed. New York: Holt, Rinehart and Winston, 1974.

Heffernan, Kevin. "Prurient (Dis)Interest: The American Release and Reception of *I Am Curious (Yellow)*." In *Sex Scene: Media and the Sexual Revolution*, edited by Eric Schaefer, 105–125. Durham, NC: Duke University Press, 2014.

Heitner, Devorah. *Black Power TV*. Durham, NC: Duke University Press, 2013.

Helm, Michael. "Ishmael Reed: An Interview." In *Conversations with Ishmael Reed*, edited by Bruce Dick and Amritjit Singh, 144–160. Jackson: University Press of Mississippi, 1995.

Hinton, James E. Audio commentary. *Ganja & Hess*, DVD. All Day Entertainment, 1973; 1998.

"Hollywood Soundtrack." *Variety*, February 22, 1984, 26.

"The Homegoing Service of William Harrison Gunn, 1889–1987" (memorial service program), 1987. Bill Gunn Papers, SCR.

hooks, bell. "The Oppositional Gaze: Black Female Spectators." In *Reel to Real: Race, Sex, and Class at the Movies*, 197–213. New York: Routledge, 1996.

Howard Sanders Advertising and Public Relations Ltd. "'Georgia, Georgia' Production Information Guide" (presskit), n.d. Maya Angelou Film and Theater Collection, WFU.

"How Negro Fares in Field of Arts." *New York Herald Tribune*, June 23, 1963, section 4, 2.

Hudson, Dale. "Vampires and Transnational Horror." In *A Companion to the Horror Film*, edited by Harry M. Benshoff, 463–482. Chichester, UK: John Wiley, 2014.

———. *Vampires, Race, and Transnational Hollywoods*. Edinburgh, UK: Edinburgh University Press, 2017.

Hunter, Marcus Anthony. *Black Citymakers: How the Philadelphia Negro Changed Urban America*. New York: Oxford University Press, 2013.

Hyams, Joe, and Jay Hyams. *James Dean: Little Boy Lost*. New York: Warner Books, 1992.

"In Memoriam: Kathleen Collins Prettyman and Bill Gunn." *Black Film Review* 5, no. 2 (Spring 1989): 5.

"International Sound Track." *Variety*, October 29, 1980, 36.

Jackson, Chuck. "The Touch of the 'First' Black Cinematographer in North America: James E. Hinton, *Ganja & Hess*, and the NEA Films at the Harvard Film Archive." *Black Camera* 10, no. 1 (Fall 2018): 67–95.

"James Baldwin to Try Movies." *Baltimore Sun*, August 6, 1972, D10.

Johnson, E. Patrick, and Mae G. Henderson. "Introduction: Queering Black Studies/'Quaring' Queer Studies." In *Black Queer Studies: A Critical Anthology*, edited by Johnson and Henderson, 1–17. Durham, NC: Duke University Press, 2005.

Jordan, Jack, to Maya Angelou, June 9, 1972. Maya Angelou Film and Theater Collection, WFU.

Jules-Rosette, Bennetta. *Josephine Baker in Art and Life: The Icon and the Image*. Urbana: University of Illinois Press, 2007.

Juzwiak, Rich. "How to Not Make a Vampire Movie: A Chat with Spike Lee & Zaraah Abrahams." *Defamer*, February 13, 2015. http://defamer.gawker.com/how-to-not-make-a-vampire-movie-a-chat-with-spike-lee-1685557174.

Kalat, David. "*Ganja & Hess* Undead: The Restoration of a Forgotten Treasure." *Video Watchdog*, no. 47 (September–October 1998): 24–30.

———. "In Search of *Ganja & Hess*." *Video Watchdog*, no. 130 (May 2007): 20–25.

Kamlot, Robert, to Gilbert Moses, March 28, 1974. "Series V: General," NYSF.

Kanefsky, Victor. Interview with the author, November 26, 2013. New York, NY.

Kanefsky, Victor, and David Kalat. Audio commentary. *Ganja & Hess*, DVD. All Day Entertainment, 1973; 1998.
Kangalee, Dennis Leroy. "Flowers for Bill Gunn: Remembering an Outlaw Artist." *Dennis Leroy Kangalee: The Passion of an Outsider Artist* (blog), July 18, 2014. https://dennisleroykangalee.com/tag/bill-gunn/.
"Kathleen Collins." *Losing Ground* (presskit), Milestone Film & Video, 2015. https://cdn.shopify.com/s/files/1/0150/7896/files/LosingGroundPK.pdf?287858186427911770.
Kelly, Quentin. Interview with the author, May 22, 2012. Princeton, NJ.
Kelly-Jordan Enterprises Inc., "Congratulations Diana Sands" (advertisement). *Variety*, April 5, 1972, 23.
———. "Double Possession" (advertisement). *Atlanta Daily World*, September 14, 1975, 10.
———. "Double Possession" (advertisement). *Boxoffice*, March 3, 1975, E-3.
———. *Double Possession* (pressbook), 1975. Production Files, MHL.
———. "An EAGER New Audience..." (brochure), n.d. Bill Gunn Papers, SCR.
———. "Ganja & Hess" (advertisement). *New York Times*, April 19, 1973, 50.
———. "Ganja & Hess" (advertisement). *New York Amsterdam News*, April 21, 1973, D8.
———. "Ganja & Hess" (advertisement). *New York Times*, April 23, 1973, 41.
———. "Georgia, Georgia" (advertisement). *Variety*, March 29, 1972, 39.
———. "The Inheritance" (advertisement). *Variety*, May 17, 1972, 23.
———. Invitation to *Georgia, Georgia* premiere. March 10, 1972. Maya Angelou Film and Theater Collection, WFU.
———. "Summer Is Already Here!" (advertisement). *Variety*, April 5, 1972, 21.
Kelly-Jordan Enterprises Inc. and Federation of Addiction Agencies. *Ganja & Hess* program, April 19, 1973. Bill Gunn Papers, SCR.
"Kelly-Jordan Has Zaire Bout." *Variety*, November 13, 1974, 30.
"Kelly-Jordan to Release Three Films." *New York Amsterdam News*, April 20, 1974, B5.
Kendrick, James. "Phantom Cinema: Illuminating the Structuring Absences of Film History." *Quarterly Review of Film and Video* 30, no. 1 (2013): 62–73.
Kenna, Laura Cook. "Making Exploitation Black: How 1970s 'Blaxploitation' Discourse Marginalized Industry History and Constructed Black Viewers' Tastes." In *Beyond Blaxploitation*, edited by Novotny Lawrence and Gerald R. Butters Jr., 201–224. Detroit, MI: Wayne State University Press, 2016.
Kernan, Michael. "Ishmael Reed's Video Voodoo." *Washington Post*, March 5, 1982, B7.
King, Greg. "'Bus' Is Stalled, But This L.A. Black Group's Determined to Get It Rolling." *Daily Variety*, April 8, 1971, 3.
Kleiman, Dena. "'Cosby' Producers Plan 2 Similar TV Series." *New York Times*, October 30, 1985, C26.
Klein, Woody. *Westport, Connecticut: The Story of a New England Town's Rise to Prominence*. Westport, CT: Greenwood, 2000.
Klotman, Phyllis R., to Bill Gunn, May 17, 1983. Bill Gunn Papers, SCR.
Korwin-Pawlowska, Bethany. "'Personal Problems': New Black Soap Opera." *Oakland Tribune*, December 12, 1980, n.p. Bill Gunn Papers, SCR.
Kostrzewa, John. "Secrets of the Tower: The Betrayal of Marquette Credit Union: Growth, Greed Take Control." *Providence Journal*, June 15, 1992, A-01.
Kouvaros, George. *Famous Faces Yet Not Themselves: The Misfits and the Icons of Postwar America*. Minneapolis: University of Minnesota Press, 2010.

Kroll, Jack. "Black-and-White Picture." *Newsweek*, January 20, 1975, 83.
Landis, Ilene, to Bill Gunn, May 19, 1986. Bill Gunn Papers, SCR.
Landry, Robert. "Black Pix: 'Menial' to 'Mean.'" *Variety*, August 23, 1972, 5, 22.
Leeming, David. *James Baldwin: A Biography*. New York: Alfred A. Knopf, 1994.
Leki, Ilona. "Bill Gunn." In *Afro-American Writers after 1955: Dramatists and Prose Writers (Dictionary of Literary Biography)*, edited by Trudier Harris and Thadious Davis, 109–114. Detroit, MI: Gale Research, 1985.
Lewis, Barbara. "The Black Critic: A High Wire Acrobat." *New York Amsterdam News*, August 20, 1977, D8.
Lewis, Jon. "Presumed Effects of Erotica: Some Notes on the Report of the Commission on Obscenity and Pornography." *Film International* 6, no. 6 (November 2008): 7–16.
"'Liberty' Lively $14,000, L'ville; 'Couple' Soft 3½G." *Variety*, March 20, 1974, 8, 12.
Lierow, Lars. "The 'Black Man's Vision of the World': Rediscovering Black Arts Filmmaking and the Struggle for a Black Cinematic Aesthetic." *Black Camera* 4, no. 2 (Spring 2013): 3–21.
Lino, Hector, Jr., and R. Bryan. "Interview with Bill Gunn." *Impressions: A Black Arts and Culture Magazine* 1, no. 2 (Spring 1975): 14–16, 45–49, 52, 56, 59, 61–62.
Lipsitz, George. "Genre Anxiety and Racial Representation in 1970s Cinema." In *Refiguring American Film Genres: History and Theory*, edited by Nick Browne, 208–232. Berkeley: University of California Press, 1998.
Lor [Lawrence Cohn]. "Archive Film Review: *Stop*." *Variety*, July 4, 1990, 26.
Lorde, Audre. "Uses of the Erotic: The Erotic as Power." In *Sister Outsider: Essays and Speeches*, 53–59. Trumansburg, NY: Crossing, 1984.
Lowenstein, Adam. *Shocking Representation: Historical Trauma, National Cinema, & the Modern Horror Film*. New York: Columbia University Press, 2005.
"'L. S. Fields' ('Derby') Really Quentin Kelly; Quits Group W for Pix." *Variety*, July 28, 1971, 1, 31.
Lucas, Tim. *Mario Bava: All the Colors of the Dark*. Cincinnati, OH: Video Watchdog, 2007.
Lucas, Tim, and David Walker. "The Savaging and Salvaging of an American Classic," *Video Watchdog*, no. 3 (January–February 1991): 38–57.
Lynn to Joseph Papp, "GAMES by Bill Gunn" (reader report), February 24, 1977. "Series II: Play Department," NYSF.
Macfarlane, Steve. "Corrupted Affections: Bill Gunn in the Rear-View." *Cinema Scope*, no. 75 (Summer 2018): 22–24.
Martin, Alfred L., Jr. "Blackbusting Hollywood: Racialized Media Reception, Failure, and *The Wiz* as Black Blockbuster." *JCMS: Journal of Cinema and Media Studies* 60, no. 2 (Winter 2021): 56–79.
Martin, Michael T., and David C. Wall, eds. *From Street to Screen: Charles Burnett's* Killer of Sheep. Bloomington: Indiana University Press, 2020.
Martin, Michael T., David C. Wall, and Marilyn Yaquinto, eds. *Race and the Revolutionary Impulse in* The Spook Who Sat by the Door. Bloomington: Indiana University Press, 2018.
Mason, B. J. "New Films: Culture or Con Game?" *Ebony*, December 1972, 60–62.
Massa, Robert. "Sightlines." *Village Voice*, April 18, 1989, 97–98.
Metz, Walter. "From Harlem to Hollywood: The 1970s Renaissance and Blaxploitation." In *Beyond Blaxploitation*, edited by Novotny Lawrence and Gerald R. Butters Jr., 225–245. Detroit, MI: Wayne State University Press, 2016.

———. "*Ganja and Hess*: Men Overtaken by Racism." *Walter's World: Film Criticism, Powered by Learning* (blog), December 2, 2015. http://waltermetz.com/ganja-and-hess-1973/.
Michener, Charles. "Black Movies." *Newsweek*, October 23, 1972, 74–82.
Miller, D. Quentin. "Lost and . . . Found? James Baldwin's Script and Spike Lee's *Malcolm X*." *African American Review* 46, no. 4 (Winter 2013): 671–685.
Milliken, Christine. "Rate It X? Hollywood Cinema and the End of the Production Code." In *Sex Scene: Media and the Sexual Revolution*, edited by Eric Schaefer, 25–52. Durham, NC: Duke University Press, 2014.
Mishkin, Leo. "On the Set with 'The Landlord.'" (*New York*) *Morning Telegraph*, August 30, 1969, n.p. Hal Ashby Collection, Department of Special Collections, MHL.
Mitchell, Lionel. "Bill Gunn's 'Rhinestone' Shines Brilliantly in Superior Production" (review). *New York Amsterdam News*, December 4, 1982, 12.
———. "Busy Weekend: Screening and Theatre Viewing." *New York Amsterdam News*, November 22, 1980, 41.
Molleson, John. "Real-Life Struggle of the 'One in Ten.'" *New York Herald Tribune*, June 23, 1963, section 4, 1–2.
"MOMA Sets Screening of 'Ganja and Hess.'" *New York Amsterdam News*, December 15, 1973, D13.
Monaco, James. *American Film Now: The People, the Power, the Money, the Movies*. New York: Oxford University Press, 1979.
———. "Blood and Blackness: An Untimely Death." *Village Voice*, March 14, 1974, 75.
———. "Lost Films: Bill Gunn's 'Ganja and Hess,'" n.d. "Series II: Play Department," NYSF.
Monaco, James, to Bill Gunn, January 17, 1974. "Series II: Play Department," NYSF.
Moon, Michael. "'The Gentle Boy from the Dangerous Classes': Pederasty, Domesticity, and Capitalism in Horatio Alger." In *Curiouser: On the Queerness of Children*, edited by Steven Bruhm and Natasha Hurley, 31–56. Minneapolis: University of Minnesota Press, 2004.
———. *A Small Boy and Others: Imitation and Initiation in American Culture from Henry James to Andy Warhol*. Durham, NC: Duke University Press, 1998.
Moore, Jacqueline. "Actress Discusses Her Goals and Roles." *Chicago Defender*, May 8, 1972, 19.
Morra, Anne, to Sam Waymon, June 7, 1990. "Series III: Scripts," NYSF.
Murphy, A. D. "50 More Potential Black Theme Films Counted." *Variety*, September 20, 1972, 7, 20.
Murray, Derek Conrad. *Queering Post-Black Art: Artists Transforming African-American Identity after Civil Rights*. London, UK: I. B. Tauris, 2015.
Murray, James P. "Black Movies and Music in Harmony." *Black Creation* 5, no. 1 (Fall 1973): 9–11.
———. "A Futuristic Fable." *Black Creation* 4, no. 2 (Winter 1973): 43.
———. "Reel Images—The Film Scene." *New York Amsterdam News*, April 21, 1973, D5.
———. "The Subject Is Money." In *Black Films and Film-Makers: A Comprehensive Anthology from Stereotype to Superhero*, edited by Lindsay Patterson, 247–257. New York: Dodd, Mead, 1975.
———. *To Find an Image: Black Films from Uncle Tom to Super Fly*. Bobbs-Merrill, 1973.
Museum of Modern Art. "New Films from Seven Countries at Museum: Anna Karina and Bill Gunn to Make Personal Appearances" (press release), December 1973. https://www

.moma.org/momaorg/shared/pdfs/docs/press_archives/5066/releases/MOMA_1973_0137_102.pdf.
"NAACP Blasts 'Super-Nigger' Trend." *Variety*, August 16, 1972, 2.
"The Newest Hottest Spike Lee Joint." *Kickstarter*, July 22, 2013. https://www.kickstarter.com/projects/spikelee/the-newest-hottest-spike-lee-joint.
Newman, Kim. "*Ganja & Hess*" (review), *Video Watchdog*, no. 179 (May–June 2015): 48–50.
———. *Nightmare Movies: A Critical History of the Horror Film, 1968–88*. 2nd ed. London: Bloomsbury, 1988.
"New York Sound Track." *Variety*, April 18, 1973, 25.
"New York Sound Track." *Variety*, July 11, 1973, 26.
"New York Sound Track." *Variety*, April 21, 1982, 14.
Nicholson, David. "A Commitment to Writing: A Conversation with Kathleen Collins Prettyman." *Black Film Review* 5, no. 1 (Winter 1988–1989): 6–15.
"N. Y. Critics' Opinions." *Variety*, April 25, 1973, 16.
"N. Y. Easter Joy Gone." *Variety*, May 2, 1973, 10, 20.
"N. Y. Rolls (Also Lays) Easter Eggs." *Variety*, April 25, 1973, 8, 12.
"Obituaries: Duane Jones." *Variety*, August 17, 1988, 55.
O'Farrow, Julia. "A Letter: Kudos to Black Critics." *New York Amsterdam News*, February 15, 1975, D3.
Olney, Ian. *Euro Horror: Classic European Horror Cinema in Contemporary American Culture*. Bloomington: Indiana University Press, 2013.
O'Malley, Hayley. "Another Cinema: James Baldwin's Search for a New Film Form." *James Baldwin Review* 7 (2021).
———. "Art on Her Mind: The Making of Kathleen Collins's Cinema of Interiority." *Black Camera* 10, no. 2 (Spring 2019): 80–103.
"Only 2 Films, But He's Known." *New York Amsterdam News*, August 18, 1962, 19.
"Our Company." *WorldWater & Solar Technologies*. Accessed June 17, 2021. http://www.worldwatersolar.com/our-company/.
Papp, Joseph, to Max Roach, January 24, 1974. "Series II: Play Department," NYSF.
Pavlić, Ed. *Who Can Afford to Improvise? James Baldwin and Black Music, the Lyric and the Listeners*. New York: Fordham University Press, 2016.
Petersen, Christina. "The 'Reol' Story: Race Authorship and Consciousness in Robert Levy's Reol Productions, 1921–1926." *Film History* 20, no. 3 (2008): 308–324.
Peterson, Maurice. "Diana Diana." *Essence*, June 1972, 34–35, 72.
———. "A Flood of Black Films." *Essence*, September 1972, 28.
———. "Interview with Bill Gunn." *Essence*, October 1973, 27, 96.
Pierson, Eric. "Blaxploitation, Quick and Dirty: Patterns of Distribution." *Screening Noir* 1, no. 1 (Fall–Winter 2005): 126–152.
"Plan 'Partisan' Pic." *Daily Variety*, September 29, 1970, 3.
Poggiali, Chris. "The Endangered List (Case File #5): *Stop!*" *Temple of Schlock*, November 29, 2008. http://templeofschlock.blogspot.com/2008/11/lost-and-still-not-found-case-file-5.html.
———. "Roundtable Discussion: *Georgia, Georgia*." *Temple of Schlock*, August 22, 2009. http://templeofschlock.blogspot.com/2009/08/round-table-discussion-georgia-georgia.html.
———. "Slinking through the Seventies: An Interview with Marlene Clark." *Temple of Schlock*, January 20, 2011. http://templeofschlock.blogspot.com/2011/01/slinking-through-seventies-interview.html.

Pollard, Samuel. Interview with the author, November 26, 2013. New York, NY.
Prettyman, Michele. "Close-Up: The New York Scene: Controlling the World within the Frame: Julie Dash and Ayoka Chenzira Reflect on New York and Filmmaking." *Black Camera* 10, no. 2 (Spring 2019): 69–79.
Prettyman (Beverly), Michele. "Phenomenal Bodies: The Metaphysical Possibilities of Post-Black Film and Visual Culture." PhD diss., Georgia State University, 2012.
Reed, Ishmael. "Bill Gunn: Director." In *Airing Dirty Laundry*, 112–119. Reading, MA: Addison-Wesley, 1993.
———. "The Black Artist Money Couldn't Buy." *Criterion*, August 27, 2020. https://www.criterion.com/current/posts/7073-the-black-artist-hollywood-couldn-t-buy.
———. *Personal Problems* (untitled press release), n.d. Bill Gunn Papers, SCR.
Rich, Frank. "Theater: 'Rhinestone,' Racism in Hollywood." *New York Times*, November 23, 1982, C11.
Richard Allen Center for Culture and Art. "*Rhinestone*" (mailer), n.d. Charles H. "Chiz" Schultz/Fireside Productions Collection, SCR.
"Rights to Biopic of Bessie Smith Stalling Filming." *Variety*, April 11, 1973, 1, 69.
Riley, Clayton. "*Black Picture Show*" (review), January 16, 1975. "Series VII: Press Office," NYSF.
Rising Sun Productions. *The Afrikan Sun* (press release), n.d. "Series II: Play Department," NYSF.
Ritter, Carolina. "Soap to Alter TV's Complexion." *Encore American & Worldwide News*, November 1980, 46.
"Rival Bessies, Flack vs. Parks." *Variety*, March 13, 1974, 4.
Robe [Robert B. Frederick]. "*Ganja and Hess*" (review). *Variety*, April 18, 1973, 30, 32.
Robinson, Jean L. *How to Survive in Spite of Your Family: This Story Has Never Been Told*. Philadelphia: Topaz, 1996.
Robinson, Jean Love, to Chiz Schultz, April 24, 1989. Charles H. "Chiz" Schultz/Fireside Productions Collection, SCR.
Robinson, Major. "Negro Actors Resent His Success: Says Star Sidney Poitier." *Pittsburgh Courier*, June 12, 1965, 5.
Rogers, Jamie Ann. "Diasporic Communion and Textual Exchange in Beyoncé's *Lemonade* and Julie Dash's *Daughters of the Dust*." *Black Camera* 11, no. 2 (Spring 2020): 130–157.
Rosenbaum, Jonathan. "Two Weeks in Another Town." *Jonathan Rosenbaum* (blog), October 22, 2018. https://www.jonathanrosenbaum.net/2018/10/two-weeks-in-another-town-2/.
Rouget, Gilbert. "Notes on the Recordings" (LP liner notes). *Music of Equatorial Africa*, Folkways Records, 1950. https://folkways-media.si.edu/liner_notes/folkways/FW04402.pdf.
Royalton. "Re: *Stop* (Bill Gunn, 1970)." *Criterion Forum* (blog), April 4, 2010. http://www.criterionforum.org/forum/viewtopic.php?f=6&t=9515.
Russo, Vito. *The Celluloid Closet: Homosexuality in the Movies*. 1st ed. New York: Harper & Row, 1981.
Ryfle, Steve. Audio commentary. *Georgia, Georgia*, DVD. Scorpion Releasing, 1972; 2012.
———. "The Eclipsed Visions of Bill Gunn: An African-American Auteur's Elusive Genius, from *Ganja & Hess* to *Personal Problems*." *Cineaste* 43, no. 4 (Fall 2018): 26–31.
———. "Georgia, Georgia on My Mind" (liner notes). *Georgia, Georgia*, DVD. Scorpion Releasing, 1972; 2012.
———. "Glorious Ganja: An Interview with Actress Marlene Clark." *Shock Cinema*, no. 39 (2010): 28–31, 46.

———. "Uplifting Black Film: An Interview with Director Michael Schultz." *Shock Cinema*, no. 39 (2010): 33–37, 46.
Schraufnagel, Noel. *From Apology to Protest: The Black American Novel*. DeLand, FL: Everett/Edwards, 1973.
Schultz, Chiz. Audio commentary. *Ganja & Hess*, DVD. All Day Entertainment, 1973; 1998.
———. Interview with the author, May 21, 2012. Tarrytown, NY.
Schultz, Chiz, to Harry Belafonte. "Projects," June 6, 1968. Charles H. "Chiz" Schultz/Fireside Productions Collection, SCR.
Schultz, Chiz, to Mike Merrick, September 23, 1968. Charles H. "Chiz" Schultz/Fireside Productions Collection, SCR.
Sconce, Jeffrey. "'Trashing' the Academy: Taste, Excess, and an Emerging Politics of Cinematic Style." *Screen* 36, no. 4 (Winter 1995): 371–393.
Sege [Frank Segers]. "*Honeybaby, Honeybaby*" (review). *Variety*, October 9, 1974, 19.
Segers, Frank. "5th Blacklight Fest Slates 30 Pics; Trade Importance Seen Growing." *Variety*, July 23, 1986, 6.
———. "Quent Kelly Enterprises Succeeds Two-Tone Producing Partnership; No 'Head-Busting' of Whites." *Variety*, November 20, 1974, 3, 22.
Shafrazi, Tony. "Dennis Hopper, 1999." *Index Magazine*. Accessed May 6, 2021. http://www.indexmagazine.com/interviews/dennis_hopper.shtml.
Sherrod, Harrison M. J. "The Blood of the Thing (Is the Truth of the Thing): Viral Pathogens and Uncanny Ontologies in *Ganja and Hess*." In *Beyond Blaxploitation*, edited by Novotny Lawrence and Gerald R. Butters Jr., 102–113. Detroit, MI: Wayne State University Press, 2016.
"Show Out of Town: *Black Picture Show*." *Variety*, December 11, 1974, 56–58.
Sieving, Christopher. *Soul Searching: Black-Themed Cinema from the March on Washington to the Rise of Blaxploitation*. Middletown, CT: Wesleyan University Press, 2011.
Simon, John. "Music of the Squares" (review). *New York*, January 27, 1975, 51.
———. "Myself When Young, Twice" (review). *New York*, April 17, 1989, 80–81.
Sinclair, Abiola. "'The Forbidden City' Season's Best" (review). *New York Amsterdam News*, April 8, 1989, 24.
Sloan, Margaret. "Keeping the Black Woman in Her Place." *Ms.*, January 1974, 30–31.
Smith, Helen C. "Major Plays Will Come from Blacks, Gunn Says." *Atlanta Constitution*, March 21, 1980, 23B.
Splawn, P. Jane. "Bill Gunn (1934–1989)." In *Contemporary African American Novelists: A Biobibliographical Critical Sourcebook*, edited by Emmanuel S. Nelson, 192–197. Westport, CT: Greenwood, 1999.
Staiger, Janet. "With the Compliments of the Auteur: Art Cinema and the Complexity of Its Reading Strategies." In *Interpreting Films: Studies in the Historical Reception of American Cinema*, 178–195. Princeton, NJ: Princeton University Press, 1992.
Stallings, L. H. "'Redemptive Softness': Interiority, Intellect, and Black Women's Ecstasy in Kathleen Collins's *Losing Ground*." *Black Camera* 2, no. 2 (Spring 2011): 47–62.
Stanbrook, Alan. "*Ganja and Hess*." *Films and Filming*, no. 395 (November–December 1988): 22.
Stevens, Brad. "Bodies Off: *Ganja & Hess*, Bill Gunn's Under-the-Skin Flick." *Sight & Sound*, July 23, 2016. http://www2.bfi.org.uk/news-opinion/sight-sound-magazine/comment/bradlands/bodies-off-ganja-hess-under-skin-flick.

Stockton, Kathryn Bond. *The Queer Child, or Growing Sideways in the Twentieth Century.* Durham, NC: Duke University Press, 2009.
Stone, Laurie. "All That Glitters" (review). *Village Voice*, November 30, 1982, 117.
"*Stop!*" *Adam Film World* 2, no. 8 (October 1970): 80–89.
"*Stop!*" *Knight* 8, no. 6 (October 1970): 68–73.
Strub, Whitney. "Archival Spotlight: The Baraka Film Archive—The Lost, Unmade, and Unseen Film Work of LeRoi Jones/Amiri Baraka." *Black Camera* 7, no. 1 (Fall 2015): 273–287.
Stuart, Fred. "Bill Gunn's Play a 'Mental Trip,' No 'Sounder' or 'Jane Pittman.'" *Philadelphia Bulletin*, n.d., n.p. Bill Gunn Papers, SCR.
Sweeney, Louise. "On Location in Lindsayland." *Christian Science Monitor*, July 14, 1969, 6.
"Talladega College Celebrates the Black Arts." *The Talladegan*, February 1976, 1.
Tate, Greg. "Bill Gunn, 1934–89." *Village Voice*, April 25, 1989, 98, 153.
Taylor, Clyde. "Bill Gunn . . . Climbing the Seven Monied Medias." *Black Renaissance/Renaissance Noire* 10, nos. 2–3 (Summer–Fall 2010): 98–105.
Taylor, Robert. "Biracial Film Company Debuts." *Oakland Tribune*, April 16, 1972, n.p. Maya Angelou Film and Theater Collection, WFU.
T. E. K. [Kalem]. "The Blame Game." *Time*, January 20, 1975, 92.
"Television Review: *The American Parade: Sojourner.*" *Daily Variety*, March 31, 1975, 17.
"'Territory' Gearing Up for N. Y., Canada Shoot." *Variety*, October 16, 1985, 85, 229.
"Theatrical Spotlight." *New York Amsterdam News*, August 17, 1974, D2.
Thompson, M. Cordell. "New York Beat." *Jet*, June 15, 1972, 63.
"Three Kelly-Jordan Films Ready for Spring Dates." *Boxoffice*, April 22, 1974, 7.
"3 Kelly-Jordan Pix; Add Exorcism to 'Ganja'; Diana Sands' Finale." *Variety*, April 17, 1974, 4.
"Till They Listen: Bill Gunn Directs America." *Artists Space*. Accessed June 17, 2021. https://artistsspace.org/exhibitions/bill-gunn.
Tudor, Andrew. *Monsters and Mad Scientists: A Cultural History of the Horror Movie.* Oxford, UK: Basil Blackwell, 1989.
"Umea Fest Skeds Kumel, Hong Kong Spex." *Daily Variety*, August 29, 1988, 8.
Underhill, Connie. "Action . . . Lights . . . Camera." *San Juan Star Magazine*, January 11, 1970, 6–7, 22.
"United Artists 'Black Hand Side' Draws Big Promotional Budget; Some 'Hip' Black Mags 'Bored'?" *Variety*, February 6, 1974, 5, 24.
Valkhn Communications. "*Rhinestone*" (flyer), February 7, 1983. Charles H. "Chiz" Schultz/Fireside Productions Collection, SCR.
Verrill, Addison. "Black Film Explosion." *Variety*, January 9, 1974, 30.
———. "Pledges Kinney Alert WB Team & Tight Budgets." *Variety*, February 18, 1970, 15.
———. "TV-Bearish WB Cupboard." *Variety*, March 29, 1972, 3, 36.
Walker, David. "Fima Noveck." *Video Watchdog*, no. 3 (January–February 1991): 50–53.
Walker, Joe. "'The Black Picture Show,' an Epic Drama." *Muhammad Speaks*, February 7, 1975, 20.
Wall, David C., and Michael T. Martin, eds. *The Politics and Poetics of Black Film: Nothing but a Man.* Bloomington: Indiana University Press, 2015.
Warner Bros. "Fall 1972" (advertisement). *Film Bulletin*, December 1971, 15–28.
———. "Warner Bros. Presents the Future" (advertisement). *Daily Variety*, November 4, 1970, 7–10.

Waymon, Samuel. Audio commentary. *Ganja & Hess*, DVD. All Day Entertainment, 1973; 1998.
———. Interview with the author, July 1, 2015. Nyack, NY.
Waymon, Sam, to Chiz Schultz, March 2, 1982. Charles H. "Chiz" Schultz/Fireside Productions Collection, SCR.
Waymon, Sam, to Chiz Schultz, March 20, 1985. Charles H. "Chiz" Schultz/Fireside Productions Collection, SCR.
Waymon, Sam, to Chiz Schultz, May 14, 1990. Charles H. "Chiz" Schultz/Fireside Productions Collection, SCR.
Weatherby, W. J. *James Baldwin: Artist on Fire*. New York: Donald I. Fine, 1989.
Weiler, A. H. "Bill Gunn, Actor and Playwright, to Direct Film." *New York Times*, November 26, 1969, 37.
———. "Forever 'Fantasticks.'" *New York Times*, June 11, 1972, D13, D22.
———. "*Ganja and Hess*" (review). *New York Times*, April 21, 1973, 19.
Weller, Sheila. "Work in Progress: Maya Angelou." In *Conversations with Maya Angelou*, edited by Jeffrey M. Elliot, 10–17. Jackson: University Press of Mississippi, 1989.
West, Hollie L. "Makers of Black Films Stand at Crossroads." *Los Angeles Times*, January 28, 1973, Calendar section, 18, 67.
Weston, Jay. "Tortured Incubation of a Hit: Or Billie Holiday Sings—At Last." *Variety*, January 3, 1973, 58.
Wexman, Virginia Wright. "Masculinity in Crisis: Method Acting in Hollywood." In *Movie Acting, the Film Reader*, edited by Pamela Robertson Wojcik, 127–144. New York: Routledge, 2004.
"Who's Who in the Cast." *Playbill* (program for *The Immoralist*). Royale Theater, February 1, 1954, 20. Bill Gunn Papers, SCR.
Wilcox, Michael A., to Bill Gunn, May 9, 1987. Bill Gunn Papers, SCR.
Wilderson, Frank B., III. "Video Tape Soap Operas." *Black Collegian*, October–November 1980, 190–192.
Williams, John. "Bill Gunn (1929–1989): Black Independent Filmmaker, Scenarist, Playwright, Novelist—A Critical Index of the Collected Film, Dramatic, and Literary Works." *Obsidian II: Black Literature in Review* 5, no. 2 (Summer 1990): 115–147.
———. "Bill Gunn (1929–1989): A Checklist of His Films, Dramatic Works, and Novels." *Black American Literature Forum* 25, no. 4 (Winter 1991): 781–787.
———. "Bill Gunn: Portrait of the Artist." *Black Film Review* 5, no. 2 (Spring 1989): 11–12.
Williams, John, to Louise Gunn, February 16, 1990. Bill Gunn Papers, SCR.
Williams, John, to Chiz Schultz, May 17, 1990. Charles H. "Chiz" Schultz/Fireside Productions Collection, SCR.
Williams, Paul, and Brian Edgar. "Up against the Wall: Primal Therapy and 'The Sixties.'" *European Journal of American Studies* 3, no. 2 (2008). http://journals.openedition.org/ejas/3022#article-3022.
Winsten, Archer. "'Ganja and Hess' Opens at the Playboy Theater." *New York Post*, April 20, 1973, 21.
Wise, Ron. "'Black' and 'Other Action' Rule Loop; Chi's Downtown Not for Varied Fare." *Variety*, January 3, 1973, 48.
Wolf, William. "Films." *Cue*, April 21, 1973, 7.
Wolfinger, James. *Philadelphia Divided: Race & Politics in the City of Brotherly Love*. Chapel Hill: University of North Carolina Press, 2007.

Woolsey, Morgan. "Hearing and Feeling the Black Vampire: Queer Affects in the Film Soundtrack." *Current Musicology* 106 (Spring 2020): 9–27.
"Yank Presence at Cannes." *Variety*, April 25, 1973, 3, 24.
Yarrow, Andrew L. "Brooklyn Series to Study Black Images in Film." *New York Times*, January 1, 1988, 9.
Zvi. "NYSF Play Report: Territory, Bill Gunn (A Screenplay)," January 31, 1974. "Series II: Play Department," NYSF.

INDEX

Page numbers in *italics* refer to figures.

Abrahams, Zaraah, *230*, 230, 233
Adams, Janus, 71, 90, 186
Afrikan Sun, The. *See* Gunn, Bill, unproduced or unpublished projects
Alberta Hunter Story, The (Gunn documentary), 209
Albertson, Chris, 26, 209
Alger, Horatio, 40, 242n26
Ali, Muhammad, 28, 52, 204–205
Allen, Billie, 45–46, 217
All the Rest Have Died (Gunn novel), 33, 37, 48, 90; autobiographical references in, 39, 42–44, 242n26; racial themes in, 184–186, 203
Alston, Pastor Elizabeth, 131, *133*, 135, 250n160
American Parade, The: "Sojourner" (Gunn teleplay), 208
Angel Levine, The (Gunn screenplay), 50–51, 53, 72, 183
Angelou, Maya, 17, 26–27, 36, 68; and *Georgia, Georgia*, 18–22, 240n44. *See also* *I Know Why the Caged Bird Sings* (book)
Apple Bee Farm Estate, 77, 81–82, *82*
art cinema, 3, 7, 14, 25, 55, 59, 71, 146–147, 152, 160, 163, 167, 170–177, 179–180, 188–189, 254n120; art house distribution, 146, 153, 197, 234, 236; movements: French New Wave, 180, 218–219; Italian neorealism, 194
Ashby, Hal, 49–50, 219. *See also The Landlord*
Association of French Film Critics, 150–151
Autobiography of Malcolm X, The, 24, 231. *See also* Baldwin, James

Baker, Josephine, 15, 29, 152
Baldwin, James, 1, 15, 33, 36, 52, 183, 188, 225; *Another Country*, 24; *The Autobiography of Malcolm X* (screenplay), 24, 231–232; *Blues for Mister Charlie*, 15, 24, 47, 113; *Giovanni's Room*, 24, 49; *The Inheritance*, 18, 24–26, 68, 241n57; on "pleading the blood," 135
Baraka, Amiri, 52, 86, 183, 186, 231
Barney, Betty, 130
Barrie, Scott, 72
Bava, Mario, 156, 206
"Bedlamite, The" (Gunn short story), 48–49, 183, 200
Belafonte, Harry, 13, 50–51
Bell, Edward, 54, 57, 59–60, 65, 199, 217
Benshoff, Harry, 61, 163–164, 187
Bergman, Ingmar, 55, 59, 151, 172
Bessie. *See* Gunn, Bill, unproduced or unpublished projects
Björkman, Stig, 16, 18–22, 26, 176. *See also Georgia, Georgia*
Black arts movement, 86, 183, 194, 255n146
Black directors, 5–7, 9–11, 16–17, 21, 31, 53, 63–64, 67–68, 178, 180–182, 192–194, 197, 210, 223, 226–229, 256n7
Black Film Center/Archive, 196
Black movie boom, 4, 8–14, 16–18, 22, 24, 26, 30–31, 71–72, 176–179, 188–189, 197–198
Black Picture Show (Gunn play), 29, 52, 90, 117, 185–186, 191, 206–207, 210, 217, 222, 225, 258n68, 261n37; analysis of, 199–204
Black press, 8–9, 22–24, 30, 48, 52, 66, 90, 149, 151, 158, 166, 171, 178, 191–193, 216, 243n53, 258n68
Blacula, 16, 67, 161, 163–164, 261n21
Bland, Edward, 7, 103
blaxploitation, 8, 11–13, 16–17, 64, 71–72, 146, 160, 172, 177–179, 188, 197–198, 206, 227, 229, 239n3
blood: addiction to, 68, 75–76, 78, 80, 89, 103, 112, 129, 163, 230, 234; "blood memory," 164; "blood politics," 165

281

Blood Couple, 1, 6, 77, 84, 89, 91, 106, *107*, 112, 120, 128, 131, *131*, 137–138, *138*, 146, 154–158, 175, 192, 248n87, 248n97, 248n105, 252n50, 254n96. See also *Double Possession*
Blood (Is the Truth of the Thing). See *Ganja & Hess*: early titles
Blood of Jesus, The, 7, 180
"blues woman," 101, 169–170, 209
Bogle, Donald, 171, 178, 193, 198
"Bongili Work Song." *See* "Bungelii Work Song"
Bowser, Pearl, 3, 6, 146–147, 153, 194–195, 214
Brooklyn Museum, 75, 78, 84, 176, 195, 247n62
Bryant, Celia, 72
Buck and the Preacher, 11, 13, 16, 72
"Bungelii Work Song," 85, 97, 129, 247n68
Burnett, Charles, 197, 257n23. See also *Killer of Sheep*

Caged Bird. See *I Know Why the Caged Bird Sings*
Caldwell, Ben, 194, 257n23
Camus, Albert, 55–56, 62; *The Fall*, 221
Cane, 180
Cannes Film Festival, 19; screening of *Ganja & Hess*, 1, 89, 146, 150–153, 192, 194, 227, 246n13, 252n28
Cannon, Steve, 209–210
CARA (Classification and Ratings Administration), 60–62, 166
Carter, John, 73, 77
Castleman, Cynthia, 77, 105
Celebration, The (Gunn play), 49
Chameleon Street, 7, 189
Chenzira, Ayoka, 227, 256n7
Christianity, 78, 80, 143, 224; Black uses of Christianity, 75, 130–132, 134–136, 158, 181, 186–188, 231
Cinerama Releasing Corporation, 14–15, 17, 22, 148
civil rights movement, 10, 15, 86, 218
Clark, Marlene, 98–99, 148, 193, 209, 226, 230; *Ganja & Hess* performance, 2, 23, 67, 73, 99, *100*, 101, *104*, 105, *106*, 109, *110–111*, 113–14, *113*, *115–116*, *118–119*, *122–123*, *125*, *127*, *127–128*, *137–138*, *140*, *141*, *142*, 150, 159, 166, *174–175*, 249n136, 252n25; *Stop* performance, 55, 60, 99
Claudine, 13–14
Clift, Montgomery, 46
Collins, Kathleen, 66–67, 193–194, 196, *196*, 206, 217–218, 225. See also *Losing Ground*
Columbia Pictures, 4, 13, 17, 24–25, 53, 151, 205, 222, 229, 231
Cosby, Bill, 13, 17, 208, 259n101
Cosby Show, The, 208, 259n101
Cotton Comes to Harlem, 8, 13, 16, 53
Cotton, Walter, 210–211
Cronos, 163, 253n77
"crossover film," 198
Cunningham, Scott, 72, 97

Darrett, Renoir, 72
Dash, Julie, 7, 182, 228, 261n10. See also *Daughters of the Dust*
Da Sweet Blood of Jesus, 3, 104, 230–234, *230*, *233*, 236
Daughters of the Dust, 7, 181–182, 227, 261n10
David, Marlo D., 3, 61, 101, 105, 108–109, 169–170, 209
Davis, Ossie, 9, 16, 52–53. See also *Cotton Comes to Harlem*
Dean, James, 43, 46
DeCarava, Roy, 109
DeMille, Annie, 72
Derby, 14
Dessisso, Ed, 72
Diawara, Manthia, 3, 74, 169, 175, 181–182, 187, 196, 226–228, 239n3
Double Possession, 1, *157*, 157–158, *159*, 252n50. See also *Blood Couple*
Dracula, 67, 161, 167
drug abuse, 55, 58, 68–69, 94, 97, 161, 181, 194, 251n7
Du Bois, W. E. B., 186
Dunbar, Paul Laurence, 207

Egyptian Murals. See Gunn, Bill, unproduced or unpublished projects
European art cinema. See art cinema
Evangel Revivaltime Church, 131–132, 135, 143
excess, 147, 160, 173, 176, 181–182
Exorcist, The, 135, 156, 161, 198

Fales, Enrico, 95, 96
Fallen Angels, The, 75, 76, 78, 80
Fame Game, The. See Gunn, Bill, unproduced or unpublished projects
Family Employment. See Gunn, Bill, unproduced or unpublished projects
Festival of Independent Black American Cinema, 194–195
Field, Allyson Nadia, 6, 182, 194
Fisher, Terence, 17, 161
Five on the Black Hand Side, 12, 153
Forbidden City, The (Gunn play), 199, 207, 226, 258n93
Ford Foundation, 72
Forster, Nicholas, 67, 214, 239n4
Foster, Gloria, 101, 207
Franklin, Wendell, 10–11, 13
Friendly Warning. See Gunn, Bill, unproduced or unpublished projects
Friends. See Gunn, Bill, unproduced or unpublished projects

Gaddis, William, 95, 115, *116*
Games. See *Rhinestone*
Ganja & Hess (Gunn film): academic reception, 3–5, 67–68, 71, 73–74, 78, 101, 108–109, 114, 164–166, 169–171, 173, 175, 178, 180–183, 186–187, 193, 196–197, 209, 226–227, 239n3, 250n154; critical reception, 1, 3–4, 76, 94, 145–152, 158, 160, 162, 165–167, 170–173, 176–179, 187, 239n2, 251n20, 252n25, 252n50, 252n73; documentary influence on, 77, 86, 97, 132, 173, 187, 194; early titles, 17, 23–24, 66–67, 147; European art cinema influence on, 146, 163, 171–177, 179–180, 188–189; frame enlargements, *76*, *79*, *83*, *85*, *87–88*, *91–92*, *95*, *98*, *100*, *102*, *104*, *106*, *108–111*, *113–116*, *118*, *123*, *127–128*, *133–134*, *136–137*, *140–143*, *168*, *174–175*, *180*; as horror film, 3, 24, 66–70, 80–81, 86, 93–94, 97, 108, 129, 146, 153, 160–167, 169, 188, 190, 226; "multimodality" of, 147, 160, 165, 173–174, 176, 181, 188–189; narrative ambiguity in, 66–67, 70–71, 74–75, 77–78, 80, 83–84, 86, 88–89, 91, 94–95, 97–98, 102–103, 105–106, 111–113, 117, 119–120, 124, 128–129, 137, 139, 143, 154–155, 174–176, 179, 181–182; outtakes from, 77, 83, *84*, 91, 106, *107*, 111–112, 117, *119*, 120–121, *121–122*, 124–125, *124–126*, 127, 131, *131*, 137–139, *138*, *140*, 154, 248n105, 249n121; post-release screenings, 1, 3, 69, 146, 190, 192–195, 197, 229, 235–236, 256n7, 256n18, 257n28, 261n37; promotion for, 2, 18, 23, *23*, 66, 147–148; racial themes in, 80–81, 89–90, 95, 101, 105, 107–110, 125, 130, 164–168, 177–188; script drafts, 4, 67, 69–70, 74–75, 85–86, 89, 91, 94, 97–99, 101–103, 112, 115, 117, 119, 124–126, 128–130, 136–137, 139, 141, 154–155, 165, 186, 246n21, 246n23; sexuality, representations of, 101, 103, 105, 117, 121–122, 127–128, 166–170, 254n96; theatrical distribution, 1, 145–150, 152–153, 192, 234; video distribution, 3, 6, 158, 160, 190, 195, 235, 239n3, 250n144. See also *Blood Couple*; *Double Possession*
Gelmiş, Joseph, 148, 171, 253n73
genre hybridity, 61, 160, 163, 165, 181, 188–189, 214
Georgia, Georgia, 15–16, 18–26, 29–30, 66, 71, 176, 240n36, 240n42, 241n48; "Georgia on My Mind" (plot outline), 19–20
Gerima, Haile, 7, 197. See also *Sankofa*
Gillespie, Michael B., 178, 181, 189
Greatest, The (Gunn screenplay), 4, 190–191, 204–205, 217
Greaves, William, 7, 9, 73, 194
Gries, Tom, 205. See also *The Greatest*
Grosvenor, Vertamae, 210, 212, 240n44
Guerin, Terry, 149, 178, 252n25
Gunn, Bill, *35*, *38*, *196*; acting career, 42–48; and age discrepancy, 34, 44–45; authorship status and characteristics, 5–6, 33, 44, 49, 53–54, 56–58, 67, 70, 95, 101, 114, 125, 165, 183–184, 191, 206–207, 209, 219–220, 232; autobiographical material in the work of, 34, 37, 39–44, 90, 200–202, 204–205, 207, 221, 244n98, 246n31, 252n28, 258n93; and the Black bourgeoisie, 33–34, 36–37, 81, 95, 177, 182, 207–208, 218, 223–224; childhood and adolescence, 36–42, 89, 161, 242n26; critics, responses to, 145, 149–150, 172, 255n144; death, 4, 206, 225–226, 235, 260n6; direction of actors by, 57–58, 73–74, 96, 101, 105, 113–114, 126–127, 134–135, 211–212,

249n129; European influence on, 55–56, 78, 102, 146, 163, 171–174, 177, 179, 184, 254n113; and genre, 55, 65–70, 94, 97, 146, 160–164, 172–173, 182, 206, 214, 232; and Hollywood studios, 4, 32, 45, 49–51, 53–55, 59–64, 68, 190–191, 200–201, 204–205, 226, 228; influence of, 5, 191, 194–197, 226–229, 234–237, 261n10, 261n37; and Kelly-Jordan Enterprises, 1, 17, 23–24, 26, 29, 66–71, 100, 152–153, 189, 191–192, 200, 202, 246n13, 246n25; race and identity politics in the work of, 33, 41–42, 49–50, 53, 62, 65, 90, 107, 110, 125, 164–168, 177–188, 202–203, 214, 217–218; screen appearances by, 45–47, 75, 83, *84*, 87–88, 89–90, *91*, 148, *159*, 211, *212*, 217, 243n51, 243n53, 259n101; sexual identity and, 40–41, 61, 101, 164, 167–170, 243n30. See also *The Alberta Hunter Story*; *All the Rest Have Died*; *The American Parade*; "The Bedlamite"; *Black Picture Show*; *The Celebration*; *The Forbidden City*; *Ganja & Hess*; *The Greatest*; *Johnnas*; *Marcus in the High Grass*; *Personal Problems*; *Rhinestone*; *Rhinestone Sharecropping*; *Stop*; "To the Black Male Children"; *Watch Your Mouth!*

Gunn, Bill, unproduced or unpublished projects, 5–6; *The Afrikan Sun* (film), 216–217; *Bessie* (film), 23, 26, 100, 209, 241n64; *Egyptian Murals* (novel), 162; *The Fame Game* (film), 50; *Family Employment* (play), 162, 206; *Friendly Warning* (film), 218–219; *Friends* (film), 50; *House of Flowers* (film), 51; *Jeanne Duval* (film), 209; *The Lena Horne Show* (TV series), 208–209, 259n101; *Men of Bronze* (TV miniseries), 208; *Moon* (film), 50; *The Owllight* (play), 49; *The Partisan* (film), 65–66, 246n3; *Renaissance* (play), 207; *Territory* (film) 4, 6, 183, 191, 219–223, 229; *The Wonderful Ice Cream Suit* (film), 51

Gunn, Bill, Sr., 37, 39, 42, 226
Gunn, Louise Alexander, 37, 39, 208, 226, 258n93

Hammer Films, 17, 161–162
Harlem Audiovisuals Inc., 86, 132

Harris, Richard, *123–124*, 126–127, *127–128*, *141–142*, *159*, 166, 226, 250n151
Harrison, Paul Carter, 149, 166–167, 187, 251n20
Harrow, Richard. See Harris, Richard
Haynes, Ulric, 95, 115, *116*
Haynes, Yolande Toussaint, 95, 115, *116*
Hefner, Hugh, 147, 153
Heller, Paul, 53, 55, 58
Heritage Enterprises, 1, 77, 153–158, 175, 191–192, 195, 250n144
Hinton, James E., 67, 72, 87, 91, 96, 102–103, 106, 108–109, 111, 114, 120, 127, 155, 235, 247n33, 249n136, 250n154, 261n10; documentary background of, 86, 132, 134, 173, 248n71
Hoffmeister, John, 56, 75, *79*, 115, *116*, 226, 235
Holiday, Billie, 13, 152
Honeybaby, Honeybaby, *23*, 23, 25, 27–29, 71
"hood" cycle, 227, 229
hooks, bell, 169–171
Horne, Lena, 208
horror genre, 68–69, 81, 97, 156, 160–167, 188–189, 225; Black horror films, 12, 24, 146, 160, 164–165, 172, 188. See also vampire subgenre
House of Dark Shadows, 81
House of Flowers. See Gunn, Bill, unproduced or unpublished projects
Hudson, Dale, 165, 167
Hunger, The, 163, 253n77

I Am Curious (Yellow), 160
I Know Why the Caged Bird Sings: Angelou book, 17; *Caged Bird* (Kelly-Jordan project), 17, 23, 26–27, 246n13; television film, 27
independent Black cinema, 3, 6–7, 9–10, 12–14, 151–152, 158, 180–182, 189, 194–195, 214, 223, 226–228, 236; "New York Scene," 67
Inheritance, The, 18, 23–26, 71, 241n57, 246n13
In the Cross, a Trembling Soul: The Inheritance. See *The Inheritance*
Invisible Man, 180, 255n139

Jackson, Horace, 10, 13
Jackson, Leonard, 72, 105–106, *106–107*, 109, 110, 140, 142, 174, 211

Janov, Arthur, 138–139
Jeanne Duval. See Gunn, Bill, unproduced or unpublished projects
"Jesu, Joy of Man's Desiring," 94, 117, 154
John, Tom, 82, 124, 155
Johnnas (Gunn play), 39–41, 49, 90, 184, 242n5, 242n25, 243n30
Jones, Duane, 76–77, 162, 206, 217, 225; *Ganja & Hess* performance, 2, 23, 67, *79*, 84–85, *87*, 91, *92*, *95*, *100*, *104*, *108*, 109, *111*, 115–116, *118*, 122–124, 133–134, 134–135, 136–137, 148, 150, *159*, *168*, *174*, 226, 248n97, 249n136
Jordan, Jack, 14–22, 24–30, 70–71, 115, 147, 152–153, 156, 241n79

Kadár, Ján, 51. See also *The Angel Levine*
Kalat, David, 71, 74, 78, 154–155, 160–161, 188; and All Day Entertainment, 3, 235
Kanefsky, Victor, 67, 72–73, 77–78, 80, 88–90, 100, 102, 105, 107, 117, 122, 128, 154–155, 171–172, 192, 218, 230, 235, 247n62, 250n144
Kangalee, Dennis Leroy, 227, 234
Kazan, Elia, 49, 54
Kelly-Jordan Enterprises, 1, 21–26, 66, 68–71, 100, 104, 146–147, 150, 153, 155, 166, 176, 188–189, 191, 197, 201–202, 232, 250n144, 251n4; demise of, 26–27, 30; founding of, 14–18
Kelly, Quentin, 14–17, 19, 21–22, 24–30, 66–71, 147–148, 152–153, 156, 158, 200–201, 246n25; and Quentin Kelly Enterprises, 28
Kendrick, James, 5–6
Killer of Sheep, 7, 181, 227
King, Mabel, 84, *85*, 100, *116*, 156
King, Martin Luther, Jr., 36
King, Tony, 72
Klotman, Phyllis, 3, 66, 73–74, 169, 175, 187, 196, 239n3, 246n23
Kroll, Jack, 185, 202–203

Lachman, Ed, 218, 223
Lady Sings the Blues, 11, 26, 151–152, 198, 228, 240n16, 244n79
Lamentation over the Dead Christ, 103
Landlord, The (Gunn screenplay), 49–51, 53, 99, 183, 200, 219–220, 244n74

Lane, Tommy, 96, *131*
Lardner, Ring, Jr., 205
Lee, Spike, 3, 66, 73, 94, 191, 228–236, 261n21; *BlacKkKlansman*, 234; *4 Little Girls*, 73; *Joe's Bed-Stuy Barbershop: We Cut Heads*, 197; *Malcolm X*, 231–232; *Oldboy*, 230; *Red Hook Summer*, 230; *School Daze*, 229; *She's Gotta Have It*, 7, 197, 228–229, 232. See also *Da Sweet Blood of Jesus*
Leki, Ilona, 184–185
Lena Horne Show, The. See Gunn, Bill, unproduced or unpublished projects
Lennon, John, 139
Lincoln Center, 49, 197, 199, 202–203, 222, 236
Lipsitz, George, 163–164
Lockhart, Calvin, 23, 27
Loden, Barbara, 172
Los Angeles rebellion, 7, 194, 197, 257n23
Losing Ground, 7, 181, 183, 217–218, 225, 227, 236
Love at First Bite, 69
Lucas, Tim, 3, 71, 146, 154–156, 173, 187, 239n3
Lumumba, Patrice, 23, 26

Major, Anthony, 72
Marcus in the High Grass (Gunn play), 49, 183, 207
Marsh, Linda, 54, 57, 59–60
Men of Bronze. See Gunn, Bill, unproduced or unpublished projects
Method acting, 46–47, 113–114
Metz, Walter, 71, 78, 254n118
Micheaux, Oscar, 6–7, 9–10, 193–194, 214, 228
Monaco, James, 74, 149, 151, 155, 173, 180, 193, 239n2, 255n139
Moon. See Gunn, Bill, unproduced or unpublished projects
Moore, Carman, 211
Morton, Joe, 206, 208, 222
Motion Picture Production Code, 54, 167
Motown Productions, 26, 151–152, 198, 222, 240n16
Murray, James P., 8–11, 30–31, 149, 171, 197–198, 224
Museum of Modern Art, 1, 3, 190, 192–193, 195, 200, 220, 222, 235–236, 250n144, 256n7

Nader, Saladin, 28, 153
National Educational Television, 73, 77, 208
National Endowment for the Arts, 71, 210–211
Nation of Islam, 205, 258n68
Neal, Larry, 86, 178, 183
"New Hollywood," 64, 98, 197, 219, 223
Newman, Kim, 160, 162, 167
New York Shakespeare Festival, 4, 45, 199, 206, 220
Night In . . . Night Out (Story of an Obsession). See *Ganja & Hess*: early titles
Night of the Living Dead, 76–77, 162, 225, 253n73
Noveck, Fima H., 77, 83, 89, 120, 146, 154–156, 158, 167, 175, 192, 231, 254n96
Nyack Center, 132, *132–133*

O'Jay, Eddie, 218
Owllight, The. See Gunn, Bill, unproduced or unpublished projects

Page, Geraldine, 222–223
Papp, Joseph, 45, 199, 203–204, 206–207, 222
Parks, Gordon, Sr., 26, 53. See also *Shaft*
Partisan, The. See Gunn, Bill, unproduced or unpublished projects
Pastore, Lou, 71, 73
PBS, 208–209, 211, 215–216, 218, 236
Perl, Arnold, 231–232
Perlin, Jacob, 236, 261n37
Personal Problems (Gunn video), 4, 52, 191, 209–216, *212*, *215*, 218, 224, 235–236
Perspective: "Crossroads," 45–46
Pinter, Harold, 55, 60, 105
Playboy Theater, 147, 149–150, 152–153, 192, 234
Play Misty for Me, 107
Poitier, Sidney, 9–12, 46, 48, 213. See also *Buck and the Preacher*
Polidori, Robert, 211
Pollard, Samuel, 73, 77, 172, 193, 230
post-Blackness, 183–184, 255n146
Premice, Josephine, 95
primal scream therapy, 138–139
problem pictures, 32–33
Public Theater, 199, 204, 206–207, 226

Qamar, Nadi, 103
queerness, 34, 61–62, 167–170; "queer childhood," 40–41, 89

race movies, 6, 10, 194, 210, 214
ratings system, 54, 60–62, 166. See also Classification and Ratings Administration
Reed, Ishmael, 26, 34, 46, 48, 204, 209–212, 214–216, 218, 235–236, 261n32
Renaissance. See Gunn, Bill, unproduced or unpublished projects
Resnais, Alain, 55, 172, 254n114
Revson, Ancky, 29
Rhinestone (Gunn play), 52, 199, 204, 206–207
Rhinestone Sharecropping (Gunn novel), 37, 54, 191, 198–199, 204–205, 237, 244n98, 246n31, 255n144, 258n88
Richard Allen Center for Culture and Art, 77, 206, 225
Riley, Clayton, 193, 200, 204
Roach, Max, 199, 218, 226, 249n111
Robertson, Hugh A., 16, 19, 22, 27, 73
Robinson, Jean Love, 225
Roizman, Owen, 55, 156
Romero, George, 76–77, 162–163. See also *Night of the Living Dead*
Route 66: "Goodnight Sweet Blues," 45–46

Sands, Diana, 13, 19, 22, 23, 24–25, 27, 29–30, 50, 101
Sankofa, 182
Schomburg Center for Research in Black Culture, 4, 37
Schultz, Chiz, 34, 50–53, 68, 70–72, 77, 81–82, 105, 127, 134–135, 143, 147–148, 155, 218, 222, 225–226, 229–230, 235, 250n144, 258n93
Sconce, Jeffrey, 158, 160
Scott, Seret, 217
"sexploitation," 59–60, 149, 160, 167
Shaft, 8, 16, 30, 96, 178, 245n112
Sherrod, Harrison M. J., 3, 165–166, 187
Shigekawa, Joan, 71
Shining, The, 161, 253n74
Simon, John, 61, 202, 207
Simone, Nina, 36, 52, 82, 223
slavery, 80, 91, 93, 163–164, 179, 182, 187, 217
Smith, Bessie, 23, 26, 37, 100, 169, 209

social realism, 25, 147, 176, 178
"social uplift," 178, 210
Sound and the Fury, The, 45, 243n53
Sounder, 11, 16, 178–179
"spatial narration," 181–182
Spook Who Sat by the Door, The, 7, 72, 178
Steloff, Skip, 153–154, 192
St. Jacques, Raymond, 13, 46
Stop (Gunn film), 3–5, 24, 36, 52–66, 99, 122, 127, 149, 156, 162, 183, 191, 201, 209, 220, 235, 244n98, 245n112, 253n74; *Mandala* (early script draft), 55
Strasberg, Lee, 46–47, 113
Sugar, Joseph, 14–15, 17, 20
Super Fly, 8–9, 11–12, 16, 31, 178, 198–199
Susskind, David, 98
Sweet Sweetback's Baadasssss Song, 7–9, 11, 16, 22, 30–31, 149, 176, 178, 180–181, 192, 198, 226, 228, 255n139

Take a Giant Step, 44–45
Tarpley, Candece, 96, 98, *131*
Tate, Greg, 5, 226
Territory. See Gunn, Bill, unproduced or unpublished projects
"There Is a Fountain Filled with Blood," 143–144
Third World Cinema Corporation, 13–14
Third World Newsreel, 195–196
Thirst, 163, 253n77
Thompson, Judith, 95, 115, *116*
"To the Black Male Children" (Gunn poem), 89–90, 126, 186, 235
Trinity, The, 122, *123*
Trip, The, 55
Turner, Nat, 91, 93, *93*
Turrentine, Stanley, 89

Vampires of Harlem, The. See *Ganja & Hess*: early titles
vampire subgenre: conventions of, 1, 67, 70, 80–81, 93–94, 97, 129, 146, 154, 156, 160–163, 166–167, 181, 188, 226; vampirism as metaphor, 66, 68–69, 84, 90, 117, 161, 163–169, 187, 234

Van Peebles, Melvin, 7, 9, 16, 26, 36, 53, 176, 180–181, 228. See also *Sweet Sweetback's Baadasssss Song*
video production, 191, 209–211, 213–214, 216, 236

Walker, David, 3, 71, 146, 154–156, 173, 187, 239n3
Walker, Drake, 16, 72
Wanda, 172–173
Warhol, Andy, 149, 174, 201
Warner Bros., 4, 12, 14, 36, 55, 58–63, 65, 151, 156, 161, 201, 217, 235
Warner Bros.–Seven Arts, 53–54
Washington, Fredi, 37, 170
Watch Your Mouth! (Gunn teleplays), 208, 259n98
Wattstax, 12, 151
Waymon, Samuel, 52, 63, 68–69, 71, 73, 85, 94, 99, 107, 110, 151–153, 155, 166, 195–196, 199–200, 205–206, 211, *212*, 218, 222–223, 226–228, 231–232, 235–236, 247n66, 261n37; *Ganja & Hess*, performance in, 67, 115, *116*, 130–131, *133*, 134–135, *159*; *Ganja & Hess* score, 67, 80, 94, 100, 103–104, 114, 117, 128, 130, 137–139, 144, 154, 249n109, 249n111, 249n112
Weiler, A. H., 148, 150, 166
Welles, Orson, 36, 174, 210
Whitney Museum: New American Film and Video series, 63, 235
Wilde, Oscar, 86
Williams, John, 226, 235
Williams, Stephen Tyrone, 230, *230*
Williams, Tennessee, 49, 113, 207, 259n94
Wilson, August, 162
Winsten, Archer, 148, 150, 166, 170, 176–177
Wiz, The, 198, 257n42
Wonderful Ice Cream Suit, The. See Gunn, Bill, unproduced or unpublished projects
Wretched of the Earth, The, 185
Wright, James, 210–211, 214

X, Malcolm, 231–232

"You Got to Learn," 94, 104, 114, 117, 130, 144, 231

CHRISTOPHER SIEVING is Associate Professor in the Department of Theatre and Film Studies at the University of Georgia. He is the author of *Soul Searching: Black-Themed Cinema from the March on Washington to the Rise of Blaxploitation.*